# ABRAHAM COWLEY

Mr: Abraham Cowley

# A B R A H A M
# COWLEY

*THE MUSE'S HANNIBAL*

*By*

ARTHUR H. NETHERCOT

NEW YORK / RUSSELL & RUSSELL

*' Shall I be thought fantastical if I confess that the names of some of our poets sound sweeter, and have a finer relish to the ear—to mine, at least—than that of Milton or Shakespeare? . . . The sweetest names, and which carry a perfume in the mention, are Kit Marlowe, Drayton, Drummond of Hawthornden, and Cowley.'*

CHARLES LAMB

FIRST PUBLISHED IN 1931

REISSUED, 1967, WITH ADDITIONAL NOTES

BY RUSSELL & RUSSELL

A DIVISION OF ATHENEUM HOUSE, INC.

BY ARRANGEMENT WITH ARTHUR H. NETHERCOT

L. C. CATALOG CARD NO: 66–24739

PRINTED IN THE UNITED STATES OF AMERICA

# PREFACE

THE purpose of this, the first attempt at a complete account of the life and works of a man whose position as a major English poet was considered by his contemporaries to be as secure as Shakespeare's own, is to study and evaluate Abraham Cowley in all of his aspects as poet, playwright, Royalist and spy, physician, educational theorist, early member of the Royal Society, and friend of Sir John Evelyn, the Duke of Buckingham, and the Earl of St. Albans, rather than to discuss him simply as a 'Metaphysical Poet', as it has been the general custom to regard him. The result, it is hoped, will be to relieve him somewhat from the stigma of his past reputation, and to present him as a figure of some interest and importance from a less narrow point of view.

Specifically, on the biographical side, this book may claim to offer considerable new material on the tantalizing mystery of Cowley's return to England from his French exile (two full years before the date ordinarily given), on his activities as a secret agent of the Stuarts, on his 'recantation', on his disfavour under Charles II, and on his true income at the end of his life. On the critical side, the book may claim to present a new picture of the struggle between the two phases of Cowley's nature, culminating in a partly forced victory for the side of simplicity and true philosophic imagination against that of fantastic elaborateness and 'metaphysical' display. But during this struggle he succeeded in composing the first religious epic in English, in virtually inventing the Pindaric or irregular ode and the Anacreontic, in devising a new and more liberal theory of translation, in becoming one of the three or four important English critics before Dryden, and in writing the first real familiar essays in the language.

In the biography itself, quotations from seventeenth-
and eighteenth-century books and documents have been
modernized in spelling, punctuation, and capitalization,
but in the appendix the wills, indentures, and other
records have been reproduced as exactly as ordinary
typography will permit. The full titles of works referred to in abbreviated form in the foot-notes will be
found in the bibliography, which also endeavours to
point out the earlier works which contain important
information on the biography of Cowley.

The illustrations have been selected with a view to
giving the reader an opportunity of forming a physical
picture of Cowley at different stages in his life, as well
as showing various places and objects which have been
associated with his name. An account of the portraits
here reproduced will be found in the appendix. Manning and Bray's augmented history of Surrey in the
British Museum is the source of the holograph copy of
Cowley's poem to Evelyn as well as of the views of his
house at Chertsey—the twentieth-century photograph
excepted. The view of Westminster about 1650 has
been used in Sargeaunt's *Annals of Westminster School*.
The monument in Westminster Abbey is the adaptation
of the actual marble which is given, with slight varia-
tions, in all editions of the works from 1681 to 1721.
The scene from *Cutter of Coleman-Street* is taken from
volume ii of the 1707 edition.

For valuable aid in discovering some of these documents, my thanks are due to Mrs. A. May Osler, of
London. I likewise wish to thank Professor Leslie
Hotson, of New York University, for the document
bearing on Cowley's position at the Duke's Theatre,
and Professor R. S. Crane, of the University of Chicago,
who interested me in Cowley some fifteen years ago and
who has continued to aid me with critical advice ever
since that time. Finally, I must make special acknow-
ledgements to Professor J. Loiseau, of Toulouse, France,

for generously letting me see the manuscript of his recently-completed Sorbonne dissertation on Cowley, in exchange for my sending him a manuscript copy of the present book. Although this exchange did not take place until after our two works had been completed and submitted to publisher and examining faculty, the result has been to our mutual profit in the matter of supplying further details concerning some phases of Cowley's life.

A. H. N.

EVANSTON, ILLINOIS

*May* 1, 1930.

# CONTENTS

# CONTENTS

# ILLUSTRATIONS

# ADDENDA

*P.* v, *l.* 8. Here and hereafter throughout the book, Evelyn should be divested of the title *Sir* which I have conferred on him.

*P.* 6, *n.* 1. *add:* William Oldys, Norroy King-of-Arms and antiquary (1696-1761), in his ms. notes inserted in the copy of Gerard Langbaine's *An Account of the English Dramatick Poets* (Oxford, 1691), I, 103, in the British Museum (B.M. MS, C28, g, as transcribed by my colleague Bergen Evans), says, "See the reg. of St Dunstan in the West for his birth & his father's name." He then adds that Walker Cowley, ironmonger, had his coat of arms granted or confirmed by W. Camden, Clarencieux, "8 Sept. 42. Eliz."

*P.* 11, *l.* 11. *add:* Dunstan Gale's *Pyramus and Thisbe* had also been published in the same year, if not earlier.

*P.* 13, *n.* 3. *add:* R. W. Chambers, *Thomas More* (London, 1935), pp. 56-57, explains this story of "Antony pigs" with reference to St. Antony's School, not Westminster School.

*P.* 15, *n.* 2. *add:* Oldys, I, 107, referring to Robert Wilde's *Iter Boreale*, says that Cowley was never whipped at Westminster.

*P.* 25, *n.* 1. Ruth Nevo, in *The Dial of Virtue   A Study of Poems on Affairs of State in the Seventeenth Century* (Princeton, 1963), p. 26, quotes the last eight lines of this poem as "Cowley's first juvenile effort at panegyric," and refers to many other of his poems of political import in illustration of her topic. In her introduction she names him as one of the eleven of "the century's excellent poets, even of its greatest," who wrote significantly on the subject of her book.

*P.* 30, *n.* 1. *add:* As a further evidence of this Jonsonian influence, see my note, "Milton, Jonson, and the Young Cowley," *M.L.N.*, XLIX (1934), 158-62, based on an epigram, "On Abraham Cowley the Young Poet Laureat," by Nicholas Oldisworth, a minor member of the Jonson circle.

*P.* 26, *l.* 6. *add as n.:* A writer to the *Times Literary Sup.* for Dec. 5, 1936, believes that still another "uncollected" occasional poem, signed only "A.C.," was very likely by Cowley. It appeared among the various commendatory poems prefixed to the 1633 ed. of Phineas Fletcher's *The Purple Island* and was entitled "On the Most Accurate Poem, Inscribed *The Purple Island.*"

*P.* 49, *l.* 18. *add n.:* L. C. Martin, *M.L.R.*, XXVII (1932), 93, points out that a ms. version of Crashaw's translation dated 1637 is extant.

*P.* 49, *n.* 2. *add:* However, Frank Kermode, in "The Date of Cowley's *Davideis*," *R.E.S.*, XXV (1949), 154-8, argues interestingly, though not conclusively, that "the whole poem was written after 1650 and finished before 1654."

*P.* 53, *n.* 3. *add:* A. L. Korn, in "*MacFlecknoe* and Cowley's *Davideis*," *Huntington Library Quarterly*, XIV (1941), 99-127, finds a further influence of Cowley on Dryden: ". . . among the epics of Dryden's time the *Davideis* was a much more important and pervasive influence upon the style and design of *MacFlecknoe*, and on what might be termed its burlesque iconography, than has commonly been recognized."

*P.* 63, *l.* 26. *add:* He might also have been familiar with Thomas Randolph's unacted and unpublished *The Drinking Academy*, which Samuel A. Tannenbaum and Hyder E. Rollins in their introduction to their edition of the play (Cambridge, Mass., 1930) think could well have been composed for presentation at Westminster School itself about 1624-6. Richard Brome, too, had introduced a School of Compliment into his *The Sparagus Garden*, acted in 1635. The original progenitor of all these burlesque schools and academies may well have been Aristophanes' satire on the school of Socrates in *The Clouds*.

*P.* 63, *l.* 30. *add n.:* For a thorough account of the current seventeenth century educational theories, see Wilson and Forbes, *Gabriel Harvey's Ciceronianus.*

*P.* 75, *n.* 2. *add:* Autrey Nell Wiley, in "The Prologue and Epilogue to Cowley's *Guardian*," *R.E.S.*, X (1934), 443-7, shows that these two pieces were printed without the play in 1642 as by "Francis Cole" (a pseudonym for Cowley?). But there was a Francis Cole, bookseller, in London at the time. There are slight differences between this version and the later ones.

*P.* 83, *l.* 32. *add:* Oldys, I, 113, says that some copies of the *Satire* "are said to have his name at length."

*P.* 118, *n.* 2. *add:* Martin, p. 94, on the authority of F. J. Routledge, points out that in this letter Cowley himself is specifically mentioned by name as being in the plot.

*P.* 120, *n.* 2: *add:* According to the *Bulletin of the Institute of Historical Research*, XVI (1938), 138, seven letters of Cowley from Paris in 1949-50 were advertised by Sotheby (25. vii. 1938). Howard P. Vincent, in "Three Unpublished Letters by Abraham Cowley," *M.L.N.*, LIV (1939), 454-8, presented another letter of the series, dated "Paris, Apr. 8: 1650," and addressed to "the right Honble Mr Long." It concerns (1) internal affairs in France, especially the siege of Bellegarde, (2) the Scotch treaty proposed by Charles II, and (3) the accidental burning of the key to Long's cipher. This letter, with one to Evelyn, belongs to the Pennsylvania Historical Society. J. Simmons, in "An Unpublished Letter from Abraham Cowley," *M.L.N.*, LVII (1942), 194-5, gives the text of another letter in the same series, now in the Bodleian. Dated "Paris. March 13, 1650," it concerns the printing of French and Latin translations of letters between Charles and Montrose on the Scotch treaty. Other similar letters may still turn up. Abraham Cowley was a very busy secret correspondent during these years.

*P.* 135, *l.* 34. *add n.:* For a discussion of the position and characteristics of Cowley's Pindarics in the history of the European ode, see Carol Maddison, *Apollo and the Nine/ A History of the Ode* (Baltimore, 1960).

*P.* 144, *l.* 9. *add n.:* For a discussion of Thurloe's activities, not only as Secretary to the Council of State but as head of the English intelligence system throughout Europe, see D. L. Hobman, *Cromwell's Master Spy/ A Study of John Thurloe* (London, 1961).

*P.* 144, *n.* 1. *add:* In the Clarendon State Papers (*Calendar*, III, 21) there is another letter of Bampfield's which probably refers to Cowley.

*P.* 175, *n.* 1. *add:* C. T. Sonnichsen, in a Harvard dissertation on Sprat, points out that John Dart, in his *Westmonasterium* (London, 1723), II, xliii, states expressly that Sprat and Cowley first met at Buckingham's, after Sprat had become chaplain there subsequent to the Restoration. But Jacob's story sounds more circumstantial, and is certainly more dramatic.

*P.* 176, *ll.* 10-13. *Delete* reference to Lord Wilmot since, in spite of the fact that he showed himself as a rival to Cowley in precocity by receiving his M.A. at Wadham in 1661 at the age of a mere fourteen, he was obviously too young in the middle '50's to have made much of a reputation "for wit and poetry."

*P.* 182, *n.* 1. *add:* Oldys, I, 105, comments: "That Discourse in one edn in 12° goes by the name of *Grebners Prophecies.* ('tis in the Harleian Library) & is the same as his Visions, but with a preface; and there is no preface to that edit. printed 12°. 1661."

*P.* 196, *l.* 13. *add new paragraph:* According to Oldys, I, 106, 114, and on the authority of Arthur Onslow, who, following what was almost a family tradition, was Speaker of the House of Commons from 1728 to 1761, Cowley for a time had even "been led into hopes of being made a Secretary of State." But, even if this much later tale can be accepted, the poet soon learned that he had aspired too high, in spite of his spying services under Thurloe, who had recently been reappointed Secretary of State, even though he had been accused of high treason to the new government by his enemies.

*P.* 211, *ll.* 30 *passim.* It is even more likely that the King's Yard refers to the royal dockyard at Deptford, a neighborhood long associated with the Cowleys (see E. S. de Beer, *History*, XVI, n.s. (1931), 284).

*P.* 237, *n.* 2. *add:* C. William Miller, in "Cowley and Evelyn's *Kalendarium Hortense*," *M.L.N.*, LXIII (1948), 398-401, proves that Evelyn had also dedicated the first edition of the book to Cowley, in spite of the fact that the page is missing from the twenty-two recorded copies of it. Howard P. Vincent has also communicated to *M.L.N.* a letter (now owned by the Pennsylvania Historical Society) which Cowley wrote to Evelyn from London, March 7, 1664, thanking him for this dedication and referring to his own life in the country and to his illness.

*P. 240, n. 1. add:* The play was published late in April, since the *Mercurius Publicus* for April 23-30, 1663, carried the following announcement: "Cutter of Coleman-street. A Comedy. The Scene London, in 1658. Written by Abraham Cowley. Sold by Henry Harringman etc." (See Sybil Rosenfeld, *PMLA,* LI (1936), 129.)

*P. 247, n. 1. add:* This grant is referred to by Oldys, I, 106, as dated April 7, 1665, "as appears in the Hanaper Books that year. (a MS. vol. late in the possession of Chs Grimes Esqr)." Oldys adds later (I, 114), again on the authority of Onslow: "Cowley . . . had 400 p Annum allowed him: was no great oeconomist or strict philosopher in his living at Chertsey; but would very sociably and freely enjoy his friends and bottle there: did not lead that melancholy discontented retired life he has been said to do."

*P. 253, l. 8. add:* Oldys (I, 114) draws a more restrained picture of the estate than Cowley himself did: "Nor was his seat at Chertsey so elegant and alluring as it has been represented. See Aubrey's Surrey & Postboy robbed of its Mail etc., 8° 1704 (I. p. 66) for the country people's robbing him of his hay. . . ."

*P. 269, l. 31. add fn.:* For a brief controversy over the extent of the influence of the Royal Society and its theories on Cowley's manner of writing, see R. F. Jones, "Science and English Prose Style in the Third Quarter of the Seventeenth Century," *PMLA,* XLV (1930), 998-1001, with its postscript by Arthur H. Nethercot and Richard F. Jones, "Concerning Cowley's Prose Style," *ibid.,* XLVI (1931), 962-6.

*P. 273, n. 3. add:* Further investigation reveals that this poem by Sprat, in spite of its new and misleading title, is really only a variant of his earlier ode to Cowley.

*P. 277, n. 5. add:* This eulogy was also ridiculed. In 1853 Henry Campkin contributed to *Notes and Queries,* V, 267-8, a copy of an anonymous ms. burlesque in his possession. Campkin and Wood both attribute the original to Scarborough.

*P. 280, n. 4.* For Cowley's role and position as a "Metaphysical Poet," see Robert Lathrop Sharp, *From Donne to Dryden The Revolt against Metaphysical Poetry* (Chapel Hill, 1940), *passim.*

*P. 285, n. 1. add:* Oldys, I, 111-12, gives a list of "characters of Cowley," some previously unnoticed.

*P. 289, l. 18. add:* The culmination of the attempt to rehabilitate Cowley for the twentieth century has been Robert B. Hinman's *Abraham Cowley's World of Order* (Cambridge, Mass., 1960), which does not hesitate to make continual comparisons between Cowley and Milton and comes close to establishing the former once more as a genuine rival to the latter.

*P. 330, l. 30. add:* Oldys, I, 113, states: "A good head in my Lord Oxford's Collection, with one hand visible, pointing to his left.*
"*Query if now in the possession of Lord Chesterfield or Mr West.
"Mr Vanblake has also got a painting of Cowley very like to prints of him; but very coarsely executed.
"Mr Vertue tells me of another painting of him."

*P. 331, l. 27. add:* Moore-Smith, *op. cit.,* p. 337, calls attention to a "beautiful portrait (head and shoulders) in the lodge of St. John's College, Cambridge."

# ERRATA

P. 26, *ll.* 31-2. *For* Dean of the School *read* Dean of Westminster.

P. 37, *l.* 3. *For* masters *read* fellows.

P. 40, *l.* 26. *For* quadriennium *read* quadrivium.

P. 58, *ll.* 9-10. *For* con-dered *read* con-sidered.

P. 66, *l.* 14. *For* college *read* university, *and add fn.:* Cowley's name appears in the university Ordo for 1639/40 (see G. C. Moore-Smith, *English Historical Review*, XLVII (1932), 336-7).

P. 70, *l.* 11. *For* March *read* May.

P. 74, *l.* 18. *For* Discipulus *read* Dominus.

P. 85, *l.* 13. *For* Yorkshire *read* Northumberland.

P. 94, *l.* 26. *For* 1636 *read* 1646.

P. 114, *n.* 1. *For* 1676 *read* 1646.

P. 120, *n.* 2. *For* Count Lauderdale *read* Earl of Lauderdale.

P. 191, *l.* 23. *For* March *read* May.

P. 277, *l.* 12. *For* Pindus *read* Pindarus.

P. 293, *l.* 10. *Add fn.:* For corrections of some of these expansions, see Moore-Smith, *op. cit.*

P. 334, *l.* 3. *For* or *read* of.

P. 338, *l.* 15, *For* Vol. I *read* Vols. I, III.

P. 365, *l.* 8. *For* Sir *read* Alfred Lord.

# I

## 'FIT SURCULUS ARBOR'

ON July 24, 1618, in the parish of St. Michael le Quern, Cheapside, one of London's solid middle-class citizens lay dying. Prosperous, respectable, pious, 'of a virtuous life', as Bishop Sprat was later to write,[1] he had applied himself so conscientiously to his business of stationer, perhaps also supplementing this with an equally satisfactory trade as grocer, that he had no occasion for humility when he looked about him at his neighbours in 'the Cheap' and compared his estate with theirs—except, perchance, that of the goldsmiths, whose blazing shops along the main highway through the district were soon to make such an impression on Charles I that he was to order all the other tradesmen who had encroached on these buildings to turn their property back at once to the original owners.

In this British respect for caste may lie the explanation of a trace of pardonable snobbery in the dying Thomas Cowley's nature, for he seems to have preferred to be known as 'stationer' only, although antiquarian Anthony à Wood and gossipy John Aubrey both designated him 'grocer';[2] in fact, Aubrey even went so far as to begin one of his scraps of notes with 'grocer, at the sign of . . .', but here was compelled to break off, his information having apparently been exhausted. For this reason, in the light of other evidence, his further statement that the 'grocer's' residence was in Fleet Street near the end of Chancery Lane (at what is at present No. 192)[3] may also be disregarded as an obvious error. The Fleet Street address, in the parish of St.

[1] Sprat, 'Account', *Works of Mr. Abraham Cowley* (1668), n.p.
[2] Wood, *Fasti*, in *Ath. Oxon.*, iv, ii. 209; Aubrey, *Brief Lives*, i. 189.
[3] G. Cunningham, *London*, p. 244.

Dunstan's in the West, would seem to denote a later
home to which the family removed after the father had
died. Thomas Cowley unquestionably specified his
parish as that of St. Michael le Quern.[1]

There were, indeed, many Cowleys in London in
1618; and many records of births, deaths, marriages,
lawsuits, and wills still preserve their names, though
not their relationships, for posterity. Nor is 'Thomas'
a Christian name of any distinction. Consequently,
Aubrey and Wood may possibly have confused a
stationer and a grocer of the same name, especially
since at least two contemporary documents are extant,
dealing only with a Thomas Cowley, grocer: the first,
dated April 8, 1608, is a joint bond between him and
John Bate, 'cives et groceros' of London, to pay to one
Alice Isburd, of the parish of St. Mary Colechurch, or
her heirs, the sum of 'two hundred and ten pounds of
lawful money of England on the tenth day of October
next coming after this date';[2] and the second, dated
October 20, 1645, is a will made by Thomas Cowley,
'citizen and grocer', of the parish of St. Giles, Cripple-
gate, and proved on December 11.[3] These two papers
may or may not have been made by the same man, but
since the will mentions a debt to be paid from the
estate, the makers would seem to have been of the same
habits, although the two signatures look to be quite
different. Moreover, the fact that, some fifty years
later, the will of Thomas, one of the sons of the Thomas
Cowley who lay dying in 1618 and who called himself
'stationer', bequeathed one hundred pounds 'To the
Company of Stationers towards the building of their
hall' would serve to confirm the suspicion that the
grocer and the stationer were not the same person.[4]

[1] See his will, Appendix no. 1.
[2] State Paper Office, James I, vol. xxxii, no. 30; also Cal. State Papers,
Dom., 1603–10.        [3] Prerogative Court of Canterbury, 147 Rivers.
[4] See Appendix no. 3.

This conclusion is borne out by the Stationers'
Registers, which show that a Thomas Cowley had been
a member of the Company since September 3, 1599.[1]
His career, including the taking of an apprentice on
September 1, 1600, his paying of a minor fine, and his
being admitted to the freedom of the Company on
June 30, 1604, may be traced in these records.[2] The
reason for Thomas, Jr's., bequest also appears when it is
noted that on March 26, 1640, when he must have been
about twenty-four or twenty-five years of age, he too
joined the profession of his father, and set up a shop at
the sign of the Grayhound in St. Paul's Churchyard;
this sign remained hanging until his death.[3] The wills
of both father and son prove clearly that they prospered
at their business.

It cannot be stated dogmatically, however, that this
Thomas Cowley had only one trade, or had never been
occupied with another. A slight bit of evidence, indeed,
exists to suggest that at one time he may have followed
a still different calling. On the eighteenth of December,
1581, according to the records of Edmonton, Middlesex, one Thomas Cowley, carpenter, espoused Thomasine
Berrye, spinster, of All Hallows, Staining, a parish just
a little to the east of Cheapside.[4] Now it happens that
the wife of the sick man also had the rather unusual
name of Thomasine, and therefore it is not impossible
that the union consummated thirty-seven years before
was only now, in 1618, reaching its close.

During the years of her marriage, Thomasine Cowley
had borne her husband at least six children who were

[1] See binding books of the Stationers' Company, cited by J. L.
Chester in *Notes and Queries*, iv, ii. 340. These facts have been called
to attention in J. Loiseau's dissertation, described in the preface.
[2] See Arber's *Transcript of the Registers of the Company of the
Stationers of London*, ii. 248, 875, 840.
[3] Ibid., iii. 688; McKerrow, *Dictionary of Printers and Booksellers*,
p. 314; Plomer, *Dictionary of Booksellers and Printers*, p. 55.
[4] Foster, *London Marriage Licences*.

still alive; and even now, in her old age, she was nearing
her time with a seventh. It is true, however, that if
these two Thomasine Cowleys married to two Thomas
Cowleys were the same, then Thomas must have followed the not uncommon Elizabethan custom of
taking to wife a girl bride of some fifteen or so years of
age, who in 1618 would be in her fifties. And there is
no evidence against this supposition. Mistress Cowley,
by Sprat's statement, died in her eightieth year, and
was seemingly a person of much energy and vitality.

But this Thomas Cowley had entered himself on the
church register as a carpenter. And on July 24, 1618, a
Thomas Cowley, stationer, lay dying. Whether he was
the carpenter who had pledged his faith to Thomasine
Berrye in 1581, or whether he was the grocer who had
been forced to sign a promissory note in 1608, or whether
he was a stationer quite different from these, this man,
foreseeing his own end, had taken all the necessary steps
to provide for his wife and his numerous family. His
estate seemed to be clear and relatively unencumbered,
and, thanks to his business acumen, he had a comfortable
sum to dispose of. At this hour, then, his thoughts were
concerned with his family and with a fond anxiety as to
their welfare after his death, which he suspected was
imminent—with these, and with the security of his
own soul.

Accordingly, he had resolved to make his will.
Master John Sharpe and Master George Brittridge were
come as witnesses. A scrivener had been summoned to
take the dictation, since the dying man seems to have
been too weak to do more than scrawl his signature.
The formal preamble completed, he continued with
these words:

. . . I, Thomas Cowley, citizen and stationer of London and of
the parish of St. Michael at Quern, London, being sick in body
but in good and perfect memory (thanks be to God), do make
this my last will and testament in manner and form following,

that is to say: First, I commit my soul to Almighty God with full assurance of remission of all my sins through the merits and passion of Jesus Christ, my Saviour and Redeemer, and my body to be buried at the discretion of my executor hereafter named; and as for the disposing of that worldly estate as God hath bestowed upon me (my debts being satisfied) I give and bequeath the same in manner and form following, that is to say—

Did he pause here, and did his mind fly to his family, dwelling with peculiar tenderness upon his wife Thomasine, who perhaps even then stood near? At least, a man of his character might well have done so in view of his next words:

First, my will and mind is that whereas God hath blessed me with six children besides the child or children which Thomasine my wife now goeth withal, viz. Peter Cooley, Audrey Cooley, John Cooley, William Cooley, Katharine Cooley, and Thomas Cooley, and to the child or children which my wife goeth withal, I give and bequeath to every of them severally the sum of one hundred and forty pounds apiece of lawful money of England, and if either or any of them shall happen to die or decease this mortal life that then his, her, or their portion so deceasing to be equally divided amongst the rest of them surviving, to be paid at their several ages of one and twenty or day of marriage.

Yes, family ties were strong with Thomas Cowley (or Cooley, as the name was often spelled, and certainly always pronounced). His own immediate domestic circle was large, but he remembered his other kin also. Through the list he went: five pounds apiece to Richard Milwood and Margery Milwood, his sister's children; five pounds to his sister Elizabeth Pierce; and five pounds apiece to his brothers-in-law, Humphrey Clarke, Humphrey Clare, Henry Moorton, and Rowland Squire (though the first two are very likely the scrivener's blunder in naming the same man twice). These bequests, or rather tokens of esteem and affection, concluded, he appointed the last-named men as overseers

of his will, 'desiring them to be aiding and assisting to
my well-beloved wife, my executor hereafter named'.
Thomas Cowley had full faith and confidence in his
'dear and well-beloved wife', as he later called her, for to
her he left the residue of his estate and made her his
'full and sole executrix'. And when he had signed his
name and used the waxen seal, and when the two witnesses had placed their signatures below, he had no
further cause to worry, except for the safe birth of the
child which his wife then bore within her. None of his
affairs were much involved, so far as his will would indicate, and he was leaving behind him a competency, if
no more. If this should fail, he could surely rely on his
brothers and sisters to care for his family.

Thomas Cowley never saw his seventh child and
fifth son. He died soon after making his will, for on the
eleventh of August Mistress Cowley proved the document before Magistrate Edmund Pope in the Prerogative Court of Canterbury, promising to administer the
estate well and faithfully; and in Somerset House the
will still lies. Some time between that date and the end
of the year (probably old style) her child was born.
Sprat is the authority for the statements that the birth
was posthumous and that it took place in 1618.[1] Of
course, it is extremely unlikely that the event could
have occurred between July 24 and August 11, and have
still allowed the mother to appear in court on the latter
date. Unluckily, however, not even the baptismal
records of the family are extant, for the church of St.
Michael le Quern was one of the many destroyed in the
Great Fire of 1666. Yet it is certain that the boy was
baptized, and that if he had no father he had a godfather who took a father's place as completely as a
godfather could. Thus, significantly enough, even at
this early age the boy found a friend just when he most
needed one—a friend who gave him his own name,

[1] Sprat, 'Account'.

Abraham. But except that this godfather's last initial was 'B' and that he was a City man like Thomas Cowley, no other facts are known. To suggest that the letter stood for 'Berrye' would be merely an attractive speculation. The boy's genuine love for him, however, was later shown in his juvenile poem, 'To His Very Much Honoured Godfather, Master A. B.'

These were the circumstances under which Abraham Cowley was born—Anthony à Wood's 'prince of poets',[1] Dryden's 'noble author',[2] Pope's 'fine poet, in spite of all his faults',[3] and Johnson's last, chiefest, and therefore most ridiculed of the 'metaphysical race'.[4]

Cowley's childhood may be reconstructed with some certainty of outline. Although he was the youngest of seven children, left early without a father, he was not allowed to run wild, even had he had a disposition to do so. Mistress Cowley was obviously a woman of strong personality, and the boy, in Sprat's telling phrase, 'was bred up under' her 'discipline' until he went away to school.[5] Yet her firm hand in no way impaired her son's love, for, again in Sprat's phrase, 'he gratefully acknowledged her care of his education to her death, which was in the eightieth year of her age'. She was not one to let the atmosphere of the household change merely because her husband's influence was removed. The baby Abraham must have sensed from the first that life was a serious affair and that much was expected of him. Instead of the nursery rhymes, ballads, and fables of the more liberal and frivolous families, he was accustomed to see about him and to hear read books of devotion which, as he says in 'Of Myself', comprised the only sort of reading done by his mother all her life.

[1] Wood, *Ath. Oxon.*, iii. 85, 825–6; ii. 494.
[2] Dryden, *Essays* (ed. Ker), ii. 108–9.
[3] Pope, in Spence, *Anecdotes*, p. 173.
[4] Johnson, 'Cowley', *Lives*.          [5] Sprat, 'Account'.

Yet the Cowleys do not seem to have been Puritans, or
'sectaries', as Dr. Johnson speculated.[1] They may have
had some Puritan ideas and ideals, not admitted as
such even to themselves, but Cowley was from the start
too violently anti-Puritan in his sentiments to leave
any question that his allegiance was always with the
genuine state church.

Mistress Cowley probably supervised her children's
education herself, though she may have had the assistance of a nurse, in accordance with the custom even in
middle-class families of the seventeenth century. But
a nurse could not have sufficed Master Abraham long.
His mother must early have perceived the signs of
his extreme precociousness—that precociousness which
stamped him as perhaps the most remarkable child in
all English literature and before which even Pope was
compelled to beat a quick retreat. Thomasine Cowley
surely watched the development of her last-born with
a pride which she would probably try to conceal as
sinful, if not idolatrous; but she could never do so.
Here was the result of all her pains and training—a
development for which she could rightly claim some
credit. It is not at all unlikely that Cowley was put to
his horn-book at less than three years of age, inasmuch
as the normal child began to study his alphabet in this
form at three or four. Nor is it likely that many trans-
formations of the horn-book into a convenient paddle
for chastisement were necessary before he was able to
proceed to his Bible and Psalter, and then to his Latin
accidence. Child prodigies in learning were common in
those days, and seem to have got as much pleasure from
their books as other children did from their toys and
games. Nevertheless, it must not be thought that Cowley at once grew into a detestable, dried-up little
pedant. Never in his life was he accused of that. Nor
could a child with six brothers and sisters fail to learn

[1] Johnson, *Lives* (ed. Hill), i. 2.

how to play, as references to various childish sports in
his juvenile writings will testify.

It happened, also, that on the table in his mother's
parlour there lay a book quite different from the rest
of the volumes of the household—a book for the
presence of which in such an environment he always
confessed himself totally unable to account. While he
was just learning his letters he probably paid no attention to it, accepting it as a child would any of the
fixtures or furnishings of a room. But one day, when he
had begun to read 'and to take some pleasure in it', as
he says[1]—when he was scarcely ten years of age, says
Sprat's Latin life[2]—he chanced to look at the book with
new eyes. Spreading the large pages open, he began to
read.

'A gentle knight was pricking on the plain', ran the
first line. It was not enough. He must have more.
And so he read on:

> . . . Y-clad in mighty arms and silver shield,
> Wherein old dints of deep wounds did remain,
> The cruel marks of many a bloody field;
> Yet arms till that time never did he wield.
> His angry steed did chide his foaming bit,
> As much disdaining to the curb to yield:
> Full jolly knight he seemed, and fair did sit,
> As one for knightly jousts and fierce encounters fit.

This was like nothing which had ever yet befallen
him. He was fascinated, even a little dazed—it was a
sphere of life so far removed from anything he had
before seen or heard of. He 'was infinitely delighted
with the stories of the knights, and giants, and monsters,
and brave houses' which he found there. The 'tinkling
of the rhyme and dance of the numbers' got into his

[1] In 'Of Myself'.
[2] Sprat, 'De Vita . . . A. Couleii', *Poemata Latina*, n.p.; also Sprat,
'Account'.

head and would not leave it. Strange and rare old
Edmund Spenser! The unfamiliar atmosphere without
doubt chiefly charmed the lad at first, and yet even
without his knowing it ('my understanding had little to
do with all this', says he in 'Of Myself') perhaps his
quick mind perceived the bond of moral earnestness
and allegory between *The Faerie Queene* and the works
upon which he had been suckled. At any rate, the book
no longer lay unopened in solitary dignity in Mistress
Cowley's parlour. Before he was twelve, Abraham had
read it 'all over'. He was thus made a poet 'as immediately as a child is made an eunuch'. He had decided
upon his career.

Nor at this age was he one to delay after a decision
had been taken. 'Begin; the getting out of doors is the
greatest part of the journey', he wrote thirty-five years
later, in 'The Danger of Procrastination'. He too
would create a poem. Perhaps, indeed, the earliest
extant composition from his pen does not represent
his most rudimentary stumblings among rhymes and
numbers; for this poem is so nearly perfect in form that
such a full-fledged birth is almost incredible. Nevertheless, in 1636, after his first volume had reached a
second edition, he himself asked his readers' indulgence
in these terms: 'I should not be angry to see any one
burn my *Pyramus and Thisbe*, nay, I would do it myself,
but that I hope a pardon may easily be gotten for the
errors of ten years' age.' If, then, the boy's pride has
not betrayed him into an exaggeration, he must have
written this little narrative within a year or so of the
time that Spenser made him a poet.

It has been questioned whether this poem is to be
judged as an imitation of Spenser.[1] Certainly Cowley
has not played the 'sedulous ape'; and yet it is possible
to write under the influence of a man without slavishly

[1] Cf. *Cambridge History of English Literature*, vii. 71; and Sparrow,
*Mistress*, pp. xv–xvi.

imitating him. As a matter of fact, Cowley could not
have been a mere tyro in versification, although Spenser
was the first *English* poet to make much impression on
him. Grosart's suggestion, indeed, that he was familiar
with the scenes displaying Bottom and his crew in *A*
*Midsummer-Night's Dream* seems quite unfounded.[1]
On the other hand, Cowley's choice of a subject proves
incontrovertibly that his Latin studies had already introduced him to Ovid (for there is no indication that he
knew the translation of the *Metamorphosis* which George
Sandys had published in 1626). The boy's version of
the Pyramus and Thisbe tale does not differ in any
material respect from that found in the fourth book of
Ovid, although he has introduced Venus as a sort of
malevolent *dea ex machina* and, rather knowingly for a
boy of ten, has dwelt much more fully on love's 'longed
for, yet untasted joy' than Ovid did. Similarly, Cowley's stanza, a not unsuccessful invention of his own,
rhyming ABAABB, shows his further independence; in
fact, never in his life did he use Spenser's favourite
form. Yet, contrariwise, many years later Dryden
attributed Cowley's use of triplets and Alexandrines in
heroic verse to the example of Spenser, and furthermore
suggested that his use of hemistichs might also have
come from Spenser as well as Virgil.[2] In some other
respects than his own admission of discipleship, then,
Cowley may be regarded as a limited Spenserian.

The two hundred and twenty-six lines of *Pyramus*
*and Thisbe* certainly deserve better treatment than their
author himself accorded them when he grew up and
refused to let them be reprinted in any of his collections. Pedestrian and perfectly regular nearly
always, they flash now and again into phrases that
no older poet would need be ashamed of. Cowley has

[1] Grosart, *Cowley*, i. xxxv, quoting Gosse, 'Cowley', *Seventeenth
Century Studies.*
[2] Dryden, *Essays*, ii. 229.

already discovered the spell of the paradox, when he writes:

> Thus Beauty is by Beauty's means undone,
> Striving to close these eyes that make her bright.

The sententious couplet has also attracted him:

> Who lets slip Fortune, her shall never find.
> Occasion once passed by, is bald behind.

Finally, the epitaph inscribed on the tomb of the dead lovers is, in spite of its false rhymes, not devoid of charm:

> Underneath this marble stone,
> Lie two Beauties joined in one.
>
> Two whose loves Death could not sever,
> For both lived, both died, together.
>
> Two whose souls, being too divine
> For earth, in their own sphere now shine.
>
> Who have left their loves to Fame,
> And their earth to Earth again.

Whatever Cowley's mother may have thought of all this infatuation, she nevertheless had not forgotten that an education was necessary even for a lad of such faculties as her son's. The other children might get along with the ordinary schooling given to young people in their position. Some of them, indeed, had probably already set up for themselves, since, for instance, there is a record extant of the marriage of a Peter Cowley to a Magdalen Droyt on October 3, 1628.[1] But Abraham must have the best training within her power, and this best was represented by Westminster School, which had had the great Camden as its head master thirty years before and which numbered Ben Jonson, George Herbert, and Giles Fletcher among its illustrious graduates. Through some influence

[1] Foster.

Sala Regalis cum Curia Westmonastery *alias* Westmanster haall.

WESTMINSTER IN 1647

not fully known—perhaps Cowley's godfather, Abraham B., had something to do with the result—she eventually procured the boy's admission to the school, though the exact date of his entrance is nowhere recorded.[1] He himself, however, refers, in his 1656 preface, to the poems which he 'wrote at school from the age of ten years till after fifteen'—a statement which would indicate that he entered Westminster in 1628 or earlier, and that *Pyramus and Thisbe* was composed there, though his first poetical inspiration was received at home.

He had not remained in the school long before he was made one of the King's Scholars. Perhaps if the statutes had not prevented such an appointment before a year of residence had expired, he might even have entered in that capacity. According to these regulations, moreover, none under eight years of age might be elected. The other bases of choice, however, being intellect, learning, character, and want of means (though the last was sometimes waived for applicants who knew the right people), Cowley was probably able to qualify easily on all four scores. At any rate on a list of the Scholars dated July 1, 1630, his name appears last,[2] so that thereafter he was, by Elizabeth's general provisions, allowed three pounds and tenpence a year for commons and two marks for the long gowns in which the Westminster boys were clothed.

'Anthony's pigs', the boys of St. Peter's College, Westminster, were called in the cant of the day, in contradistinction to 'Paul's pigeons', the students of the rival school maintained in connexion with St. Paul's Cathedral; and as one of these 'pigs' Abraham Cowley began his formal education.[3] The lodgers were

[1] Sprat, 'Account'; Birch, *Royal Society*, ii. 220; Welch, *List of Queen's Scholars*; Sargeaunt, *Annals*; Grosart, i. xii.

[2] Tanner MS. 69, f. 137, at Bodleian; quoted by Loiseau.

[3] For the details of the following picture, cf. Sargeaunt.

awakened at five in the morning by a loud 'Surgite!' from one of the monitors, and lengthy Latin prayers followed immediately. Still in a daze, the boys made their beds and swept the floor of their bare-walled dormitory—an old stone granary, with a habitable tower, which had been made over many years before. Two by two they trooped into the cloisters to wash, the thoroughness of the job being passed upon at six by the Second Master as they returned for further prayers. Lessons began at seven. Usually sometime between eight and nine a 'bever', or exceedingly light breakfast of bread and perhaps small beer, was allowed—whereupon lessons began in earnest, were continued till twelve, were interrupted for dinner and prayers, were resumed at one, and extended till six, when supper, seasoned with prayers and graces, was served. The boys were quite ready for bed at eight, even though they might already have availed themselves of the privilege of holding up their hands during study hour, muttering 'Dor!' and receiving permission to drop their heads upon their arms on the wooden forms.

When Cowley entered, Lilly's Latin grammar was undoubtedly familiar to him, and perhaps some of the other conventional text-book material, such as Vives, Dionysius Cato, Aesop, or even Terence, all of whom were usually taught in the first two or three forms. Erasmus, Cicero, Sallust, Caesar, Virgil, Livy, Horace, and others came later. One of Westminster's specialties, however, was its Greek, which was begun as early as the fourth form with Cleonard's grammar, and continued through Lucian, Plutarch, Isocrates, Demosthenes, and Homer. In the last form, also, Hebrew was begun.

From the start, however, Cowley's masters found that they had acquired a peculiar case to deal with. Years later, one of his favourite reminiscences was to tell how his teachers could never prevail on him, 'by any persuasion or encouragements, to learn without book the

common rules of grammar', and were finally forced to
grant him a special dispensation, because they found
that he 'made a shift to do the usual exercise' out of his
'own reading and observation'.[1] Nor was he recalcitrant,
or in any sense a 'problem', as his poems and dedications
to his masters prove. Anything of a mechanical or
exacting nature bored him, and he preferred to get at
the essential—the command of the language—in his
own fashion. As Sprat described the process, 'having
got the Greek and Roman languages, as he had done
his own, not by precept but use, he practised them, not
as a scholar but a native'.

The clever youngster must have been both a perplexity and a joy to his masters. His relations with
them were both cordial and intimate, and yet seasoned
with the proper respect and regard for their dignity.
And the schoolmasters of those days, with their long
gowns of plush, sometimes furred at the edges, their
broad, starched collars, and their flat velvet hats or
skull caps, were such as to inspire veneration. On
Cowley's entrance, the Dean of Westminster, who by
virtue of this position was ultimate head of the school,
was John Williams, to whom the boy was soon respect-
fully to dedicate his first volume. Contrary to Grosart's
implication,[2] Cowley was never a student under Dr.
Richard Busby, the famous bewigged 'whipping
master' who became temporary head of the school in
1638[3] and who subsequently, after being confirmed in
his appointment, boasted that sixteen of the bishops
then on the bench had been birched with his 'little rod'
—not to mention the fact that Dryden was one of his
pupils. Williams, however, had occupied his place since
1620, and on the fall of Francis Bacon in 1621 had also
been appointed Lord Keeper of the Great Seal and
Bishop of Lincoln. This impressive person Cowley

[1] Cowley, 'Of Myself'; Sprat, 'Account'.
[2] Grosart, Cowley, i. xv, n.; xxiv.      [3] Sargeaunt, p. 19, *passim*.

must have often seen going back and forth, and idolized
with the unenvious worship he always had for the
great, even though he knew that the Lord Bishop was
not so highly esteemed by Charles as he had been in
James's reign.  As time went on, too, he must have
noted the more and more disconcerting signs of the
Bishop's inclination toward the cause of the Commons against the King—an attitude quite opposite to
his own.

But the actual head of the school was Master Lambert Osbalston, or Osbaldeston, a person of very definite
character,[1] whom Cowley called his 'very loving master'
in dedicating *Pyramus and Thisbe* to him in 1633.
Most of all, however, the boy was later drawn to
Master John Jordan, the second master, appointed in
1631,[2] and when Jordan died, about ten years after,
Cowley honoured him with one of his sincerest elegies.
Jordan, seemingly a Belgian by birth, must have been a
teacher of the ideal type—an excellent person to have
direct charge of all the King's Scholars as one of his
chief duties—kind and yet firm, learned and yet not
pedantic—one 'Whose government ne'er stood me in a
tear', one for whose students 'Father itself was but a
second name'.  Thus again, having outgrown the care
of his mother and his godfather, Cowley found a friend
to take his own dead father's place.

Yet all was not books and schoolmasters at Westminster School.  Sports were not encouraged there
overmuch, but Cowley played his share with the rest.
His youthful play, *Love's Riddle*, he tells us, was written
in time 'Stol'n . . . from cat, or ball'—the latter probably
being a primitive form of football.  Other favourite
games of the school were 'trap', 'span-farthing',
marbles, boxing, and wrestling.  Stage plays were also
popular forms of recreation—professional and amateur.
The Westminster boys had their favourites among the

[1] Cf. Sargeaunt, *passim*.                    [2] Ibid.

adult companies, as Cowley's dedication of his own first play shows, in its allusion to

> . . . a part for Robinson, whom they
> At school account essential to a play.

Why they especially admired Richard Robinson is a question difficult to answer, since he was not an outstanding member of the King's Men at this time. However, the fact that he had made his first reputation as a child actor, praised by Ben Jonson as an 'ingenious youth' in 1616, may have attracted the boys to him. Moreover, Cowley may have felt a sort of family interest in the man, since Robinson, after serving his apprenticeship under Burbadge himself and later marrying Burbadge's widow, had seemingly stepped into the adult vacancy left by Shakespeare's fellow-member, Richard Cowley, in 1619.[1] There is, however, no definite evidence to show that Richard and Abraham Cowley possessed anything more than a fairly usual surname in common, though the Cowleys were friendly with a Robinson family, as is shown by the will of Abraham's brother Thomas. So there may have been some professional dramatic tradition in the Cowley circle. As for amateur theatricals, at school itself an annual Latin play was given by the boys and was regarded as one of the most prized customs of the place, though scenery was absolutely lacking.

One of Cowley's friends who was interested in the drama was John Nichols (or Nicholas), a boy who showed his interest by going up to Cambridge a little ahead of the other and producing a play of his own there.[2] Still another, Robert Meade, later wrote a comedy, *Love and Friendship*, which was printed posthumously; Meade, like Cowley, was the son of a stationer, at the

---

[1] Cf. Baldwin, *Shakespearean Company*, pp. 224–5, &c.
[2] See Cowley's 'Answer to an Invitation to Cambridge'; and Moore Smith, *College Plays*, p. 70.

sign of the Black Lion, Fleet Street, and Wood calls him
'a learned man'.[1] Benjamin Masters was still another
interested in literature. He not only wrote commendatory poems for Cowley's first volume, but also,
according to the *Alumni Westmonasterienses*, composed
several printed sets of verses of his own.[2] One of Cowley's less intimate and non-literary schoolfellows at this
time was also Henry Bennet, son of Sir John Bennet of
Middlesex,[3] and later favourite of Charles II, who
created him Earl of Arlington for services rendered in
managing the royal mistresses.

Thus, wherever he went, Cowley was sure to make
friends, usually of a particular type. As he says in 'Of
Myself', 'Even when I was a very young boy at school,
instead of running about on holidays and playing with
my fellows, I was wont to steal from them, and walk
into the fields, either alone with a book, or with some
one companion, if I could find any of the same temper'.
Such a contemplative disposition is not at all unnatural
among schoolboys, and Cowley is not to be considered
in any respect abnormal in his daily life. In fact,
he even seems to have been not unfamiliar with the
birch, and perhaps had had the offensive but common
experience of being made to kiss it afterwards, as an
indication of his submission.

Such, in general, is a picture of his stay of seven or
eight years at Westminster. But never during this time
did he forget his ambition to be a poet. He must have
scribbled a great deal which he destroyed—such, at
least, was his custom in later life. Following *Pyramus
and Thisbe*, however, the next poem that can be dated
with any exactness is *Constantia and Philetus*, which
'confesseth me two years older when I writ it'[4]—that is,
he composed it about 1630.

[1] Wood, iii. 343.     [2] Grosart, *Cowley*, i. xiii.
[3] Sargeaunt, pp. 71, 74.
[4] 'To the Reader', 1636 ed. of *Poetical Blossoms*.

*Constantia and Philetus* is both much like *Pyramus and Thisbe* and at the same time very different from it. For subject the boy poet has chosen material which is again both a love story and a tragedy, and Venus and Cupid and the other gods still play an important part in the introduction. The scene, however, is no longer laid in Roman days but in Italian; some Italian *novella*, indeed, may have furnished the ground-plot, although the tale as Cowley tells it, with its two lovers, its rival favoured by the parents, and its sympathetic brother, each one of whom has 'gaspt out his flying sprite' at the end, is quite too conventional to allow any real identification.

Two new and important tendencies, however, appear in the poem—two tendencies which from now on strove for the ascendancy, and of which one for a long time seemed to be victorious, only to be at last unseated by the other after the struggle appeared to be over. 'What a force must he have put on himself, when he complied with the false taste of his age, in his poetical, which he too modestly thought his best, works!' exclaimed Richard Hurd a hundred and fifty years later.[1] Yet Cowley does not seem to have forced himself particularly into the style which Hurd and Johnson so much reprehended. The cleverness and dazzlement of the 'conceit' of Ovid and his school, or the bucolic simplicity and tranquillity of Horace and his—Cowley, an adult in facility of composition, but a babe in judgement, was obviously uncertain which to choose. Moreover, in England the examples of the Spenserians, William Browne with his pastorals, and Giles Fletcher, who had already brought fame to Westminster School, were before him. The head master, Osbaldeston, with his unusual emphasis on English composition, admired the latter style, as seen by the verses and orations composed by his students. Naturally enough, when faced

[1] Hurd, *Selected Works of Cowley*, ii. 58.

with the dilemma of choice, young Abraham Cowley compromised—he took them all.

The amorous 'conceits' of *The Mistress* are already present in *Constantia and Philetus*, though in his address 'To the Reader' Cowley vows, 'My Muse with tears, not with conceits, did flow'. But tears also flow from the eyes of the hitherto cold Constantia as if 'Her burning flame had melted hills of snow'; Cupid is unable to escape, because in setting the heart of Philetus on fire he had burned his own wings; the beauty of Constantia has made her lover 'blind with too much sight'; and at the end, in death, the eyes of Philetus are 'Like a fallen star, or an eclipsèd sun'. An echo song is introduced, which in artificial cleverness is not much behind the other echoists. And yet, though these various conceits confess that the author has fallen under the spell which held him in bondage during most of his life and which likewise brought him a measure of contemporary fame that for long throned him without a peer, this poem also prophesies the ending. From the first there was in Cowley a yearning for the beauties of the country and the consolations of nature. He was no Wordsworthian, as Dr. Grosart too enthusiastically suggested,[1] nor did he observe nature with the loving minuteness and individuality which distinguish the nineteenth century from the eighteenth; but even at twelve he cherished

> The crystal brooks which gently run between
> The shadowing trees, and as they through them pass
> Water the earth, and keep the meadows green,
> Giving a colour to the verdant grass.

Did he write such lines because he had read about similar scenes in his poets, or had he already begun to make trips into Kent and perhaps spend his holidays there, as he was to do later? Or perhaps, since vacations

[1] Grosart, *Cowley*, i. civ–v.

VERA

ÆTAT: SUE 13    Anno 1633

REGII ALUMNI SCOLÆ WEST                    EFFIGIES ABRA: COWLEY

Reader when first thou shalt behold this boyes
Picture, perhaps thou'lt thinke his writings, toyes.
Wrong not our Cowley so; will nothing passe
But gravity with thee? Apollo was
Beardlesse himselfe, and for ought I can see
Cowley may yongest sonne of Phœbus bee.

B. Masters comp:        Hen: Seile excu: Ro: Vaughan sculp

COWLEY AS A BOY

were almost unknown in Westminster School, he had found his delight in his walks into the countryside near by—for a few minutes' stroll in almost any direction would have taken him beyond the houses, the Parliament buildings, and the Law Courts, into the meadows of Hampstead, the marshes of Tuttle Fields, or along the brook which ran past the south wall of the school. There is, however, no way of telling exactly where he found this love for the country, unless it is permitted to reconstruct the past from the future. All that is sure is that, from this time on, the struggle between the two sides of Cowley's nature commences: shall he choose the fashionable style as his key to fame, or shall he turn away from that fascinating door and seek only the moderate pleasures of the quiet country life?

*Constantia and Philetus* is itself negligible in the light of the problem it propounds. The author himself, moreover, confesses some doubt as to the success of the poem, for he ends by saying that he will omit the 'doleful words' of Constantia's father for his dead daughter: these

> . . . my tired Muse me calls
> T' o'erpass, which I most gladly do, for fear
> That I should toil too much the reader's ear.

Not very long after this time appeared Cowley's first volume of poetry. It bore the title of *Poetical Blossoms*, and also carried the insinuating motto, '—*fit surculus arbor*': 'the sprout becomes the tree'.

## AT WESTMINSTER SCHOOL

JUST how early in its season Cowley's 'sprout' thrust itself into public view is a somewhat more debatable question than is ordinarily supposed.[1] The first extant edition of *Poetical Blossoms* is certainly dated 1633, and yet there are several evidences that the little collection was known, in some form, at least two years before.[2] Possibly Sprat made a mistake when he wrote, 'In the thirteenth year of his age there came forth a little book under his name';[3] possibly Cowley's own memory betrayed him when he spoke of an ode in 'Of Myself' as one made 'when I was but thirteen years old, and which was then printed with many other verses'. But even though Cowley's error may have misled the uncritical Sprat, how account for Benjamin Masters' commendatory poem 'To His Dear Friend Abraham Cowley, on His Flourishing and Hopeful Blossoms', with its phrase, 'Nor yet was Cato's judgement at thirteen So great as thine'?

Preparations were obviously on foot in 1631 to announce to London its youngest genius. Why else should Robert Vaughan have engraved a portrait of Cowley, which was labelled 'Aetat: suae 13' even though the date 'Anno 1633' had to be added later when the book was printed? The manuscript must have been ready and in circulation, though for some reason publication was delayed. If this situation be admitted, a sonnet written on December 9, 1631, as Gosse and Grosart have suggested, is flooded with new light:

> How soon hath Time, the subtle thief of youth,
> Stolen on his wing my three and twentieth year!

[1] Cf. Grosart and Gosse, Grosart's *Cowley*, i. xliii.

[2] Loiseau calls attention to the fact that the licence was issued on October 24, 1632—see Arber, iv. 287.      [3] Sprat, 'Account.'

My hasting days fly on with full career,
But my late spring no bud or blossom shew'th.
Perhaps my semblance might deceive the truth,
That I to manhood am arrived so near,
And inward ripeness doth much less appear,
That some more timely-happy spirits endu'th.
Yet be it less or more, or soon or slow,
It shall be still in strictest measure even
To that same lot, however mean or high,
Toward which Time leads me, and the will of Heaven;
All is, if I have grace to use it so,
As ever in my great Task-Master's eye.

Had Milton, preparing to 'go down' from Cambridge to Horton, already heard rumours of the *Poetical Blossoms* of the poet whose reputation was to rival, if not eclipse, his own and all other contemporaries' until many years after both were dead and buried? Was the Puritan, with his 'late spring', with 'no bud or blossom', already envying the young Royalist, the 'timely-happy' spirit ten years his junior, who was to take place beside Shakespeare and Spenser as one of his three favourite poets?[1]

Whatever the precedent circumstances, in 1633 Henry Seile displayed a small new quarto of thirty-two leaves for sale in his shop at the sign of the Tiger's Head in St. Paul's Churchyard. The volume, with its engraved portrait, its dedications, and its other features, was an attractive one and must have drawn the attention of many to the author pictured there in a costume which is still worn by the Captain of the King's Scholars when delivering the prologue to the annual Latin play. Cowley is pictured in the conventional tight-fitting jacket buttoned to the neck, his turndown collar being tied with small tassels, his tight sleeves encasing stiffly posed arms, and his thick hair being cut in bangs across the forehead but allowed to curl down to the neck behind. His face, more oval than square, with its stout

[1] Cf. Johnson, *Lives*, i. 154.

nose and small, rather full, mouth, was not a strikingly handsome one at this time, but it is sufficient proof that it was only his mind which had developed so much beyond his years. In externals he was like all other boys of his age.

The purchaser of *Poetical Blossoms* would have found it to be made up of three other poems besides *Constantia and Philetus* and *Pyramus and Thisbe*. The last of these, 'A Dream of Elysium,' was a sort of schoolboy exercise in which the Muse, 'whom I adore', vouchsafed the poet a visit to the Elysian Fields, where all his favourites of lesson time—Hyacinth, Narcissus, and Apollo; Ovid, Homer, and Cato; Hero and Leander, Portia and Brutus, Pyramus and Thisbe—for a brief space came to life before they dissolved as the cockcrow interrupted his dream. The other two opened to him a new field, which he was to cultivate assiduously—that of occasional verse. Both were elegies, one on the death of Dudley, 'Lord Carleton, Viscount Dorchester, Late Principal Secretary of State', an old Westminster boy who died on February 2, 1632, and the other on a death which came much nearer home, for it was that of Cowley's cousin, Richard Clerke, or Clarke, a student at Lincoln's Inn. The technic of both, with their extravagant praises and high-flown comparisons, is very similar to that of the commendatory verses prefixed to the volume by Cowley's school friends, and the poems are therefore probably good examples of the goal at which Master Lambert Osbaldeston taught his less clever pupils to aim.

If the epistle 'To the Reader' added to the second edition of *Poetical Blossoms* three years later is to be believed, some of the buyers of the book read it with censure, some with scepticism, and some with approval. A few, indeed, had even called the author 'a pipe, which never sounds but when 'tis blowed in' and had suspected him of being not 'Abraham Cowley, but *Authorem anonymum*'. But the Westminster boys knew better;

and Cowley himself, surely a bit puffed up with his distinction, went on looking for occasions upon which he could exercise his skill.

.Such opportunities were many, especially to one who seemingly from the first believed with his whole soul in the divinity which hedges a king. Charles I, now ruler of Great Britain for some eight years, had already entered troubled waters. The task of conciliating all parties, pleasing himself, and still strengthening his throne was proving more and more beyond his powers, and he was continually taking steps which alienated new groups of his subjects. His coronation at Edinburgh on June 18, 1633, was one of his errors, because of the Anglican ceremonial which accompanied it, but this fact could never be guessed from the two poems which Cowley soon afterward wrote, 'On His Majesty's Return out of Scotland'. The same thoroughgoing loyalty is evinced in the ode entitled 'In Commendation of the Time We Live under the Reign of Our Gracious King Charles', which ends with the flattery that Charles has changed

> The Iron Age of old
> Into an Age of Gold.

Nor were the verses confined to the King alone. Probably nearly every birth, death, and journey of the more prominent members of the court was hailed as grist for the industrious mills of Cowley and his colleagues in Westminster School. Often these events must have been set as 'themes' by one or another of the masters, since whole collections of poems on such topics as the birth of the Duke of York on October 15, 1633, exist in manuscript at the British Museum and otherwhere. One of this set, which is entitled *Genethliaca Ducis Eboracensis* and contains effusive contributions in Latin and English by no less than sixteen boys, is signed by Cowley,[1] as is

[1] Compare the version printed in Sargeaunt, p. 282, with that in Royal MS. 12 A. xiii, ff. 2 b–3b.

another in another manuscript on the birth of the Princess Elizabeth on Christmas Eve, 1635.[1] Since these were never included in his works during his lifetime—the former, indeed, having never been 'collected'—they plainly represent a large number of similar exercises which were lost or destroyed.

How much of all this was worship from afar cannot be said, but it should be remembered that the School was not much distant from Whitehall and the palaces. A meeting even at this age with some of his heroes and heroines is not beyond credulity; and in fact his poem 'To the Duchess of Buckingham' would suggest that such a thing had occurred. For the still beautiful duchess, widowed by the assassination of her husband in 1628, was the mother of that George Villiers, Duke of Buckingham, who left his name so deeply dyed on the pages of Restoration history and who, despite his many more weighty and still more frivolous concerns, found time to be one of the chief patrons of Abraham Cowley, the stationer's son.

There was, however, one birthday which the School did not celebrate with any versification.[2] It occurred on November 19, 1634—the day on which King Charles was thirty-four years old. One of the customs of Westminster demanded that on the King's birthday the King's Scholars post in Hall a copy of verses made for the occasion by one of their number. It is difficult to believe that Cowley composed no poem for the event, but at any rate none was posted—a fact which was later made one of the charges brought by the fanatical Laud against the moderate Bishop Williams, Dean of the School. The real cause of the failure, however, is not far to seek. Lambert Osbaldeston, a strong-willed anti-Stuart and enemy of Laud, was clearly implicated. In the preceding winter he had furthermore written several

[1] Harleian MS. 6383, f. 30, and Grosart, *Cowley*, i. cxxxix.
[2] Cf. Sargeaunt, ch. v.

forceful but incautious letters, referring to some un-
named enemy as 'Vermin, little Urchin, meddling
Hocus-Pocus'. When the letters came into the possession
of Laud and his Star Chamber in 1639 Laud chose to
consider himself as described by these ungentle epithets,
in spite of Osbaldeston's denials. As a result, the
Head Master was fined ten thousand pounds, half to go
to the Crown and half to the Archbishop, was to lose all
his appointments, and—greatest indignity of all—was
sentenced to have one of his ears nailed to the pillory in
the Palace Yard and the other similarly treated in the
Dean's Yard, with his pupils as witnesses—whereafter he
was to remain in prison during the King's pleasure.
But Master Osbaldeston thought too much of his ears to
allow them to be thus separated. He did not await
the officers. By the time they arrived he had fled, according to his note, 'beyond Canterbury'—and Cowley had
already been for two or three years at Trinity, where
the authorities were all staunch to the Stuart cause.
Osbaldeston's pupils would not be likely to write birthday odes to the King.

The year 1633, however, was more noted for the
appearance of another and more momentous volume of
poetry than the juvenilia of *Poetical Blossoms*. For the
first collected edition of John Donne's poems, which had
long been circulating in manuscript, was put into print
in that year, and it is from this time that Cowley's
discipleship (if such a thing ever actually existed except
in the minds of later critics) dates. Donne had died two
years before, while still Dean of St. Paul's Cathedral.
As a famous preacher, with his hour-glass beside him in
the high pulpit, he had very likely spellbound Cowley
with some of his sermons as he had spellbound all
the rest of London. But these poems, for the most part
the product of his unregenerate and impious youth,
were totally different from what the boy might have
heard from his lips at St. Paul's—they were harsh,

violent, passionate things, the fruit of a tortured, discontented, yet profoundly penetrating mind, which
stripped the sham from all human motives and human
emotions, and had no more mercy for the possible
sensitiveness of a mistress than for the hypocrisy of a
court usher.

The first clear sign of the influence of Donne seems
to have grown from a visit which Cowley paid to the
Law Courts at Westminster Hall. The boys of Westminster School had the privilege of listening to the
arguments there and of attending the debates in the
Commons, but apparently were not always welcomed
in those places. At any rate, one day Cowley made an
appointment with a friend to meet at Westminster Hall,
probably as much for a lark as for the instruction they
would gain. From the first, however, affairs did not
turn out as planned. The friend failed to appear, but
Cowley resolved to go on with his sport alone. No
sooner had he found a place, however, than a 'semi-
gentleman of th' Inns of Court' tried to push him out
of it. As any boy of spirit would, Cowley resisted with
some sturdiness, whereupon a 'neat man in a ruff',
whom he therefore took to be a barrister, turned on him
reprovingly, with the words, 'Boy, get you gone. This
is no school! '

Not at all cowed, Cowley answered smartly,

'Oh, no !
For if it were, all you gowned men would go
Up for false Latin! '

Shocked at such impudence, the Inns of Court youth,
in his often-pawned satin suit, struck out at Cowley,
who 'providently skipped away' to a safe distance, from
which he poured out such a stream of scathing remarks
on law students and lawyers that one must look to
Donne's first and fourth satires for the inspiration of
'A Poetical Revenge', the poem which Cowley immediately wrote in impish exultation over his victory.

The two or three early amorous verses which are extant from this period may also show a slight debt to Donne's *Songs and Sonnets*. In addition, Cowley's first love affair may be preserved in the ode, 'To His Mistress', beginning,

> Tyrian dye why do you wear,
> You whose cheeks best scarlet are ?

Another lyric, likewise dating from this time, but not printed until 1700, is perhaps addressed to the same mistress, here named Eliza; but its content is as commonplace as its title—'To a Lady Who Desired a Song of Mr. Cowley, He Presented This Following'.

Donne's poems thus set another fashionable style before Cowley, which he practised upon at intervals, but which he did not display to any extent until *The Mistress* burst upon the applauding world many years later. Only two or three times did he refer to Donne by name, but these allusions, coupled with certain imitations, are sufficient to show an intimate knowledge. In 1656, for instance, he quoted from 'Doctor Donne's' 'The Will' in his own preface; and in his early play, *The Guardian*, he made Dogrel say of Aurelia: ' . . . thou'dst be a rare wife for me. I should beget on thee Donnes and Jonsons; but thou art too witty.'

'Donnes and Jonsons'! To Cowley these seem to have been the two wittiest English poets. Both were intensely learned men, both were critics of society, and both were known for the unorthodoxness and roughness of their versification. Little of Jonson's rocky strength is discernible in Cowley, as is little of Donne's white-heat of feeling. But he read them both, and profited as well as he could, especially in his experiments in metrics. As he may have heard Donne preach, so he may even have met Jonson in the great Ben's lodgings in Westminster, or at the Dog or some other pot-house which the other frequented. William Cartwright, one of Ben's most loved 'Sons', was an old Westminster boy and student of Osbaldeston's, and may very probably have introduced this prodigy of the coming generation to the dying war-horse of the old. However this may be, the great Lord Chancellor, Clarendon, at this time simple Edward Hyde, is authority for Cowley's imitation of Jonson, who, he said in acknowledging his own youthful debt to Jonson, Selden, Falkland, and their circle, 'was the best judge of, and fittest to prescribe rules to, poetry and poets, of any man who had lived with or before him, or since: if Mr. Cowley had not made a flight beyond all men, with that modesty yet, to ascribe much of this to the example and learning of Ben Jonson'. [1] At any rate, Cowley practically forgets Spenser from this time on.

Cowley's daily life during these years must be inferred from his poems. When, on May 9, 1635, John Littleton, elder son of Sir Thomas Littleton, tried courageously to save his younger brother from drowning but was drowned himself also, Cowley wrote an elegy in honour of the lad. When Mistress Anne Whitfield, whom he seemingly knew at court, died, the elegiac Muse was again called upon, in a poem which contains one of the many reminiscences of Shakespeare to be found in his work. He convinced himself that he was paying part of his debt to his godfather by writing a poem promising some day to write another poem about his 'sponsor in baptism' which would make both their names immortal. He translated a set of verses about the 'B. Virgin'.

The life of affairs, the routine of school, the desire for fame via the path of fashionable poetry, were uppermost. And still he had not yet succeeded in strangling the other side of his character. Hidden and almost lost with only a spark or two burning, was the suspicion that perhaps his present road was the wrong one—that

[1] Clarendon, *Life*, i. 34.

another type of existence was the one for which he was
best fitted and for which he should not kill his longings.
Tucked away at the end of an eleven-stanza poem,
'A Vote', in which he recorded his abhorrence of the
sermonizing Puritan, the pedantic schoolmaster, the
fee-seeking justice of the peace, the tailor-made courtier, the psalm-singing churchman, and the rest, much
in the manner of Donne, he inserted the following
lines:

> This only grant me: that my means may lie
> Too low for envy, for contempt too high;
>    Some honour I would have,
> Not from great deeds, but good alone;
> Th' ignote are better than ill-known;
>    Rumour can ope the grave.
> Acquaintance I would hug, but when 't depends
> Not from the number, but the choice, of friends.
>
> Books should, not business, entertain the light,
> And sleep, as undisturbed as death, the night.
>    My house a cottage more
> Than palace, and should fitting be
> For all my use, no luxury;
>    My garden painted o'er
> With Nature's hand, not Art's, and pleasures yield
> Horace might envy in his Sabine field.

And to prove to 'future times' that this was his real
'soul's picture' he wrote three other odes, based partly
on his favourite classic authors and having these titles:
'That a Pleasant Poverty Is to Be Preferred before Discontented Riches', 'On the Uncertainty of Fortune',
and 'Upon the Shortness of Man's Life'. Brooks, king-
fishers, daisies, lilies, daffodils, and robin-red-breasts
brighten the lines of the second poem, and show that
Cowley, notwithstanding his submersion in the city, has
not forgotten that the country is still beautiful.

Somewhere, about this time, Cowley also acquired

the ambition to be a dramatist.[1] Westminster School itself, though never the home of a semi-professional company of child actors as were Paul's and the Chapel Royal, had had a long and honourable history in the drama, as could be expected in an institution which numbered the names of Nicholas Udall, John Taylor, and William Elderton among its past masters. The annual Latin play was still a vigorous tradition, and Cowley had undoubtedly sat with the rest of his fellows on the benches, boxes, and edges of tables in the Hall watching the mingled pride and anguish of the performers, or perhaps had even taken a part himself. He had, moreover, begun to frequent the public theatre on the days when a 'play', or holiday, was announced by the masters. The terminology of the drama had already become his in *Constantia and Philetus* when he had distinguished the stages of his story as 'the first act in 's tragedy', the 'prologue to his tragedy', and 'a full and perfect tragedy'. His habit of dropping in upon performances at the Cockpit, only a few minutes' walk to the north, appears in his slighting allusion to 'One who is ravished with a Cockpit play' in 'A Poetical Revenge' —a poem which also refers to Shakespeare's dramas and to Ruggle's *Ignoramus*, the Latin comedy which had stirred James I to such heights of enthusiasm at Trinity, Cambridge, in 1615. In his visits to the Cockpit, and the Bull, and the other playhouses he mentions, Cowley had noticed mockingly how the gallants rose conspicuously between the acts, swept the boxes with their gaze, and then cried, 'God save you, madame!' whether a belle recognized them or not; or he had criticized the 'huge, gigantic speeches' and the exaggerated posturing of the actors. What more natural, then, than that he should try a play of his own ?

Sometime toward the end of his Westminster career,

[1] Cf. my article, 'Abraham Cowley as Dramatist,' *R.E.S.*, iv. (1928), 1–8.

consequently, he began work on a pastoral drama, to be entitled *Love's Riddle*. The tradition of the pastoral, in the drama as well as the poetic romance, was an old one, but Cowley seems to be quite at home in it. Perhaps he had seen Thomas Randolph's *Amyntas* performed at Whitehall; or perhaps he had read Joseph Rutter's *The Shepherd's Holiday* when it was published in 1635; or perhaps he had felt the charm of Fletcher's *The Faithful Shepherdess*. On the other hand, resemblances to the Greek *Daphnis and Chloe* by Longus, to Guarini's *Il Pastor Fido*, to Tasso's *Aminta*, and to Bonarelli's *Filli di Sciro* have been suggested, in spite of the fact that there is no definite evidence of Cowley's knowledge of Italian. If with these 'sources', however, are put the many incidental reminiscences of Daniel, of Lyly, of Shakespeare, and of Ben Jonson, whose method of characterization by 'humours' is patent, the critic cannot fail to be impressed, if not overwhelmed, with the author's reading at an age when most boys find the task of getting their required lessons to be quite sufficient.

In *Love's Riddle* Cowley is still faced with his dilemma. His conceits, especially in the first half of the play, are plentiful, but commonplace. A lover is described as part chameleon and part salamander, the sun of love is prayed to melt the ice of a woman's heart, and nature is supposed to have 'robbed the Great to make one Microcosm'—that is, one woman. The best suggestion of Donne occurs in Callidora's short speech in the first act, beginning,

> For as the soul is nobler than the body,
> So its corruption asks a better medicine.

On the other hand, there are many passages on the comparative value of city and country life, notably in the 'Beatus ille' or 'How happy is that man' speech of Callidora in act two. Cowley, indeed, does not preserve his pastoral atmosphere as well as Randolph does, for he confuses the pastoral and the sylvan, and he has allowed himself many incongruous references to the 'City Bear Garden', to the 'fearful noise of guns', and to 'a Welchman'; nor would one expect even a mad Sicilian to exclaim, 'Pox on you!' But, taken in conjunction with Cowley's earlier passages on the country life, this pastoral comedy must clearly be admitted to have sprung from an innate longing of one side of his nature, and should not be regarded as a mere conventional imitation of earlier writers in order to show the author's precociousness and ingenuity in weaving the borrowings from a wide reading into a pattern of his own.

Without doubt, Cowley hoped that his play would attract favourable enough attention to be produced, perhaps at Westminster. The large number of songs fitted for boy singing would indicate this anticipation. Nevertheless, although the play possesses many lyrical and some dramatic passages, as well as a typical Cowleyan humour and a clever vein of satire, it was never given as he wrote it. It was, however, adapted by Daniel Bellamy for performance in a young ladies' boarding school in 1723.[1] Hapless author! Nor was it included in the second edition of *Poetical Blossoms*, issued in the spring of 1636, although a new section, entitled *Sylva, or Divers Copies of Verses Made upon Sundry Occasions by A. C.* and containing the best of his productions during the preceding three years, was added to the old. And this title, *Sylva*, would suggest that the author felt that some of the promise of the 'surculus' of *Poetical Blossoms* had begun to be realized. In the eyes of others, perhaps, he was certainly not yet a 'grove' or even a 'tree'; but few would refuse to admit that he was now a sapling.

[1] Ibid., pp. 6–7.

# III

## 'THE MUSE'S HANNIBAL'

FOR seven or eight years, then, Cowley remained one of 'Anthony's pigs'—yet not contentedly so, in spite of his poetical success. For here he was, a great fellow of seventeen, still in a preparatory school when the average age of admission to the university was but fourteen or fifteen.[1] Although at twelve or less he had probably been as mature as the ordinary college entrant, he had been forced to stick ignobly at Westminster for a long period which must have seemed a mere tedious marking of time.

Whatever the reason for this delay, whether it was the financial condition of his widowed mother forced to provide for the other members of a large family or whether it was some educational technicality or deficiency, the boy chafed under the yoke. His impatience, indeed, tempered though it was with an attempt to be philosophical, finally broke its bounds and displayed itself to public view, as friend after friend was 'sped away' to Cambridge or Oxford. The final poem in *Sylva*, entitled 'An Answer to an Invitation to Cambridge' and addressed to 'Nichols, my better self', is plain indication of Cowley's frame of mind. In it, he pleaded with Nichols, who had gone up as a Trinity scholar a year ahead of him,[2] not to tempt him with a description of the pleasures of Cambridge or he might commit the 'schoolboy's sin' of truancy. The taste of Ovid had grown insipid on his palate when he thought of the 'dainties of philosophy' awaiting him at the university, and he loathed the 'crambo' of school when he let himself reflect on 'logic's diverse cheer'. He

[1] Mullinger, *Cambridge Characteristics*, p. 28.
[2] Ball, *Admissions to Trinity College*, ii. 349.

begged Nichols not to tantalize him with the beauties
of the Cam, for fear that the last vestige of pleasure in
London's 'chief holiday', when even the dungboats were
repainted and, gay with flags, bore the merrymaking
'cits' out upon the troubled Thames, would be destroyed. 'Why do I stay, then ?' he inquired ruefully.

> . . . I would meet
> Thee there, but plummets hang upon my feet:
> 'Tis my chief wish to live with thee,
> But not till I deserve thy company.
> Till then we'll scorn to let that toy,
> Some forty miles, divide our hearts.
> Write to me, and I shall enjoy,
> Friendship and wit, thy better parts.
> Though envious Fortune larger hindrance brings,
> We easily see each other: *Love hath wings.*

A new event, moreover, was to convince Cowley that
'envious Fortune' had marked him for her own. In the
spring of 1636 he determined to announce himself a
candidate for a university scholarship. According to the
terms of Elizabeth's charter to Westminster School,
three scholars were to be elected annually from the
group of Queen's or King's Scholars to go up to Christ
Church, Oxford, and three to Trinity College, Cambridge; and this number was later increased, in spite of
the fact that sometimes the colleges did not have vacan-
cies for these new members.[1]  For some unexplained
reason, Cowley seems to have preferred Trinity to
Christ Church, although a Trinity scholarship was
worth only about half as much as one at Christ Church
—and surely this must have been an item of consideration to a boy in none too affluent circumstances.
Nevertheless, he went to Osbaldeston and declared his
purpose—one of which the head master must surely
have approved.

[1] Cf. Mullinger and Sargeaunt, *passim.*

The second Monday in Easter term arrived, and with
it the electors. The Dean of Christ Church, accompanied by one of his masters, came down to London from
Oxford; the Master of Trinity, bringing with him one
of his own sharpest examiners, was driven in from Cambridge; and all four immediately went into consultation with Osbaldeston, Bishop Williams as Dean of
the School, and one of the latter's prebendaries. The
dormitories and halls were scrubbed and shining, for on
Monday all the former Scholars were traditionally in-
vited to a banquet and on Tuesday the electors made
their annual tour of inspection. But the excitement of
the School in general could have been nothing in comparison with that of the two classes of candidates, the
'minor' and the 'major'—those who desired to go,
respectively, to St. Peter's College within their own
school or to one of the universities.

'Challenge', or the examination of the 'College'
candidates in grammar, humane letters, and composition, elicited relatively little attention in view of the
greater honours at stake. Nervous as Cowley was,
however, and wondering about the impression he had
made on the electors, he seemingly still had sufficient
control of his head to live up to his reputation as a wit
in the epigram contest at the banquet on the first night.
With the given quotation from Ovid, 'Nullis amor est
medicabilis herbis', tradition has it that he arose and
delivered the following quatrain:

> Sol Daphnis sees, and seeing her admires,
> Which adds new flames to his celestial fires.
> Had any remedy for love been known,
> The god of physic, sure, had cured his own.[1]

On Tuesday the electors visited the school, and the
boys recited their declamations, composed for the
occasion by the head master. Finally the names of the

[1] Johnson's ed. of *Cowley*, i. 356. Cf. Sargeaunt, p. 73.

fortunate candidates were read—the boys who, on the
morrow, would deliver their declamations 'up school'
before all the students and faculty and would immediately thereafter be 'sped away' to the universities. But,
when the list was announced, Abraham Cowley's name
was not on it.

The cause of his failure is perhaps not too obscure to
be found. Cowley himself has given the clue to it in his
admission that he would never get the rules of grammar
(classical Latin grammar, of course) by heart. As
Sargeaunt has pointed out, both Westminster and
Trinity were at this time very strict in this matter. As
a result, the electors chose George Younger, William
Croyden, Charles Bernard de Berg, and Thomas Yard-
ley, but failed Abraham Cowley.[1] The record reads
simply: 'A. Cowley was a candidate for Cambridge, but
not elected'.[2] The boy, however, though apparently
bearing no resentment, had his revenge; for none of the
other four ever made any figure in either the academic
or the larger world,[3] whereas Cowley soon became one
of the graduates of whom both Westminster and Trinity
were most proud.

Disappointed, even despondent, as he must have been
for the moment, he was nevertheless not to be permanently abandoned by the Fortune whom he had just
slandered as 'envious'. Perhaps at this critical juncture
one of those ubiquitous friends with whom he was
always so well provided intervened. If so, the most likely
guess is Sir Kenelm Digby, the brilliant and erratic
young man whose exploits as student, 'scientist', lover,
privateer, and courtier had excited both England and
the Continent.[4] Digby had by this date already 'discovered' his famous 'powder of sympathy', which was
attested on good authority to cure wounds if merely

---

[1] Ball, *Admissions*, ii. 352; Welch.
[2] *Alumni Westmonasterienses*, quoted by Grosart, *Cowley*, i. xiv.
[3] Sargeaunt, p. 30.                          [4] Digby, *Private Memoirs*.

brought into contact with any substance which had once touched them; the death of his beautiful and 'seeming virtuous' wife and the subsequent autopsy had made him the subject of considerable suspicious gossip when it was found that her brain was peculiarly small and when his explanation that he had been plying her with doses of 'viper wine' to increase her beauty had ɔeen heard; and he had recently provoked the remonstrance of Laud by reverting, while on a visit to France, to the Roman Catholicism of his family. Yet he was a popular and spectacular figure, as proved by many tributes and dedications, one of which was by Abraham Cowley. For when Cowley published his *Love's Riddle*, the manuscript of which he carried with him when he went up to Cambridge in spite of his failure of election, he addressed it 'To the truly worthy, and noble, Sir Kenelm Digby, Knight', with promises of 'future service' which seem to indicate the presence of a debt to be repaid. And after all, what is more probable than that Digby, called by his Oxford tutor, the mathematician Allen, the 'Mirandula' or infant prodigy of his age, should have heard of Cowley, an infant prodigy fifteen years younger, and have spoken a few words in his favour to the proper people? Furthermore, Aubrey has recorded that Digby was ever 'very kind' to the younger man.[1] Nevertheless, if Digby's influence was exerted in this particular instance, it must have been applied indirectly, as the result of an earlier acquaintance, since the older man seems to have been in France just at this moment.

Or perhaps Cowley had simply made a better impression on the Master of Trinity than he had realized. Dr. Comber may have decided that he could not fairly elect the boy as a Trinity Scholar on the terms of the Westminster competition, but he may have perceived that such gifts as Cowley's did not belong in the

[1] Aubrey, i. 226; Stebbing, *Some Verdicts of History Reviewed*, p. 53.

ordinary category, and that it would be a stupid piece
of pedantry to overlook them. At any rate, the records
of Trinity College for March 30, 1636, read as follows:
'It is ordered by the Master and Seniors the 30th of
March, 1636, that Abraham Cowley was chosen into a
dry chorister's place in reversion, and that the College
shall allow him the benefit thereof till it fall, or that he
be chosen Scholar at the election of Scholars next
following'.[1]

Thus from one of 'Anthony's pigs' Cowley became
a 'dry chorister'—a mysterious rating which Aldis
Wright has conjectured to mean a chorister who,
paradoxically, did not sing. Such an appointment and
such unusual favours as are suggested in the above-
quoted record would indicate that a strong influence of
some sort was at work in Cowley's behalf. Naturally
enough, he did not reject his opportunity; and on
April 21, 1636, under the name of 'Abraham Cooley', he
donned the purple gown of the Trinity undergraduate
and began his university career, having been assigned
to the tutorship of Mr. Caesar Williamson.[2]

Life in its externals was not very different from what it
had been before.[3] The chapel bell still rang at five, and
matins was said, followed by a short homily by one of
the Fellows. These exercises set the tone for the whole
day. As for studies, the old quadriennium was still in
force, consisting chiefly of work in Latin and Greek;
rhetoric; a little arithmetic, geometry, and astronomy;
and logic and metaphysics. These subjects were pursued under the direction of a tutor and also by attendance on the college and university lectures—though at

[1] Cf. Hill's note in Johnson's *Lives*, i. 65. Because of what he re-
gards as a contradiction between the dates of the examination and of
Cowley's admission, Loiseau suggests that the date in the Master's
Conclusion Book should be 1637 rather than 1636. He also has an
interesting discussion of the term 'dry chorister'.

[2] Ball, ii. 352.

[3] Cf. Mullinger; Godfrey, *Home Life under Stuarts;* &c.

this time the halls of the latter speakers were very meagrely populated. One of the main educational features of the day, however, was the 'disputation', in which the older students, much in the medieval manner, still measured their wits in logic combat with their own colleagues or with rivals from other colleges. In such exhibitions, however, Cowley could not have shone as brilliantly as in his private studies, for he was always recognized as a rather poor speaker—in spite of Sprat's insistence that his 'exercitia scholastica' were 'Romano foro et Ciceronis auribus digna'.[1]

Even though theology was not officially part of the curriculum, the atmosphere of the whole university was predominantly religious—nor was it therefore different from that in which Cowley had always moved. It was no oversight which had omitted doctrinal teaching from the course, but rather a fear of arousing to a dangerous pitch those combined religious and political feelings which were already undermining the foundations of the long-established order. Trinity, though thoroughly loyal to Church and King, was nevertheless in the midst of an open rebellion against the type of ritualism being propagated by Laud and his party. The year after Cowley's entrance, indeed, charges were brought against the school, of which the following were a part: '. . .they sit or kneel at prayers, every man in a several posture as he pleases; at the name of Jesus, few will bow; and when the Creed is repeated many of the boys, by some man's direction, turn to the west door'.[2] Similarly, students often made up their own extemporaneous prayers, disregarding those to be found in the Book of Common Prayer.

The whole atmosphere was a familiar one to Cowley, coming as he had done from Westminster School. It was a sort of compromise between the extremes of the Puritans and of the Catholic party within the Church

[1] Sprat, 'De Vita'.　　　　[2] Quoted by Godfrey, p. 92 ff.

of England. And when in 1637 Bishop Williams, leader
of the opposition against Laud, was sent to the Tower
to remain 'on the King's pleasure', and when in 1639
Osbaldeston saved his ears, Cowley was probably
among the many Trinitarians who sympathized with
their stand as exponents of Protestantism. At bottom,
indeed, he had many Puritan tendencies, but his heart,
as usual, belied his mind, and he remained faithful to the
old order.

As a student, Cowley quickly showed his masters that
they had made no mistake in creating a place for him
and in aiding in his support. His mother, or one of
his friends, probably made shift to find what was still
lacking in the £20 to £40 a year necessary to meet the
expenses of the average student. On June 14, 1637,
however, the College redeemed its promise, for the
records read: 'Cowley chosen and admitted Scholar by
the King's letters dispensatory'.[1] This is the first direct
evidence of Charles's possible interest in Cowley's case,
but it was an interest which was destined to endure.

The attitude of Cowley's new comrades toward him
during the first year or two of his course can only be
surmised. Very likely some of them were inclined to be
vaguely hostile toward him at the start, as boys are
likely to be toward one who has been harbingered with
such a reputation as his had been. On the other hand,
many of his old schoolmates were awaiting him at
Trinity, among whom Nichols was undoubtedly one of
the first to kiss his cheek. Among the masters was
Robert Crane, who had just been made tutor of his
college, after having been elected from Westminster in
1632.[2] Even Cowley's room mate after he had received
his scholarship was a Westminster boy several years his
senior—Robert Creswell. Creswell had been monitor
at the old school while Cowley was there, and had then
come up to Cambridge along with Crane and had re-

---

[1] Hill, in Johnson's *Lives*, i. 65; Ball, ii. 352.        [2] Ball, ii. 343.

ceived his B.A. in 1636. He was also a poet of some local repute. The special privilege of living alone with a young man like this, instead of with two or three ordinary students as was usually the custom, was granted only to boys holding scholarships, and was unquestionably appreciated by one of Cowley's temperament.[1]

Cowley made many new friends, too—and one of these is of peculiar interest.

In 1637 the third edition of *Poetical Blossoms* was printed by Henry Seile, who was certainly still congratulating himself on his acumen in having dared to issue the first of Cowley's youthful works. This new edition was very likely the occasion of the poem which commemorates the early stages of one of the most touching of literary friendships, and which at the same time reveals a friendly envy of Cowley's accomplishments not at all unlike the one suggested by Milton's birthday sonnet. When Cowley had entered Trinity as a 'dry chorister', Richard Crashaw had just left Pembroke Hall for Peterhouse.[2] Like Cowley he had attended a semi-charity school, the Charterhouse, and had then gone on to Pembroke, where he obtained his degree in 1634. Leisurely enough, perhaps being delayed somewhat by his fervent interest in Nicholas Ferrar and the quietist group at Little Gidding, he proceeded towards his M.A., and in 1637 was elected to a fellowship at Peterhouse. Perhaps he was even ordained about this time, since a letter of Queen Henrietta Maria refers to him as having been a minister in England; certainly he held some official ecclesiastical position in Little St. Mary's Church, temporary chapel of Peterhouse. Yet even a senior student such as he, was eager to seek the acquaintance of the famous Cowley and to pay tribute to his genius.

There is a poem in Crashaw's *The Delights of the*

[1] See Moore Smith, *Notes and Queries*, xii, ix, 305, quoted by Loiseau.
[2] Cf. Martin, introduction to Crashaw's *Poems*.

*Muses* with the title: 'Upon Two Green Apricocks Sent to Cowley by Sir Crashaw'. With the delicate implication that the scarce ripe fruit represented his own achievements in comparison with those of his 'sweet friend', Crashaw wrote such lines as these:

> Fain would I chide their slowness, but in their
> Defects I draw mine own dull character—

and these:

> . . . Oh, had my wishes
> And the dear merits of your Muse their due,
> The year had found some fruit early as you—
> Ripe as those rich composures Time computes
> Blossoms, but our blest taste confesses fruits.

The friendship of the two, drawn together by their similarly shy and contemplative natures, dated from this initial memorial and continued uninterrupted by all the turmoils and hatreds of the time until Crashaw's premature death a dozen years later.

The intimacy of their relationship is also attested by another poem, or rather pair of poems, in the same volume by Crashaw, published in 1646, though undoubtedly this particular work was written earlier. Cowley's contribution first appeared separately in his volume, *The Mistress*, in the following year. Apparently in one of their conversations the two youths had fallen into an argument on hope and its value. Cowley, in a cynical or at least a contrary mood, had constituted himself the attacker, and Crashaw had championed the cause of this 'virtue'. As a result, they wrote a poem, in alternate stanzas, in which Cowley tried to show that "'Tis Hope is the most hopeless thing of all' and Crashaw, with happy enthusiasm, refuted each argument and added an extra stanza of triumph at the end. In *The Delights of the Muses* the composite poem was entitled 'On Hope, by Way of Question and Answer, between A. Cowley and R. Crashaw'. In the meantime, however,

Cowley himself had written a rather ironic defence of the 'virtue' and called it 'For Hope', which he later printed with its companion piece, 'Against Hope'. These two poems furnish one of the best examples of what may be called their author's epithetic style, in which his imaginative sense and his power of comparison are found in their full stature.

But Cowley's affection for Crashaw, and even for his older friends such as Nichols, was nothing in the light of a new friendship which he formed at Trinity. Among the students of Pembroke was a certain William Hervey of Ickworth, Suffolk, who had entered college on April 5, 1636, at the age of seventeen.[1] Hervey came of a good family, his mother being Susan Jermyn, daughter of Sir Robert Jermyn; he was also first cousin to Henry Jermyn, later Earl of St. Albans. Young Hervey was therefore provided with those things of which Cowley at this period of his life was inclined to lament the lack—position and money. But in this case the difference between their situations formed no barrier. They met each other, and from then on, if Cowley may be believed, were inseparable as Damon and Pythias, or Pylades and Orestes. Next to his brothers and sisters Hervey loved Cowley best, and Cowley loved his friend's family as if it were his own— and even more perhaps, since he never mentions his own directly in his writings.

Hervey was a lad of serious disposition, and yet no prig. As Cowley described him, he had 'all the light of youth, of the fire none'.[2] The discipline of the university suited his temper as well as Cowley's, and the two knew better what to do with their time than to spend it 'in toys, in lusts, or wine'. The taverns, boxing-matches, skittle-playings, dancings, bear-baitings, cock-fights, fairs, dice, and cards, which were expressly

[1] Tilley, *Cowley's Essays*, p. xiii.
[2] Cowley, 'On the Death of . . . Hervey'.

stipulated against in the statutes had no attraction for the pair, although if the diaries of young Puritans like Simon D'Ewes may be believed, the average under-graduate much preferred such forbidden pleasures, and worse, to going about with his tutor and conversing with him in Latin, Greek, or Hebrew as the rules demanded.

In the daytime, when Cowley and Hervey could get permission to go outside the college walls, they might be seen roaming the tranquil fields about Cambridge together, much as Milton and his friends had done before them. Not a tree or a bird in the neighbourhood but was familiar to them, as they lay in the shade of the one and listened to the trillings of the other, or read and conversed together. And at night they many times talked down the stars, in

> . . . search of deep philosophy,
> Wit, eloquence, and poetry.

It was this intercourse, seemingly, this knowledge that a sympathetic friend and trustworthy critic awaited his every need, that stimulated Cowley to fresh flights of poetry.

> To him my Muse made haste with every strain
> Whilst it was new, and warm yet from the brain.

Various occasional poems in Latin and English, such as were printed in the Cambridge Συνῳδία of 1637 and *Voces Votivae* of 1640, probably had their first auditor in Hervey. But he was also present in some of Cowley's best known and most typical verses, as well as in these ephemera. The ode, 'Of Wit', for instance, which even Johnson confessed to be 'almost without a rival'[1] and which Alexander Pope was not above pilfering from,[2] was obviously written first for Hervey's eye. This poem, which is an intellectual and critical analysis of, perhaps,

---

[1] Johnson, *Lives*, i. 36.
[2] Pope, 'Essay on Criticism'; cf. Bryant, *N. Am. Rev.*, cxxiv. 382.

what wit is not rather than what it is, opens with this
couplet:

> Tell me, O tell, what kind of thing is Wit,
> Thou who Master art of it.

Whom could the final stanza fit but Hervey?

> But Love, that moulds one man up out of two,
> Makes me forget and injure you.
> I took you for myself, sure, when I thought
> That you in anything were to be taught.
> Correct my error with thy pen:
> And if any ask me then,
> What thing right wit and height of genius is,
> I'll only show your lines, and say, "Tis this'.

That Cowley actually considered his friend to possess
such wit and judgement as here described, his later ode
to Hervey is clear proof.

'The Motto', with its famous opening lines, must also
have passed under Hervey's eye:

> What shall I do to be forever known,
> And make the age to come my own?
> I shall like beasts or common people die
> Unless you write my elegy.

It was in this poem that Cowley confessed his ambition to become 'the Muse's Hannibal'. Knowing too
well that he had neither birth nor wealth to help him,
he realized that his fortune must be struck from himself alone.

> Yet I must on; what sound is't strikes mine ear?
> Sure, I Fame's trumpet hear.
> It sounds like the Last Trumpet, for it can
> Raise up the buried man.
> Unpassed Alps stop me, but I'll cut through all,
> And march, the Muse's Hannibal.

Yes, he would be the Muse's Hannibal, and conquer
the Alps of verse which had never before been scaled.
For the sake of the Muse and the elegy Fame might

write, he promised to renounce honours, wealth, estate, love, and all that might prevent him from taking a place among Aristotle, Cicero, and Virgil, the greatest writers of the past. Nor could a faithful Achates such as Hervey have failed to applaud the grandeur of the resolution and to encourage the youthful votary.

These two poems are probably to be referred to the years 1637 or 1638, if an important principle concerning Cowley's method of preparing manuscripts for publication be admitted: the *Miscellanies* particularly, and probably the *Occasional Verses* as well as the Pindarics, are arranged chronologically, perhaps having been taken directly from some bound copy-book. At any rate, every poem which, from internal or external evidence, can be dated exactly, falls into its proper order in the printed volumes, and if this be a fact, the conclusion is strongly presumptive that the intervening, undatable poems also occupy the places where they belong according to time of composition.

Cowley was now living in a deeply religious, even pious, atmosphere. The people to whom he most looked up, the masters and heads of schools he had attended, were in orders. The many virtues of his friend Hervey were swayed by 'Religion, Queen of Virtues'. Crashaw, still an Anglican, though growing more and more dissatisfied with the established Church, had strong Catholic as well as mystical tendencies. What more natural then, than that Cowley, avid for fame as he had admitted himself to be in his private poems, should decide that the noblest path to his desire lay in the direction of religious poetry? His mistake, if mistake it was, never was recognized by his contemporaries —and perhaps never by himself, though some signs exist that he later came to mistrust his earlier judgement.

Religious poetry was, patently, no new thing in England. Herbert's *The Temple* had been published in 1633, and Cowley seems to refer to it indirectly in the

opening of his next work. Yet Cowley had expressed
his ambition to be the 'Muse's Hannibal'. How could
he do so and yet be of service to religion? There was
one way. The religious epic had not yet been attempted
in English—a fact to which he called attention in the
notes to his new poem. In France, 'divine' du Bartas
had written his *Semaines* at the end of the last century,
and Joshua Sylvester had gained himself great fame and
credit by translating these ponderous works on the
Creation into English. In Italy, Marino more recently
had published his *La Strage degli Innocenti*, which was
so to attract Crashaw by both its Christian material and
its 'conceited' style that he was to translate its first
book as 'The Suspicion of Herod' in 1646. Perhaps even
at the time when Cowley's imposing idea came over
him, Crashaw had begun his work, and may even have
talked it over with his friend. For as McBryde has
pointed out,[1] there are some indications of a knowledge
of Crashaw's translation in the epic which Cowley
began about the year 1638, though he did not publish
it until almost twenty years afterward. Sprat clearly
intends to indicate that Cowley's epic had its inception
in this period, for he says that at Cambridge, 'before
the twentieth year of his age, he laid the design of
divers of his most masculine works, that he finished
long after'.[2]   And even more specifically he adds, 'His
*Davideis* was wholly written in so young an age . . . that
he had finished the greatest part of it while he was yet
a young student at Cambridge.' The first part of this
statement, however, must be regarded a bit sceptically,
as will be seen later.

The *Davideis* is a poem which was lavishly overpraised
in its own day, and lavishly overridiculed by the heavy-
handed Dr. Johnson later.[3] Cowley must have com-

[1] McBryde, *Davideis*, p. 2 ff.          [2] Sprat, 'Account'.
[3] Cf. my article, 'The Reputation of Abraham Cowley (1660–1800)',
*P.M.L.A.*, xxxviii (1923), 598 ff.

menced his composition with a great deal of enthusiasm,
and even went so far as to compile one book in both
English and Latin. And why should he not be enthusiastic, knowing that he was striking out a new trail
in English poetry and being convinced that he was
simultaneously doing religion a service? He planned to
immortalize all of the troubles of David in a heroic
poem of twelve books, 'after the pattern of our master,
Virgil' (whom he always worshipped), and to conclude
'with that most poetical and excellent elegy of David's
on the death of Saul and Jonathan'.[1] This argument he
would embellish with all his wit and learning, and furnish it with a set of notes which would allow him to
explain his theories about the epic and about versification, as well as equip it with a battery of marginal
glosses to give his authorities for the events and ideas
in the story. It was, in short, to be a sober, a noble, a
truly heroic piece of work, in which the author would
no longer appear as a sprout, or even a sapling, but as a
full grown and sturdy tree, ready to take its place in the
sacred grove of Apollo—for Cowley himself was not
overly worried by any mixture of classical and Hebrew
mythologies.

But, as usual, he made his mistake. His exuberance
and his knowledge of the national fondness for striking
and richly embellished writing led him into a series of
excesses for which even Sprat later felt himself called
upon to apologize, or at least explain. The high serious-
ness of Milton is not absent from the poem in many
passages, such as the description of the love of David
and Jonathan for one another, or the vision of the
Annunciation. But even the latter scene Cowley is
unable to leave without the insertion of a jarring conceit:

Heaven contained virgins oft, and will do more;
Never did virgin contain heaven before.

[1] Cowley, 'Preface', *Poems* (1656), n.p.

Nevertheless, Dryden rather than Johnson was right in calling attention to the hyperboles in the poem instead of to the more figurative conceits, for it is exaggeration such as the following portrait of Satan which frequently topples over into absurdity:

> Thrice did he knock his iron teeth, thrice howl,
> And into frowns his wrathful forehead roll.
> His eyes dart forth red flames, which scare the night,
> And with worse fires the trembling ghosts affright.

No one who has read the descriptions of Envy, Fancy, and their attendants in the first and second books can cavil at Pope for ridiculing them and their kind—derived originally from Virgil though they were—in the *Rape of the Lock*.

Similarly, though science was no regular part of the university curriculum, Cowley was unable to repulse the temptation to show his acquaintance with the latest scientific, or pseudo-scientific, theories. To such lines—dealing with the origins of winds, of fountains, of thunder, and of comets; with the effect of gravity on falling bodies; and with the location of hell—he called attention in the commentary of his notes. Yet though he deemed thunder 'an exhalation hot and dry, shut up in a cold and moist cloud, out of which striving to get forth, it kindles itself by the agitation, and then violently breaks it', he refused to accede to 'the old senseless opinion that the heavens were divided into several orbs or spheres, and that a particular Intelligence or Angel was assigned to each of them to turn it round (like a mill-horse, as Scaliger said) to all eternity'.

However, like Milton, Cowley specifically confessed that he was not above using an idea or belief for a poetical purpose which he would not accept as an attested fact. Perhaps it is not necessary to trace Milton's practice in this respect to the *Davideis*, though it cannot be doubted that this is the poem which made

Cowley one of the former's three favourite poets. But
many other ideas and specific passages in *Paradise Lost*
—such as the digression on the fatal qualities of gold,
the sonorous use of proper names, the description of
the division of labour in building Pandemonium, and
the picture of Satan and his staff, 'Which Nature
meant some tall ship's mast to be' (in Cowley's phrase)
—undoubtedly were suggested by Cowley's epic; so
many, indeed, that the vast difference in the success of
the two poems is more than ever to be marvelled at.

In another way than his mere choice of material,
however, Cowley must be given credit as an innovator,
an experimenter—that is, in his versification.[1] The
selection of heroic couplets for a poem of this length
and nature becomes of more moment when it is recalled
that he made his decision at least as early as 1638, about
four years before Denham's *Cooper's Hill* was published. Yet though practically all of the couplets are of
the closed type, Cowley's tendency, as always, was to
counteract the natural resulting rigidity by various
devices which would allow the more flexible effect
desirable in narrative verse. Accordingly, he inserted
many Alexandrines, especially in passages where the
sense would be illustrated and emphasized by such a
slow and dragging line. Conversely, he frequently cut
off a line or a speech with an abrupt hemistich. He
made the elision, marked by an apostrophe, a common
feature. Not one of the least bold of his innovations, in
his own opinion, was the interpolation of lyric measures
in the midst of an epic, in the form of songs—a practice
which the ultra-classic Rymer later considered one of
the objectionable features in an otherwise fine and almost
truly classical poem.[2] Cowley's rhyming, finally, with its
acknowledged influence upon Dryden's prosody[3] and

---

[1] Cf. Saintsbury, *Camb. Hist. Eng. Lit.*, viii. 260.
[2] Rymer, 'Preface to Rapin', in Spingarn, *Critical Essays*, ii. 172–3.
[3] Dryden, *Essays*, ii. 229.

with Milton's reaction against it in adopting blank verse, contrary to 'the use of some famous modern poets',[1] becomes of more importance when it is noted that he had based it on a consciously evolved set of principles, which, together with his discussion of the faults and virtues of former traditions in epic technique, he continually kept before his reader by means of his notes. These matters were probably among the ones which he and his faithful friend Hervey discussed as they strolled along the banks of the Cam or lay indolently under the fences or trees in the fields near by—indeed, in one note he recalls how he had debated a certain moot question with 'a friend of mine', who sounds much like Hervey.[2]

On the whole, however, the *Davideis* must be relegated to the number of ambitious failures in English poetry. Seemingly the author's own interest waned as he went along. Although the third book contains the attractive description of Saul's two daughters, Merab and Michol, which William Cullen Bryant for some reason thought that Scott used in his characterization of Minna and Brenda Troil in *The Pirate*,[3] the narrative skill of the poem constantly decreases and involves itself in digressions and retrospects. Cowley probably wrote for a couple of years with all the great zeal of which he was capable, and then laid his manuscript aside. He took it up again later, to be sure, and finally published it, but his project of twelve books 'after the pattern of our master, Virgil', was never more than a third realized.

Why did Cowley tire of this, the first of the great works which were to make him 'the Muse's Hannibal'? Was it because, subconsciously perhaps, he missed the opportunity to write more passages such as the following

---

[1] Milton, 'The Verse', *Paradise Lost*.
[2] Cf. my article, 'Abraham Cowley's *Discourse concerning Style*,' *R.E.S.*, ii. (1926), 390 ff.  [3] Bryant, pp. 370–3.

one in the second book—passages which let him pour
out his real nature in the place of the artificialities
which he seemed to feel were demanded of one who
wished to shine in the poetic firmament of his age?
For this is the undercurrent which runs, almost unnoticed, through all of his earlier verse:

> Fair angels passed by next in seemly bands,
> All gilt, with gilded baskets in their hands.
> Some as they went the blue-eyed violets strew,
> Some spotless lilies in loose order threw.
> Some did the way with full-blown roses spread,
> Their smell divine, and colour strangely red—
> Not such as our dull gardens proudly wear,
> Whom weathers taint, and winds' rude kisses tear.
> Such, I believe, was the first rose's hue,
> Which, at God's word, in beauteous Eden grew—
> Queen of the flowers, which made that orchard gay,
> The morning blushes of the Spring's new day.

# IV

## PLATO, AND THE LAUGHABLE SHIPWRECK

ONE of the familiar sights of Cambridge while Abraham Cowley's *Davideis* was yet but an embryo was that of a tall, thin young man, with a serene and thoughtful face slightly tinged with melancholy, with alert hazel eyes, and with a pale, slightly olive complexion. Henry More, four years the senior of Cowley, had, because of his appearance and his character, been affectionately dubbed 'the angel of Christ's' soon after he had entered Christ's College in 1631, just before 'the lady of Christ's' was ready to leave.[1] Having become one of the best liked of the college tutors after receiving his B.A. degree in 1636, he had taken his M.A. in 1639, and not long afterward was given a fellowship and ordained. His figure, indeed, was seldom to be seen on the streets, for he loved the pleasures of withdrawal from the world and preferred to walk in the college garden or to read and meditate in his room; and yet he was probably known to more people for this very reason than if he had bid for fame by thrusting himself forward on every public occasion.

Cowley can scarcely have failed to know More, although the two can be related only indirectly. But More was the centre of a group of Christian philosophers which would inevitably arouse the interest of an inquisitive pair like Cowley and Hervey. The 'angel of Christ's', after undergoing a period of scepticism and black despair, had finally worked his way back into the light—a light which illuminated his whole being when he spoke and wrote of it, and which was perhaps the outgrowth of the same sort of ecstasy as, by his own account, was sometimes induced in him when he

[1] Cf. Grosart, ed. of *More*, i. xv ff.

listened to music or played on his own theorbo. More
was a mystic, and even his body, if he may be believed,
was not like that of other men. Certain of its excre-
ments 'had naturally the odour of violets', and his
'breast and body, especially when very young, would of
themselves, in like manner, send forth flowery and
aromatic odours from them, and such as he daily almost
was sensible of when he came to put off his clothes and
go to bed'.[1] And yet More did not regard himself as set
apart, but was of a friendly, sanguine nature.

The light which had come to More and his companions was that of Plato—or perhaps even more of
Plotinus and the Neo-Platonic school. Dogmatic
Calvinism More was unable to endure, and Aristote-
lianism was as bad. Reason was to become the guide of
the soul (and consequently for a time he was an ardent
apologist of Descartes), but reason was to be checked
from scepticism by the conscience, or whatever the
individual might desire to call the divine spark within
him. The whole problem of life, in fact, lay in the
mystery of the relation of the mortal part of man to the
immortal, and in the manner wherein the divine portion
of man's nature might free itself from the earthly and
perishable and prepare itself for God. The attempt to
fuse the Christian and the pagan statements of this
doctrine had already been made by the Neo-Platonists,
and between them and the true Platonists the Cambridge men made little distinction. With a touch of
Stoicism they preached that indulgence in the pleasure
of the senses dragged one farther and farther from the
perfection of the divine ideal, and that asceticism rather
than self-gratification would eventually carry the soul
upward to its home.

Always susceptible to new ideas—in fact, almost
chameleon-like at times in his receptivity—Cowley
naturally did not escape being tinctured for the moment

[1] Quoted by Powicke, *Cambridge Platonists*, p. 153.

COWLEY AT THE AGE OF TWENTY

by Cambridge Platonism. In 1640 Henry More began
to write his *Psychozoia*, the first part of which was published by the University printer in 1642. But Cowley
could never accompany More in his pursuit of the soul
through the strange and awful caverns of life and death
into the pure and dazzling heights of immortality.
Even though More was an avowed imitator of Spenser
in both versification and language, Cowley could never
whirl with him out into the other worlds of an infinite
universe, or see in the pre-existence of the soul a proof
of the actuality of spirits, ghosts, and disembodied
beings. Cowley's touch of Platonism was of a more
orthodox and less rhapsodic nature—nearer, perhaps,
to the ideas in the series of 'commonplaces' delivered in
the Trinity chapel in 1641 by Master John Sherman,
one of the Fellows, whose theology partook somewhat
of Platonic idealism. [1]

The closest approach to Platonism to be found in the
*Davideis* occurs in the second book, in the long passage
beginning:

> What art thou, Love, thou great mysterious thing?
> From what hid stock does thy strange nature spring?
> 'Tis thou that mov'st the world through every part,
> And hold'st the vast frame close, that nothing start
> From the due place and office first ordained.
> By thee were all things made, and are sustained.
> Sometimes we see thee fully, and can say
> From hence thou took'st thy rise, and went'st that way;
> But oftener the short beams of Reason's eye
> See only, there thou art, not how, nor why.

The succeeding discussion of the differences between
the love of men for women and that of men for men,
and of the differences between love and lust, are conventional enough; but the explanatory note is more
interesting. In it Cowley makes the identification of the
Christian Trinity with Power (the Father), Love (the

[1] Cf. *Camb. Hist. Engl. Lit.*, viii. 317.

Son), and Wisdom (the Holy Ghost), whose operation together produced the world, which has since been preserved partly by them, but even more by 'the emanations and beams of them, derived and impressed in the creatures'. Here is Neo-Platonism indeed, and much more cosmic than that which appears in another poem, 'Friendship in Absence', written about 1641. But for the rest, the *Davideis* shows that Cowley had been reading Plato and his followers rather than that he considered himself one of them. Four times in his notes he refers to Plato by name and twice to Porphyry. Sometimes, indeed, his remarks are definitely slurring. Iamblichus, for instance, he says took 'the principles of his mystical philosophy from the Pillars of Mercury'; and in a discussion of miraculous cures wrought by music he classes the 'Platonics' with their 'Anima Mundi' along with magicians with their 'Colcodea' and rabbis with their 'fables and prodigies not worth repeating'.

An anti-materialistic philosophy of this sort could not make any permanent impression on Cowley, and the waning of his interest can be traced even within his epic. His significant allusions to it are all concentrated in the first two books of the poem. Twice in the third book he quotes from Plato, but not on any philosophic question. In the fourth book there is silence.

But, though failing to find an intellectual and spiritual haven among the Cambridge Platonists, Cowley seems to have found at least part of what he was looking for in another place. The poem which he wrote 'To the Lord Falkland. For His Safe Return from the Northern Expedition against the Scots' would indicate that by 1639 he had probably made the acquaintance of the young nobleman whose life and character stood in striking contrast to those of Kenelm Digby, Cowley's other friend in the seats of the great. Whereas Digby's mighty height and handsome face combined with his

spectacular bearing and actions to make him conspicu-
ous in every gathering, Lucius Cary, second Viscount
Falkland, was low in stature, his visage was not particularly attractive, and his carriage was ungraceful. But, as
his friend Hyde said, his small and unprepossessing body
contained a great heart.[1] Falkland seemingly had a
genius for making friends, from the crabbed Ben Jonson
to the theological Chillingworth, and his lovable personality cast a sort of spell over every one who came
within his range, so that he was praised for qualities and
abilities which he did not actually possess.

The exact medium through which Cowley was
recommended to the attention of Falkland may even
be traced.  On May 12, 1638, the young poet's friend
and room mate, Creswell, who had already earned the
Viscount's esteem, wrote the latter a letter thanking
him for his many favours.[2] But Creswell was not satisfied to end on a merely personal and perhaps selfish
note.  He must recommend his 'ingenious' companion
to the same kind patron, even though this friend was at
the time absent and unable to speak for himself.  And
Creswell went on to write in glowing terms of the
precocious youth who was not only already a poet in
duodecimo, but who was also preparing to publish an
augmented edition as well as a pastoral in English and
a Latin comedy 'which has been acted here'.

Cowley's poem, then, may have been undertaken at
Creswell's solicitation, and have led to an actual
meeting with Falkland.  If the two had met by 1639,
they had probably done so at Great Tew, not far from
Oxford, whither Falkland had retired to keep an open
house which drew his friends from London as well as
the best minds of Oxford to him in a constant stream.
So many were his visitors, it is said, that he never knew

[1] For a first-hand sketch of Falkland, see Clarendon, *History*, i. 443–
4; ii. 444 ff.
[2] See Rawlinson MS. Poet. 246, quoted by Loiseau.

who were in the house with him or with whom he would sit down to dinner. It was his tolerance and broad-mindedness which made him so popular, and these qualities were at this time especially applied to the solving of the religious problems vexing England and to examining them in the fair light of reason. There was no mysticism in him and his friend Chillingworth. They braced themselves firmly upon the Bible, and with that as a foundation repulsed all attacks upon a liberal Protestantism, no matter whether these were made by the sacerdotal Laud or the most Calvinistic preacher. The middle ground was his—and the middle ground was always Cowley's. It was a similarity in both spirits and studies which drew the two together, says Sprat's Latin life. This combination, added to a common dis-like of public life and especially war (into which Falk-land's conscientiousness had drawn him), appears in the poem, and Cowley's admiration is clear, no matter whether he celebrated his subject merely from general report or whether he had actually become one of Falk-land's circle while still a student at Cambridge.

Cowley's elegy on Sir Henry Wotton, one of Eng-land's most admired diplomatists and the provost of Eton College, who died in December 1639, may also have arisen from a meeting within the Falkland group, for John Hales was an intimate friend of both Wotton and Falkland, and visited them both frequently. If Cowley, therefore, did not meet Wotton in person at Great Tew, he may have heard him talked about. Moreover, Wotton's favourite angling partner, honest Izaak Walton, liked Cowley's tribute so much that, after it had been printed in 1656, he included it in the next edition of his life of Sir Henry.[1]

All these experiences and friendships would indicate that the young man was growing up—and growing into

---

[1] The *Dict. Nat. Biog.* in its account of Wotton states erroneously that Cowley's elegy was printed in *Reliquiae Wottonianae* in 1651.

a very serious person. This impression, however, would
be far from the complete truth. He was still a university
student without a degree, and he took plenty of part and
pleasure in the ordinary activities and diversions of his
companions. For one thing, he had not forgotten that
on his departure from Westminster School he had carried with him his stillborn play, *Love's Riddle*. He may
even have had hopes of seeing it produced at Trinity,
long noted as the home of the academic drama, but if
so he must have discovered soon that his pastoral did
not belong to the usual type there given. As he wrote
in his dedication, he immediately learned that Cambridge had certain traditions in comedy, such as the
stock character of a philosopher; and that it was not
wise to disregard these. The Latin drama was still
paramount at the university. Consequently, Cowley,
a fluent though a far from classical Latinist, determined
to write a Latin comedy for his college to produce.[1]

His method of proceeding to work shows how much
of an eclectic he was. Just as he had gone to Renaissance
models for his first play, so he went to the classics for his
second. In fact, the second is much more derivative
than the first, but nevertheless displays even more
ingenuity in fabricating the patchwork into a new and
not too badly boggled garment. From Plautus he
borrowed an ever-dependable 'miles gloriosus', whom
he christened Bombardomachides; a parasite named Gelasimus; and a pedant-philosopher, Gnomicus—a part
inserted seemingly in accordance with his half-promise
in the dedication of *Love's Riddle*. He provided the
alternating thrills and buffoonery of a haunted house
from Plautus's *Mostellaria*, and solved the complica-
tions in which he found himself involved by eventually
uniting two long-lost children, Aemylio and Aegle,
with their father, Polyporus, much in the fashion of
Plautus in his *Captivi* or *Rudens* or of Terence in his

[1] Cf. my article, 'Cowley as Dramatist.'

*Andria.* The scene, however, which gave the play its title of *Naufragium Joculare*, or the 'laughable shipwreck', he probably found in the *Deipnosophists* of Athenaeus, whom he had been reading at this time as various notes in the *Davideis* will testify. Similarly, in the play itself occur several references to the *Captivi* and the *Menaechmi* which clearly indicate that he had these plays in his mind as his standards (though Dr. Johnson brushed the comedy aside with the remark that it was written 'without due attention to the ancient models: for it is not loose verse, but mere prose').

Nevertheless, the fact that Cowley was more than a merely academic student of the drama must not be lost sight of. Although, as 'Of Wit' shows, he had read the 'dry chips of short-lunged Seneca', he had continued also to patronize the popular theatre and to hear

> . . . such lines as almost crack the stage
> When Bajazet begins to rage.

It is not impossible, then, that he had either seen or read Thomas Heywood's *The English Traveller* and *The Captives*, both of which had devoted passages to the 'shipwreck by land' of some drunken roisterers, not to mention the fact that the sub-plot of the first was deeply indebted to the *Mostellaria* and the main plot of the second to the *Rudens*.

English or Latin as these sources may be, a series of scenes in the third and fourth acts, upon which Cowley squandered a large part of his pains and his wit, derive either from the English or not at all. He had now been at Trinity for about three years, and was nearly ready to take his degree. An essential feature of degree-taking was, even yet, the medieval disputation, in which the candidate was expected to prove his training in logic and metaphysic by presenting and defending some theme in public. The less brilliant candidates put on their performances in the semi-privacy of the college

chapel, but the ambitious and the showy, thirsty for
fame or urged by eager masters, debated in the 'schools'
where all the world could hear. Immense enthusiasm
was often stirred up over these contests between repre-
sentatives of rival colleges. A comparison with the
gladiatorial combats of the Roman arena and the
joustings and tournaments of the Middle Ages would
not be too remote in describing the intensity of excitement surrounding these wit and tongue combats in a
day when competitive athletics were practically unknown. Royalty often came to witness the duels, and
the attendance of dukes and bishops was a commonplace.

Cowley, like Bacon, hated the still surviving Aristotelian system of the universities. He had an infinite
contempt for the tenuous mind-spinnings and quib-
blings of the schoolmen. And, though an adequate, he
was not a remarkable, speaker. He could write better
than he could talk.

Three-fifths of the way through *Naufragium Joculare*
Cowley's chief plot began to run thin. Perhaps he had
seen Shirley's *Love Tricks, or the School of Compliment*,
in which the third scene of the fifth act had been given
a special title, 'The Compliment-School'; or perhaps he
knew Middleton and Rowley's *A Fair Quarrel*, in which
the first scene of the fourth act was entitled 'The
Roaring School'. But whether he knew these, or others,
or none, he resolved to fill up the necessary five acts in
his comedy by introducing a 'schola jocandi', in which
the 'art of joking' would be taught, according to the
latest educational methods.

In these scenes, therefore, Cowley unloaded all his
satire on education, schoolmasters, and students—too
many passages, indeed, owe their existence to his rather
schoolboyish love for a 'jocus'. All those who need
instruction in major and minor premisses, fallacies,
*argumentum ad hominem*, and the Porphyrian tree,
all those who are shaky on their Ramus, Scotus,

Tostatus, Suaresius, and Suetonius, are recommended to
enroll in the school. A young scholar is entered by his
mother; a rival 'professor' of the 'ars jocandi' arrives and
demands a contest:—a series of digressive scenes like
these, in which perhaps actual Cambridge characters
were pilloried, would have a sure appeal to the audience
Cowley had in mind, especially when the whole was
interlarded with puns, with simple reminiscences of
Virgil, with allusions to Horace, Ovid, Cicero, Erasmus,
and Luther, and with random snatches of Greek, which
might be taken by the other actors as Hebrew or the
language of the 'cacodaemons'. And at the end (for the
action was contemporary and the scene Dunkirk) the
two fools, Gelasimus and Morion, together with their
pedant-tutor, Gnomicus, determine to transfer their
school to Cambridge, for 'Emptores jocorum ibi
habitant quamplurimi'.

The date chosen for the production of Cowley's
comedy was February 2 ('quarto Nonas Februarii'), and
the year was probably 1638/9, though the title-page of
the printed copy is dated 1638, in accordance with the
old-style calendar.[1] Two contradictory clues exist in
the play itself: in 'Ad Lectorem' Cowley refers to himself as 'hornus academicus', and the tone of all the prefa-
tory material is as apologetic as it would naturally be
if he had really been a 'this year's student'; but on the
other hand the dutiful dedication to Dr. Comber ends:

> Collegii nam qui nostri dedit ista Scholaris;
> Si Socius tandem sit, meliora dabit.

Cowley, the Scholar, then, is already looking forward to
the day when he may become a Fellow: he would
scarcely have been so bold if he had not expected his
bachelor's degree very quickly.

---

[1] Cf. Moore Smith, *College Plays*, p. 90. Loiseau points out fhat the
play was entered on the Stationers' Register on March 14, 1638/9. See
Arber, iv. 412.

There had been no play given at Trinity for several years, although Queens', Trinity's chief dramatic rival, had produced W. Johnson's *Valetudinarium* just the year before.[1] The great hall of Cowley's college, which could hold as many as two thousand on occasion, was therefore probably well filled—if the 'Comedy House' near the back of the Master's Lodge had not already been built, in competition with Queens', which was even then erecting its own playhouse. The usual precautions against the mischievous meddling, if not the actual attack, of jealous members of other colleges were probably taken; that is, the glass was carefully removed from the windows or else covered with netting, and special 'stagekeepers' or guards were appointed. The latter were ordinarily dressed in lace-trimmed suits of red, green, or white, and were armed with staves, swords, daggers, and steel caps, which might become useful for policing purposes as well as for decoration. The 'university music' may have been hired to play, and the auditorium was lighted with candles in iron candlesticks, or with cressets, torches, or lanthorns. The stage itself demanded no special properties for this play—the old 'comic scene' of the classics would have done very well, and placards may even have been hung up to indicate locality.[2] All that is certain is that the 'Prologus' warned his seemingly unruly audience that the author, blushing deeper than his purple gown, was peeping through a crack in the scenery in fear of his fate.

Whether Cowley acted a part in his own play is a doubtful question, though Genest, because of the statement that the playwright did not dare come before his audience 'nisi personatus' (that is, 'except masked' or 'in an assumed character'), conjectures that he did.[3] At any rate, the comedy was a success on this occasion, though seemingly never revived in its original form. After the good humour of the audience had been assured

[1] Moore Smith, p. 70.　[2] Ibid., *passim.*　[3] Genest, *English Stage*, x. 64.

by means of such refreshments as canary, burnt wine, diet bread, or oranges, and the actors were more substantially rewarded with a meal of cheese, bread and butter, loins and breasts of mutton, puddings, and beer or ale, the costumes were packed away in the special chest kept for that purpose in the Audit-Chamber. Here they lay idle until they were needed for another play, which, as it happened, was one by Cowley's friend Nichols just a year later.[1] And before the twenty-fifth of March both *Naufragium Joculare* and *Love's Riddle* were in print, bearing the stamp of Cowley's old publisher, Henry Seile.

Shortly afterward, Cowley must have proceeded to his first degree, although the college records do not show the exact date. Nevertheless, Bliss gives 1639 as the year of his B.A., and the Trinity records state that he was admitted Minor Fellow on October 30, 1640, in spite of the fact that there was no vacancy and that he was compelled to continue on his Scholar's stipend until he left the university over three years later.[2] Toward the end of 1639, however, the legacy of £140 left him by his father's will fell due, and so his circumstances were somewhat improved.

Whether there was any relationship, however, between Cowley's *Naufragium Joculare* and his appointment to a fellowship is a point on which one may well be sceptical, in spite of the amateur dramatist's rather cheeky hint to Dr. Comber.

[1] Moore Smith, p. 70.
[2] Bliss, in Wood, *Fasti*, in *Ath. Oxon.*, iv, ii. 210, n.; Ball, ii. 352; Grosart, *Cowley*, i. xvi; Hill in Johnson's *Lives*, i. 5; Lumby, *Cowley's Prose Works*, p. xiii.

# V

## THE FIRST OF THE 'TROUBLES'

IT was probably through Kenelm Digby that Cowley
made the acquaintance of Sir Anthony Van Dyck—
an acquaintance which would seem to have stimulated
in him an interest in painting, though not as a practitioner. During the latter part of his life Van Dyck had
been flattered and enticed into virtually adopting
England as his home, and in his stays at the castles of
various of the nobility as well as at the royal palaces
Cowley must have had opportunities to meet him.[1] At
the home of Digby alone these opportunities would have
been numerous, for three times in one year the painter
had portrayed the Lady Venetia Digby in allegorical
poses, and on her death in 1633 had drawn tears from
all the beholders of the portrait in which he showed her
lying as in a beautiful sleep, with a fading rose at her
side. When Van Dyck died on December 9, 1641,
therefore, Cowley again called upon his elegiac muse
to celebrate and mourn this 'famous painter'.

The qualities in the artist which had made the most
impression on the young poet, however, show no profound or technical knowledge of the art of design. The
more than lifelike effect of the figures, the truth and
permanence of the colour, the proportion and conso-
nance of the line—these were the elements of the 'art
that 's dumb' that appealed to the practitioner of the
speaking art of poetry. But character always occupied
a prominent place in Cowley's evaluations, which, it
must be confessed, disclose him to have been either a
very poor or a very partial judge.

> Nor was his life less perfect than his art,
> Nor was his hand less erring than his heart.

[1] Cf. Carpenter, *Van Dyck*, &c.

The readers of these lines, as well as those praising the beauty of Lady Mary Ruthven, Van Dyck's young widow, and his faithful love for her, must have smiled a bit ironically when they recalled how, only two or three years before, Margaret Lemon, the most beautiful of the painter's models and mistresses, had tried to maim Sir Anthony's right hand when she learned of his marriage. Yet Cowley was familiar enough with the circumstances of the family to know that only eight days before her husband's death Lady Van Dyck had borne him a daughter; and so his estimate of character could scarcely have been based on ignorance. The position of the poem in its volume also shows that Cowley wrote his elegy almost immediately after the event he described.

In this connexion, it is an interesting coincidence (if no more) that in Van Dyck's will, made on the day of his first legitimate child's birth, a Mistress Catherina Cowley was named a guardian of the infant, Justiniana Anna, with a regular stipend to be paid for the next eighteen years.[1] Whether this Mistress Cowley was any relative of Abraham—perhaps even his sister Katherine —is unknown.

The poet's interest in painting just at this period is also shown in his satirical epigram on 'Prometheus Ill-Painted' and in the passage in the third book of the *Davideis*, wherein Moab displays to David all the golden tapestries and rich mural pictures in his palace. One of the greatest disappointments in Van Dyck's career had come when his commission to execute a series of frescoes in the banqueting room at Whitehall was withdrawn because of the exorbitant price he asked. Similes and other figures drawn from the art of painting continue to be rather frequent in Cowley's writing, both verse and prose, but none are especially recondite. They show the well-instructed amateur, no more.

[1] Carpenter, *Van Dyck*, pp. 76-7.

Cowley's interest in music falls into the same category as his interest in painting. In the *Davideis* he has many times insisted on the necessity of poets being also musicians, as well as philosophers. Such they were in ancient days, and such they should continue. A rather eloquent, though rhetorical, passage in the first book, introducing David's famous song which calmed Saul's raging soul, is annotated by two sizable references to the *Liber de Arte Magna Consoni et Dissoni* of Kercherus, who 'is well worth the diligent reading'. Nevertheless, this very passage in the epic was the one which Sir John Hawkins chose in 1787 to prove that Cowley 'appears . . . to have been but little skilled in music'.[1] Here, however, Cowley was much more concerned with drawing a somewhat Platonic picture of the harmonious motions of the created universe than in showing his knowledge of music as it was actually practised in the seventeenth century; and he should therefore, as before, not be denied the position of an intelligent amateur.

In other, and more weighty, matters of the day, too, Cowley was an amateur, but not always an intelligent one. In politics as well as in poetry and religion he was faced with his dilemma. He could not have helped perceiving the quagmire in which the King had lost himself —a desperate, not unlikable, but ineffectual king whose flounderings succeeded only in plunging him ever deeper into the morass. Struggle after struggle Cowley recorded in his verse; and each one appeared a royal victory rather than a defeat. When, in the midst of the troubles of 1639, Henrietta Maria bore Charles another son, to be created Duke of Gloucester, Cowley glanced at the Scottish war-clouds, quickly averted his eyes, and reassured himself and his monarch by saying, in both English and Latin, that a new Stuart heir was worth more than an army to England. These poems, together

[1] Hawkins, quoted in Hill's Johnson's *Lives*, i. 26, n.

with similar congratulations from the other brightest
literary lights of the university—such as Crashaw,
Joseph Beaumont, and Henry More—were gathered
together, printed by the university printer, and presented to the royal parents in 1640 as *Voces Votivae*.

By 1641, however, Charles's favourites in both
Church and State had begun to fall, in rapid succession.
Laud, the archetype of sacerdotal tyranny, had at
length driven himself blindly on the rocks of impeach-
ment and confinement in the Tower, from which, in
March, he had seen Strafford, deserted at last by the
tortured Charles, led forth to the scaffold. From the
window of his cell the once-haughty archbishop had
blessed the condemned and discredited statesman, and
had then fallen fainting to the floor. On November 25,
Charles himself, after having plotted in the North both
with and against the Scots, returned to London bearing
only those concessions of his own which, in Edward
Hyde's words, had made 'a perfect deed of gift of that
kingdom'.[1] But Cowley would not let himself see the
inevitable result. Instead, in 'On His Majesty's Return
out of Scotland', he rejoiced that 'This happy concord
in no blood is writ', and that the dark menace of civil
war was for ever removed. To him, Charles was 'the best
of kings', and nothing could shake him from that view.

And yet, seemingly not more than a month afterward, he wrote his ode 'To the Bishop of Lincoln, upon
His Enlargement out of the Tower'. For as Laud's star
plunged downward into the abyss, Williams's rose again
into the zenith. For four years he had languished in
prison, and had been mulcted by fine after fine. His
friends in the moderate party were, however, many, and
Charles was eventually forced to release him on the
demand of the Lords. Indeed, in December, in a
frantic attempt to appease his subjects, the King
appointed Williams Archbishop of York, perhaps hoping

[1] Clarendon, *History*, i. 405–6.

in this way to get a new staff upon which he could lean. Cowley's congratulatory poem, however, seems to have been written before his old Dean's final elevation,[1] and for this reason would appear more clearly than ever to be the expression of a genuine admiration for Williams's character and principles. Inconsistent as this was with his thorough loyalty to Charles, Abraham Cowley gave no sign that he realized the problem facing him.

One thing is certain, however: he hated the third party with a hate which perhaps was the outgrowth of an unacknowledged fear. Never, from the time of 'A Vote' to that of *Naufragium Joculare*, had he mentioned the Puritans except in derision. Slowly his data had been accumulating. The Puritans 'deal with no oath above God's fatlikins, or by my truly; exclaim upon the sickness of drinking healths; and call the players rogues, sing psalms, hear lectures'. They pray so indefatigably that 'not a dish o' meat but will be longer a-blessing than a-roasting'. They 'banish Shakespeare and Ben Jonson out of the parlour, and . . . bring in their rooms Mar-Prelate and Prynne's works'—not to mention Sternhold and emblem literature. They go to hear Joseph ('everlasting') Knockdown preach, call each other 'Brother' this and 'Sister' that, and some even turn Brownist. Hypocrites they all are, according to Cowley's picture in *The Guardian* and his other writings, whatever exceptions he may have made in his heart.

But along with his shrewd observations of Puritan character and custom (which were not untinged, of course, by his favourite Ben Jonson's caricatures of the same sect) Cowley had been watching life at the other

---

[1] Loiseau suggests that the poem was written after May 5, 1642, when Williams was released from prison a second time, after having been incarcerated by the Commons for his defence of Conway. In this way he makes the poem a Royalist document. But in this case would it not have been addressed to the 'Archbishop of York' rather than the 'Bishop of Lincoln' ?

extreme. He had marked the lawyers, 'such civil, complete gentlemen in their satin doublets . . . and broad ruffs . . .; and courtiers, all to be laced and slashed, and fine fellows as you shall see in a summer's day'; and knights; and gentlemen. Sardonically he had marked the fashionable lady, who would 'have a dozen of French tailors, doctors, jewellers, perfumers, tire-women, to sit in consultation every morning, how I shall be dressed up to play at gleek, or dance, or see a comedy, or go to the Exchange i' the afternoon; send every day my gentleman to know how such a lady slept, or dreamed, or whether her dog be yet in perfect health; then have the young smelling braveries all adore me, and cut their arms if I be pleased to be angry; then keep my close and open coaches, my yellow satin pages, monkeys, and women, or (as they call 'um) creatures'. He had studied the 'cutters' or 'roarers', who paid no debts; drank their stingo or sack as freely as Providence would permit; respected no women; swore as if they 'would rend the house in two'; boasted of their foreign travels and battles, and yet were arrant cowards; cheated at cards and had no honour among themselves; and still knew something about Plutarch, Tom Coriat, Shakespeare, Homer, and the Muses. He had watched society of all ranks at its amusements of dicing or bowling; its excursions to witness the perpetual comedy of the mad folks at Bedlam; its outings in Moorfields, or at Bartholomew Fair; its drillings and musket-shootings in Finsbury Fields; its family trips to 'Mortlake in the Easter holidays', staggering under a shoulder of mutton, a fat pig, and a round bottle; its patronizing of tight-rope walkers, tumblers, and puppet-plays. Although he was shut up within the university most of the year, Abraham Cowley had acquainted himself with the world as well— the underworld as intimately as the upper, if his descriptions of the 'punks' of London, their rates, and their haunts may be trusted.

His interest in the theatre, too, was fresh as ever. He had listened to Tamburlaine 'roar . . . at the Bull', and he knew that Golden Lane specialized in kings and gods. He had been amused at the bear in *Mucedorus*. He had watched impecunious gentlemen 'sneak into a playhouse at the fifth act', or even, down on their luck, 'sell small pamphlets . . . or else tobacco, or else snuff candles'. And he knew what sort of women were always waiting 'i' the six-penny-room'.

The opportunity to put all this acquired experience together came without warning in March, 1641/2. Again the royal affairs had grown so muddled that the King feared to remain in London with his family. Accordingly, he set out on a sort of 'progress' into the North. On Saturday, March 5, the news reached Cambridge that one week later the young Prince of Wales, with his retinue, would pause at Cambridge on his way to York. At once Trinity College, loyal to the core, cast about for some method of making the stay of the twelve-year-old boy a memorable and a pleasurable one. The traditional manner of entertaining all great visitors was by offering them a play. Abraham Cowley was the leading dramatist of the university. There was no question of his willingness or his ability—but would there be time? For not only would the play have to be conjured out of the void, but it would have to be produced and acted, chiefly by the Scholars. The College, however, was not daunted. The particular friend of Prince Charles, the fourteen-year-old George Villiers, Duke of Buckingham, was almost ready to take his M.A., and there were other ties with the Stuart house. Cowley knew that he must not fail.

The play which he evolved was a comedy, *The Guardian*, written mostly under the influence of the 'humours' school of Jonson, although at the same time there were many reminiscences and allusions to Shakespeare, Marlowe, Kyd, and perhaps others, such as

Greene. As might be expected, the plot, dealing with the attempts of a none too scrupulous guardian, Captain Blade, to get control of his niece Lucia's fortune for either himself or his friends, was conducted largely by means of intrigues, disguises, and mistaken identities; but the true love of the priggish young Truman was rewarded in the end. The comedy, however, should not be criticized too severely for its lack of originality in material or for its frequent incoherence and loose-jointedness, for as Cowley wrote in 1656, it was 'neither made nor acted, but rough-drawn only, and repeated; for the haste was so great that it could neither be revised or perfected by the author, nor learned without book by the actors, nor set forth in any measure tolerably by the officers of the college'.[1] The last implication, however, seems somewhat of a slander, for in the Senior Bursar's record of the 'Extraordinaries' for 1642 appears this entry: 'To Mr. Willis for Ds. [Discipulus] Cooley's comedy. lxv *li*. xvi *s*.'[2] This heavy expenditure, however, must have included all the other costs for the Prince's entertainment while he was at the college.

Nor did the young Charles spend all his time at Trinity. Joseph Beaumont, Crashaw's schoolmate and fellow-poet at Peterhouse, of which he later became Master, wrote a letter describing the events of the day: 'From the Regenthouse his Highness went to Trinity College, where after dinner he saw a comedy in English, and gave all signs of a great acceptance which he could, and more than the University dared expect.'[3] Cowley, therefore, had succeeded, and must have regarded the twelfth of March[4] as one of the greatest days of his life. It is the first occasion, at least, on which he may be said to have definitely met any member of the royal family which was to become such a controlling influence in his career.

---

[1] Cowley, 1656 'Preface'.    [2] Lumby, p. x.
[3] Cooper, *Annals of Cambridge*, iii. 321.    [4] See title-page of play.

One is tempted to wonder just how much Cowley (or 'the poet Aquila', as an entry in the Douce MS. mysteriously styled him)[1] took the tastes of his prospective audience into consideration in writing his play. Certainly a comedy containing such a song as Colonel Cutter sings after tricking the Puritan heiress Tabitha into marrying him might be regarded as a bit sophisticated for the enjoyment and edification of a twelve-year-old boy. On the other hand, when it is remembered that this was the sort of atmosphere that Charles, Buckingham, and the rest were reared in—that dignified schoolmasters, pious divines, and divinity students not only applauded such college plays, but wrote and acted in them, to the horror of the Puritans—then one can more easily understand the life of the English court after the Restoration. There was no need for France to act as tutor to exiles who had been gallants from childhood.

Cowley's success obviously made him begin to fancy himself more and more as a playwright; indeed, it is not unlikely that, after having thus, by three stages, entered the field of contemporary life in the drama, he wondered whether he might not erroneously have chosen poetry as his forte rather than play-writing. At any rate, in the heat of his enthusiasm he immediately started to revise *The Guardian* very thoroughly.[2] He struck out two whole parts in the underplot, those of the 'sharking soldier', Colonel Cutter, and his jackal, the not unamusing poet, Dogrel; and probably improved the construction of the rest very considerably. What his ultimate intentions were cannot be said, but the professional theatre seems always to have been in his eye. Yet the theatre as well as the throne was already tottering. In September of this very year came the order of the Lords and Commons putting a stop to all stage performances because of the troubles of the civil wars,

[1] Cf. Moore Smith, p. 90.        [2] Cf. 1656 'Preface'.

which had now broken into the open. Cowley laid his copy away, and then, in the confusion that ensued, lost it. When the comedy was again revised almost two decades later it was a very different play from either of the earlier versions—but it had reached the professional stage.

Moreover, to the national afflictions a great personal sorrow was to be added. Cowley's love for William Hervey had continued unabated during these years, and one of his sincerest poems, 'Friendship in Absence', would seem to have been an outgrowth of it. But just before dawn of May 16, after a stormy and dismal night, the bell of the chapel began to toll. Cowley, hearing it, knew too well what it portended. Hervey, now a student at Trinity, had been stricken with an infectious fever (probably small-pox) not long before, and now he was dead.[1]

Cowley's elegy, 'On the Death of Mr. William Hervey', notwithstanding one or two conceits which mar its surface, is underneath an expression of a genuine and profound emotion. Though the elegiac convention was strong at Cambridge and had been fortified by Milton's 'Lycidas' and Crashaw's verses to his friend Herrys, poems which Cowley was undoubtedly familiar with, he wrote under no pastoral disguise or with no rhetorical apostrophe to death. He eulogized Hervey as a phoenix of virtues, it is true, and he found consolation in the thought of immortality and sainthood, but as a whole the poem is done simply and eloquently—and so forcefully that it procured for its author the enduring friendship of John Hervey, brother of the deceased, and therefore a cousin of Henry Jermyn, who was soon after created Baron Jermyn.[2] This friendship later led to Cowley's introduction to Jermyn and his becoming a member of the latter's household—an event which,

---

[1] Birch, *Royal Society*, ii, 221.
[2] Ibid.; also Sprat, 'Account'.

in the opinion of Hurd, ruined, rather than made, his fortune.[1]

Unsettled and harassed as he, like the whole university, was, Cowley continued at his books, cementing old esteems and friendships and making new ones. Diminutive Dr. James Duport, former Westminster boy and now well-loved Professor of Greek, whose foible was the composing of Greek hexameters and Latin hendecasyllabics on the most trivial as well as the most weighty occasions, formed the opinion that Cowley was England's greatest poet, just as Jonson was her greatest dramatist—and this opinion he never changed.[2] And Thomas Fotherby, in Sprat's phrase one 'of the most eminent members of that famous society' of Trinity College, did for Cowley many unspecified kindnesses.[3] It was probably through Fotherby, too, that Cowley became the friend of young Martin Clifford, the former's nephew, who entered Trinity in 1640 from Westminster[4] and soon insinuated himself into the attentions of Buckingham as well as of other members of the 'society'.

There is nothing at all improbable about Wood's statement that on March 16, 1642/3, Cowley was chosen Major Fellow of his college.[5] The fact nevertheless remains that his name appears on no such list, and that he continued to receive his stipend as Scholar until Michaelmas, 1643.[6]

Despite the congenial associations at Trinity and a few of the other colleges, Cambridge as a whole was becoming more and more intolerable to the loyalist supporters of the King. The Roundheads had infiltrated the school and town bit by bit, as well as made the whole shire one of their strongholds, whereas the

---

[1] Hurd, Cowley (1777), i. 115; cf. also Dialogues, i. 110, n.
[2] Mullinger, p. 181 ff.
[3] Sprat, 'Account'. Cf. also Cowley's will, appendix no. 2.
[4] Ball, ii. 370.   [5] Wood, iv, ii. 210, n.; cf. Grosart, Cowley, i. xvi.
[6] Lumby, p. xiii.

rival university, Oxford, had been accepted and fortified as the head-quarters of the Cavaliers and their sympathizers. Cowley was torn between two allegiances, but the choice was not equal. The cessation of payments on his scholarship in September 1643, and his close friendship during this period with Lord Falkland, who died in the same month, would indicate that he had left the university by the spring of this year or earlier—with what pain and regret his fine 'Elegia Dedicatoria ad Illustrissimam Academiam Cantabrigiensem,' written some time afterward, will witness.

On August 28 the Parliament passed its law requiring 'Monuments of Superstition and Idolatry to be Demolished'. On December 20 and 23 the commissioners visited Peterhouse, one of the worst offenders, and, as the diary of William Dowsing, one of the vandals, records, 'pulled down two mighty angels with wings, and divers other angels, and the four Evangelists and Peter with his keys over the chapel door, and about a hundred cherubims and angels and divers superstitious letters in gold', as well as 'sixty superstitious pictures, some Popes and crucifixes, and God the Father sitting in a chair and holding a glass in His hand'.[1] The sight must have been too agonizing for Crashaw to bear, for he escaped to Holland, as his letter to one of the Ferrar group, dated from Leyden on February 20, 1643/4, proves. He planned to resign his fellowship, knowing that he would lose it anyhow, and so far as can be ascertained he never returned to England, though it has been suggested that he was for a short time one of the Royalist group at Oxford.[2]

When, therefore, the Earl of Manchester and his commission arrived at Cambridge on February 5, 1643/4, to administer the Solemn League and Covenant, he found that this particular bird, like many others, such as Cowley, had already flown. Working through the colleges one by one, Manchester came to Trinity in

[1] Quoted by Martin, *Crashaw*, p. xxv ff.                [2] Ibid.

March. Those who were not present to subscribe to the oath were deemed recusant and were automatically ejected from their appointments. On April 8, Cowley, along with his friends Nichols, Robert Creswell, Thomas Cook, Thomas Croyden, Robert Crane, and many more, was formally dispossessed by the Commission.[1] Following a separate trial, for having privately dispatched to the King all of the College plate on which he could lay hands, Dr. Comber, the Master, was likewise removed from his office soon after.[2] Of Cowley's Westminster contemporaries, only William Croyden, who had obtained his fellowship in 1640, alined himself with the invaders, and as a result was appointed a Senior Fellow on November 6, 1645, on the order of the Commons.[3] Crashaw's name was stricken from the rolls of Peterhouse on April 8, 1644.

The Roundheads were in control. In the quiet chambers where Cowley and Crashaw had studied and written, the soldiers of the Puritan party were quartered. Libraries were ransacked, and porters' lodges were turned into prisons. St. John's College was rifled of its collection of ancient coins, to the weight of twenty-two pounds. In St. Mary's the Books of Common Prayer favoured by Laud were ripped and torn. The beautiful grove which Jesus College was so proud of was hewed to the ground.[4]

Only the tall, unworldly figure of Henry More continued to pace the cloisters of Christ's College, too engrossed in the world of the spirit to worry the Puritan emissaries with his loyalist sympathies; and Dr. Duport, unnoticed because his name did not appear on the list of Fellows at Trinity, remained unmolested to deliver a series of lectures on his cherished Theophrastus. William Croyden became one of the university proctors.

[1] Walker, *Sufferings of Clergy*, ii. 160–1; cf. Gough, *Cowley's Essays*, pp. xiii–xiv.    [2] Hill in Johnson's *Lives*, i. 4.
[3] Ball, ii. 352.    [4] Mullinger, p. 171 ff.

# VI

## OXFORD AND THE VIRGILIAN LOTS

AT Oxford just then the Royalists were, on the whole, as optimistic of their ultimate success as the Puritans·had been of theirs at Cambridge. Magdalen and Christ Church were the chief head-quarters of the young Cavaliers, but Cowley seems to have settled at St. John's, a college which had profited greatly from the benefactions of Laud during the latter's Chancellorship of the University and which was not long after to become the repository of the body of the beheaded prelate. Here, in Sprat's words, Cowley 'prosecuted the same studies with a like success',[1] though one may well doubt whether studies pursued in such a troubled and feverish atmosphere were productive of any very permanent results.

The atmosphere of Oxford was indeed a peculiar one. Ladies and belaced gentlemen filled every college and hall, and turned the beautiful grove of Trinity into a mimic Hyde Park. The pitiful diversions and dissipations of a court trying to force itself into seeing only what it wished to see alternated with forays and expeditions into Cornwall and the West Riding, which in turn succeeded sober philosophical and political discussions among the best minds of the party. These included such men as Edward Hyde, who had just been made privy councillor and knighted, and Falkland, whom, much against the young man's will, Hyde had persuaded to accept a secretaryship of state only a year before—at the age of thirty-two.

Great Tew was but a short distance from Oxford, and here the most intelligent and earnest of the court —Cowley among them—were accustomed to repair in

[1] Sprat, 'Account'.

the intervals of the skirmishings between Cavaliers and
Roundheads. Again in Sprat's words, Cowley 'speedily
grew familiar to the chief men of the court and the
gown, whom the fortune of war had drawn together.
And particularly, though he was then very young, he
had the entire friendship of my Lord Falkland. . . .'[1]
The acquaintance may, then, have commenced at this
late date rather than at the time of Cowley's poem to
his friend in 1639, but if so it must always have been
tinged with sadness. For Falkland, introspective and
hating all strife and conflict, had for many months been
brooding over the sickly posture of affairs in his loved
England. By the time of Cowley's arrival, he had come
to despair of a happy outcome, whichever party should
be victorious. England would lose—in fact, had lost—
no matter which party should win. It is noteworthy
that Cowley's admiration was for a man of this type,
even more than for a dashing Cavalier such as Digby.

Courtiers, soldiers, writers, ecclesiastics, physicians—
all had crowded into Oxford to show their allegiance to
the monarchy, and all left their mark on the sensitive
young poet. Perhaps his interest in medicine dates from
this period, for two celebrated doctors whom he afterwards extolled were in the city at this juncture—one
at the height of his fame, the other but anticipating his.
Dr. William Harvey's insistence on the circulating of
the blood was now generally accepted, and he had become a close attendant on the King in consequence of
his pre-eminence in the field of physic. Nor did the
turmoil of war divert him from his zest for experiment,
for at Trinity College he set up his laboratory and performed his tests there. There, too, Cowley's friend
Dr. Charles Scarborough was to be found, at work with
his master. The story of the companionship of the
sixty-five-year-old Harvey and the youthful Scarborough
has been succinctly but vividly told by Aubrey: '. . . at

[1] Sprat, 'Account'.

Oxford Harvey grew acquainted with Dr. Charles
Scarborough, then a young physician; and whereas
before he marched up and down with the army, he
took him to him, and made him lie in his chamber,
and said to him: "Prithee, leave off thy gunning and
stay here; I will bring thee into practice." [1] Harvey's
guarantees were never chimerical. Scarborough eventually gained one of the best practices in England.

Robert Meade, Cowley's old Westminster panegyrist,
had also been in Oxford studying medicine ever since
being elected to Christ Church in 1634. But young
Meade displayed one of the qualities his friend lacked—
the spirit of a soldier. He soon became a captain in the
King's army, and distinguished himself in various
battles more than he had ever done in literature. [2]

Another association which Cowley renewed for a few
months was that with Archbishop Williams, who for a
short time supported Charles at Oxford, but who soon,
on catching the King in an act of typically weak perfidy,
went over to the Commons, with whom his sympathies
had for a long period lain. But this act was too late to
influence Cowley, whose allegiance was now secure—
how secure may be judged from the first poetical work
which he had published since Love's Riddle.

The Puritan and the Papist, published in 1643 as the
work of 'a Scholar in Oxford' and signatured at the end
with the initials 'A. C.', is one of the most immoderate
defences of a moderate position ever written. Although
Cowley never included it among his acknowledged
works, the discussion of its authorship by the publisher
of Wit and Loyalty Revived in 1682 is conclusive
enough, and it is also assigned to Cowley by several
contemporary manuscript copies. [3] Nor should the
savageness of the satire on the two extreme religious
parties disturb the champion of the unquestionable

[1] Aubrey, Brief Lives, i. 299.        [2] Wood, iii. 343; also Welch.
[3] Cf. Sparrow, Mistress, p. 200.

Cowley canon, for the poet had already shown his talent for penning such invectives in some of his early imitations of Donne. Various topical references indicate that the poem was probably dashed off in the heat of the summer and certainly before the death of Pym in December. Such a stinging piece of rough, witty abuse cannot have failed to draw the applause of the coterie at Oxford, except, perhaps, of the Roman Catholic supporters of Queen Henrietta Maria. Spurred on by this applause, and, it may be, recalling his acid sketches of Puritan females in *The Guardian*, Cowley may even have drawn 'The Character of an Holy Sister'.[1] No attack on the honesty, good faith, or morals of the Puritans was too harsh for the poet at this time. Only as he grew older did he perceive the ephemeral nature of controversial and polemical writings.

The habit of sometimes merely initialing his early works with an arrogant 'A. C.', as if confident that the letters alone would sufficiently advertise the author, was once or twice to get him into embarrassments which he would have preferred to escape. Even before *The Puritan and the Papist*, in fact—late in 1642, to be specific—his name had been involved in political verse pamphleteering. For in that year, at London, an eight-page broadside entitled *A Satire against Separatists, or the Conviction of Chamber-Preachers and Other Schismatics contrary to the Discipline of This Our Protestant Religion* had pushed itself forward under the protection of the signature 'A. C. Generosus', and continued to be attributed to Cowley in its various reprints until as late as 1675, as the longhand ascription in the British Museum copy of that date shows. And the *Satire*—orphan or bastard, though more likely the former—provoked an answer soon afterward in *A Satire against the Cavaliers, Penned in Opposition to the Satire against Separatists*. Marprelate was abroad again

[1] Printed tentatively by Grosart, though rejected by A. W. Waller.

for a time, and his doings were as mysterious and fly-by-night as ever.

Whether he always wished to acknowledge his off-spring or not, Cowley was now, with the possible ex-ception of John Denham, the chief poet of the Cavalier party at Oxford—Edmund Waller having been caught by the Parliament in his absurd little Royalist plot, and then having cringingly escaped any worse punishment than exile, which was his reward for betraying his friends to their deaths. And Cowley now conceived a much more ambitious project than any reprobate verses. In spite of Sprat's loyal but vague statement that 'Nor in the meantime was he wanting to his duty in the war itself, for he was present and in service in several of the King's journeys and expeditions',[1] Cowley was no fighter, though he may have forced himself into one or two encounters, as Falkland did into many. He probably had his own case in mind when he wrote, in a flatulent description of the battle of Edgehill:

> Here Learning and th' Arts met; as much they feared
> As when the Huns of old and Goths appeared.
> What should they do ? Unapt themselves to fight,
> They promised noble pens the acts to write.[2]

Consequently Cowley planned to compose a history of the Civil War in heroic couplets, beginning with a sketch of the proud wars of old in which England had engaged, and then extending his account from the year 1641 forward as long as these present lamentable and shameful struggles should last. Of the authenticity of this pedestrian work—which is, like all of Cowley's disputatious writing, sometimes questioned—there is no need to doubt, although it was not printed until 1679, a dozen years after his death. Nevertheless, in the preface to his 1656 edition he himself confessed to having composed, 'during the time of the late troubles',

---

[1] Sprat, 'Account'.      [2] Cowley, *Poem on Late Civil War*, p. 14.

'three books of the Civil War itself, reaching as far as
the first battle of Newbury, where the succeeding misfortunes of the party stopped the work'. This is not a
completely accurate description of *A Poem on the Late
Civil War*, as the first publisher entitled it, but he was
probably right in considering it 'unquestionably a part'
of the longer work. To whom the manuscript from
which he said he printed it belonged, he did not state.
Very likely, however, since he did not claim that it was
in Cowley's own hand, it was a copy made by one of the
Oxford circle, perhaps before the author had brought
his work beyond the summer campaign of Newcastle in
Yorkshire in 1643, with which the present fragment
ends. A glancing allusion to *The Puritan and the Papist*
in the first paragraph would also aid in fixing the
authorship, as would the characteristic hemistich, 'But
tears break off my verse', just after a eulogy of the
wounded Cornish commander, Sir Ralph Hopton. If
Cowley himself witnessed any of the engagements
which he celebrated, the victory of Hopton, Grenville,
Digby, and others over Stamford at Stratton would,
from the tone of the description, seem the one most
likely.

But even in the midst of his most exultant pictures
of Royalist successes, in the midst of his pride at dwelling in the same town which sheltered the great Charles,
Cowley could not forget the sad remembrance of the
university which he had left. Oxford, in spite of her
glories, was to him but 'the British Muse's second
fame':

> O happy town, that to loved Charles's sight
> In these sad times giv'st safety and delight, . . .
> Amidst all the joys which heaven allows thee here,
> Think on thy sister, and then shed a tear.[1]

And the joys of Oxford too were soon to turn into

[1] Ibid., p. 21.

sorrows. Defeats and deaths all around him were
sufficient to throw Cowley into new doubts. He could
act the poet laureate to a cause of whose triumph he
was confident, but he could not drive his muse to
commemorate failure. He was the Muse's Hannibal,
not her Charles I. Though loyal as ever to the King,
he wrote no more of his rhymed history—fortunately,
perhaps, since his genius did not lie in that direction.
The war, however, had even so early begun to divert
him from the path which he had marked out for himself
since childhood.

Unwittingly, too, he was to become a minor, but
important, agent in confirming the King's increasing
forebodings of ultimate discomfiture, if no worse.
While the Royalist rival Parliament was sitting at
Oxford about this time, according to an anecdote told
by Dr. Edward Lake (and in different versions by
other writers),[1] the King, tired out with business and
afflictions, and having exhausted all the amusements
which had been transplanted from London, looked
yearningly for some new sort of distraction for his
weariness. Nothing seemed to offer except the books
of the Bodleian; so there he went, accompanied by
Falkland and others. While there (he himself being not
unsuperstitious), he happened to notice some of the
young noblemen who were still ostensibly students at
the University 'pricking in Virgil' for their fortunes—
in other words, trying the *sortes Virgilianae* or Virgilian lots.

Somewhat incautiously, he resolved to try his fate.
But he would nevertheless have the way sounded out,
and he motioned to Falkland to go first. The latter
obeyed, whatever his feelings, averted his eyes, and
pushed open the *Aeneid* to the one hundred and fifty-

---

[1] See *Diary of Dr. Edward Lake*, quoted by Grosart, *Cowley*, ii. 353;
Aubrey, *Anecdotes*, pp. 108–10; Wellwood, *Memoirs*, pp. 93–4; Chet-
wood, in Dryden's *Works*, xiii. 316; Gildon, *Miscellany Poems*, p. 26.

second verse of the eleventh book—an ominous passage
which Dryden was to English thus:

> O Pallas, thou hast failed thy plighted word,
> To fight with caution, not to tempt the sword;
> I warned thee, but in vain, for well I knew
> What perils youthful ardours would pursue;
> That boiling blood would carry thee too far,
> Young as thou wert to dangers, raw to war.
> O curst assay of arms, disastrous doom,
> Prelude of bloody fields and fights to come!
> Hard elements of unauspicious war,
> Vain vows of heaven, and unavailing care!

The passage was menacing, for Falkland's morbid-
ness on the subject of the war and his rash valour in
battle were known to all.  But the King would not be
deterred.  Calling for the book, he too thrust his pin
into it, reckless of consequences.  Then, already beginning to repent for having thus exposed himself to
possible ill-news, he gazed at the passage upon which
his finger rested.  He would have closed the volume
then and kept what he had seen to himself.  But it was
too late, for his attendants were already craning their
necks to see.

> At bello audacis populi vexatus et armis,
> Finibus extorris, complexu avulsus Iuli,
> Auxilium imploret, videatque indigna suorum
> Funera; nec, cum se sub leges pacis iniquae
> Tradiderit, regno aut optata luce fruatur,
> Sed cadat ante diem, mediaque inhumatus arena.

It was Dido's curse of Aeneas, in book four of the epic.
The King looked concerned; the nobles looked concerned and embarrassed.  But Charles, once committed,
would not turn back.  He would have the verses rendered into English; moreover, he would have the translation done by one who was master of both Latin and
English poetry and who, besides, did not know whose

lot was being forecast. He would have the job done by
Mr. Cowley.

As he glanced about, his eye lighted on Henry
Jermyn, who seemingly had already become a sort of
patron to the poet. To him the King delivered the
mission of having the fortune Englished. When Jermyn
returned from St. John's (Lake says Christ Church,
perhaps because Westminster boys ordinarily went
there), he bore with him the following version of the
lines:

> By a bold people's stubborn arms oppressed,
> Forced to forsake the land which he possessed,
> Torn from his dearest son, let him in vain
> Seek help, and see his friends unjustly slain;
> Let him to base, unequal terms submit,
> In hope to save his crown, yet lose both it
> And life at once; untimely let him die,
> And on an open stage unburied lie.

If Cowley actually wrote these couplets from such an
original, his chambers at St. John's must have been
swept just then by a cloud of wandering fumes from
Delphi, for his prophecy was to be fulfilled to as exact
a detail as was Dido's curse. His bravery, moreover, is
to be admired as much as if he had actually led a charge
of Prince Rupert's horse, for he could scarcely have
failed to perceive the application of the passage to his
sovereign's fortunes, and yet he conscientiously rendered
his translation.

Charles's behaviour on receiving the paraphrase has
not been recorded. If his promise to Cowley of the
mastership of the Savoy, one of the sinecures which
would return to his control as soon as his throne should
cease to totter, was made in this general period (Cowley, in a statement of his case after the Restoration,
said that it was made 'in a letter to the Queen' while the
King 'was at Oxford')[1], Charles showed himself to be

[1] See ch. xiv.

as magnanimous as his usually tolerant character would lead one to expect. But whether he would have kept the promise which would enable the poet to retire and pursue his scaling of the poetical Alps, untroubled by financial cares, is another matter.

Cowley's intimacy with Falkland, however, was fated to come to an even more abrupt end. The latter's fit of melancholia deepened as the weeks hurried past. The outcome would have been the same whether the tale of his trial of the *sortes Virgilianae* is true or mythical. His death was a virtual suicide. Though no military man, he had exposed himself to every danger that offered at Gloucester, but his life seemed charmed. On September 20, 1643, however, just before riding into the battle of Newbury, he told his friends that he was sure he would at last find peace. Purposely spurring his horse past a gap in a hedge which was swept by the rebels' musketry, he was immediately shot to death. Nor was his loss one of the least which the Royalists suffered in the tactical defeat which resulted—their first important one in the rebellion.

The end of Cowley's former panegyric may also stand as his valedictory to his hero:

> He is too good for war, and ought to be
> As far from danger as from fear he's free.
> Those men alone (and those are useful too)
> Whose valour is the only art they know,
> Were for sad war and bloody battles born:
> Let them the state defend, and he adorn.[1]

Too late both he and Falkland found that war is no respecter of talents.

[1] Cowley, 'To the Lord Falkland'.

# VII

## LOVE'S COLUMBUS

FOR two years ('per biennium', says Sprat's Latin life) Cowley remained at Oxford, trying to study, trying to write, but continually being led farther and farther astray by the court life into which he had been thrown. At first he did not resist too much. He had always worshipped the royal family, and now he was associating with it on more and more intimate terms. He was dazzled by finding dukes and earls and knights as his daily companions, and he saw how men of humble birth might become favourites and rise to positions of honour and importance. What more natural than that his ambition should be stirred in a new direction, especially since the old now seemed to be blocked? Henry Bennet, for instance, another Westminster boy, had become secretary to Lord Digby in 1643 and was now acting as a private messenger between the Queen and Lord Ormonde in Ireland. Jermyn himself, of good (though not high) birth, had risen with phenomenal speed after having attracted the attention of the Queen while in his early twenties. Although only a scholar and a poet, Cowley knew that he possessed abilities as great as theirs; and through John Hervey he had already gained the confidence of Baron Jermyn.

Abraham Cowley became the secretary of Baron Jermyn, and, consequently, of Queen Henrietta Maria.[1] This seemed to be the only road open to him, and after all, under the circumstances, only a very strong-minded man with a clear view of his own destiny would have been justified in refusing. Cowley's character, however, was not of this type.

The exact date of his accepting the position cannot

[1] Sprat, 'Account'.

be set. Henrietta Maria left England for the last time
on April 3, 1644, never to see her husband again. She
had been a good wife to him, after the assassination of
the elder Buckingham had removed this barrier between
them, although she had been hated by the people for
her Catholicism. He had been a good husband to her,
according to royal standards, and she had borne him
three sons and three daughters, as well as three other
children who died in their infancy. He had not objected to her fondness for Jermyn, and she had not
objected to his occasional frivolities; in fact, their unalloyed affection for each other was proverbial throughout Europe. Besides, toward the end of the preceding
period, she had been fully occupied in furthering the
affairs of the Roman Church in England, and in gaining
aid from the Pope, from her relatives in France, and
from Holland. Her march through England ('her she-
majesty generalissima', she smilingly called herself) to
join the King near Oxford—at Kineton, as Cowley described the meeting in his rhymed history—had been
one of the dramatic episodes of the 1643 campaign, and
the affectionate meeting of the two had been followed
by the birth of their last child at Exeter, just before her
hair's-breadth escape to France.

When she went, ill in health and despondent in mind,
Jermyn went with her as her secretary, and was appointed Governor of Jersey in the same year. Whether
Cowley accompanied them at this time is not demon-
strable. Sprat's statements on the matter cannot be
absolutely reconciled chronologically with others that
he made on other events, but on the whole they suggest
that Cowley left England in 1644. 'During the heat of
the Civil War', he says in his English life, Cowley 'was
settled in my Lord St. Albans' family, and attended
her Majesty the Queen Mother when, by the unjust
persecution of her subjects, she was forced to retire into
France'. In his Latin life he also wrote: 'In familiam

illustrissimi Comitis Sancti Albani adscitus, reginam
Mariam, regno per nefas extorrem, in Galliam secutus
est'. His statements concerning Cowley's twelve-year
stay in France likewise seem to be based on the as-
sumption that the other left England in 1644, although
—as will be shown later—the actual absence was only
about a decade. At any rate, some time before the
surrender of Oxford to the Parliamentary forces in
June 1646, Cowley was firmly established in the household of Jermyn at Paris.

Exactly what he expected to find on his first view of
Parisian society he has not recorded, but he probably
anticipated his introduction to this new life with considerable zest, being of an inquisitive and observant
nature. Hurd, in his *Moral and Political Dialogues*,
later imagined Cowley describing his expectations to
Sprat in this strain: the poet found himself in 'a country
which piques itself on all the refinements of civility.
Here the world was to appear to me in its fairest form
and, it was not doubted, would put on all its charms to
wean me from the love of a studious, retired life. . . . All
that the elegance of polished manners could contribute
to make society attractive was to be found in this new
scene'.[1]

But, eager as Cowley was, he was too thoroughly
English in temperament to discover in France what he
had hoped for. As Sprat explained the situation, 'He
had a great integrity and plainness of manners, which
he preserved to the last, though much of his time was
spent in a nation and way of life that is not very famous
for its sincerity'.[2] This passage Hurd later elaborated
on by making Cowley speak as follows: 'Yet shall I
confess my inmost sentiments of this splendid life to
you ? I found it empty, fallacious, and even disgusting.
. . . All was ambition, intrigue, falsehood. Every one
was intent on his own schemes, frequently wicked,

[1] Hurd, *Dialogues*, i. 79–80.                    [2] Sprat, 'Account'.

always base and selfish. Great professions of honour, of friendship, and of duty; but all ending in low views and sordid practices.' [1]

Actually, however, Cowley could not have been quite so disillusioned as all this. He had lived with the English court at Oxford, and near it while at Westminster; and courts do not at bottom differ greatly from one another. Nor could he have been totally unfamiliar with the condition of France on his arrival. Henrietta Maria's brother, Louis XIII, had died just about the time that the English court had gone to Oxford. Richelieu, as great a tyrant as Laud had ever been, but an infinitely greater statesman, had preceded his weak master by half a year. Maria de Medici, the intriguing and exiled Queen Mother, had died in destitution during the same six months. As a result, Henrietta Maria's nephew, Louis XIV, a boy of but six or seven years of age, now occupied the throne. Over him, as regent, sat his mother, Anne of Austria, daughter of Philip III of Spain, at first so eager to please all parties that the pleasure-loving Cardinal de Retz one day remarked bitingly that the French language had been reduced to five words: 'The Queen is so good!' But over her ruled Cardinal Mazarin, an Italian prelate trained in the school of Richelieu. With such a combination, and with a populace as restless and distrustful of the nobility as the French were at this time, what could be expected but intrigues, hatreds, and civil and international wars? Everywhere in Europe there was conflict, though in Germany the Thirty Years' War had almost exhausted itself.

Anne granted her unfortunate sister-in-law a suite in the Louvre.[2] Another, in the same building, she gave to Henrietta's chamberlain, Lord Jermyn, and it was here that Cowley was established when he reached Paris.

[1] Hurd, as before.
[2] Taylor, *Henrietta Maria*; Haynes, *Henrietta Maria*.

So far as creature comforts were concerned, he had a
good master. Ostentatious, a lover of the lusts of the
flesh, Jermyn was almost the only one of the English
exiles in Paris to keep open house and to live with as
much splendour and display as if his King were not
being harried and hunted from place to place in England like a badger. Even after Prince Charles, after an
exciting escape from England under the convoy of
Sir Edward Hyde, reached France, Jermyn kept up his
former style, though the Prince's household was soon
reduced almost to penury.

But notwithstanding his deficiencies, Jermyn must
have had some good qualities to retain the lifelong
devotion and confidence of persons like Cowley and the
beautiful Queen. Gambler and roué as he was, he must
have been a good and understanding friend, as well as a
patron of the arts. Sprat, who also later reaped the
benefit of Jermyn's generosity, likewise bore testimony
that in Cowley's 'long dependence on my Lord St.
Albans, there never happened any manner of difference
between them'.[1] For the poet did not presume to
criticize individuals, though many times in his life he
could not have approved their conduct and often assailed court and diplomatic life in general.

Nor was Cowley the only poet to profit from Jermyn's
liberality. In 16⅚6 Will Davenant, another of Henrietta's favourites because of the plays and masques he
had written for her and the English court in the old
days, returned from a mission to Charles with which
she had entrusted him. Although the King had scorned
his wife's suggestion that he 'part with the Church for
his peace and security', Jermyn, to whom religion
meant little except in its political aspects, installed the
merry Will in more of his chambers at the Louvre, and
the recently knighted dramatist sat down to continue
the writing of his new epic, *Gondibert*, which was to be

---

[1] Sprat, 'Account'.

constructed on the plan of a five-act play and would set
new rules and standards for all succeeding heroic poems.[1]

Jolly Will, who was the godson of Shakespeare and
was not averse to admitting a much closer relationship
while in his cups, must have been a more congenial
companion to Jermyn than was the quiet Cowley. The
contrast was striking: Cowley, with his calm, rather
placid face, and his deliberateness in conversation,
opposite the noseless Davenant, volatile, dissolute, and
reckless in speech and action. The one was gentle and
sensitive; the other seemed to have no deep personal
feelings, and could jest about the decay of his nose as if
the 'mischance', which Suckling's *Session of the Poets*
attributed to one of his French amours, had actually
occurred to another man. If, moreover, Wood's
counter-story about the 'handsome black girl in Axe-
Yard, Westminster', is correct,[2] Davenant seems to
have been brazen enough even to insert his Dulcinea
into the third book of the third canto of his unfinished
epic.

*Gondibert* furnished the topic for many conversations
between its author and Cowley, who praised the design
and encouraged the work.[3] All of the English men of
letters in Paris—and there were many of them—discussed it and criticized it. According to Aubrey,
Davenant's enthusiasm toward his poem later excited
the derision of Denham and other courtiers, and even
the philosopher Hobbes was drawn into the argument,
though, on the whole, on Davenant's side.[4]

Thomas Hobbes, in his own words 'a man of feminine
courage', had been the first of the prominent Royalists
to flee to Paris, fearing that some of his early utilita-
rian works on politics and the state, which had been
circulating in manuscript, would lodge him in the

---

[1] Davenant, 'Preface' to *Gondibert*.                    [2] Wood, iii. 804.
[3] Davenant, 'Preface'; and Cowley, 'To Sir William Davenant.'
[4] Aubrey, *Brief Lives*, i. 207.

Tower along with Laud and Strafford. Cowley's attraction to a solid, unorthodox thinker of this sort is proof of his own versatility of mind.[1] Moreover, Hobbes's general philosophical position, being quite opposite to that of the Platonists, seems to have accorded with what young Cowley had been working out gradually by himself. Hobbes, as a young man, had known and talked with Bacon—and Cowley ardently admired Bacon. During his youthful travels, too, Hobbes had become acquainted with the scientific methods of Galileo and Kepler, and had become interested in Montaigne. Later, in his middle age, he had been a member of the circle of Gassendi and, in some measure, of Descartes—and even now, at the University of Paris, Gassendi was giving his famous lectures and publishing his books on the Epicurean philosophy. Materialistic ideas, based on conceptions of pleasure and self-interest as the mainsprings of human life and action, began to seep into Cowley's consciousness and to assimilate themselves slowly with the Horatian hedonism which had been his from childhood.

Edmund Waller, whose well-advertised love for 'Sacharissa' had left him still romantically interesting to the ladies in spite of his ignominious rejection, his subsequent second marriage, and his unsavoury behaviour in the plot which had resulted in his banishment, was another prominent figure among the exiled Cavaliers. Still wealthy, he was the only Englishman who, after finally settling in Paris, made any pretence at keeping up with Jermyn in setting a table and showing a front.[2] According to Aubrey, his head was 'but small, brain very hot, and apt to be choleric', his body was thin and not robust, his face oval, and his eyes were 'popping out and working'.[3] He had already tickled the

[1] Cowley, 'To Mr. Hobbes'.
[2] Cf. Thorn-Drury, ed. of *Waller*, i. lviii–lix.
[3] Aubrey, *Brief Lives*, ii. 276.

Queen's ears with his complimentary verses in England, and now, for a time at least, he acted as her chamberlain. This was the man who was to be Cowley's chief rival as a love poet for many years.

It was probably not until 1646 that the two men met in Paris, though they may have known each other slightly in person—and certainly by reputation—in England. For in the autumn of that year Waller reached the capital from a trip through Switzerland and Italy, and with him he brought his companion on the journey, John Evelyn.

Of all the great people whom Cowley numbered among his friends during his whole life, Evelyn was, with the possible exception of Falkland, the one who proved the most kindred spirit. Neither man was in real temperamental harmony with most of the persons among whom he was compelled to live. Evelyn had already displayed his unfitness for a career of action by obtaining the King's permission to desert the scene of the war in October 1643. He counted himself a Royalist, and yet he would have sacrificed anything for peace. He loved his books and he loved the quiet and solace of a sheltered, well-tended garden. On all of these scores Cowley found himself in agreement, and there is little doubt that the lovely intimacy between the two grew up at this time.

But these people, exiles though they were, were all living in comparatively comfortable circumstances and all moved in the great world. Soon after Cowley's arrival, however, the miserable tale of another English exile was brought to him—an exile who, being a 'mere scholar' and a poet to boot (according to Wood) and having neither rank nor wealth, had fallen into wretched straits.[1] Investigating the story he had heard, Cowley found the friend of his Cambridge days, Richard Crashaw. Prayers, and fasting, and meditation, con-

[1] Wood, iv, ii. 5.

H

tinued late into the night as well as through the day,
in accordance with the discipline of his Little Gidding
comrades, had convinced Crashaw that he could find his
peace nowhere but upon the steadfast bosom of Rome,
but his conversion had brought him only spiritual
comfort. He had made no friends. His soul was redeemed, but his body was wasted and uncared for.
Utter destitution was not far off when Cowley found
and rescued him.

Crashaw, however, was an apostate, and Cowley had
written many harsh lines about the subjects of Rome.
What should he do? There was probably never any
question in his mind. What he had written, against
both Puritan and Papist, he had written against people
whom he had never really known. There is no record
of his ever attacking a person with whom he had had
even a slight acquaintance; and his writings actually
suggest a grudging admiration for Cromwell himself
after he had met the man. The personal equation was
everything to Cowley—and he had loved Crashaw.

No one could have asked for a kinder welcome than
Queen Henrietta Maria, through Cowley's mediations,
gave Richard Crashaw. The latter had written verses
about her in England, it is true (his panegyric had been
the longest of all the congratulatory poems in *Voces
Votivae*), but even supposing that these had met her
eyes, she was by this time pretty well inured to flattery
—as much so, at least, as a fascinating woman can ever
become. Cowley's advocacy had much to do with his
friend's reception, but perhaps an even greater reason
was that the Queen saw in the shabby convert an indication that her sincere but ill-timed efforts to Catholi-
cize England were still bearing fruit, sparse as it was
in comparison with what she and those who had
fostered her match with Charles had once expected.

Crashaw, for his part, saw in Henrietta Maria a veritable saint on earth. Though her beauty as a fifteen-

year-old bride had long ago begun to fade, her dark eyes—
as Van Dyck's portraits clearly show—were as sparkling
as ever and her bearing as gay and vivacious. Her oval
face, with its rather too pointed chin and full mouth,
was set off by the peculiar frame of symmetrically
frizzed ringlets which she had made the fashion. Her
costume, though not so gorgeous as she had dazzled her
alien subjects with in England, was still admirably calculated to set off her special beauty, for the pension of
10,000 crowns which her royal sister-in-law had granted
her on her arrival had not yet been withdrawn because
of the woes of France.[1] But all these things—and the
similar attractions of her ladies—probably made little
impression on Crashaw in comparison with her spiritual
qualities and her intense devotion to her religion.
Their mutual interest in St. Teresa, too, must have
furnished them with a topic for fervent discussion,
though probably Crashaw's mysticism was as foreign to
her temperament as it was to Cowley's.

Here, among the literary coterie of expatriates but
not of them, Crashaw dwelt for a year or so, depending
on the bounty of his friends. The ill-tempered Prynne,
indeed, charged that the Queen and her ladies had
actually taken up a purse for this 'peevish, silly seeker'
who had let himself be 'transplanted to Rome'.[2] But
if so, Crashaw did not fail to make them some return,
though in less material currency, for he dedicated his
*Carmen Deo Nostro* to Lady Denbigh, one of the Queen's
household, who was already wavering along his own
path. In the end, with a letter to Pope Innocent X
written, on September 7, 1646, in Henrietta's own
hand,[3] he passed on to Rome, where, according to
Dr. John Bargrave, he became a *seguita* or attendant to
Cardinal Palotta.[4] Through the whole affair Cowley

[1] Haynes, p. 220.                [2] Prynne, *Legenda Lignea*, p. cxxxviii.
[3] In Martin, *Crashaw*, p. xxxiii.
[4] Bargrave, *Pope Alexander*, p. 37.

had been the moving spirit, though he was never one to boast of his charities.

Perhaps it was the stimulation of all these associations which caused him to take up his pen again, on a subject which was neither polemical nor religious. Or perhaps the initial inspiration had come even earlier, while the buzz of the more light-hearted members of the court at Oxford had entranced and seduced him from his more serious projects. At any rate, chameleon-like, Abraham Cowley forgot his resolve to be 'the Muse's Hannibal' and to write the first religious epic in English. He had a new enthusiasm. He would become—as he wrote in 'The Prophet'—'Love's Columbus', and he would take as his motto, 'Haeret lateri lethalis arundo'. He would celebrate the fatal arrow and the blind bow-boy in a manner which would, he secretly hoped, bear comparison with Ovid and even drive the fashionable Edmund Waller himself to cover—Waller, whose rather formal verses to the Earl of Leicester's daughter every young Cavalier had got by heart long before their publication to the world in 1645.

> I'll fix thy title next in fame
> To Sacharissa's well-sung name—

promised Cowley to his mistress in 'The Given Love'.

He had already made one or two tentative excursions into the realm of amorous verse, as in 'To a Lady Who Made Posies for Rings', written not long before *The Guardian*. But now he set out to compose an entire new cycle of love poems—though he was not yet in love. Moreover, he was never quite sure of what he wanted to do—whether he wished to reveal a story in verse or whether he preferred to descant in general upon love's blisses and pains. The result was that through the series of sixty or so poems which he turned out and circulated in manuscript among his admiring friends there ran only a sufficient thread of plot to

cause the reader to wonder whether after all the whole
thing was merely an artificial pose and whether perhaps
among the ladies of the Queen there was not one whom
the poet kept at least in his mind's eye, just as a painter
requires some sort of model from which to work.

When Dr. Johnson remarked sarcastically, 'The compositions are such as might have been written for
penance by a hermit, or for hire by a philosophical
rhymer who had only heard of another sex', he was perhaps too ready to take advantage of the openings which
Cowley himself gave.[1] In the very initial poem, 'The
Request', in fact, Cowley admits that he has often
'wished to love', but in vain; and in 'Resolved to be
Beloved', 'Resolved to Love', 'The Dissembler', and
other poems scattered through the whole series he
reiterates the same point of view. But in the second
poem, 'The Thraldom', the arrow pierces his heart, as
he has requested, and from that point the story develops.

The third poem, 'The Given Love', outlines the
situation. Bold in imagination only, the poet argues
with the lady, to whom he refuses to give a name, not to
let his lowness of position and her greatness keep them
apart.
> I'll flatter or oppose the King,
> Turn Puritan, or anything,

he swears—mighty promises from Cowley, all except
the first, and lines which might well have been written
at Oxford. And so he goes through the whole catalogue.
His lady leaving him, he will see no spring till she re-
turns. He sends her a letter 'Written in Juice of Lemon'.
He defends himself, perhaps to another sweetheart,
against the charge of inconstancy, and then, Donne-
like, abuses his lady for falsehood, foulness, and pride.
He sees her 'Clad All in White'. He finds her cold, and
loves her 'first because she could love nobody, afterwards loving her with desire'. He wagers with some

[1] Johnson, *Lives*, i. 41–2.

male friend that in spite of the latter's gravity and 'streaks . . . of divinity' an invitation from the lady would dissolve all his sobriety. He despairs, and thinks of escaping from 'this great hive, the city'—and meditates even on death.

Then, in 'The Bargain', comes the introduction of the first real complication, one which might have some basis in actuality. A wealthy competitor enters the field, and entices the lady with his money. Again he appears, in 'The Rich Rival'. And that some such event did actually occur, Cowley's ode addressed many years later to Lord Broghill, Earl of Orrery, would seem to prove; for it contains these lines:

> I wrote and wrote, but still I wrote in vain,
> For after all my expense of wit and pain,
> A rich, unwriting hand carried the prize away.

Then comes 'The Parting', which might well betoken the removal of the lady to France with the Queen. Cowley gives her his picture, but still fears to confess his love. But they are soon reunited, and the description of episodes in the affair in 'Resolved to Love' could easily fit the Louvre. He is falsely accused of being unfaithful and loving her waiting-maid. He carves his lady's name on a tree, which promptly withers from the heat. And so, although every other observer perceives his plight, the lady herself remains blind, and the poet is reluctantly compelled to write 'Love Given Over'. The citadel of his heart has been sacked and burned (the number of military figures in the cycle directly reflects the time of composition), and therefore he need never fear another hostile attack.

If Cowley had any basis of actuality for these poems, it was a very slight one. According to Sprat's Latin life, he played with, or counterfeited, love-adventures ('De amoribus lusit') with the ease and ingenuity of Ovid and Catullus, and his own modesty. Yet one *affaire du*

*cœur* he seems to have had, though there is no agreement as to when in his life it occurred or with whom.
In 'Of Greatness' he himself wrote, 'If ever I were to
fall in love again'—a statement which would indicate
that he had been in love at least once before. Barnes's
story ('quod ex certa relatione accepimus') was that
only once had Cowley been in love, and then, though
living in the same dwelling ('in iisdem aedibus') with
his mistress, because of his bashfulness he had never
dared to address his suit to her.[1] But this story is
essentially the same as that told by Cowley's own poems,
and would easily fit his stay in the Louvre. Alexander
Pope, however, gossiping with Spence, attempted to
embroider on the anecdote by stating dogmatically that
the lady involved here and in the most famous of
Cowley's love poems, 'The Chronicle', which was not
published until long after the rest, became the wife of
Sprat's brother.[2] Unfortunately for Pope's tale, however, it is extremely unlikely that these two ladies were
the same, since Sprat was seventeen years younger than
Cowley and the two men did not meet until nearly a
decade after the main series of the lyrics was published
in 1647 as *The Mistress, or Several Copies of Love Verses*,
from a floating manuscript in England—and, if the
publisher's note is to be believed, without the author's
knowledge. Nevertheless, the fact that when Cowley
himself later included the cycle in his first collected
edition he changed the poems virtually not at all
would indicate that the manuscript was a very correct
and authentic one, if it were not actually furnished by
him.[3]

   *The Mistress*, however, is more a hodge-podge than
the preceding summary would suggest. The story itself
does not develop consistently, but is interrupted by

[1] Barnes, *Anacreontius*, p. 32.
[2] Pope, in Spence's *Anecdotes*, pp. 285–6.
[3] Cf. Sparrow, *R.E.S.*, iii. 22–7.

many love poems of a general rather than a specific
nature, and by many more, such as 'Resolved to be
Beloved', 'The Welcome', and 'The Inconstant', which
present the speaker as a promiscuous lover, unable to
resist any woman who may look at him.

> I never yet could see that face
>     Which had no dart for me;
> From fifteen years to fifty's space
>     They all victorious be.
> Love, thou'rt a devil, if I may call thee one;
> For sure in me thy name is Legion.

Or, on the other hand, in 'The Dissembler' he does not
attempt to disguise the real truth—that he has been
feigning his sad condition:

> Unhurt, untouched, did I complain,
> And terrified all others with the pain. . . .
>     Darts, and wounds, and flame, and heat,
>     I named but for the rhyme or the conceit.

The lack of unity in *The Mistress* is also emphasized
in other ways. For instance, in 'Love Given Over', the
'wretched Cowley' admits to having wasted three of his
'lustiest' and 'freshest' years in his luckless pursuit, but
in other poems periods of five years or one year are
mentioned. Nor do the lyrics themselves seem to
belong to the same stratum of his work. 'Against Hope'
and 'For Hope', for example, had already been printed
in 1646 by Humphrey Moseley, Cowley's new publisher and the nation's leading dealer in *belles lettres*, in
an edition of Crashaw's poems. Similarly, 'The Motto',
an early poem, later removed to another section of
Cowley's works, first appeared as a postscript to *The
Mistress*.

If, however, Cowley's own confession be accepted,

> My lines of amorous desire
> I wrote to kindle and blow others' fire,

the discrepancies begin to disappear. Such an admission, moreover, should not be taken to indicate that Dr. Johnson's too-well-quoted sarcasms have provided the last word on Cowley's love lyrics. For Cowley was too true a poet always to write badly even on a theme which life had not yet fitted into his deepest experience. Many of his conceits, with their burning glasses of ice, their flaming hearts, and their hailstones of cold tears, would do credit to an old-fashioned valentine, and often a poem with a striking and seemingly sincere opening, such as 'My Heart Discovered', dissolves into a sequence of stale figures and recondite allusions.

But some of his best poems—and some of the best poems of his age, in fact—were written in these forced attempts to amuse the new friends he had made at court. Probably some of the more libidinous verses, which were later cited by the Reverend Edmund Elys for lasciviousness,[1] were inserted simply to pander to a common taste, which Cowley had already recognized in *The Guardian*; but on the whole the series was much purer than many erotic cycles of the day. Though there are some traces of Platonic ideas, as in 'Clad All in White' and 'My Heart Discovered', Cowley is now emphatically no Platonic.

> Indeed, I must confess
> When souls mix 'tis an happiness;
> But not complete till bodies too do join,
> And both our wholes into one whole combine:
> But half of heaven the souls in glory taste
> Till by Love in heaven at last
> Their bodies too are placed.

Such are his ideas in 'Platonic Love'. Similarly, in 'Answer to the Platonics', he jeers, 'When I'm all soul, such shall my love too be'. The same insistence on the physical aspects of love, without the exclusion of the

[1] Cf. Grosart, i. li.

spiritual, appears in the last lines of 'The Soul'. The
doctrine of the Stoics, says 'My Fate', is a 'sad and cruel
one; and 'The Enjoyment', the most outspoken of all
the lyrics in the first edition, confesses outright, 'In
love there's none too much an Epicure'.

> Nought shall my hands or lips control:
> I'll kiss thee through, I'll kiss thy very soul.

Such a couplet furnishes the clue to Cowley's philosophical position in *The Mistress*. Influenced as he may
have been by Shakespeare in 'Not Fair', or by Drayton
in 'Love Undiscovered', he was a follower of Donne—
and not a mean one—in his best poems at this time.
John Sparrow, a more orderly and much more sympathetic critic than Dr. Johnson on this subject, has discussed Cowley's direct debts to Donne so competently
that another discussion would be mere repetition.
Cowley has caught the Dean's preoccupation with the
eternal strife between the soul, the mind, and the body;
again and again he opens his poems with abrupt
irritated plunges into the midst of the situation; he
abuses and rails at his mistress as if he were a true
Elizabethan, and then repents and castigates himself
with penances; he brings the science of the atom, the
motions of the earth, the septennial renewal of the body,
the Salic law, and the principles of logic into his verses;
he is cynical in the midst of his most abandoned passion.
His epithetical style, with its exuberant faults and its
apt virtues, appears at its best in such rhapsodies as
'Beauty', with its striking first line, 'Beauty, thou wild
fantastic ape'.   There is genuine emotion, though perhaps not always consistently maintained, in the majority
of *The Mistress*.  Cowley has not succeeded in convinc-
ing his readers that he was himself more than tentatively
in love (if even so much as that), but he has provoked
them to new thoughts on the subject and sometimes

¹ Sparrow, *Mistress*, pp. xv–xvii, xx.

has created an enduring metaphysical poem which is
more than a mere conceit, as in 'The Separation':

> Ask me not what my love shall do or be
> (Love, which is soul to body, and soul of me)
>   When I am separated from thee;
>   Alas, I might as easily show
> What after death the soul will do;
> 'Twill last, I'm sure, and that is all we know.
>
> The thing called soul will never stir nor move,
> But all that while a lifeless carcass prove;
>   For 'tis the body of my love.
>   Not that my love will fly away,
> But still continue, as, they say,
> Sad troubled ghosts about their graves do stray.

Cowley was not satisfied, however, to base his claims
to being 'Love's Columbus' on *The Mistress* alone. His
experiments with paraphrasing eleven of the poems
wrongly attributed to Anacreon and with writing an
'Elegy upon Anacreon, Who was Choked by a Grape-
Stone' seemingly were made at about the same time, or
a very little later. What more natural than that, as
Sprat said, after counterfeiting Ovid and Catullus,
Cowley should turn to the most popular of the Greek
poets associated with love and wine ?[1] And in introducing the Anacreontic, with its characteristic measure
of seven or eight irregularly accented syllables, into
English, Cowley was not only much more of a Columbus
than he had ever been in *The Mistress*, but he achieved
a success which not even the calumniators of the larger
collection have denied.

In these light, graceful little lyrics, moreover,
Cowley sketched in vague outlines the same character
and story as he had presented in *The Mistress*. In 'Love'
the first of the group, he told, in the person of Anacreon,
how he had resolved to write of heroes and of kings, but

[1] Sprat, 'De Vita'.

how his lyre had refused to answer to these 'mighty
numbers':

> Farewell, then, heroes, farewell, kings,
> And mighty numbers, mighty things:
> Love tunes my heart just to my strings.

He poured an oblation to 'Beauty' in both series, and in
'The Duel' he told how Love's arrow had pierced his
once stubborn heart and Love himself had conquered
the citadel. In 'Gold' he lamented that the greatest
pain of all 'is to love, but love in vain', especially since

> Gold alone does passion move,
> Gold monopolizes love!

The Epicurean tone of *The Mistress*, likewise, became
more vocal in the Anacreontics, though it was the popular type of 'The Epicure':

> Fill the bowl with rosy wine,
> Around our temples roses twine,
> And let us cheerfully awhile
> Like the wine and roses smile.
> Crowned with roses, we contemn
> Gyges' wealthy diadem.
> To-day is ours; what do we fear?
> To-day is ours; we have it here. . . .

And in 'Another' on the same topic he wrote:

> Let me alive my pleasures have;
> All are Stoics in the grave.

The most famous of all Cowley's love lyrics, however,
is 'The Chronicle', which Johnson himself extolled as 'a
composition unrivalled and alone: such gaiety of fancy,
such facility of expression, such varied similitude, such a
succession of images, and such a dance of words, it is in
vain to expect except from Cowley'.[1] Appearing in the
*Miscellanies* in a position which would indicate that it,
with its two companion imitations of Horace's ode to
Pyrrha and of one of Martial's epigrams, was written

----
[1] Johnson, *Lives*, i. 36.

between 1642 and 1650, and probably after 1647, 'The Chronicle' would seem to have been itself suggested by Cowley's own version of Anacreon's 'The Account'. In this 'Ballad of Mistresses', as the *Spectator* later called it,[1] Cowley gave a playful catalogue of all the women he had ever loved—not to the number of thousands, as Anacreon had done, but only a score or so by name. This catalogue, however, has a remarkable feature, which tantalizes the critic into a desire for more knowledge than he is ever likely to get: for a great many of these names are identifiable with persons in one way or another connected with the author's life or works. Here are Katharine, Audria, and Thomasine— Cowley's two sisters and his mother.[2] Here is Elisa— and among the juvenilia published after his death is a song to 'Eliza'. Moreover, Elisa in 'The Chronicle' is not unlike the heroine of 'Not Fair' in *The Mistress*. Here is Ann—and Cowley had published a poem to Mrs. Anne Whitfield in his juvenilia. Catherine, Susanna, and Isabella are named—and these were the names of Van Dyck's three sisters. A 'gentle Henrietta' and a 'Mary' are named together—and Cowley was in the court of Henrietta Maria. (As it happens, there is extant in Nahum Tate's *Poems by Several Hands*, published in 1685, an 'Ode Written by Mr. Abraham Cowley for Her Majesty, Queen to King Charles I'— an ode which has apparently never been reprinted in this form.) And 'Black-eyed Bess', Susan's 'viceroy maid', reminds one curiously of 'The Waiting-Maid' in *The Mistress*. The temptation to suggest that the rest of the names in the list also had originals in Cowley's own life is irresistible, though an attempt to identify only one of them has been made—that by Pope, when he told Spence that Heleonora, the last of the roll, represented Cowley's only real passion, and that she married Sprat's brother.[3]

[1] No. 311.    [2] Cf. Grosart, *Cowley*, i. xi.    [3] Spence, pp. 285–6.

Yet even now, swept away as he was by this new temporary enthusiasm, Cowley was still troubled with doubts concerning the course he had chosen, or which had been forced upon him. Years later, in 'Of Myself', he commented as follows upon this portion of his life:

With these affections of mind, and my heart wholly set upon letters, I went to the University, but was soon torn from thence by that violent public storm which would suffer nothing to stand where it did, but rooted up every plant, even from the princely cedars to me, the hyssop. Yet I had as good fortune as could have befallen me in such a tempest; for I was cast by it into the family of one of the best persons and into the court of one of the best princesses in the world. Now though I was here engaged in ways most contrary to the original design of my life, that is, into much company, and no small business, and into a daily sight of greatness, both militant and triumphant (for that was the state then of the English and French courts), yet all this was so far from altering my opinion that it only added the confirmation of reason to that which was before but natural inclination. . . . I met with several great persons, whom I liked very well, but could not perceive that any part of their greatness was to be liked or desired. . . . Though I was in a crowd of as good company as could be found anywhere, though I was in business of great and honourable trust, though I ate at the best table and enjoyed the best conveniences for present subsistence that ought to be desired by a man of my condition in banishment and public distresses, yet I could not abstain from renewing my old schoolboy's wish in a copy of verses to the same effect.

And so, just as before he had quoted from 'A Vote', now he quoted from 'The Wish', a poem which had appeared quite incongruous in its original setting in *The Mistress*:

> Well then, I now do plainly see
> This busy world and I shall ne'er agree;
> The very honey of all earthly joy
> Does of all meats the soonest cloy,

And they, methinks, deserve my pity
Who for it can endure the stings,
The crowd, and buzz, and murmurings
    Of this great hive, the city.

Ah, yet, ere I descend to th' grave,
May I a small house and large garden have!
And a few friends, and many books, both true,
    Both wise, and both delightful too!
And since Love ne'er will from me flee,
A mistress moderately fair,
And good as guardian-angels are,
    Only beloved, and loving me!

O founts! Oh, when in you shall I
Myself, eased of unpeaceful thoughts, espy?
O fields! O woods! when, when shall I be made
    The happy tenant of your shade?
Here's the spring-head of pleasure's flood;
Here's wealthy nature's treasury
Where all the riches lie, that she
    Has coined and stamped for good. . . .

Notwithstanding this poem, however, during the
'forties Cowley had not gained quite such a clean-cut
conception of his own character as he possessed when he
wrote his essay. He could never definitely make up his
mind, and he flitted from one poetical blossom to another like a veritable honey-bee. Substitute 'genius' or
'spirit' for 'love' in the last stanza of the second 'Resolved to Be Beloved', and Cowley has drawn his own
portrait as well as it can ever be drawn:

When it does hardness meet, and pride,
My love does then rebound t'another side;
But if it aught that's soft and yielding hit,
    It lodges there, and stays in it.
Whatever 'tis shall first love me,
    That it my heaven may truly be,
I shall be sure to give 't eternity.

# VIII

## EXILES IN THE LOUVRE

THAT the 'eternity' which Cowley so lavishly promised to all the subjects touched by his pen was not simply the traditional expression of a desire rather than a reasonable certainty is proved by the issuance in England, in 1648, of a small volume of rough, controversial verses entitled *The Four Ages of England, or the Iron Age. With Other Select Poems*, one of which was the derelict *Satire against Separatists*. The fact that the book contained a 'Postscript. To His Judicious Friend, Mr. J. H.' [John Hervey?], which was signed 'A. C.' (the title-page having actually read, 'Written by Mr. A. Cowley'), coupled with the fact that Cowley himself wrathfully disowned the work at the first opportunity, would indicate that some crafty publisher was trying to take advantage of the acknowledged fame of the exiled poet. Similarly, in 1650 *The Guardian* was pirated in Dublin and put into print for the first time— a public exposure of his 'hasty first-fitting' of a play in which Cowley also disclaimed any share, though he was not unpleased to learn later that his comedy had been several times acted 'privately during the troubles' while the regular theatres remained legally sealed.[1]

On the whole, however, Cowley had little time for writing while he was in France. The 'business of great and honourable trust' which he referred to in 'Of Myself' was after all—excluding his own character—the greatest obstacle to his programme that he had yet encountered. For five years ('per quinquennium'), says Sprat, he managed the secret correspondence which was continually maintained between the Queen in France and King Charles in England. If this figure may be trusted, he must have accompanied Henrietta when she left

[1] 'Preface' to *Cutter of Coleman-street*.

England in 1644, since in 1649 the King suffered the same fate as he had permitted to Strafford eight years before.

And so, 'In that weighty trust', Cowley 'behaved himself with indefatigable industry and unsuspected secrecy. For he ciphered and deciphered, with his own hand, the greatest part of all the letters that passed between their Majesties, and managed a vast intelligence in many other parts, which for some years together took up all his days and two or three nights every week'.[1] As a proof of his claims, Sprat added that almost all of this royal correspondence was still extant, 'manu propria describens'.[2] Perhaps the fact that this, the third and most elaborate of the Queen's ciphers, consisted entirely of numbers representing either letters or complete words and disguised names, accounts for the difficulty in recognizing the writing of Cowley—or often, indeed, of any one—in the correspondence which has survived.[3] In the letters themselves, Henrietta and Charles frequently mentioned the necessity of absolute secrecy, even Jermyn being several times specifically excluded from participation. But when the Queen's health or eyesight failed her, as sometimes happened, she was compelled to call in outside assistance for the dull and onerous task of transliterating the messages in both directions. It was here that Cowley's duty must have lain, although his name, unlike that of Davenant, Denham, and many others, never appeared in her printed correspondence. Henrietta's own letters were written in French; those which were in English were probably composed by either Cowley or Jermyn under her direction.

Nor were Cowley's labours confined to the Queen's service alone. He was primarily in Jermyn's household,

[1] Sprat 'Account'.  [2] Sprat, 'De Vita'.
[3] Cf. *Letters of Queen Henrietta Maria* (ed. Green) and *Lettres Inédites de Henriette-Marie* (ed. de Baillon).

and Jermyn also had many friends and agents to keep
in touch with. The following letter, for instance, is probably typical of this aspect of Cowley's activity. It is
the earliest of the poet's letters to be extant, so far as has
been discovered; it is now among the Clarendon State
Papers in the Bodleian, nor does it ever seem to have
been printed.[1] All of the document, with the exception
of the opening, the closing, and two or three incidental
phrases, is in the peculiar combination of numerical and
literal cipher which is endorsed on the outside of the
paper as Sir John Berkeley's, but the decipherer has
written in the proper letters just above their symbols.
The recipient was Lord Culpepper.

Paris, Apr. 20, 1646.

My Lord,

There is news come this morning, which my Lord would write
to you, but that he is gone in haste to St. Germain to let the
Queen know it and therefore he commands me to give your
Lordship notice of it. It is, that the business of your last letters
to Oxford is resolved upon, and that the King is resolved to put
himself into the Scots' army and for that end hath sent Montreul
with letters to the Scots' army and another to the governor of
Newark to deliver the town into the Scots' hands if they think it
fit to receive it. He hath likewise promised as soon as he shall be
in their army to send for the releasement of Duke Hamilton and
a command to the Marquis of Montrose to retire into France
for a while. This is the sum of Sir R. Murray his letter to the
Cardinal, with which he presses him to be mindful of those
promises he made of assistances to the Scots in case the parliament shall not agree to an accommodation.

The post is so instant upon parting that I dare not trouble
your Lordship with more lest I should not trouble you at all,
which in this occasion is necessary; I remain,

My Lord,
Your Lordship's most faithful and most humble servant,
A. Cowley.

The issue of these plans is well known.

[1] Clarendon State Papers for 1676: 27, f. 147.

Unfortunate poet! Reduced to acting as amanuensis and translator of secret documents! But yet his position was no menial one, though Milton as a secretary was a person of enormously greater consequence than he. Many of the Cavaliers, indeed, held it an honour to engage in similar subterranean operations. Evelyn, for instance, after marrying the twelve-year-old daughter of Sir Richard Browne, the English 'resident' at the French court, had returned to England in 1647 and, in spite of making his peace immediately after, had maintained a secret correspondence with his father-in-law in the intervals between translating de la Mothe le Vayer's Of Liberty and Solitude and other Epicurean and libertin works. Thomas Killigrew, indeed, had no fewer than six ciphers for the conduct of his private and diplomatic business, and in one of these 'Abr. Cowley' is assigned a special numerical symbol, in the expectation that his name will be used frequently.[1] And Cowley too was greatly trusted and confided in— even being sent off on long missions of importance when a particularly responsible messenger was demanded. In this fashion he made journeys into Flanders, Holland, Jersey—and even back into Scotland itself, 'or wherever else the King's troubles required his attendance'.[2] The first of these voyages which has been traced occurred shortly after his letter to Culpepper. At the very time Cowley was writing, Prince Charles had arrived in Jersey, and showed little disposition to rejoin his mother in Paris. Consequently, in June a large party, under the leadership of Jermyn, was sent out to reclaim the young man, and of this party Cowley was a member.[3] If this period in his life was arduous, and often tedious, it was also a time of romance and adventure. Though he

---

[1] Brit. Mus. Addit. MS. 33596, ff. 21-32. Cf. Harbage, Killigrew, pp. 103-4.      [2] Sprat, 'Account'.
[3] See letter written by counsellors of King on Oct. 19, 1646, in Clarendon State Papers, vol. xxviii, no. 2339; quoted by Loiseau.

was not a soldier, there was risk in any mission he assumed which would take him into the Channel islands or into Britain again. He seemingly served faithfully and well.

Only once, it appears, was the steady flow of correspondence detected by the enemy. Occupying a similar position to Cowley's at the other end of the system was Sir John Denham, who, while a loyal Royalist, still had the faculty of retaining a friend or two on the Puritan side. In 1647 he had obtained admission to Charles, who, his armies defeated and scattered, was then in the custody of the Parliament. On this occasion Denham had conveyed intelligence from the Queen to her husband, and had been unsuspected, perhaps because, as he said, he had been 'furnished with nine several ciphers' for carrying on the business.[1] But shortly afterward distrust fell upon him—not because of any fault of his own, but because some one among the Parliamentarians accidentally recognized Cowley's handwriting in a letter. Denham, however, was warned in time and decamped into France in 1648, where he was a not unwelcome addition to the body of literary exiles already in Paris. He may or may not have had something to do with the exciting escape of the young Duke of York from London into France in April of that year. Nevertheless, after reaching the Continent he resumed his activity as an agent, helping to maintain contact between the Queen in Paris and the Prince of Wales as the latter moved wearily from place to place in his vain search for aid for his cause and a comfortable refuge for his shabby retinue. In these duties Denham's acquaintance with Cowley ripened and deepened into a respect which convinced him, too, that his friend was as great a poet as the world had yet seen.

One of the several reasons for Henrietta Maria's

[1] Cf. Johnson's *Lives*, i. 13, and Hill's note; also *Camb. Hist. Engl. Lit.*, vii. 69, 71.

failure to obtain any essential aid for her husband's cause from the French. Government was that within three or four years of her arrival her native country was in almost as perilous a state as her adopted one. The civil war which broke out in 1648 and which took its name of the 'Fronde' from the fact that the sling had been the favourite weapon used by the Paris mob in stoning the windows of Cardinal Mazarin and his friends, had some superficial resemblances to the struggle which had been occurring between Court and Parliament in England, but soon degenerated into a series of intrigues and factional disturbances among the more ambitious and arrogant of the French nobles. As a result, the little court of banished English, which before had managed to exist in at least comparative comfort, fell suddenly into absolute destitution, when for six months Henrietta's pension from her young royal nephew failed to be paid.

The second earliest extant letter of Abraham Cowley, discovered by Grosart and dated from Paris on January 8, 1648/9, sketches a vivid picture of the besieging of Paris at that time by the meteoric young Condé.[1] At three o'clock on the preceding Wednesday morning all the city had been astounded at the sudden departure of 'the King, the Queen Regent, Duke of Orleans, Prince of Condé, and almost all the great persons, men and women', for St. Germain-en-Laye. As a result, the whole town was alarmed with it, and with great disorder and confusion began to put themselves into a posture of defence'. In relative bodily safety (for Henrietta Maria was not unpopular among the French citizenry in spite of her close associations with the court), the English watched the mystery develop. Indeed, most of the campaigns of the Fronde were actuated by mysterious and obscure motives—this one, to Cowley, being no exception. He saw the Royalists

[1] In Grosart, *Cowley*, ii. 352 3.

blockading the roads into Paris so that no provisions
might enter the town, and he read the counter-demand
of the Parliament that Mazarin 'should leave the Court
in one day and in eight the kingdom of France, or else
to be prosecuted as a traitor'. The English could scarcely
have failed to be reminded of Strafford and Laud and
the long sequence of disasters which even now was
resulting in the imprisonment of Charles by his subjects
and in the extreme jeopardy—how extreme none of
them suspected—of his life.

On the other hand, though the English exiles were
not likely to be harmed, their situation was desperate
enough. Cowley wrote, and without exaggeration, that
Henrietta had been 'left here without one penny of
money to buy her bread for to-morrow', and that Jermyn
had not yet returned from St. Germain with aid.
Cowley's master, indeed, was not quite so thoroughly
trusted by others as he was by the Queen,[1] and when
assistance was finally to come it was to do so from
another quarter.[2] Though the season was January, she
was unable to afford even a small fire and had been compelled to keep her little daughter Henrietta, born just
before the flight from England and later smuggled over
to France, in bed for warmth. Fortunately this was the
occasion which De Retz, coadjutor bishop and a person
of influence among the Frondeurs, chose to pay a call.
Overwhelmed by the straits of the daughter of his
former king, he begged the French Parliament for help
and succeeded in getting a generous grant for the English Queen, which tided her over until the affairs of her
nephew righted themselves.

Nor were these hardships the worst of the blows
which she had to bear. In England on the thirtieth of
January, contrary to the beliefs of all but those in the

---

[1] In 1646 he had even been accused of high treason and of negotiating
the sale of Jersey to France. See the letter of Hyde, Carteret, &c., in
*Clarendon State Papers*, quoted above.          [2] Haynes, pp. 252-3.

innermost councils of the English Parliament, King
Charles I was beheaded at Whitehall. The news pene-
trated Paris only after some delay, for the blockade still
prevented the entrance of letters into the city. But
rumours began to circulate, of the truth of which the
courtiers became convinced before any hint had reached
the ears of the Queen. Jermyn, whose intimacy with her
made him the natural person to break the news, finally
did so with the diplomacy which was one of his best
qualities, and her complete desolation and reaction to
the shock did much to combat certain scandalous tales
concerning her relations with her chamberlain. The
fact that no suggestion of any of these ever appears in
any of Cowley's references to the pair would be an
additional proof of their falseness, even though stories
of a secret marriage were afterward diffused.

The death of Charles I and the consequent establishment of the young Charles II in his place as leader of the
Royalist cause made a considerable difference in the
situation of the English court in Paris, for Henrietta
was regarded by some as occupying a somewhat similar
position in relation to Charles as her sister-in-law Anne
held over her son Louis—that is, although Henrietta
was never appointed regent, she was still respected or
feared—according to the sympathies of the individual—
as her son's leading adviser. And at first many displayed
the utmost anxiety as to whether she would obtain
ascendancy enough to embroil him in the Roman
Catholic schemes which she was still prosecuting in
Rome with the aid of Sir Kenelm Digby, now growing
middle-aged and fat, and, in the opinion of many,
madder than ever. The Church of England constitu-
tional party, headed by Sir Edward Hyde and Sir
Edward Nicholas, were especially worried by the power
of Jermyn and his friends, Lord Culpepper and Henry
Percy; but they soon found that the young King, as well
as his brother James, had no intention of shifting

allegiance to Rome at this time, no matter what other
religious ideas he might hold.

The death of Charles I and the removal of Charles II
into the Low Countries to perfect his plans for regaining his father's throne naturally altered Cowley's
secretarial duties somewhat, and the intelligence service
between the new King and Henrietta passed into other
hands.[1] However, Cowley immediately became engaged in a fresh correspondence which was to keep the
Queen in touch with her second son, James, Duke of
York, whose journeyings back and forth across the Continent were almost as mercurial as his brother's had been.
Shortly before this time Cowley's old schoolfellow,
Henry Bennet, had joined the Royalist group in Paris,
and having already been secretary to Digby and having
had other useful experiences in various campaigns and
travels, had been given a position in James's party
headed by Sir George Carteret, much like that held by
Cowley under Jermyn. As a result of these facts, an
official correspondence of some extent (perhaps partly
in cipher) grew up between the two men, Cowley's side
of which, consisting of some fourteen or fifteen letters,
was preserved, and printed by Tom Brown in 1702 as
part of his *Miscellanea Aulica*.[2] These letters furnish a
very valuable picture of the life and opinions of the
English in Paris during the time of the 'Princes' Fronde
and Charles's ill-fated Scotch expeditions.

[1] Sprat, 'Account'.
[2] Loiseau questions whether all of these letters, especially the twelfth,
thirteenth, and fourteenth, are to Bennet, and cites internal evidenc
showing that they were probably to other correspondents. Accordin
to various references and documents, the recipients of Cowley's letter
included the following persons: Carteret, Berkeley, Culpepper, Charle
May, Count Lauderdale (see Brit. Mus. Addit. MS. 23113, dated Mar. 10
1650), and of course Bennet. A letter dated Feb. 12, 1651, to an un
known correspondent was printed in Maggs Bros.' catalogue 23, item
502, and Loiseau mentions another, dated Feb. 10, 1646, in th
Clarendon papers. Hyde wrote to Cowley from Madrid on July 12
1650 (see *Clarendon State Papers*, vol. xl, f. 104).

On the thirtieth of April 1650, when the first of these letters was written, the Scotch treaty was the matter of paramount importance. Aware as Cowley was of Charles's disposition to forfeit any or all of his religious or political principles in order to obtain military aid for his cause (as a reference to 'two or three mighty tender consciences' about the King shows), and until the very end sceptical of the consummation of any agreement, Cowley was now persuaded that terms would soon be reached at Breda, whither the King had gone. Nor did he blush to reveal the reason for his conviction, though he had been 'one of the last hopers': for 'Virgil has told me something to that purpose'. There seems to be no question that the fulfilment of the two prophecies from the *Aeneid* in the old Oxford days had so impressed Cowley that he had again consulted the Virgilian lots on this important occasion. Contemptuous as he was of superstition on most matters, he could not entirely escape its taint.[1]

Primarily interested as the exiles were in the news of Cromwell's campaign in Ireland, of the blockade of Prince Rupert's fleet in the Road of Lisbon by fifteen Parliamentary ships, and of the prospect of a new war in England with Lord Fairfax as leader of the hostile forces, they were also not inactive on their own part and had various projects afoot, from which they expected favourable results. Henrietta herself, whose misfortunes had forced her to look more and more for consolation to her retreats with the Carmelite nuns of St. Teresa, had begun her plans for founding an order of her own at Chaillot, but her new role as a *dévote*, which caused her to dress, in all sincerity, in a garb of sombre black and white, did not prevent her from formulating other schemes of a political nature.

The chief of these had to do with strengthening the loyal colony of Virginia in the New World by sending a

[1] Cf. Johnson's sneering comment, *Lives*, i. 8–9.

group of artificers and mechanics there to help develop its industries. And since there were plenty of such persons unemployed in France and since Will Davenant's labours on his *Gondibert*, which had begun to pall upon him as well as upon his friends, had recently terminated in the publication of the first two books of the epic by a Parisian bookseller, she pitched upon the idea of out-fitting a ship for him and dispatching him to America. This, at least, is the usual explanation given for the expedition, although evidence has recently been pro-duced which would indicate that Davenant's mission was really to supplant Lord Baltimore as Lieutenant-Governor of Maryland and to try to overcome the effects of the latter's activities as a supporter of the Parliamentarian cause.[1] The interest of the exiles in the plan, whatever it was, was high, for at last they seemed to be doing something tangible; and Cowley's postscript to his letter of May 10 reveals his own anxiety for his friend, who had sailed, epic and all, from a port in Normandy not long before.

It must have been just preceding this time that Cowley had written his important critical poem, 'To Sir William Davenant. Upon His Two First Books of *Gondibert*, Finished before His Voyage to America', for the verses, accompanied by a similar set of Waller's, appeared first in the 1650 edition of the epic, and were also referred to by Davenant in his preface, dated January 2; moreover, the last four lines indicate that hopes for a successful colonization were still strong. Perhaps Cowley composed his poem as a sort of final message to his friend before sailing. At any rate, the poem, with its inveighing against the introduction of 'gods, devils, nymphs, witches, and giants' into the 'fan-tastic fairyland' of the Italian epic romances, and its insistence on the necessity of planting 'men and manners' in their place, has patently been written under the

[1] Campbell, *M.L.N.*, xviii. 238–9.

influence of Hobbes and his theory of *vraisemblance* in poetry. Forgetting his earlier admiration of Spenser and his own practice in the yet unpublished *Davideis* (an inconsistency which Dryden was not slow to note),[1] forgetting—or repenting—his own earlier style and its florid conceits, Cowley declared whole-heartedly for the naturalistic principles of the aged Hobbes and the performance of the latter's disciple, Davenant. Again, as had happened many times before in his career, he had seen a new path open out before him, and had resolved to follow it—until another and more fascinating one offered itself.

For over two weeks after Cowley's letter no news of Davenant's fate came to Paris. From the Netherlands arrived the exciting information that the Scotch treaty had been concluded with the commissioners, though on very hard terms, and that Charles intended to cross the Channel in about a month, where he would join his ablest Scotch supporter, the gallant Lord Montrose. Then, in Cowley's letter of May 28, the blow falls: 'Be pleased to let him [Sir George Carteret, governor of Jersey] know the misfortune that is befallen to Sir Will. Davenant (in which I believe he has a share); it is that he is taken, and now prisoner with all his men in the Isle of Wight.' And then Cowley adds gloomily, 'We are strangely pursued in all things, and all places, by our evil fortune; even our retreats to the other world (except by death) are cut off.'

Such was his common mood in those dreary days— and yet even in these depths he could not resist the temptation of a play on words when it offered itself.

The year 1650 was perhaps the most dismal in Cowley's whole life, if the tone of his letters is any guide. On May 28 he wrote Bennet that Montrose had suffered misfortunes in Scotland, that Holland had recognized the new English republic, that Ireland had been ruined

[1] Dryden, *Essays*, i. 154.

by jealousies, and that Cromwell would very likely reach Edinburgh before Charles could even cross the Channel, so slow were the Scotch commissioners in advancing the money they had promised. In Paris, too, local affairs were as bad: '. . . the whole kingdom's as much discontented as ever, and so great are the wants of the court that this very day the Swisses are in a mutiny for their pay, refuse to do duty, and threaten to march away to-morrow.' Nor was this all that Henrietta's royal nephew had to fear, for an actual war with the English commonwealth threatened, the English having already, privateer-fashion, captured many French ships, 'among which the Cardinal's own, given him by the Queen of Swedeland, is said to be one'.

On June 11 the situation was, if possible, worse. 'The appearances of great disorders suddenly to happen in this kingdom . . . do increase daily, and nothing but the hand of God (which at this time seems likelier to fall heavy upon this place than to relieve it) can avert them.' The Spaniards had advanced from Flanders to within twenty miles of Compiègne, where the French court still tarried. But, most paralysing of all, 'This day news is come that at Edinburgh they have hanged, drawn, and quartered the Lord Montrose in a cruel and barbarous manner.' Cowley took this calamity almost as a personal one—'I am confounded with the thought of it.'

By the twenty-first, however, Charles had at last got away—and then for over two months the exiles had no news of their king. Rumours were bandied about—that he had landed in the Orkneys, accompanied by Buckingham and other English lords; that his chief supporters among the Scottish nobles had been banished by the Scotch Presbyterian leaders; that he had reached Edinburgh; that he had landed near Aberdeen; 'that being pursued by ten Parliament ships, he put himself and most of his company into three fishermen, and so got thither, whilst his own ships were still followed by the English, who knew not that he had quitted them.' During June and July rumours were as plentiful as supplies were scanty. Cromwell, having forced Fairfax to retire, had been 'received with great triumph and magnificence at London' and was to 'have some new great title conferred upon him (as Protector of the People's Liberty, or some such like)'. Cowley's references to Cromwell were always edged keenly with irony.

To pass the time and also to strengthen the bonds between the French and the English Royalist parties, some of the English lords volunteered their services against Turenne and the Spanish. In one of these engagements Digby and his troop distinguished themselves, and not long afterwards the young Duke of York joined the forces of his cousin Louis, while his brother Charles, having at last reared his standard in England and even weakly taken the Covenant, was entangling himself deeper and deeper in Cromwell's spider-web.

The Low Countries were being torn as much as France and England. In August the Prince of Orange, Henrietta's son-in-law, tried in vain to capture Amsterdam; and simultaneously Paris was split in two as to the 'question whether this town and Parliament should continue in obedience to the King or join with those of Bordeaux'. .In November the Prince of Orange was dead, suddenly smitten with the small-pox, and Charles had lost another ally. No one knew what might happen next—or, indeed, what had already happened.

None of Cowley's letters is more gloomy than that of November 18, written after Bennet had been detached from the Duke of York's party and sent to Italy. For this is the picture he was compelled to send his friend of the Duke's plight in Brussels—a plight so desperate that the latter's advisers had suggested a journey to

Germany, or even to Japan or the West Indies, as an improvement of a situation which could not be more bleak: 'Sir G. Ratcliff is the controller of his household, and orders the whole business of two dishes a meal for the Duke in his chamber.'

Two dishes a meal! And served privately so that the world would not see the Duke's penury! Bennet, a man who always knew on which side his bread was buttered, surely congratulated himself on his good luck in escaping into more merry surroundings, the effect of which had seemingly suffused his letters. It was as the result of this that for a few moments in his correspondence Cowley regained an echo of the gay raillery which had once distinguished his writings. 'My Lord gives you many thanks for your truffles,' he wrote in acknowledgement of a present from the epicure in Italy to the epicure in Paris, 'and Mrs. Gardiner for your care of her beauty; the former I had some part in, the latter I am sure I never shall.' Yes, Bennet had already commenced to develop that eye for charming women which later got him his title from Charles for services rendered. And Cowley was not slow to play up to him slyly, as his postscript to his letter of December 5 will prove: 'Be pleased to present my humble service to Mr. Marcess; Mrs. Marcess is come to town, but I have not seen her, nor know where she lies. . . . I have this afternoon received yours of the 26th of November; your present to Mrs. Gardiner and your questions too upon it make her blush. Your truffles were excellent good, as I wrote you word before; as for the Piedmont wine, we are now such moderate men as to content ourselves with that of the Rhine, in which I hope suddenly to drink your health.'

Unfortunately for posterity's knowledge of Cowley's familiar letter writing, however, the correspondence, so far as is known, here broke off abruptly, with the exception of one political letter three years later; for Henrietta had ordered Jermyn, and therefore Cowley, into Holland 'to condole, congratulate, and advise with' the Princess Royal of Orange over the death of her husband, the birth of her son, and her future attitude toward the cause of her brother Charles. Not long after this, too, the Fronde wore itself out, and the real reign of Louis XIV began.

# IX

## PINDAR IN JERSEY

THE year 1651 was a busy one for Jermyn's secretary
in his capacity of confidential agent for the royal
party, and yet it also saw the inception of one of his
most original ventures as a poet. From the Netherlands, Cowley's business carried him first on a very
dangerous trip to Scotland, with letters for the King
there. Leaving the Continent early in February,
Cowley succeeded in eluding the Parliamentarian
patrol in the Channel,[1] and by the first of March he
had passed through La Haye on his return journey, in
the company of Rainsford, another agent, bearing
letters from the King for the princes in France.[2]

Scarcely had he had time to recover from this mission
before he found himself again in Jersey, which had remained a Royalist stronghold throughout the Rebellion
—and was, in fact, the last spot of any importance to
fall into Parliamentarian hands. The steep, bold cliffs
on the north, combined with the sandy bays and
marshes on the other three sides, had enabled Sir
George Carteret, its lieutenant-governor for six or
seven years, to harbour the Prince of Wales in Elizabeth
Castle for two months on his way to France, from which
he had returned, in October 1649, to sign his declaration of rights to the throne left vacant by the behead-
ing of his father. Now, in 1651, the royal exiles were
again in need of money, and in May, Jermyn was
machinating for the sale of part of the Crown lands in
Jersey for allaying this need.[3]

[1] See letter of Sir Edward Nicholas to Lord Hatton, Feb. 8, 1651, in
*Nicholas Papers*, i. 219. This and all further references to the *Nicholas
Papers* were first quoted by Loiseau.

[2] Ibid., pp. 222, 228; letters dated Mar. 1 and 12.

[3] See letter of Carteret to Nicholas, June 9/19, 1651, in *Nicholas
Papers*, i. 258.

The two men who were assigned the task of carrying out this delicate and seemingly tainted job were Cowley and Sir John Berkeley.[1] Carteret, whose own powers of extortion had certainly not endeared him to the islanders, was so alarmed at the methods employed that he wrote a protest to Sir Edward Nicholas, describing them thus: 'The commission for the sale of the 200 pistoles a year was to this effect, that the money should be paid into the hands of M. Cowley, whereof he was to pay 2,000 pound to Lord Jermyn for his interest in the said lands. . . . I saw a warrant from the King to pay 300 pistoles of that money to M. Long, and the two commissioners were to have a fleece of it'. Carteret feared, and rightly, that not many of the proceeds would remain for the defence of the island or for other legitimate purposes.

In such malodorous transactions—the sort in which Jermyn was too frequently engaged—Cowley seems to have been able to stuff his scruples in his pocket, and to take his 'fleece' along with the rest of the crows. Or perhaps he felt that his responsibilities as business agent for his master released his own conscience from any burden. Whatever the explanation, these activities were not calculated to raise him in the esteem of Hyde's faction. On the other hand, some of his duties as Jermyn's representative involved him in more straightforward kinds of affairs, all the way from handling bills of exchange for 20 pistoles, or 1,124 guilders and 14 sols, to signing a receipt for 12 cases of 150 agates which Jermyn had bought from Buckingham during one of the latter's penurious moments.[2]

[1] Ibid.
[2] These documents are quoted by Loiseau. The first, dated Paris, Apr. 4, 1649, is in the possession of Lady Margaret M. Verney, and was probably addressed to Sir Henry Verney. The second, dated Apr. 10, 1651, is in the *Nicholas Papers*, i. 235. The third, dated Mar. 1, 1651/2, is in the possession of Mr. Charles Cottrell Dormer.

A more savoury result of Cowley's visit to Jersey was 'An Answer to a Copy of Verses Sent Me to Jersey', one of the most amusing of his satirical and critical poems. It was obviously written at this time, since it alludes to the capture of Davenant by Green in 1650, and since the island citadel finally capitulated to Parliament on December 15, 1651, following the rout of Charles's forces at Worcester on September 3.

Who the writer of the letter 'Fraught with brisk, racy verses' was, cannot be stated—perhaps Waller or Denham—but at any rate it aroused Cowley to a reply replete with rich colloquial humour and good critical sense. Though Jersey might well have appealed to him as a haven of peace and retirement after his feverish years in France, it in fact struck him only as a barren shred of ground on which neither verse nor sack could, or did, prosper. Only William Prynne, his old scorn, had tried to immortalize Mount Orgueil in bombastic verse, with the result that he had been acclaimed a new Homer by the rough, unlettered islanders. But at any rate, Cowley reminded his anonymous friend, if the soil of Jersey refused to bear tropes and figures (it was probably known even then for its potatoes), the land was 'undefiled with clinches yet' as well as with the 'actual crying sin of bombast'—two things with which he swore the English Muse was stained and soiled.

As a place of human habitation, indeed, Jersey seems to have made such a profoundly unpleasant impression on him that its memory lingered in such passages as his description, in the fourth book of the *Davideis*, of the 'low, small island' 'midst the main',

> Assaulted round with stormy seas and skies,
> Whilst the poor heartless natives, ev'ry hour,
> Darkness and Noise seems ready to devour.

The evidence, however, would suggest that for the first time in a great number of years Cowley had many free

hours on Jersey to do with as he pleased.  Naturally, he
turned again to poetry, which he had cultivated only
sporadically since *The Mistress*.  It is noteworthy, too,
that the last three poems which he later published as
part of his *Miscellanies* (all of which would seem to have
been written about 1651) deal with religion as he had
never before dealt with it.

Dwelling as he had done for years in the midst not
only of the Roman household of Queen Henrietta
Maria but also of a Roman Catholic nation like France,
it would have been remarkable if Cowley had not given
much serious thought to the tenets of the Church of
Rome.  The tale preserved as follows by the antiquary
Hearne reveals the sort of rumour which trailed many
who had lived in Paris with Henrietta and her favourite
convert, the Abbé Walter Montagu: 'Mr. Cowley was
after his death said by some to have died a Roman
Catholic; but this was only a malicious story: for Mr.
Joyner [probably William Joyner, author of *The Roman
Empress* in 1671], who knew him well, has told me that
he could not be drawn into that communion all the time
he was in France, which was about ten years, but that
he continued firm to the last.' [1]  But besides Wat
Montagu, once a prominent member of the circle of
Falkland at Great Tew, there was Dr. Stephen Goffe,
a Royalist agent, who eventually became a Brother of
the Oratory and chaplain to the Queen.  According to
Wood's seemingly erroneous story, it was Goffe who
befriended Cowley at Paris and placed him in the family
of Lord Jermyn. [2]  It would, therefore, be only a strongly
Protestant mind which could withstand these and other
influences, but this time at least, like Henrietta's own
sons Charles and James, Cowley does not seem to
have wavered.

The poems on Davenant and Jersey had both referred

---

[1] Hearne, *Remarks and Collections*, i. 246.
[2] Wood, *Fasti*, in *Ath. Oxon.*, ii, ii. 494; and iv, ii. 210.

to the usages and claims of the 'Romish church', but 'The Tree of Knowledge', with the sub-title, 'That There Is No Knowledge. Against the Dogmatists', was Cowley's first complete poem on such a religio-philosophical topic. Its occasion was not at all unlikely the appearance of the last part of the *De Theologicis Dogmatibus* of D. Petavius in 1650, and Cowley's conclusion, reached through two tortuous introductory stanzas, was that by eating of the forbidden fruit

> The only science man by this did get
>   Was but to know he nothing knew:
>   He straight his nakedness did view,
> His ignorant, poor estate, and was ashamed of it;
>   Yet searches probabilities,
>   And rhetoric, and fallacies,
>   And seeks by useless pride
> With slight and withering leaves that nakedness to hide.

The second poem of the series he named 'Reason. The Use of It in Divine Matters'—the sort of subject which Culverwel, with his Cambridge Platonist tendencies, had talked and was soon to write so ably about. And there is more than a likelihood that Cowley, in his scoffings at those who induced visions and inspiration by fastings and sleepless vigils, had the spiritualistic tendencies of Henry More and his type in mind. No, held Cowley (perhaps reflecting some of his talks with Hobbes):

> When we trust men concerning God, we then
>   Trust not God concerning men. . . .
>
> In vain, alas, these outward hopes are tried;
>   Reason within 's our only guide.
> Reason, which (God be praised!) still walks, for all
>   Its old original fall.
> And since itself the boundless Godhead joined
>   With a reasonable mind,
> It plainly shows that mysteries divine
>   May with our reason join.

And so, as might be expected, Cowley balked at the last step of scepticism, just as Bacon had done—he admitted that the same tests should not be applied to faith and to the 'Holy Book' as were applied to other branches of human belief. Reason is the infallible guide to the mysterious gates of faith—no more. But it is a matter for the individual to control; it is not to be relinquished to the church.

Last among these *Miscellanies* (last because he wrote it last, and not because, as many critics have maintained, he considered it—justly—his best) Cowley wrote his touching elegy, 'On the Death of Mr. Crashaw', with its famous opening couplet,

> Poet and Saint! To thee alone are given
> The two most sacred names of earth and heaven.

Poor Dick Crashaw had not found rest so soon as he had expected in the Roman church. For a full year after his arrival in Italy, he had not even obtained financial help—as Digby's note of remonstrance to the Pope in the Queen's name shows.[1] In addition, if Bargrave may be believed, Crashaw had been so sickened by the wickedness of Cardinal Palotta's retinue, where he was finally placed, that he had at length been sent, on April 24, 1649, to the miracle-working shrine at Loretto as a canon of the church.[2] On April 28 he was admitted to the third of the four degrees maintained there, that of 'beneficiatus'. And within four months he was dead—of a fever, probably, though Bargrave suggests poisoning, because of the other's outspoken criticism of the corruption and depravities of many of the Italian ecclesiastics.

Crashaw had found his rest at last, but the news of his decease was very slow in getting back to England and France. This is probably the reason that Cowley did not write his monody until two years afterward.

[1] Cf. Martin, introduction to *Crashaw*.    [2] Bargrave, p. 37.

'On the Death of Mr. Crashaw', although undoubtedly an outpouring of very sincere feeling, is nevertheless more interesting as a landmark in Cowley's spiritual biography than as a lyric. The writer has undergone somewhat of a revulsion and has found himself back in the days when he started his sacred epic, which he had so long laid aside—the days when Hervey, and perhaps Crashaw himself, had encouraged and even aided him in his pious labours, rather than the days in which he had spun out artificial love lyrics for the court ladies and gentlemen. He was convinced of his own guilt in helping to debase the exalted powers of poetry by fastening on too much of the chaff of heathendom instead of bringing the Muses back to their true 'Holy Land'.

> Nay, with the worst of heathen dotage, we
> (Vain men!) the monster Woman deify:
> Find stars, and tie our fates there in a face,
> And Paradise in them by whom we lost it, place.
> What different faults corrupt our Muses thus?
> Wanton as girls, as old wives fabulous!

And so the whole poem becomes a plea for sacred poetry such as Crashaw had written—irrespective of creed or church.

> Pardon, my Mother Church, if I consent
> That angels led him when from thee he went,
> For even in error sure no danger is
> When joined with so much piety as his.

Reason after all is weak, and human wills are wilful; faith is less important than works. And from this time on, Cowley swears to 'learn of things divine' by recalling the greatness of his friend.

Perhaps the broad tolerance expressed in this, the best of Cowley's many elegies, may have lent strength to the rumour of his leanings toward Rome, but there is not the slightest evidence that he ever considered severing his allegiance to the Church of England. The postscript of his letter to Bennet on July 9, 1650, after the holding of Anglican services in the Louvre had been forbidden by Queen Anne (on the suggestion, it was hinted, of the fanatical Wat Montagu), proves his steadfastness: 'Pray present my humble service to Mr. Crowder [the former chaplain?], and tell him that he has left our church here like a rat, for it is since quite fallen. The Queen of France at her last visit to ours desired her most earnestly to suppress it, saying that she conceived (upon most deep and solid grounds) that her son's late troubles had been in part caused by the public permission of heretical worship in his own palace; so that now we are interdicted.'

Cowley's stay on the uncongenial isle of Jersey may have been lightened by the writing of the three poems just discussed, or they may have been composed soon after his return to France. On the other hand, a much more influential series was almost certainly conceived and begun there—a series which for a time again demonstrated his claims to be considered the 'Muse's Hannibal'. In 'a place where he had no other books to direct him', according to Sprat,[1] he accidentally happened upon a copy of Pindar's works, was struck with the novelty and inspiration of the odes, and determined not so much 'to let the reader know precisely what he spoke, as what was his way and manner of speaking; which has not been yet (that I know of) introduced into English'. In other words, this accidental meeting with Pindar on an occasion when Cowley's mind was not pre-occupied with military and political matters (and where could this have been but Jersey?) led to what was practically the invention of the Pindaric or irregular ode in English.

At least, Cowley's words in the preface to his Pindarics imply that he regarded his work as quite original, though Ben Jonson had already experimented tenta-

[1] Sprat, 'Account'.

tively with the form in his 'A Pindaric Ode on the
Death of Sir H. Morison'. But there was a great difference between Jonson's ode and Cowley's Pindarics.
Jonson's was formed and moulded, and divided into
the 'Turn', 'Counter-Turn', and 'Stand'—it was at
least regular in its irregularity; Cowley's odes were
'loose and unconfined', as Sprat described them. No
strophe, antistrophe, and epode echoed and repeated
each other as Congreve and Gray were to make them
do, in the true Pindaric manner. Cowley's were
'enthusiastical', filled with digressions, and decorated
with bold figures of speech, in the manner of their
original; [1] but they were not Pindar.

And yet to conclude, as most critics have done, that
Cowley was ignorant of the strict rules of the Pindaric
is to do an injustice to his scholarship which is not
upheld by the evidence.[2] Robert Shafer has demonstrated very clearly that Cowley's purpose was 'to try
merely to infuse the *style* and *manner* of Pindar into
poetry that was in all other respects of his own age' and
that consequently 'he made no attempt to imitate in
English verse the form of Pindar's odes', which was
well known among English critics and readers and
which Cowley's own preface implies that he understood
and appreciated.[3] The choice of a 'free' verse form he
was not much concerned with, since many poets in
England and France, from Spenser to Crashaw and
Corneille and Racine, had used irregular metrical
effects and rhyme schemes. Even though both he and
Sprat felt called upon to defend his prosody for its
'near affinity with prose' and to warn readers that the
lines, like Pindar's, might seem rough if not pronounced,
accented, or elided correctly, he was still more con-

---

[1] Cowley, 1656 'Preface', and 'The Praise of Pindar'.
[2] Cf. my article, 'The Relation of Cowley's "Pindarics" to Pindar's
Odes,' *Mod. Phil.*, xix. 107–9.
[3] Shafer, *The English Ode*, pp. 123–57, *passim*.

cerned with a theory of translation which he had evolved
—quite by himself, though Sprat grudgingly admitted
that 'others had the good luck to recommend it first in
print'.[1]

The word-for-word, literal type of translation,
Cowley held, was actually the least literal of all. For
the lapse of time between different ages changes the
colours of poetry as much as of painting; and the 'no
less difference betwixt the religions and customs of our
countries, and a thousand particularities of places,
persons, and manners' merely confuse the eye without
aiding the understanding.[2] Moreover, Greek versification to a Greek, French to a Frenchman, or Italian to
an Italian, means something entirely different from
what it means to an Englishman, no matter how familiar
the latter may be with the language. Consequently,
all that is left, since a translator must necessarily rob
his subject of many qualities, is to recompense him in
some measure with new ones—to add, leave out, or alter
whatever may seem desirable in order to naturalize the
original in the new language. And this sort of translation, imitation, or whatever it may be called, is
preferable to the exact rendering of foreign authors
because, though 'originals both in painting and poesie'
may be 'much more beautiful than their natural objects',
a copy can never be better than an original and is
usually much short of it. For this reason, in Cowley's
opinion, the Psalms of David, to the Hebrews of David's
time 'the most exalted pieces of poesie', had never
been satisfactorily put into English, even by Sandys or
Buchanan, who was 'the best of them all, and indeed a
great person'.

Having thus shown himself to be one of the first of
English critics to grope toward the historical point of
view in criticism, Cowley then proceeded to illustrate
his own principles by imitating, or paraphrasing, or

[1] Sprat, 'Account'.        [2] Cowley, 'Preface' to 'Pindaric Odes'.

naturalizing Pindar's second Olympic and first Nemean odes, and by furnishing them with an imposing array of notes and comments, as he had done before with the *Davideis*. But again he proved himself to be a better explorer, a better Columbus, than a practitioner. Again he was fated to give an idea to hundreds of poets, most of whom were naturally vastly inferior to himself, but a few of whom, including Wordsworth and Tennyson, were destined to write irregular odes (not translations, of course) which in height of feeling and truly enthusiastic intensity far excelled anything that Cowley did in imitation of Pindar or in application of his theory to material of his own. For, on the whole, all that he succeeded in catching in his work was the superficialities, the tricks, of the Greek poet. Notwithstanding his obvious desires, Cowley's nature had little in common with his original's, and such an affinity is always obligatory for achieving anything better than journeyman work. The possibilities of accommodating sound to sense were unlimited, but Cowley was too much inclined to abuse his own liberty. Digressions, addresses to the Muse, allusions to myth and history, omitted transitions, discussions of art versus nature (with the preference always given nature) in the poem itself—all these are present as in Pindar, and yet the poems fail to stir the reader deeply. Short passages strike and impress him, but the odes as a whole leave him cold.

Under the impetus of this most recent enthusiasm, it is quite impossible to say how many 'Pindarics' Cowley was immediately delivered of. The number may have been dependent on the length of his stay in the 'place where he had no other books to direct him'. Inasmuch, however, as the third of the odes in his printed collection, 'The Praise of Pindar', is a paraphrase or imitation of his favourite Horace, he either knew his Horace as well as he knew himself or else postponed his admiration

until his return to a more 'civilized' community, where
books and poets were no longer a nine days' wonder.

Even at the outset of his career as the reincarnation
of Pindar, indeed, Cowley recognized his own inade-
quacies and unfitness for the new campaign he had
undertaken in the conquest of his poetical Italy. Horace,
too, had drawn the comparison between Pindar's
sweeping flights into the empyrean and his own humble
earthliness, but in 'The Praise of Pindar' Cowley elaborated on the other's hints in the following passage, so
typical of his suppressed self:

> . . . alas, my timorous Muse
> Unambitious tracks pursues;
> Does with weak, unballast wings
> About the mossy brooks and springs,
> About the trees' new-blossomed heads,
> About the gardens' painted beds,
> About the fields and flowery meads,
> And all inferior beauteous things,
>    Like the laborious bee,
> For little drops of honey flee,
> And there with humble sweets contents her industry.

From this time on to the publication of the first collected edition of his *Works*, in 1656, Cowley seems to
have devoted his poetical labours to new Pindaric
junketings and to a resumption of the task involved
in the continuation of the yet unpublished *Davideis*.
The ageing manuscript of the once cherished epic, it is
likely, had been recalled to its author by the resolves he
had made in his elegy on Crashaw, and he had gone at
the job of completing it and its notes with a spurt of
vigour. He may even have allowed parts of it to be
copied out and circulated among his friends, as a passage
in one of the gossipy letters of Dorothy Osborne seems
to attest; for in 1654, on the presumptive date of
June 15 or 18, she wrote in this fashion to Sir William
Temple: 'Here are some verses of Cowley's. Tell me

how you like them. 'Tis only a piece taken out of a new thing of his; the whole is very long, and is a description of, or rather a paraphrase upon, the friendships of David and Jonathan. 'Tis, I think, the best I have seen of his, and I like the subject because 'tis that I would be perfect in.' Since the reference is indubitably to the second book of the *Davideis* and since there is no jot of evidence to suggest that the poem was in print at this time, one must conclude that this 'new thing' by Cowley had, in part at least, reached England by 1654.

Preceding biographers have known nothing of the poet's whereabouts between September 13, 1653, and April 12, 1655, though Dorothy Osborne's letter might have given them a clue. On the former date, however, the last of his printed diplomatic letters—an isolated one to Bennet—was headed from Paris, and contained the usual budget of news concerning the health of Charles, the state of affairs in Holland, Scotland, and Ireland, and the doings of the 'ridiculous Parliament'. The personal note in the letter has increased, in spite of its business nature, and Cowley appears on terms of easy equality with Bennet, Sir John Berkeley, and others of the chief figures among the English exiles.

To these last years in France, such Pindarics as 'The Resurrection' and 'The Muse' are probably to be attributed. The combination of adverse fortune and plentiful intercourse with many brilliant minds had deepened Cowley's philosophical interests and sharpened his critical faculties. Consequently, in 'The Resurrection' he revealed his continued concern in the theories, here chiefly physical, of Epicurus and Lucretius, as well as his customary contempt for Pythagorean metempsychosis, which, in his judgement, was much better suited to poets than to philosophers. Similarly, 'The Muse', though quite uninspired as a poem, summarized the result of his conversations and reflections on the

subject of poetry. Cowley's position as one of the
leading critics of his age is illustrated in such compositions as this, with their accompanying notes and comments. So, in 'The Muse', he conjured with all the
terms and concepts which were soon to bulk so large in
French and English criticism. Allegorically visioning
the Muse as entering her chariot, drawn by the winged
steeds of Fancy, Judgement, Wit, Eloquence, Memory,
and Invention, and lackeyed by Nature, Art, Figures,
Conceits, Sentences, 'pleasant Truths', and 'useful Lies',
he saw his 'Queen' sweep grandly into the heavens,
along the way of the Past, Present, and Future, all of
which, the actual as well as the imaginary, belonged
equally to her by the same rights as those of God. For
the province of poetry, in Cowley's eyes, was infinite,
just as its span was eternal: '. . . it makes what choice it
pleases out of the wrack of time of things that it will
save from oblivion.' [1]

On the night of April 12, 1655, along with several
other suspected Royalists then in London, 'the memorable M. Abraham Cowley, more famous by his pen than
by his sword' (according to *The Weekly Intelligencer of
the Commonwealth*), was apprehended by a party of
Cromwell's soldiery and thrown into prison, where he
was afforded sufficient opportunity to continue his
meditations on the value and functions of poetry and
philosophy. The wings of the new 'Theban swan' were,
momentarily at least, clipped.

[1] Cowley's note to 'The Muse'.

# X

## SPY AND APOSTATE

THE barb in the *Intelligencer's* 'memorable M. Abraham Cowley, more famous by his pen than by his sword' must have struck deep. None of the other news sheets of the week, however, sought revenge in similar irony. The *Mercurius Politicus, The Perfect Diurnal of Some Passages and Proceedings of, and in Relation to, the Armies in England, Scotland, and Ireland, The Faithful Scout*, and *The Weekly Post* merely identified him as 'late secretary to the Lord Jermyn in France'; and *Perfect Proceedings of State-Affairs* and *Certain Passages of Every Day's Intelligence* contented themselves with listing a 'Mr. Colley' among the prisoners taken in the raid. *The Weekly Intelligencer, The Faithful Scout*, and *The Weekly Post*, however, probably through faulty reporting, gave both 'Mr. Colley' and 'Abraham Cowley' in their roster of captives.

The sudden appearance of Jermyn's secretary in London at this juncture demands some explanation, especially since the date anticipates by a year that given by all biographers except A. B. Gough and J. Loiseau for Cowley's return to his native land.[1] Sprat was later to describe the circumstances as follows:[2] After Charles II left France, and Henrietta Maria remained behind, Cowley's duties as confidential secretary 'passed of course into other hands. Then it was thought fit, by those on whom he depended, that he should come over into England and, under pretence of privacy and retirement, should take occasion of giving notice of the posture of things in this nation'. In other words, he was to become a spy, still in the service of Jermyn and the Queen Mother.

The means by which he was to achieve this 'privacy

[1] Gough, p. xviii.                    [2] 'Sprat 'Account'.

and retirement' have never been explained, though some
light can now for the first time be thrown upon them.
The whole episode is obscure, full of contradictions—
and rather unpalatable. Most likely he intended to
take advantage of the Act of Oblivion, as many of his
friends had already done. Evelyn had been at Sayes
Court since 1652; Davenant had been released from
Cowes Castle and was in good standing; Hobbes had
made his peace about the same time; the 'easy turncoat',
Waller, had been allowed to come back from his banishment in 1651; and even Buckingham had secretly begun
to negotiate with Cromwell's agents for his restoration.
Cowley, therefore, probably intended to work through
them or some other influential friends for a similar
forgetfulness of the past.

But it was not in 1655 that he returned to London,
for this purpose or in accordance with arrangements
already made. When he was arrested on April 12, he
had already been in England for nearly a year. In spite
of Sprat's implications that his friend broke his exile in
1656, Cowley actually took up his residence in London,
with the full knowledge and consent of Cromwell himself, in the summer of 1654, seemingly in plenty of time
for Dorothy Osborne to quote his 'new thing' in her
letter to her stately young sweetheart.

Among the Rawlinson manuscripts at the Bodleian
are the official copies of many of the warrants and passports issued by the Protector to various persons and for
various purposes. One of these passports reads thus:
Oliver P.

> These are to will and require you to permit and suffer
> Mr. Abraham Cowley to transport himself with his
> necessaries from France to England without any your
> lets, hindrances, or molestations: Given at Whitehall
> this first of May, 1654.

To all our Admirals, &c.[1]

[1] MS. Rawlinson A. 328, f. 35.

Did Cowley at once take advantage of this permission,
for which he apparently had been in wait? There is
evidence to prove that he did—and, besides, that he
passed back again to France and then returned once
more to England, all within a few months.

In the same Rawlinson collection are two other very
interesting documents. The first is in the volume of
Secretary Thurloe's state papers which is dated July
1654. The paper is endorsed: 'Information concerning
Mr. Rainsford and Denham writing to the King and to
Paris, &c.'—and is described in the Bodleian catalogue
as 'Information [from Colonel Bampfield] respecting
the movements of many Royalists in England'.[1] This
Colonel Joseph Bampfield was the clever renegade who
had first been a trusted spy of Charles I, but in this very
month of July 1654, after having been suspected of
treachery by the Royalists, had secretly but definitely
entered the service of the Commonwealth. The
following extract from his report refers to Cowley:
'Cowley I have not seen. I was at his lodging, but he
made himself to be denied: I fear your friend who
obtained your consent to his coming over was not ingenious with you'. Since the document is not addressed,
one can only surmise who 'you' and 'your friend' were,
though perhaps one of the two was Dr. Charles Scarborough, who openly enters into the story later on, and
the other either Jermyn or Buckingham, the latter
being the more likely.[2] For although Cowley, like all
of the devious Jermyn's friends, was at first treated well
in England,[3] Jermyn specifically disavowed any part
in his former secretary's venture, and in April 1655
asserted that he had not even heard from Cowley for
three months, adding that he had just learned that the
same person as had procured Cowley's passport had

---

[1] MS. Rawlinson A. 16, f. 351.      [2] Loiseau favours Buckingham.
[3] See Hatton's letter to Nicholas, June 8, 1655, in *Nicholas Papers*,
ii. 345.

also procured Buckingham's, and that he had tried to put the poet on guard against the Duke.[1] Nevertheless, as will be seen in a moment, Buckingham remained in close touch with his erstwhile schoolmate and soon made use of his services.

One thing, therefore, seems so far to be clear: in July 1654 Cowley was living in London, but in spite of the fact that he had been vouched for by some person in authority, he was still in touch with certain of his wavering friends abroad, at the same time as he was already suspected of duplicity by the Cromwellians. As the actor of a part, then, he was not displaying himself as much of a success.

The second of the two documents referred to above is another passport, slightly more detailed than the first, but to the same effect: on August 18, 1654, Oliver Cromwell writes to 'all our Admirals and Commanders at Sea, and to the Officers of our Ports, and Customs, &c.' that they should allow Mr. Abraham Cowley and all his 'necessaries' safe conduct 'from France to any port in England'.[2] The presence of this second passport somewhat complicates matters, but if the dating of Colonel Bampfield's report and Dorothy Osborne's letter may be trusted, the simplest explanation is that Cowley crossed the Channel again sometime in July and was ready to recross it in August. Nor did the mystery of this restlessness escape the members of the English court in Paris. Their comments and speculations upon it may be inferred from a passage in a letter which Lord Hatton wrote to Nicholas on October 2, 1654; the passage runs as follows: 'At the English court here they cry down Scotland much; there is sure some treaty on post, for Mr. Cowley is parted hence for England.'[3]

[1] See letter of Bennet to Charles II, dated Apr. 6, 1655, among the Ormonde papers in the reports of the *Historical MSS. Commission*, new series, i. 315; quoted by Loiseau.
[2] MS. Rawl. A. 328, f. 122.　　　　　[3] *Nicholas Papers*, ii. 92.

From August or September, then, Cowley may be imagined as again living nervously in London and attempting to carry out the terms of his mission, whatever these were.  But he was constantly under surveillance by both parties, though his next actual move cannot be detected until the spring of the following year—and Buckingham is very much involved in it.

The story is contained in a letter written by 'Infallible Subtle' Daniel O'Neill to the King on March 8, 1655.[1]  The events may be described somewhat in this manner: Several days before, the Duke of Buckingham had arrived at Dover, from France.  There he had been met by one of Cromwell's men, and the two had been closeted together for six hours.  Soon afterwards the Duke had returned whence he had come. Though O'Neill could not find out the subject of their conference, he was sure the meeting was not for the King's good.  And—here is the fatal information—the man who had arranged this understanding between them was 'the red-haired clerk of Mr. Jermyn', a poet and one of the King's enemies.

Charles was naturally much aroused.  In his name, Bennet demanded an explanation from Jermyn, who— as has already been shown—disclaimed all connexion with the affair by insisting that Cowley had gone to England 'upon his own private occasions', though at the same time assuring the King that he was certain Cowley had not had an interview with Cromwell.[2] But the harm was done.  Whether guilty or not, Cowley was from now on (if he had not been before), like Buckingham, a suspicious character.

Distrusted by the most powerful of the Royalists, he was in just as bad repute among the Parliamentarians, and before he could rehabilitate himself with either, fate—his usual adverse fate—intervened.  Within a

[1] *Nicholas Papers*, ii. 219.
[2] Ormonde papers in *Hist. MSS. Com.*, n.s., i. 315

month he found himself seriously involved in an affair
which, if his own statements may be accepted, was of
the nature of the very affairs he had come over to
combat. In March an uprising had been fomented by
the Yorkshire Royalists, centring at Salisbury. This
had proved abortive, and the ringleaders had most of
them been seized and committed to prison, where the
jury of the grim Cromwell had sentenced them to be
hanged, drawn, and quartered. Let *The Faithful Scout*
take up the story from this point:

'Some further discovery being made about an additional plot against his Highness and the present
Government, orders issued out for the apprehending
of divers persons about London, supposed to have a
hand therein; and accordingly a party of sword men
were drawn out, and apprehended these gentlemen
following.' The names of those caught in the dragnet
included, besides Abraham Cowley, those of 'Sir
Thomas Armstrong, who obscured himself in London
by the name of Dr. Wilson, and was formerly a commander of horse under the Marq. of Ormonde in
Ireland' (he probably being the 'gentleman of considerable note' for whom Cowley, according to Sprat,
was mistaken),[1] 'M. Waldron' (probably Cowley's faithful man-servant [2]), 'M. Rich. Nichols, a gentleman belonging to the Duke of York', and 'Mrs. Eliz. Prince, a
young maid (as supposed), poor soul! Is her sex not to
be pitied?'

All of these dozen or so suspects were haled to Whitehall on the next day and examined personally by
Cromwell and Secretary Thurloe, though only the
newspaper records of the trial are extant. The interview
plainly made a profound impression on at least one of
the accused—the poet Cowley. Some of the passages

[1] Sprat, 'Account.'
[2] Cowley's will makes careful provision for his servant, Thomas
Waldron.

in the *Vision* which he later wrote about Cromwell are
so vivid that they seem to be a clear reflection of an
affecting experience. To him the Protector was a
'prodigious man'. Sometimes, indeed, he filled the poet
'with horror and detestation of his actions'. But at
other times (like this one, perhaps), Cowley was 'inclined a little to reverence and admiration of his
courage, conduct, and success'. There can be no doubt
that the prisoner's manner at his examination was
conciliatory. He has, indeed, furnished an excellent
clue to his behaviour when, in the *Vision*, he replied to
the Angel 'as if I had spoken to the Protector himself in
Whitehall' and 'desired him that his Highness would
please to pardon me, if I had unwittingly spoken anything to the disparagement of a person whose relations
to his Highness I had not the honour to know'.

But neither Cowley's tongue nor his pen could serve
him in this situation. They were as ineffective as his
sword had been before. Moreover, though perhaps
Sprat's statement that his friend had been arrested 'by
a mistake' is true, the fact remains that Cromwell
showed no disposition to make amends for his error.
Several of the gentlemen who had been swept up in the
raid without cause were promptly released, but Cowley was committed to prison, pending a further investigation of his case. He was obviously regarded as a
valuable and important catch.

Here was a new dilemma. Should he let himself
languish in confinement, stiff-necked, proud—but
loyal?—or should he bend himself to the will of the
conqueror who had overcome all opposition, and had
even done away with Parliament itself? Should he
remain faithful to Charles and the Cavalier cause,
perhaps putting his head in the way of a noose, certainly bottling himself up so that nothing in the form of
his mission could be accomplished—or should he turn
his coat, recant or at least pretend to do so?

The reasons for, and benefits of, submission were eloquently presented by Sprat many years afterward in an endeavour to extenuate his friend's course. 'Upon his coming over he found the state of the Royal Party very desperate. He perceived the strength of their enemies so united that till it should begin to break within itself all endeavours against it were like to prove unsuccessful. On the other side he beheld their zeal for his Majesty's cause to be still so active that it often hurried them into inevitable ruin. He saw this with much grief. And though he approved their constancy as much as any man living, yet he found their unseasonable showing it, did only disable themselves, and give their adversaries great advantages of riches and strength by their defeats. He therefore believed that it would be a meritorious service to the King if any man who was known to have followed his interest could insinuate into the usurpers' minds that men of his principles were now willing to be quiet, and could persuade the poor oppressed Royalists to conceal their affections for better occasions. And as for his own particular . . . he saw it was impossible for him to pursue the ends for which he came hither if he did not make some kind of declaration of his peaceable intentions.'[1] All of which was very true—and perhaps represented what Cowley really thought when he found himself in his cell once more; or perhaps represented merely what Sprat pretended to think that Cowley thought, for the purpose of defending his friend's memory. If the first alternative is true, then the reasoning illustrates the effect of a long training in court diplomacy on Cowley's character; if the second, it may be regarded partly as a bit of personal pleading, for Sprat, too, was one who had once confessed himself in print to be as ardent an admirer of the Lord Protector as he later became of King Charles II.

The situation, however, was not quite so simple as

[1] Sprat, 'Account'.

Sprat would have it. Probably Cowley did not give way at once. The many examinations 'before the usurpers' which Sprat alludes to undoubtedly took place, as did their attempts 'to make him serviceable to their ends' in 'all imaginable ways'. But that Cowley remained totally unmoved by their arguments is not to be believed. There are too many hints in his own works, and too many stories afloat about his alleged recantation to doubt that eventually a change began to occur. In fact, some of the literary evidence would suggest that the impetus toward the arrangements finally consummated came as much from Cowley's side as from that of the authorities.

Nor is such an outcome an occasion for unmitigated amazement and for accusations of perfidy and treachery. Cowley was inconsistent, easily swayed by his environment, even weak-willed—but there had always been a side of his character which secretly sympathized with many of the principles for which the Commonwealth stood. His observations on court life and manners had not pleased him or attracted him. The integrity and virtues which a pious Christian gentleman like himself would admire had not revealed themselves to him in unalloyed purity and clarity during his experiences with kings, queens, and their retinues. And, most of all, queer new ideas about government and ethics had been invading his mind ever since he had been exposed to Epicurean and *libertin* trains of thought, all of which culminated in his enthusiastic discipleship under Thomas Hobbes.

As a public confession of this discipleship Cowley wrote his Pindaric ode, 'To Mr. Hobbes'. The poem is obviously the product of this particular part of his career, and may well have been composed while he was in prison and desirous of showing his admiration for and agreement with a great person who was also in high favour with Cromwell and his party. For Hobbes, after

publishing his *Leviathan* in 1651, had, by the ideas of
government which he reiterated there, estranged himself thoroughly from the outcast heirs of the English
throne and, by virtue of the same ideas, recommended
himself to the autocrats of republicanism who now held
the country under complete control.  A dictator like
Cromwell could not but welcome a man who, with
forceful language and apparently flawless logic, once
his premises were granted, had proved that absolute
monarchy was the ideal government of the state and
that the conqueror, by means of the 'social contract'
represented in him for the people, is the sole and
rightful ruler and law giver.

These political and social doctrines, so speciously and
dazzlingly put, struck and overcame Cowley as thoroughly as their author's literary theories had formerly
done.  He bestowed on Hobbes a new version of the
title which he had once claimed for himself—'Thou
great Columbus of the golden lands of new philosophies'.
He swore that, of all the 'Vast bodies of philosophy' he
had seen and read, only that of Hobbes displayed a
'living soul', and was neither a dead corpse nor an artificial creation.  He traced philosophy from Aristotle,
through Greece, Rome, and Arabia, to its vanishing in
the empty words of the Schoolmen; and then announced
its rebirth in the mind of Hobbes.  The new conclusions,
he held, were indubitable and inevitable:

> And if we weigh, like thee,
> Nature and causes, we shall see
> That thus it needs must be. . . .

As poetry, 'To Mr. Hobbes' is not great.  As biography, to the reader who perceives its implications, it
is highly important, because it contains a definite statement of faith.  And one of its notes, too, deserves
mention, for in criticizing one of his own conceits
Cowley quoted Seneca's stricture upon Ovid, 'Nescivit

quod bene cessit relinquere', and translated it, 'When
he met with a fancy that pleased him, he could not find
in his heart to quit or ever to have done with it'.
Some forty-five years later, in the often-quoted
'drag-net' simile, Dryden was to sum up his judgement
on 'the darling of my youth, the famous Cowley', in
almost the same words.[1]

In his next two odes, 'Destiny' and 'Brutus', Cowley,
under the veil of different allegories, continued the recantation he had begun. Those whom he wished to
understand could do so with ease, and those who would
be enraged could be told that their interpretations
were erroneous and unintended by the author. How
else explain the first stanza of 'Destiny' than by referring
the allusions of its chess game to Cromwell, the Royalists,
and Charles?

> Strange and unnatural! Let 's stay and see
>> This pageant of a prodigy.
> Lo, of themselves th' enlivened chessmen move;
> Lo, the unbred, ill-organed pieces prove
>> As full of art and industry,
>> Of courage and of policy,
> As we ourselves, who think there 's nothing wise but we.
>> Here a proud pawn I admire,
>> That still advancing higher
>> At top of all became
>> Another thing and name.
> Here I'm amazed at th' actions of a knight
>> That does bold wonders in the fight.
>> Here I the losing party blame
>> For those false moves that break the game,
> That to their grave, the bag, the conquered pieces bring,
> And above all, th' ill conduct of the mated king.

In the stanzas following this, the influence of Hobbes's
mechanistic philosophy is also apparent. In them

---

[1] Dryden, *Essays*, ii. 108–9.

Cowley strikes a new note of pessimism—or rather of fatalism or even determinism—which sounds a hollow undertone beneath virtually all his writings of this period. There is no free will. 'Destiny plays us all.' Why, therefore, reasons Cowley, try to be what Fate has not willed ?

> Thou neither great at court, nor in the war,
> Nor at th' Exchange shall be, nor at the wrangling bar.
> Content thyself with the small, barren praise
>    That neglected verse does raise.

And he comforts himself with the thought that all of his 'great forefathers . . . from Homer down to Ben' suffered a similar neglect at the hands of Fortune.

'Brutus', the next ode, was even more open in its underlying suggestions, and was, in fact, often called in question by the King's party after the Restoration. For Brutus was a regicide as well as a republican. Though Cowley had seemingly always admired him, it was nevertheless a bold stroke to single him out for praise at this juncture, with an allegory which all too plainly identified him with Cromwell, Caesar with Charles I, and Rome with England. And when these parallels were supported by allusions to the proposal to constitute Cromwell king, by references to secret attempts upon the Protector's life (being perhaps a side glance at the Salisbury plot), and by a prediction that 'new philosophies' would bring about an ending like that deserved by Brutus rather than that which he suffered, Cowley had gone a long way toward putting himself in countenance with the Cromwellian government.

For certainly these poems were circulated by those of Cowley's friends who were interested in obtaining his release, just as was the fourth book of the *Davideis*, which he either wrote or extensively revised at this time. The art of cloaking a modern political allegory in

a Biblical narrative was still to be brought to perfection
by Dryden, but in the first half of the fourth book of his
epic Cowley provided his successor with an excellent
example of how the thing could be done. The 'argument'
itself, with its references to 'the change of government
in Israel', 'the state of the Commonwealth under the
Judges', and 'the motives for which the people desired
a king', indicated clearly enough the viewpoint from
which the poem was to be read. David's speech to
Moab was replete with allusions to such matters as 'a
Civil War', the 'frequent curse of our loose-governed
State'; the dispossessing of the kings by 'special men,
armed with God's warrant'; the death of Eli at home,
while his sons were abroad; the threats of a 'rough,
neighbouring war'; and other similarities whose point
lay in their cunning phrasing even more than in their
facts. Most significant of all, however, was the extended
discussion of the advisability of surrendering the commonwealth form of government under the Judges for a
revived monarchy—the same question that was agitating
all England at the time. The wise Samuel, in whose
person Cowley would seem to be flattering Cromwell,
apparently voiced Cowley's own opinion when he advised against such a course and favoured the retention
of the republic. In addition to unmistakable references
to the attempts of Charles II against the Commonwealth
and to the weak characters of Cromwell's sons, Cowley
drew an astonishingly prophetical picture of what was
actually to happen to the nation after the monarchy
was restored.

So many opportunities for allegorical interpretation
could not have been mere chance. They were not co-
incidences. Moreover, if all these things were done
with the purpose of disarming suspicion and of preparing
conditions for Cowley's career as a spy, he certainly
went much farther than necessary and farther than any
of his principals intended. In fact, he knew so well

what he was doing, and did it so skilfully, that one is
tempted to read a parable into his two Old Testament
odes, 'The 34 Chapter of the Prophet Isaiah' and 'The
Plagues of Egypt', both of which are jeremiads concerning the degenerate condition of Israel. But whether
there was any lesson for England intended here or not,
the latter poem clearly affords many effective passages,
descriptive and otherwise, which may well be remembered when one reads Milton's *Paradise Lost*. In the
second poem, too, Cowley's knowledge of Hebrew
appears in the notes.

These political readjustments, whether regarded as
voluntary or as forced, could not but bring about a
bitter revulsion, a thorough disgust with life, in the
once light-hearted poet. 'Life and Fame', 'The
Ecstasy', 'To the New Year', and 'Life' all confess this
pessimism. Life is 'thou Nothing's younger brother';
the shadows that man takes for things are 'but the
empty dreams which in Death's sleep we make'; instead
of wishing to live long, 'The ripened soul longs from his
prison to come'; old age finds nothing but 'Sourness and
lees' left within the cup; and the man who would desire
to pry into the future and thus 'seek to antedate our
misery' is frankly styled a fool. A peculiar mixture of
Platonic and Epicurean ideas appears in these odes, but
the dominant tone is one of utter depression and soul
weariness. Pity, rather than condemnation, is the
emotion uppermost in the reader's mind as he comes
upon these poems in their proper context—pity that
circumstances should have forced upon a man like
Cowley a part so repugnant to his temperament and
abilities.

But even these manifold evidences of conversion were
not sufficient to satisfy the Oliverian officers. They were
hard-headed men, and did not put too high a premium
on mere words. Besides, Cowley was a poet, and Sprat
himself later suggested that what poets said need not

necessarily be taken as an index to what they believed.[1]
Bampfield even wrote to Thurloe from Paris on
November 22, 1655, to the effect that '839 has told a
friend of mine that Cowley shall apply to you, and pretend to serve your interest to secure and free himself'.[2]
Money was heavier than air, which words consisted of,
and Cromwell's agents evidently considered that a
heavy bond was a better guarantee of good behaviour
than any number of anti-Royalist poems. At any rate,
Cowley's release came only after he had found some one
to go his bail for a thousand pounds—a huge ransom,
it would seem, for a mere poet, whose sword, unlike
that of his poetic rival, John Cleveland, was quite
worthless.

The friend who, as usual, appeared at this opportune
time was Dr. Charles Scarborough,[3] whose acquaintance
Cowley had probably first made at Cambridge (Scarborough had been a fellow contributor to *Voces Votivae*
in 1640) and had then renewed at Oxford when both
men were there with the King. Scarborough, however,
after having been in a sense adopted by Dr. Harvey, and
being more interested in medicine than warfare, had
soon dropped out of the Royalist ranks and had made
his peace with the Puritans, among whom he had dwelt
ever since in increasing prosperity.[4] Whether he had
cancelled all his Royalist affiliations or not is another
question. (He was knighted after the Restoration and
became one of Charles's personal physicians.) His
appearance at this point as Cowley's sponsor, however,
may have been the result of some prearrangement connected with the granting of the passports, or his good
nature may simply have asserted itself when he discovered a friend in distress. Nor did Cowley fail to
reward the other in such a way as was in his power, for
the ode 'To Dr. Scarborough' would seem to be the

[1] Sprat, 'Account'.                [2] See Thurloe, *State Papers*, iv. 233.
[3] Sprat, 'Account'.                [4] Wood, iv, ii. 97.

outcome of this episode.[1] The poem is notable, then, partly because of its tribute to the author's benefactor, even more because of the proof it gives of Cowley's new knowledge of and interest in medicine, but most, perhaps, because of its memorable concluding couplet:

> Let Nature and let Art do what they please;
> When all 's done, Life is an incurable disease.

[1] On Apr. 8, 1656, Scarborough wrote to the Earl of Oxford, sending him Cowley's new book as a testimony of his friend's 'incomparable merit', and promising to bring the poet to the Earl for a 'second visit' in the summer. See MSS. of James Round in *Hist. MSS. Com.* (London, 1895), p. 280; quoted by Loiseau.

# XI

# CHAINED TO THE BODLEIAN

ONLY one thing remained to clench Cowley's severing from his former allegiance: a public admission, under no veil of allegory, of his defection from the cause of Charles. In pursuance of his recently taken resolve to seek no further fame than that which the Muse whom he had tried in vain to forsake had brought him, he had spent the several months ('paucis . . . mensibus', in Sprat's phrase) [1] of his imprisonment not only in writing new poems but also in preparing for the press the first collected edition of his works. [2] While still under duress, he composed the preface for his volume, and in this preface he inserted the twenty or thirty lines which he was to spend most of the remainder of his life repenting.

The passage was tucked away in the middle of this introduction as an explanation of why he had suppressed certain of his earlier works, particularly his juvenilia and his partisan writings on the Civil War, but to those whose eyes were eagerly on the watch for obnoxious and censurable material the words must have stood out as if printed in black letter. They are important enough to demand quotation verbatim:

. . . Now though in all civil dissensions, when they break into open hostilities, the war of the pen is allowed to accompany that of the sword, and every one is in a manner obliged with his tongue as well as hand to serve and assist the side which he engages in, yet when the event of battle and the unaccountable will of God has determined the controversy, and that we have submitted to the conditions of the conqueror, we must lay down our pens as

[1] Sprat, 'De Vita'.
[2] Loiseau points out that this, as well as 'Davideis . . . Libris Quatuor', was registered by Humphrey Moseley on Sept. 11, 1655; see *Transcript of Registers . . . 1640–1708*, ii. 12.

well as arms, we must march out of our cause itself, and dis-
mantle that, as well as our towns and castles, of all the works
and fortifications of wit and reason by which we defended it.
We ought not, sure, to begin ourselves to revive the remembrance
of those times and actions for which we have received a general
amnesty as a favour from the victor. The truth is, neither we
nor they ought by the representation of places and images to
make a kind of artificial memory of those things wherein we are
all bound to desire, like Themistocles, the art of oblivion. The
enmities of fellow-citizens should be, like that of lovers, the
redintegration of their amity. The names of party and titles
of division, which are sometimes in effect the whole quarrel,
should be extinguished and forbidden in peace under the notion
of acts of hostility. And I would have it accounted no less un-
lawful to rip up old wounds than to give new ones; which has
made me not only abstain from printing any things of this kind,
but to burn the very copies, and inflict a severer punishment on
them myself than perhaps the most rigid officer of state would
have thought that they deserved.

Now if what did happen in 1660 had not happened,
this statement of the situation would probably have
been accepted as eminently fair and sane. Only fanatics,
who never change their minds once they have made them
up, only absolutists, who believe in an eternal and im-
mutable standard of life and action, could disagree with
it. Cowley, however, was a relativist, which is a less
ugly-sounding word than opportunist, and the absence
of any extreme doctrines in this document will illustrate
his position. Nevertheless, to his own age and that
immediately succeeding, when party loyalty bulked so
large, even so mild a recantation as this assumed
gigantic proportions, and as late as 1712 an antiquary
like Thomas Hearne could be surprised by this 'very
remarkable passage concerning the late Rebellion, which
Mr. Cowley excuses himself from writing against, and
indeed speaks much more for the Republicans and
Oliverians than either the present Bp. of Worcester or
the late Dean of St. Paul's, Dr. Sherlock, did for the

late Revolution and in defence of all the illegal acts of that kind that ever were done'.[1]

If Cowley had known how fatal to his future prospects these statements were to be, he would certainly have been more guarded in what he said and perhaps would never have trusted them to the forthrightness of prose at all. For he now—though he may have been unaware of the fact—put himself anew under the suspicion of both parties, though some of the Royalists still trusted him. Edward Hyde, however, was one of those who did not, as a passage in a letter which he wrote from Breda to Lord Ormonde 'this 10 of May after midnight', 1656, shows: 'I never reckoned upon the French money for the discharge of your debts at Cullen. If you have a good account of all that hath been received, it is as much as I look for: my intelligence is not good, if 2,000 li. be not this last post returned to you, and if 4,000 were returned into England to Mr. Cowley. You will think it strange after you have read the preface to his book.'[2] The rest of the letter concerns other aspects of the Royalist system of 'communication'.

There is, moreover, other cause to believe that even after his release Cowley attempted (or pretended—one cannot say which) to carry out his original mission. At the Bodleian, among the Clarendon manuscripts themselves, is preserved a series of three 'cant' or 'disguised' letters which remain from what internal evidence shows to have been a group of four.[3] They are all in the same hand, which could easily be a conscious distortion of Cowley's own, but they all bear different signatures: 'J.T.', 'J.H.', and 'W.R.' The first, dated from London on April 21, contains no address; the second, dated the 27th, is addressed on the outside to 'Monsieur le Fleure, Tailleur François dans le Faux-bourg St. Germains à Paris', but was actually received

---

[1] Hearne, iii. 415–16.    [2] MS. Clarendon 51, f. 269.
[3] Ibid., ff. 211, 248, 277. See appendix no. 6.

by Nicholas Armourer (one of the King's gentlemen, later knighted) and endorsed, 'This is Mr. Cow. letter to me'; and the third, dated May 1, is addressed to a Mr. Binns. The contents of these letters, coupled with Armourer's abbreviated identification, Hyde's almost simultaneous announcement of the dispatch of money to London, and another document which will be referred to shortly, make it not improbable that here are further tracks in the devious trail of Cowley as a secret agent.

The exact purport of these letters, nevertheless, cannot be interpreted, since the key to fictitious names and veiled allusions is missing. Charles, however, was himself sometimes referred to in other similar correspondence as 'Mr. Ellis', and mercantile terms such as 'business', 'gloves', 'trading', and so on have always been common disguises for diplomatic and military proposals. The drift of the letters, then, would suggest that the writer was in touch with several people, especially a Mr. Conyers, who were not unwilling to participate in a certain 'business' if suitable arrangements could be made, but that he could not understand why his communications were not being answered. In the last note, there is a strong suggestion that the writer intends to leave London soon, perhaps for France.[1]

The reason for the delay in reply seems obvious: the persons at the other end of the chain were debating whether their man was to be relied upon any further, or whether—like Colonel Bampfield—he had been tampered with by the other side and was perhaps playing the game with both hands. But the opposition was just

---

[1] In Birch's *Thurloe State Papers*, v. 366, 414, 469, appears a series of intercepted letters which perhaps form a continuation of the one described above. They are from various places on the Continent; have different signatures, all indefinite; are dated Sept. 9, Sept. 15, and Oct. 11; and all contain references to Conyers, Binns, gloves, cinnabar, &c.

as uncertain of its man, as another report from Bampfield sent from Paris on November 2, 1656 (new style),
and now in the Rawlinson collection, would indicate:[1]
'. . . Some project I am certain is hatching which I may
in a short time discover; I believe 63: 20: 9: 35: 37:
[deciphered 'Axcot' or 'Ascot'] is gone back into England, from whence he came lately, and has been since
in Flanders. He passes to and fro very often; he uses to
lie privately in Aldersgate Street, and is a great con-
federate of 7: 50: 73: 41: 59: 2: 82: [Cowlyes]. There
is likewise of this company one Colonel 66: 61: 44: 32:
64: 20: [Rogers] with a 23: 47: 19: 82: 83: 27: 94: 22:
[glass eye] who walks privately in London and lies
about Doctor's Commons. At my arrival in this place
905 [Jermin] discoursed with me at large, and very
freely, about the business of 54: 22: 20: 37: 8: 41: 33:
30: [Lestolfe] where he said there was good landing, the
town the best affected of any in England, and the
country all about the like; that it was upon the entrance
into an island' called Loyingland; that it was about
eight hours from Dunkirk; and that an army of ten
thousand could hold it against a force three times as
great. The whole passage of course refers to the suspected Royalist scheme to invade England with an
armed body in this year. But whatever came of the
plot, Cowley was not caught in it.

From all this conflicting evidence, each reader can
draw his own conclusions. There is at least nothing to
show that the suspected man ever actively aided the
Cromwellians, unless his pen may be considered a
weapon, as so many of the Royalists—including the
King and his chief councillor, Hyde—insisted on re-
garding it. And certainly Cowley had not brought himself to all these circumvolutions and admissions without
considerable agonizing and perhaps self-condemnation.
Very likely it was the feeling that he had betrayed his

[1] MS. Rawl. A. 44. f. 33; also Birch, *Thurloe State Papers*, v. 512.

own genius while gaining his bodily freedom that led
him to what is probably the most startling statement in
the entire preface of his new book; that is, that he was
now to be regarded as poetically dead—that he would
never write any more poetry—and that he intended, in
accordance with a long-standing hope, to retire 'to
some of our American plantations, not to seek for gold,
or enrich myself with the traffic of those parts . . . but
to forsake this world for ever, with all the vanities and
vexations of it, and to bury myself in some obscure retreat there (but not without the consolation of letters
and philosophy). . . .' Let Dr. Johnson scoff at this confession as he will,[1] or let any other captious critic point
out that the announcement is scarcely to be reconciled
with Cowley's programme of acting as a Royalist spy
in England, the fact remains that the poet was from his
point of view quite justified in his desires. The picture
which he draws of himself and the world in which he
has been forced to live and move is an eternally vivid
one of any artist, sensitive to beauty and truth, dropped
without recourse into an environment thoroughly at
variance with his temperament and inimical to his
development.

For, speaking of poets, Cowley wrote in the same preface: 'And if in quiet and flourishing times they meet
with so small encouragement, what are they to expect
in rough and troubled ones ? If wit be such a plant
that it scarce receives heat enough to preserve it alive
even in the summer of our cold climate, how can it
choose but wither in a long and a sharp winter ? A
warlike, various, and a tragical age is best to write of,
but worst to write in.' These valid and rather advanced and Hobbesian critical ideas on the poet's
environment he supplemented with equally valid ones
on the poet's mental state. 'Neither is the present
constitution of my mind more proper than that of the

---

[1] Johnson, *Rambler*, no. 6.

times for this exercise, or rather divertisement. There is nothing that requires so much serenity and cheerfulness of spirit; it must not be either overwhelmed with the cares of life, or overcast with the clouds of melancholy and sorrow, or shaken and disturbed with the storms of injurious fortune; it must, like the halycon, have fair weather to breed in. The soul must be filled with bright and delightful ideas, when it undertakes to communicate delight to others, which is the main end of poesy. . . . The truth is, for a man to write well, it is necessary to be in good humour; neither is wit less eclipsed with the unquietness of mind than beauty with the indisposition of body. So that 'tis almost as hard a thing to be a poet in despite of fortune as it is in despite of nature.'

The key to Cowley's essential character and poetic theory is to be found in that phrase, 'The soul must be filled with bright and delightful ideas.' As often as he had been misled into the morasses and sucking quicksands of didactic and controversial verse, he was convinced that the chief purpose of poetry was not to instruct, but to delight. Yet not since the days of his boyhood, with few exceptions, had he been allowed to write as he wished—to express the 'bright and delightful ideas' which were within him. The struggle between King and Commons had taken care of that.

The remainder of his preface he devoted to a description of the contents of his volume, and to a running fire of comments on his own work and on poetry in general. Critically, then, this section is an interesting and important document, for it marks its author as one of the few conscious English critics before Dryden.[1]

The first part of the book was to consist of his *Miscellanies*, many of which were written in his youth. The second was to be *The Mistress, or Love-Verses*, 'for so it is, that poets are scarce thought Freemen of their

[1] Cf. my article, *R.E.S.*, ii. 385–404.

Company without paying some duties and obliging themselves to be true to love'. Perhaps in recollection of his diatribe against amorous verse in his elegy on Crashaw, however, he felt called upon to defend his inclusion of these poems, and he did so by reminding the reader that poetry is not necessarily 'the picture of the poet, but of things and persons imagined by him. He may be in his own practice and disposition a philosopher, nay, a Stoic, and yet speak sometimes with the softness of an amorous Sappho'. Yet he neither affirmed nor denied that he had been in love when he wrote his verses. Moreover, though apologizing for any 'obscenity or profaneness' in 'some expressions (if such there be) which may happen to offend the severity of supercilious readers', he silently added seven new poems to the collection which had first appeared in 1647—and these seven, dealing with such subjects as 'Honour', 'The Innocent Ill', 'Dialogue. After Enjoyment', and 'Bathing in the River', were much more risqué in both material and outspokenness than any in the former edition. Otherwise, the second text is so close to the first as to indicate that the printer worked directly from the latter, although Cowley never acknowledged that he had had anything to do with the earlier version. In this connexion, it may be worth noting that Humphrey Moseley was the publisher of both volumes.

The third part of the collection was to be the Pindaric odes, concerning the reception of which Cowley was so doubtful as to provide a special explanatory preface in addition to the paragraph devoted to them in the general introduction.

But the most important part of the volume, in Cowley's mind, was obviously the fourth and last—the part which comprised the still unfinished *Davideis, a Sacred Poem of the Troubles of David*. Representing different strata of his work for a period of over fifteen years and revealing many signs of revision (several notes even in the first two books refer to Pindar, and one note in the second book refers to one of his own Pindarics), the epic was the first and weightiest sign of the accomplishment of his vow to the memory of Crashaw.

The invocation, to Christ himself, contains the following lines:

> Lo, with pure hands thy heavenly fires to take,
> My well-changed Muse I a chaste Vestal make!
> From earth's vain joys and Love's soft witchcraft free,
> I consecrate my Magdalene to Thee!
> Lo, this great work, a Temple to Thy praise,
> On polished pillars of strong verse I raise! . . .
> Too long the Muse's lands have heathen been;
> Their gods too long were devils, and virtues, sin . . . .

And this idea, with its possible glancing allusion to Herbert's *Temple*, was the one on which he dwelt at great length in his preface. Poetry, the greatest of the arts, had too long neglected the 'many . . . bright and magnificent subjects' which 'the Holy Scripture affords'. It was 'not without grief and indignation' that he beheld 'that divine science employing all her inexhaustible riches of wit and eloquence either in the wicked and beggarly flattery of great persons, or the unmanly idolizing of foolish women, or the wretched affectation of scurril laughter, or at best on the confused, antiquated dreams of senseless Fables and Metamorphoses'. The list was a tacit 'mea culpa', for of all these sins Cowley himself had been guilty—and of some of them he was to be again. His enthusiasm, indeed, led him even to a condemnation of classical mythologies, as well as 'their worthy successors, the knights errant'. 'All the books of the Bible are either already most admirable and exalted pieces of poesy, or are the best materials in the world for it.' With such magnificent ideals for the salvation of poetry—ideals which, he said, Quarles and Thomas Heywood, for instance, had dismally failed to reach, and which, he

recognized, even he himself had fallen far short of—
Cowley closed his preface, which furnishes a most faithful portrait of his vacillating character and of his
dilemma at this period.

Sometime early in 1656, the *Poems* of Abraham
Cowley were offered to the public by Humphrey
Moseley, 'at the Prince's Arms in St. Paul's Church-
yard'. The motto on the title-page was from Virgil's
*Georgics*:

> Tentanda via est, qua me quoque possim
> Tollere humo, victorque virum volitare per ora.

Following the title-page Cowley had placed his Latin
'Elegia Dedicatoria, ad Illustrissimam Academiam
Cantabrigiensem' as a sign of his love for his old school.
But on June 27, mindful of his last dwelling-place before
departing for France, he himself carried a copy of his
work to Oxford, 'the Muses' Paradise', and, in accordance with the custom, chained it to one of the shelves
of the Bodleian, where it is still to be found. Not content with this evidence of his affection for the second of
his universities, he inscribed in the volume a new
Pindaric ode, in his own hand, entitled 'The Book
Humbly Presenting Itself to the University Library at
Oxford', in which, with becoming modesty, he apolo-
gized for the appearance of his work among such august
company and suggested that if fate had left him to
follow his own devices instead of forcing him to a life
of action and unrest he might have produced something
more worthy of the honour accorded him.

# XII

# DOCTOR OF MEDICINE AND LITERARY IDOL

THE composition of the Bodleian ode is sufficient indication that Cowley did not persist very long in his resolution to desert the Muse whose Hannibal he had once sworn to be. Nor probably had any one taken him very seriously. He was of a resilient temperament, and after his release from gaol the whole complexion of affairs seemed to change for him. He had been a famous figure even while his reputation depended mostly on *The Mistress* and those poems which he had been circulating in manuscript. Now, after the publication of his book, he was acclaimed everywhere and lionized by every one who pretended to any sort of entrée into the Muse's court. Not even Waller could boast of a higher place in the literary public's esteem than that in which Cowley basked. Only a few disgruntled political malcontents did not join the chorus—persons who, moreover, would not dare lift their voices in criticism for fear of betraying themselves to the government.

Cowley's own serio-comic 'Ode, Upon Occasion of a Copy of Verses of My Lord Broghill's' soon publicly marked his recognition of the foolishness of his vow, besides showing how completely he had been taken up by another of Cromwell's most trusted supporters. Broghill, later Earl of Orrery, who had for some time oscillated between monarchy and republicanism and had finally become a staunch and even confidential friend of the Protector, had written a poem in Cowley's defence and particularly in praise of the *Davideis*.[1] This poem

[1] This poem, entitled 'To Mr. Cowley on His Davideis', was considered lost until Loiseau found it in the collection of the Marquis of Bath, at Longleat.

lone was, from Cowley's adulatory view, more than nough to atone for all his disappointments in love and poetry, more than enough to make him wish to recall he Ovid, the Horace, the Homer, and the Virgil which he had bitterly pitched out of the window, more than nough to make him swear a new and eternal service o the Muse.

In the fourth stanza of this ode, also, Cowley introduced a rather long medical figure, which signalized a new stage in his career. Sprat, as usual, is the expositor. According to his story, when Cowley returned to England on his 'mission', 'he was advised to dissemble the main intention of his coming over under the disguise of applying himself to some settled profession'.[1] Who the adviser was cannot be definitely said, but all the signs point to Charles Scarborough, who had already bailed the poet out of prison. For Scarborough was a physician, and a noted one; and it was to 'physic' that Cowley turned. This interest was not a new one, for medical references displaying some knowledge of theory and terminology may be traced in his earlier works; but he now decided to go into it thoroughly, and actually to seek a degree. His first step was to undertake 'many anatomical dissections', probably under the tutelage of Scarborough. Then, after he had familiarized himself with anatomy, he 'proceeded to the consideration of simples', and, as a good doctor should, resolved to study this aspect of medicine not merely from books[2] but in nature itself. Consequently, 'he retired into a fruitful part of Kent, where every field and wood might show him the real figures of those plants of which he read'.

The exact location of Cowley's first place of retirement in Kent is unknown, but it was probably not

---

[1] Sprat, 'Account'.
[2] Loiseau points out that among these botanical books were the complete works of Aldrovande. These, as well as other volumes, Cowley gave to the Trinity library in 1665, where they still remain.

very far from London—perhaps, indeed, near Greenwich or Deptford, where he would be within reach
of Sayes Court, which was the home of Evelyn and in
which Evelyn had recently written his translation of
and essay upon the first book of Lucretius. Hasted's old
history of Kent asserts that the place was Deptford—
'so fruitful to the herbalist'; [1] and Cowley's 'Ode.
Sitting and Drinking in the Chair Made out of the
Relics of Sir Francis Drake's Ship' would confirm the
belief, since this chair was first kept at Deptford and
only later presented to the Bodleian by John Davis—a
gift celebrated by Cowley some time after. And certainly this neighbourhood, in the seventeenth century,
if not exactly comparable to a spot in 'some of our
American plantations', would have offered just the
sort of quiet and peace which he craved, without
forcing upon him any of the really primitive conditions
and deprivations which he could not have endured.

The result of this course of study, which could not
have consumed much more than two years at the most,
was that Cowley was created 'doctor of physic' by the
University of Oxford on December 2, 1657. [2] Anthony
à Wood, in commenting rather crabbedly on the event,
explained it by stating that Cowley had complied 'with
some of the men then in power', and added, 'whereby
he gained the ill-will of some of his friends'. [3] The
episode is obviously part and parcel of the larger
'recantation' affair, and seems further to confirm the
former evidence upon Cowley's position. But nevertheless there is one charge which none can, with justice,
bring against him: he made no attempt to exercise his
new and quickly gained power by practising upon

[1] Hasted, i. 10.

[2] Loiseau confirms this date by referring to the Register of Convoca-
tion (Reg. T., ff. 304, 305) for July 2, 1657, and the Register of Congre-
gation (Reg. Qa., f. 182) for 'Terminus Michaelis, 1657'.

[3] Wood, iv, ii. 209; Walker, ii. 160–1.

iling and defenceless humanity. The only consequences
f his studies were his new title of 'Dr.' by which he
vas from now on often addressed, and a long series of
otanical verses, written in Latin a year or two later.

The 'Ode. Upon Dr. Harvey', also of this period,
ιay similarly have sprung from a desire to pay a per-
ɔnal obligation, for Harvey was Scarborough's patron
ιd master, and therefore may not unlikely have been
f some assistance to Cowley too. The poem, in spite of
rather unfortunate basic metaphor for a scientific sub-
ɛct, must certainly rank high, in ideas at least, among
ɔowley's works. It must have been written not long
efore Harvey's death on June 3, 1657, for the last
.anza suggests that all realized that his end was near.
'he important feature of the ode is that, after recalling
ιe other's experiments with the circulation of the
lood, with the growth of the embryo, and especially
ith the incubation of the egg, performed in the old
ays with George Bathurst at Oxford, Cowley took
ιarvey as typical of the new scientific spirit of the age:

> Thus Harvey sought for truth in truth's own book,
>     The creatures, which by God himself was writ;
>         And wisely thought 'twas fit
>     Not to read comments only upon it,
>     But on th' original itself to look.

'his criticism upon the cramping medieval methods
ill in vogue Cowley then went on to apply to the arts
. general, which

>         dance like fairies a fantastic round,
>     But neither change their motion nor their ground.

'he poem closed with an allusion to the greater accom-
ιishments Harvey might have achieved if the tumults
f the Civil War had not interfered with his work.

Scientific as Cowley's chief pursuits were at this time,
ɛ did not neglect his literary associations. One of the
ost significant, though sometimes slightly amusing,

phenomena of the day was the emergence of women—
'learned ladies', as Myra Reynolds has called them[1]—
into the field of active literary composition and art
Among the first of the blue-stockings was the youn,
Mrs. Katherine Philips, the famed 'matchless Orinda'
in the language of her coterie. Shortly after his repatria
tion Cowley met this attractive young paragon, sti
in her twenties, and promptly wrote his 'On Orinda'
Poems. Ode'. His acquaintance with her could no
have been very lengthy, since most of her time wa
spent at her husband's home in Wales, among he
Society of Friendship, with their stilted, artificial name
of Antenor, Rosania, Lucasia, Palaemon, Policrite, &c.
but he knew her well enough to praise her 'forehea
smooth' as well as her 'sparkling' eye. And indeed he
extant portraits and busts show her to have been nc
without some physical charms, with large but goo
features, a full bosom, a rather thick neck, and hai
sometimes falling in curls to her shoulders and some
times caught up in a sweep behind. She seems to hav
had a partiality for earrings and a tight necklace.

These matters could not have been entirely negligibl
to a poet who still had the reputation of being one c
England's best penners of love verses, even though h
had tried to forgo it; but Cowley was most impressec
according to his ode, by her wit, her 'well-knit sense
her 'numbers gentle', and her 'fancies high'. Here wa
a woman's writing which at last would bear compariso
with a man's. ''Tis solid, and 'tis manly all,' he criec
Moreover, it was not only instructive but also pure, an
for this reason he was prepared to place her abov
Sappho herself, her only rival, whose 'ill manners' ha
sadly soiled her fame.

Though to-day it may seem a little difficult t
account for Cowley's ardent championship of 'Orinda
the fact remains that in her own time she was lavish!

[1] Reynolds, *The Learned Lady in England*, 1650–1760.

praised by such diverse characters as Lord Broghill, Henry Vaughan, the Earl of Roscommon, Jeremy Taylor, and Dorothy Osborne (then Mrs. Temple), and was welcomed into their different circles. Perhaps the vision of a transplanted and modified *précieuse* coterie, such as he had known in France, helped to attract Cowley. Orinda's favourite theme of 'Honour and Friendship', though somewhat Platonic in derivation, would also have appealed to him and elicited his approval. To him, though he had a sense of humour, the English *précieuses* would not seem too ridiculous.

In the meantime he was finding himself less and less alone in his apostasy from Charles. The latest of the deserters was no other than the King's former boon-companion, the Duke of Buckingham. Despairing of the exiled monarch's ever regaining his inheritance (and in this belief differing not at all from the majority of Charles's former adherents), he had presumed so far on the royal decay as to press his suit to the widowed Mary, princess of Orange, the King's sister. Repulsed there and also having had a financial disagreement with his proposed brother-in-law, he had completed his negotiations with Cromwell and had returned to England in 1657. He was a dashing figure, and few thought the worse of him for his conduct in love, war, or politics—or if any did, they wisely reserved their opinions.

Buckingham and Cowley must have met soon after the former's arrival, and have renewed, even increased, their former intimacy. Consequently, Cowley must have watched the Duke's actions with interest and curiosity, particularly his courtship of the sweet young Lady Mary Fairfax, the daughter of the man to whom his confiscated lands had been granted. Lady Mary, though already pledged to the Earl of Chesterfield, had lived such a retired life on her father's estate at Nun-appleton that she was captivated by the bold and dissipated young man. Buckingham, of course, saw no

objection to regaining his lost inheritance by such a
match, even with the daughter of a former enemy and
Parliamentarian general, the great Lord Thomas Fairfax. If Andrew Marvell had not ceased to be the tutor
of Lady 'Moll' three or four years before, he would
undoubtedly have celebrated the event of the marriage
with some caustic verses, in spite of his admiration for
the family. But Marvell had by this time become the
assistant of Milton in the foreign secretaryship under
Cromwell's government, and the office of laureate was
left to Abraham Cowley. If Sir Clements R. Markham
may be believed,[1] Cowley was not only present to
commemorate the occasion in verse, but was actually
Buckingham's best man. All the chief families of the
county thronged Percy Bolton Church on that fifteenth
of September, 1657, and Cowley's latest Pindaric ode
distributed graceful flatteries among all who were
involved.[2]

His picture of the Fairfaxes, though much briefer
than that left by Marvell in several poems, nevertheless
agrees with it in all essentials. Thomas Fairfax was
undoubtedly a great general and an unselfish and wise
leader, though he let himself be pushed into retirement
by Cromwell. Mary Fairfax's face was of the sort to
cause many 'gentle triumphs'. But Marvell is the one
to have left the real portrait of her, in his stanzas at the
end of 'Upon Appleton House, to My Lord Fairfax'.
It is the kind of picture that Cowley himself might have
drawn, if he had only had the gift of drawing people as
he drew idyllic nature:

> 'Tis she that to these gardens gave
> That wondrous beauty which they have;
> She straightness on the woods bestows;
> To her the meadow sweetness owes:

[1] Markham, *Life of ... Fairfax*, p. 372.
[2] Cowley, 'To the Duke of Buckingham, upon His Marriage with
the Lord Fairfax His Daughter.'

> Nothing could make the river be
> So crystal-pure but only she;
> She yet more pure, sweet, straight, and fair
> Than gardens, woods, meads, rivers are.

Buckingham was fortunate in gaining such a wife, but it is doubtful whether her virtues were the kind which he could long appreciate. The 'second part' of Buckingham's 'tragicomedy', to which Cowley called his ode the 'prologue', was perhaps more tragedy than comedy to Moll Fairfax, though for a long time amusing enough to her husband. For the poet, however, the epithalamium marked his appearance as the 'servant of the person' who was to remain one of his chief patrons and admirers to the end of his life. The friendship of Cowley and Buckingham is difficult to account for, but that it existed there are dozens of proofs. Either one or the other had a side to his character which the world in general could catch in only fleeting glances. Moreover, the worst of Buckingham's traits had not as yet developed themselves as they were later to do.

There was another person whom Cowley met about this time and with whom the bond of kindred dispositions would seem to be much stronger. And yet this person, too, through Cowley's agency, was introduced to the Duke and was taken up by him and aided to many ecclesiastical appointments. This person was young Thomas Sprat, a youth still at Wadham College, Oxford, and the future biographer and literary executor of the poet.

Giles Jacob, not always a very trustworthy authority, is the source of the only story describing the circumstances under which Sprat and Cowley met;[1] and yet his account, taken in conjunction with one of Sprat's own poems, is so plausible that it is probably correct. The placing of Cowley's poems in the Bodleian must have made considerable stir in Oxford literary circles,

---

[1] Jacob, *Historical Account*, pp. 194–5.

but it impressed no one more than it did young Thomas
Sprat, who, though born seventeen years later than his
hero, already had a literary reputation to maintain. The
son of a small country clergyman, he had come to Wadham to study for orders, had been appointed scholar in
1652, at the age of seventeen, and had taken his B.A.
in 1654. At the time Cowley presented his book, Sprat
was only a year from his M.A., and had often earned
the approval of the warden, Dr. John Wilkins, for his
scientific as well as classical attainments. He and the
boy, Lord Wilmot, soon to succeed to the title of Earl of
Rochester, had already made Wadham famous for wit and
poetry, though most of it had so far been quickly dead.

But Sprat's soul was completely ravished by the
divine writings of the great man who had honoured
Oxford with his gift. There was no doubt in his mind,
as there was in Cowley's, as to which had been the more
honoured by the affair—the poet or the University; and
as a consequence he celebrated the event with a three
hundred line ode, 'Upon the Poems of the English
Ovid, Anacreon, Pindar, and Virgil, ABRAHAM COWLEY
in Imitation of His Own Pindaric Odes.'[1] In flattering
contradiction of the humble tone of Cowley's ode to
the Bodleian, Sprat began his as follows:

> Let all the meaner rout of books stand by,
>   The common people of our library;
> Let them make way for Cowley's leaves to come,
> And be hung up within this sacred room:
>   Let no profane hands break the chain,
> Or give them unwished liberty again.
> But let this holy relic be laid here
>   With the same religious care
>   As Numa once the target kept
>   Which down from heaven leapt . . . .

[1] Perhaps this is the ode which Jacob describes as having been written
when Sprat presented a copy of Cowley's *Poems* to the Wadham College
Library.

Gathering momentum as he went, he gave full rein to his Pindaric steed, letting it plunge with 'headlong haste' from long line to short in the newly invented fashion, spurring it on with learned allusions to Arion, Prometheus, and Amphion, and embellishing it with a panoply of conceits copied from his model. With meticulous care he praised each section of Cowley's book, from its recommendation of sacred poetry in the preface, through the *Miscellanies*, *The Mistress*, the *Pindarics*, and the *Davideis*. From this time on, Cowley was his god and he became a humble devotee.

It was through this ode, according to Jacob, that Sprat made the acquaintance of Cowley, 'who liked him and his compliment so well that he most effectually recommended him to the patronage of the late Duke of Buckingham, his great benefactor'. If this explanation of their meeting is correct, it is a likely rebuttal of Alexander Pope's story that Cowley's only real love, mentioned as 'Leonora' 'at the end of that good ballad of his on his different mistresses', was the lady who married Sprat's brother. For 'The Chronicle' had been written and printed some time before there is any evidence that Cowley had ever heard of the Sprats, however much he was to have to do with one of them from this point on.

On the other hand, if Pope's tale be admitted for the sake of romance, Cowley had his revenge. Perhaps he did meet his mysterious Heleonora before he had heard of the Sprats, and perhaps he even introduced her to the only brother of his new friend. Perhaps, abandoning hope that the bashful middle-aged poet would ever confess his flaming heart, she finally listened to the protestations of this brother, whose name, curiously enough (though other precedents are known), would seem also to have been Thomas Sprat, according to a comparison of the wills of Bishop Sprat,[1] his wife Helen,

---

[1] In *Some Account of . . . Sprat* (1715).

and his son likewise named Thomas.[1] Perhaps she mar
ried this Thomas, brother of the bishop-to-be. But i
she did so, she had plenty of opportunity to repent he
choice and her impatience. For the only one of th
Sprat family to prosper was Cowley's Boswell, an
when the latter died in 1713 he was compelled to re
commend his brother, along with divers other 'poo
relations', to the generous care of his son, then Arch
deacon of Rochester. Nor have a good many hours o
research revealed the true name of Heleonora, the need
brother's wife. None would know to-day that she an
her husband had lived, if Alexander Pope had not bee
an incorrigible gossip.

[1] See Prerogative Court of Canterbury, 109 Plymouth and 14
Shaller, respectively.

# XIII

## THE RECALL OF THE STUARTS

ON September 3, 1658, Oliver Cromwell, Lord Protector of Great Britain, died at Whitehall—the day being the anniversary of his former triumphs at Dunbar and Worcester. The condition of the realm, like his own health, had changed profoundly since those battles less than a decade before—but not more greatly than it had altered, beneath the surface, since Cowley's return and submission only four years past. Outwardly, up to the day of his death, Cromwell was entrenched as firmly as ever. His autocratic character and power had enabled him to ride down all opposition, to dismiss Parliament when it failed to do his pleasure, to appoint his own judges, levy his own taxes, and direct his armies as he would. He was as great a tyrant, as great an enemy to democratic and representative government, as he had once been a crusader in the cause of the Parliament against the King. But beneath, his government was undermined with countless tunnels of approaching dissolution. The Commonwealth was swarming with factions; only a small part of it was content. Laws had been made and methods inaugurated which could be enforced only by the Ironsides or the iron hand. And no one was left to succeed to the office of 'protecting' England but Cromwell's unambitious son, Richard 'the Little'.

Cowley could see the dangers as well as any one, but not even he could pierce far enough into the future to predict the recall of the Stuarts. He could, however, perceive that Oliver Cromwell was not actually such a great man as he had once believed—or, for a time, had pretended to believe. Signs exist, indeed, that even after the situation became fairly obvious he still delayed

altering his position publicly until he was absolutel
certain how the wind would blow. Wood, for instanc
recorded that Cowley 'made a copy of verses on Oliver
death', implying that they were commendatory ones;
and William Stebbing has even speculated on th
possibility of this poem having later been turned int
prose by its author and put into the mouth of th
Satanic angel in the *Vision* concerning Cromwell whic
Cowley published after the Restoration.[2] Such a hypc
thesis may be a bit too daring, but it should be remen
bered that the old dependable, Edmund Waller, joine
with the two young bloods, Thomas Sprat and Joh
Dryden, to publish a panegyric ode apiece on the dea
Protector in 1659, and that these indiscretions were nc
seriously held against them later. In all his tergiversa
tion, if such it was, Cowley was doing nothing whic
hundreds of his contemporaries were not doing wit
sufficient impunity.

Whatever justification or explanation he made t
himself, he has left a graphic enough picture of th
splendid public funeral by which, on November 23, tl
body of the Protector was carried from Somers
House to Westminster, from which it was remove
after the Restoration and was subjected to all sorts
vengeful degradation. According to the *Vision*, Cowle
although he 'bore little affection either to the memoi
of him or to the trouble and folly of all public pagea
try, ... was forced by the importunity of [his] compar
to go along with them and be a spectator of th
solemnity'. Who composed Cowley's 'company'
unknown, though Sir John Evelyn, who has also left
vivid description of the scene, may have been one. Ce
tainly both men in their accounts regard the event
the same sarcastic manner.

There was [according to Cowley] a mighty train of bla
assistants, among which, too, divers princes in the persons

[1] Wood, iv, ii. 210.  [2] Stebbing, p. 62.

their ambassadors (being infinitely afflicted for the loss of their brother) were pleased to attend; the hearse was magnificent, the idol crowned, and (not to mention all other ceremonies which are practised at royal interments, and therefore by no means could be omitted here) the vast multitude of spectators made up, as it uses to do, no small part of the spectacle itself. But yet, I know not how, the whole was so managed that, methoughts, it somewhat represented the life of him for whom it was made; much noise, much tumult, much expense, much magnificence, much vain-glory; briefly, a great show, and yet, after all this, but an ill sight. At last (for it seemed long to me, and, like his short reign too, very tedious), the whole scene passed by; and I retired back to my chamber, weary, and, I think, more melancholy than any of the mourners.

Yes, Cowley's mind was still wavering between admiration and hatred when he dreamed his dream—and perhaps there was more admiration at this particular moment than he wished to confess later on. His hatred probably really grew as he saw the muddle into which affairs were quickly plunged by 'Richard the Little'. Evelyn's account, which was much richer in detail, on the other hand displayed no melancholy in its author's mind, as the entry in his diary will show:[1] 'It was the joyfulest funeral that ever I saw, for there were none that cried but dogs, which the soldiers hooted away with a barbarous noise, drinking and taking tobacco in the streets as they went.' And for this spectacle the state paid £60,000.

The speedy realization of Richard Cromwell's approaching failure as ruler probably hastened Cowley's critical sense and, according to the 'Advertisement' preceding the *Vision* as finally printed, he planned a series of three discourses which would show England her present and future miserable state—two to be in the form of dreams and the other to be 'after the manner of the prophetical threatenings in the Old Testament'.[2]

[1] For Oct. 22, 1658.
[2] Loiseau has discovered in the British Museum, which has no copy

The last two he never completed—or even started, for
new developments in the political situation intervened.
Instead, perhaps to furnish distraction for himself in his
forebodings and anxieties, he turned again to comedy, a
form of writing which he had totally neglected since
his revising of *The Guardian* in the old Cambridge days.

There are two clues as to the time and circumstances
surrounding the inception of this new project. First,
Pepys, in his diary for December 16, 1661, stated that
the play was 'made in the year 1658'—a fact which is
partially confirmed by the phrase on the title-page of
the printed edition of 1663: 'The Scene London, in the
Year 1658.' In the second place, in his preface, Cowley
wrote that, finding himself 'for some days idle, and
alone in the country', he decided to occupy the time by
rewriting the old *Guardian*, which had never satisfied
him. The result was *Cutter of Coleman-Street*, a
thorough revision of his juvenile comedy, which would
seem to differ considerably from the former revision
which he had made and lost after the college performance before Prince Charles. The cast of *Cutter* clearly
does not correspond with the changes which, according
to the 1656 preface, he made in his play following his
initial dissatisfaction.

The spirit of *Cutter* is quite plainly anti-Puritan, but
on the other hand it is none too obviously pro-Cavalier.
The playwright is, in a way, making comic capital of
both parties and holding up neither to any special
admiration. This attitude would accord rather well

of the ordinary 1661 edition, a pamphlet with the same text but with
a different title-page and preface. The title-page reads: *The Visions
and Prophecies concerning England, Scotland, and Ireland, of Ezekiel
Grebner, Son of Obadiah Grebner, son of Paul Grebner, Who Presented
the Famous Book of Prophecies to Queen Elizabeth*. Although this work
was also published by Herringman in 1661, Loiseau considers it, with
its preface describing Ezekiel Grebner and the plan of the book, to be
an earlier form of the *Vision*, showing Cowley's intentions of once
becoming a pamphleteer in the Royal cause.

with his state of mind during the brief Protectorate of Richard the Little, when he saw the ruin lurking beyond every new political turning; whereas if he had written the play after the Restoration, as is supposed by most critics except A. W. Waller,[1] he would probably have been a bit more careful not to hurt the sensibilities of many of the newly rehabilitated gentry. Why, moreover, should he have selected 1658 rather than 1660 or 1661, when no portion of the plot actually demanded the earlier date? It is likewise fairly certain that Cowley was still living in Kent in 1658 (that is, 'in the country'), whereas there is no evidence that he had begun his final withdrawal from London, after the Restoration, until the early part of 1662. Pepys's phrase, 'made in the year 1658', may therefore be at least tentatively accepted, as representing a piece of gossip which he may have picked up around the theatre on the night of the performance three years later. In 1658, however, Cowley could have considered his comedy as nothing but closet-drama, written for his own diversion and having no likelihood of production.

One other project, which he embodied in writing, was high in his mind about this time—and one which reflects more credit upon him than some of his more obscure manœuvres. This had to do with the movement which eventually led to the establishing of the Royal Society of London for Improving Natural Knowledge and which was one of the most important scientific activities of the day.[2]

Since 1645 a small group of men had been meeting, usually at Gresham College, London, for the purpose of holding discussions and performing experiments of a scientific or pseudo-scientific nature. The name by which they went, 'The Invisible College', would suggest that the society was built on hermetic or even Rosi-

[1] Ed. of *Cowley*, ii. vi.
[2] Cf. Sprat's and Birch's histories of the Royal Society.

crucian models, but actually there seems to have been nothing of a mysterious character connected with it. During 1648 and the following years, some of its members being at Oxford, a series of meetings were held in the home of Dr. Wilkins, of Wadham, and in this way Thomas Sprat grew interested in it, though he was still too young to become a full-fledged member. At the same time, a considerable interest in educational reform manifested itself in England—most of it laying a new stress on 'natural philosophy' and experimental science rather than on the old humanities and dialectics.

Cowley himself had shown this interest in educational institutions and methods in the passage which he had devoted to the Hebrew Prophets' College at Naioth, in the first book of the *Davideis*. He now planned to digest all his new ideas on the subject and put them into a plan or prospectus for the founding of a 'Philosophical College' just outside of London—a college which would base its curriculum and methods properly on 'things' rather than 'words', on observations rather than preconceptions, just as Harvey had done. The general idea may have come to him from various sources. In 1648 William Petty had published *The Advice of W.P. to Mr. Samuel Hartlib for the Advancement of Some Particular Parts of Learning*. Of course, Francis Bacon's Utopian description of Solomon's House in the *New Atlantis* would also suggest itself, especially to any one who knew Cowley's admiration for the great Lord Chancellor. And even though Cowley specifically disclaims such a source, Bacon's influence nevertheless appears in a few places, such as Cowley's classification of knowledge (with divinity excluded from the same sort of rational examination as is given to science), his sketch of the gallery and museum which would be found in his second quadrangle, his plan to have four of his twenty professors continually travelling through Europe, Asia, America, and Africa in order to keep in

:ouch with all discoveries there, and his specification
:hat the curriculum should include 'all things contained
n the Catalogue of Natural Histories annexed to my
Lord Bacon's *Organon*'. Almost simultaneously with
Cowley's writing, too, Evelyn was drawing up a scheme
ınd sending it in a letter, dated September 3, 1659, to
Robert Boyle the chemist, already a member of the
Invisible College'. All of these plans had their central
features in common.

But it is with Milton's well-known tractate *Of Education* (1644) that Cowley's *Proposition* challenges most
comparison. It seems extremely unlikely that the latter
writer could have been unfamiliar with the former
work; certainly the two men had a mutual esteem for
Samuel Hartlib, the English-Polish writer on education
ınd agriculture, to whom Milton addressed his pamphlet and Cowley later alluded with admiration in his
essay, 'Of Agriculture'. The two also agreed that the
contemporary school system not only wasted too much
:ime in its attempt to teach Latin and Greek rhetoric
ınd barren logic to immature minds but also began at
the wrong end, inasmuch as it commenced with abstract
words and ideas instead of with things and objects.
Cowley, however, stressed this point rather more than
Milton did, as he also did the teaching of agriculture;
but otherwise on these matters the two were in clear
ıccord. Both men would similarly not neglect the
bodies of their students for their minds; but above all
both would inflame their boys with a love of and a
pleasure in the pursuit of genuine knowledge.

On the whole, as Hurd was to point out, Cowley's
plan was 'better digested' and 'less fanciful' than
Milton's.[1] His estimates of salaries and operating
expenses were worked out to the last pound. His
buildings were laid down with the meticulous enthu-
iasm of all amateur architects. His provisions governing

[1] Hurd, *Cowley*, i. 185, n.

academic tenure and appointments, the relationship
between instructing staff and trustees (or 'governors')
weekly faculty meetings, frequent written reports o:
progress of accomplishments in experiments, celibacy
devoting time to other pursuits in addition to regula:
teaching, and similar matters, all show that he realizec
many of the problems which still persist in university
life. Nor would Cowley's curriculum put quite such a
strain upon his two hundred young pupils (they woulc
enter the school at about thirteen years of age) a
would Milton's, which, as the latter himself said of hi
desired teachers, 'will require sinews almost equal tc
those which Homer gave Ulysses', and which guaranteec
to make Sir Philip Sidneys, if not greater paragons, o
all students who would remain in his school fron
twelve to twenty-one years of age. For althougl
Cowley suggested that his students be shown anatomy a
a 'divertisement', he had self-control enough not tc
suggest (as Milton did) that, in addition to the standarc
subjects, the boys 'may easily have learned, at any odc
hour, the Italian tongue', have mastered Hebrew as a
side course in theology ('Whereto it would be no im
possibility to add the Chaldee and Syrian dialect')
and have absorbed a knowledge of fugues and sym
phonies in the 'interim of unsweating themselve:
regularly, and convenient rest before meat'. The sani-
tariums of to-day could probably not have held the
patients which would have been made if Milton'
scheme for making 'brave men, and worthy patriots
dear to God, and famous to all ages' had been adoptec
by the government. But Cowley's *Proposition* woulc
have turned out some able scientists, who at the same
time would not have been ignorant of the arts anc
humanities.

This scheme Cowley seems to have worked out in al
its details and then to have entrusted the manuscript tc
some friend of his—who is not otherwise known thar

A SCENE FROM *CUTTER OF COLEMAN-STREET*

by his initials, 'P.P.'—to keep until further directed. So, at least, the dedication of the *Proposition* when printed some two years later would indicate. For Cowley was again leaving England. Sprat's account is as brief and as tantalizing as usual: 'Yet, taking the opportunity of the confusions that followed upon Cromwell's death, he ventured back into France; and there remained in the same station as before, till near the time of the King's return.'[1]

There is, indeed, nothing to prove that Cowley crossed the Channel before Richard's abdication on May 25, 1659. By this time Buckingham, after irrepressibly fomenting a new Presbyterian plot, had been released from his resulting imprisonment in the Tower and at Windsor, on his father-in-law's security of £20,000, and had had sufficient opportunity, in spite of his word, to set on foot new plans for the recall of Charles and his own pardon for his errors in judgement. Markham, indeed, states—without overt· evidence— that Cowley accompanied the Duke during his enforced stay at Windsor Castle and helped provide entertainment there.[2] This might easily have been the case.

Various questions, however, have been raised at different times as to the motives lying behind Cowley's return to France, when he might as well have remained in England with Buckingham. Nor is Sprat's facile description of the episode to be accepted at quite its face value, with its implication that the poet resumed his service under Jermyn and the Queen Mother on the old terms. There is even a suggestion of 'bond jumping' in the affair, though no details concerning the ultimate disposal of Scarborough's guarantee have been discovered. Three alternative explanations seem to lie open: either Cowley had his bondsman's consent to

---

[1] Sprat, 'Account'. Sprat's 'De Vita' states that Cowley returned to France 'Paulo post sub Cromvellii mortem' and remained 'usque ad . . . Caroli . . . reditum'. [2] Markham, p. 374.

break the terms of his contract; or the 'confusions that followed Cromwell's death' were so great that he expected to escape detection and forfeiture of bail;—or else there was some new consideration which made the other consequences quite negligible in the light of its greater importance.

The mystery is at least partly solved in a series of letters found by C. H. Firth in the Carte MSS. at the Bodleian in 1893.[1] Oddly enough, this discovery has been overlooked by practically all of Cowley's critics and biographers, and the speculation as to what happened there in France has gone on as before.

This correspondence involves the most prominent and influential members of the little court which was now bubbling with new hopes of power and felicity in its native land, from which it had been so long separated. Not only do the names of Charles and Jermyn figure conspicuously therein, but the glittering title of the Marquis of Ormonde adds itself to the list, and Mart Clifford appears as a messenger and intermediary.

Whether Cowley was actually summoned to France by Jermyn when the recall of the Stuarts seemed certain is a question which cannot be positively answered. But there is an undercurrent running through the letters which suggests that the poet's conduct throughout was dictated by his old friend and master, who saw the necessity of Cowley's re-establishing himself in Charles's good graces after those rather shady activities in Puritan England. But the process of re-establishment did not prove quite so simple as the King's generally forgiving nature and present difficult situation might have led every one to believe. For Charles had either found time himself to read the volume of poems which Cowley had set loose three years before, or some of the officious busybodies always to be found near every influential

[1] MSS. Carte 30, ff. 515, 517, 518; and 213, ff. 598, 634; printed n *Academy*, xliv. 296.

person had at once rushed it to his attention. This volume, it will be recalled, not only contained several poems of a very ambiguous import, but—more important because the meaning of prose is less capable of 'interpretation' than that of poetry—it was introduced by a preface which, in Charles's opinion, was prejudicial not simply to his interests but to his person and even his life.

The letter which Cowley wrote from Paris on the day after Christmas, 1659, to Ormonde, at the royal headquarters at Brussels, seems honest and candid enough:

My Lord:

Having been told by Mr. Clifford of the favourable expressions your Excellency was pleased to make concerning me, I think it very unfit either to omit or defer my most humble thanks for them. It was a consolation that came most seasonably to relieve in some measure that great affliction which His Majesty's displeasure had brought upon me. And as your Excellency's former goodness might justly give me hopes of it now upon this occasion, so that of his Majesty gave me so little fear of this misfortune, as made it fall more heavily upon me. For I did not believe it had been possible for me ever to do anything even by mistake (so far was I from evil intentions) that might give offence to his Majesty, whose service I always accounted the chief duty, and favour the chief happiness, of my life. But though I am fully satisfied in conscience of the uprightness of my own sense in those [two] or three lines which have been received in one so contrary to it, and though I am sure all my actions and conversation in England have commented upon them according to that sense of mine, and not according to the interpretations of others, yet because it seems they are capable of being understood otherwise than I meant them, I am willing to acknowledge and repent them as an error, hoping that his Majesty, to whom God has given so great and necessary occasions of clemency and a bounty of nature fitted and proportionable to them, and who appears so ready to forgive his most outrageous enemies, will pardon the slip of that man's pen in one expression, who calls Almighty God to witness that he never did, spoke, or thought, anything to the prejudice either of his Majesty's person or interests, and who on the contrary has made it the whole business of his life according to the utmost of his capacity to serve both. And I do so far, my lord, comfort myself with the opinion of your belief in this point that I hope you will please to represent it to his Majesty, and do therein not only a great justice in respect of my innocency, but in regard too of my present trouble of mind, the greatest charity to,

My Lord,

Your Excellency's most humble and most obedient servant,

A. Cowley.

Paris, Decemb. 26, 1659.

Ormonde, however, though protesting his high esteem of the 'correspondence and conversation' he had had with the poet, was not fully convinced of Cowley's sincerity, as his reply of January 17 proves. The King, he gracefully assures the petitioner, is doing himself an injury in depriving himself of the other's services, but nevertheless will not be persuaded to a reconcilement unless a clean breast of the affair is made. The marquis, perhaps remembering Hyde's letter to him three years before, therefore advises his correspondent either to furnish some new and plausible interpretation of the offending lines in the preface and 'find means by some address to the King to make it as public as those lines have been', or else to frame 'an ingenuous and frank recantation', which will certainly please his friends and probably have the desired effect on the King.

For over a month Ormonde waited in vain for an answer to his suggestion. He wrote to Jermyn, voicing his perplexity, since he had undertaken the affair on the latter's instigation. To an unprejudiced reader of the correspondence, the delay would imply that Cowley and his master were doubtful as to which course should be pursued. The poet had already recanted once too often, and it was possible that an insistence on complete innocence would eventually be more effective than an

admission of guilt. This plan, at least, was the one finally
adopted, and on February 19 Jermyn wrote to Ormonde
to tell him that a second letter had been drawn up—a
letter in which Cowley 'is far from justifying the error
of his words of his preface; he only justifies himself from
the malice of them and he cannot do otherwise without offending God and his own conscience, for without
doubt he had no malice'. And the baron closes on a
peculiar personal note by stating that he needs Cowley's
private service for himself if his own service to the King
is to be of any value.

The new letter must have been a slight improvement
over the old, though the King was far from being
pacified by it. But it seemed to be the best apology he
could get, and he grudgingly decided to allow Cowley
to resume his former duties with Jermyn. Even yet,
however, according to Cowley's letter of gratitude to
Ormonde, dated March 2, the poet dared not 'venture
to write to his Majesty' and was forced to confine himself to the hope of kissing the royal hands 'about a
month hence at London'.[1]

This blissful day, nevertheless, had to be postponed a
month or so longer than he had estimated. On March 29,
1660 (Charles's thirtieth birthday), the new ruler,
having been proclaimed King three weeks before in his
absence, reached London and was received with wild
acclaim by all factions, from the steadfast Royalists to
former Parliamentarians like Monk and Fairfax, the
latter of whom Buckingham claimed to have won over
to an active support of the Stuart cause. On May 31,
Cowley, again in England and perhaps recalling the
earlier royal ambition for a public statement of loyalty,
published his nineteen-page-nineteen-stanza Pindaric,

[1] A letter from Col. Robert Whitley to Nicholas, Mar. 9, 1659/60,
in *Nicholas Papers*, iv. 195, also quotes Davenant to the effect that
Charles had actually refused to give his hand to Cowley to kiss, in spite
of the solicitations of Jermyn, who presented him.

'Ode, upon the Blessed Restoration and Return of his Sacred Majesty, Charles the Second,' in which he inquired ironically,

> Where 's the impostor Cromwell gone ?
> Where 's now that falling star, his son ?

and compared the returning monarch to the ideal hero of epic poetry:

> So when the wisest poets seek
> In all their liveliest colours to set forth
>     A picture of heroic worth
> (The pious Trojan or the prudent Greek),
> They choose some comely prince of heavenly birth
>     (No proud gigantic son of earth,
> Who strives t' usurp the god's forbidden seat);
> They feed him not with nectar and the meat
>     That cannot without joy be eat.
> But in the cold of want, and storms of adverse chance,
> They harden his young virtue by degrees;
> The beauteous drop first into ice does freeze,
> And into solid crystal next advance.
> His murdered friends and kindred does he see,
>     And from his flaming country flee.
> Much is he tossed at sea and much at land,
> Does long the force of angry gods withstand.
> He does long troubles and long wars sustain,
>     Ere he his fatal birthright gain.
>     With no less time or labour can
>     Destiny build up such a man
>     Who 's with sufficient virtue filled
>     His ruined country to rebuild.

In this style Cowley, along with the rest of England, welcomed the King whose family he had served so long and arduously in·France. If he had seemed to waver in his allegiance for a while, so had thousands of others in the crowd which had cheered the former exile—and Charles, in his general amnesty, had promised to sink all the past in oblivion. Cowley's fortunes, aided by his mighty ode, were, he thought, like those of England, to enter on a new phase from this moment.

Edmund Waller, however, had anticipated Cowley by getting *his* congratulatory ode displayed in the book-stalls and sold upon the streets one full day before his less clever and more ingenuous rival's.[1]

[1] Hill, Johnson's *Lives*, i. 12; quoting Masson, *Milton*, vi. 12–13.

# XIV

## 'THE MELANCHOLY COWLEY'

AND so back they trooped—the whole gay, seedy crew, resolved to compensate themselves for their years of penury and discomfort abroad. Buckingham, of course, through his alliance with Fairfax, was already living in all his old style, and Jermyn, whom malicious rumours still credited with being the Queen Mother's lover, if not husband, in spite of her new life as a religious, had never forsaken his favourite luxuries. His immediate elevation to the title of Earl of St. Albans, however, gave him greater opportunities for display than ever before. Henry Bennet, Cowley's diplomatic correspondent, returned with the stragglers a few months later, and was at once rewarded by being made Keeper of the Privy Purse, a position which enabled him to prosecute with ease and enthusiasm his commissions as chief pander to the priapean monarch. So satisfactorily, indeed, did he execute these duties, especially with Lady Castlemaine, that he was made Baron Arlington in 1663. Assisting him was another of Charles's self-made favourites, Baptist May, familiarly known throughout the country as 'Bab May' and styled frankly by Pepys, himself none too puritanical in morals, a 'court pimp'. May, a relative of the Charles May whose name appeared frequently in Cowley's letters from Paris, was appointed Registrar in the Court of Chancery in August 1660, but proved such a good pupil to Bennet that he succeeded to the Privy Purse in 1665. Rochester, the Killigrews, Davenant, Hobbes, and dozens of others were taken up by the King and, for varying causes, loaded with marks of his favour.

What wonder, then, that Cowley confidently relied on a similar recognition and guerdon for his past services? 'Plenty he sowed below, and cast about him light', he wrote of Charles.

> For every tree and every herb around
>   With pearly dew was crowned,
> And upon all the quickened ground
> The fruitful seed of heaven did brooding lie. . . .[1]

What mattered his momentary weakness and temptation? Even Waller, aided by his nimble tongue and wit, had been readily forgiven, for when Charles had rather sharply asked why his ode on the Restoration was inferior to his earlier one on Cromwell he had replied, with his usual effrontery, 'Sir, we poets never succeed so well in writing truth as in fiction.'

The royal purse-strings, however, loosened themselves none too promptly when Cowley's own pockets were in their vicinity, although there were sufficient signs of relaxation to lure him into continued hope. For instance, the fellowship at Trinity from which the Puritans had ejected him might now naturally return to him. It still had seven years to run before he would be required to take orders. It was a small plum, to be sure, but attractive enough as a stopgap to an impecunious poet with almost nothing in his purse. Charles saw the justice of this request (the granting of which would of course cost him nothing), and in January 1660/1, commanded the college to reinstate Cowley in his appointment, as the following entry in the Admission Book of Trinity, dated February 11, 1660/1, shows:

Whereas we received a letter from his Majesty dated the last of January in the behalf of Mr. Abraham Cowley, fellow of Trinity College, for the continuance of his seven years before taking holy orders, in regard of his being ejected immediately after his taking degree of Master of Arts, in those troublesome times, we have thought it good to record this in our conclusion book, that it may be considered as a special case, and so his

[1] Cowley, 'The Complaint'.

Majesty makes it expressly in his letters, and not to be drawn hereafter into example.

H. Ferne.

The payment of dividends thus authorized by the Vice-Chancellor began in 1661 and continued until the third quarter of 1667, being terminated only by the poet's death.[1]

The Savoy, however, was the richest plum upon which Cowley had his eye.[2] In fact, he had been watching it intermittently ever since the first Charles had written his wife a letter from Oxford promising her the appointment for her protégé. On January 30, 1653/4, moreover, Charles II had confirmed his father's grant in writing, and after the Restoration had similarly assured St. Albans that the Earl's former secretary should have the place.[3]

But promises came easily to the new king, who was immediately faced with the problem of finding sinecures for several times as many applicants as there were places. And promises, even if unfulfilled, were much more useful for keeping doubtful persons in good humour than downright refusals would be. There was unquestionably much competition for the Mastership of the Savoy, even though the foundation had fallen into considerable decay during the Commonwealth. Dr. Thomas Warmstry was a strong candidate, for he was supported by General Monk; and Dr. Gilbert Sheldon, prebendary of Gloucester and former Warden of All Souls, Oxford, was another. Cowley seems never to have had a real chance. Sheldon also boasted a promise of the place during Charles's exile, and in 1660 was allotted a whole string of appointments, among which was the Mastership.[4]

[1] Cf. Lumby, pp. xvii–xviii; and Hill, Johnson's *Lives*, i. 5, n.
[2] Lloyd, [*Memoirs*,] p. 620, quoted by Peck, *Collection*, p. 82, n., says that Cowley also tried for the Charterhouse.
[3] See below.                [4] Cf. Loftie, *Memorials of the Savoy*.

The news was a blow to Cowley, but he did not despair, for he saw Sheldon made not only Dean of the Chapel Royal but also, within a year, Bishop of London. Obviously, one man could, or should, not continue to administer so many offices. So, when the story of a new appointment commenced to circulate even while Sheldon was holding the famous Savoy Conference on the Prayer Book at his lodgings in 1661, he resolved to press his case once more. That he had powerful rivals, he knew, and so, looking back into the past as well as on into the future, he drew up the following analysis of his claims, which is still preserved in the State Paper Office: [1]

Abr. Cowley's Case concerning the Mastership of the Savoy.
His Majesty of blessed memory, when he was at Oxford, promised in a letter to the Queen that he would bestow upon Abraham Cowley the Mastership of the Savoy as soon as the disposal of it would come into his power.
His Majesty (whom God long preserve) gave him a warrant for the said Mastership bearing date Jan. 30, 1653.
His Majesty at his coming into England was graciously pleased to confirm the said grant by word of mouth to the right Honourable the Earl of St. Albans.

> If it be said that the late King
> had formerly promised the place,

That is only said; but the other grant is under the hand of two Kings.
Secondly, it is humbly conceived that the promise of giving any small preferment is satisfied by the giving other great ones instead of it.

> If it be said that the place
> belongs only to a Divine,

First, there are several precedents to the contrary.
Secondly, it is affirmed by good lawyers that the statutes require no more but Deacon's orders.

[1] Chas. II, vol. xlvii, no. 94; see also Cal. State Papers, Dom., 1661–2, p. 210.

Thirdly, it is a royal foundation, and the King's pleasure is legally a dispensation of the statute.

Fourthly, Holy Orders are so far from being necessary for the execution of the Master's office that even the Minister's place there has been lately suppressed.

Fifthly, if it be thought fit that the Mastership should be appropriated and annexed to the clergy, yet it is humbly conceived to be but reasonable that the person who hath the present right should have equal compensation for the loss of it.

> Notwithstanding all which the
> said Abraham Cowley, having missed
> of the said Mastership or any
> compensation for it, his case is this:

That he, having had the honour during all the times of distress and banishment to serve her Majesty the Queen Mother, the late King of blessed memory, and his Majesty (during all his abode in France, without ever putting him to one penny's expense) in matters of considerable trust and labour, and having by his Majesty's happy restoration seen all men else who had served abroad in the like kinds, rewarded with profitable employments and honours, nay, almost all his old contemporaries at the University before, advanced far above him at a time when all the preferments of three nations were disposed of at once, hath been so far from being able to get any share therein that all which he had in the world (and that no great fortune, yet the reward of twenty years' service from two Kings) hath been taken from him without any the least recompense or consideration for it, and he not only ruined by the hope thereof, but exposed to the shame of a general interpretation that this could not have happened to him but either as the punishment of a great criminal or the casting away of a most worthless person.

A 'great criminal' or a 'most worthless person'? No one, not even Charles himself, would accede to this hyperbolic alternative. A 'little criminal' or a 'slightly tainted person' would probably better suit the situation. The King seems certainly to have regarded Cowley in such a light. The story is told that about this time Cowley actually broached his case to the Lord Chan-

cellor, the faithful and wise Edward Hyde, who had
been created Earl of Clarendon in 1661. After hearing
the poet's petition for some preferment or reward for
his services and sufferings for the King, the Chancellor
turned upon him a severe countenance and said, 'Mr.
Cowley, your pardon is your reward'.[1]

Anthony à Wood asserted that Cowley failed in his
solicitations because of 'certain persons, enemies of the
Muses'; and many, commenting on the episode, have
wondered why Clarendon, who in his *Life* stated that
Cowley had 'made a flight beyond all men' and even
excelled his master, Jonson, should in this case be an
enemy of the Muse's representative.[2] The Chancellor
was of course no admirer of Buckingham, St. Albans,
Arlington, and the poet's other friends in the King's
private circle, but his nature was far above allowing
personal animosities of this kind to sway his actions
toward individuals only indirectly related to them. Dr.
Humphrey Prideaux, thorough-going Anglican and
Tory, seemingly quoting the anecdote from some unknown source some sixty years later,[3] offered what would
seem to be the commonly accepted explanation of
Wood's phrase [4] and Clarendon's rebuke. It was the un-
lucky ode on Brutus, and the other poems of that period,
even more than the 1656 preface, which made the King
continue to avert his face, for he was still living in some
fear that the fanatical supporters of the dead Republic
might make an attempt against his life. Charles could
forgive affronts, lampoons, pasquinades, and anything
having to do merely with his private character. He
could even pretend to forget all that had been said

[1] See Prideaux, *Judgement*, pp. 41–2, quoting some unknown
source.
[2] Cf. Wood, iv, ii. 210; Disraeli, *Calamities*, i. 61; Stebbing, p. 63;
Gough, p. xx; Lumby, p. xix; Clarendon, *Life*, i. 34.
[3] See Prideaux, above.
[4] For additional comment see unsigned letter to Wood in MS.
Rawlinson, D. 912, f. 562.

or written in championship of his enemies. But he could not forget incitations which might endanger his personal safety. The existence of Cowley's Pindaric was a perpetual reminder to the disaffected that assassination was a method which had been used in the greatest days of Rome to rid the state of a ruler objectionable to part of the populace.

Moreover, another incident had happened just about this time which, all undeservedly, had strengthened the opposition of the 'enemies of the Muses' toward Cowley. For among the first steps taken by the Cavaliers in their thirst for amusement and distraction was the re-establishment of the theatre—and Cowley had a satirical comedy among his manuscripts, as well as a long-standing ambition to invade the professional stage.

The monopoly of the legitimate drama was invested in two playhouses, to which Charles had issued patents (although the final closing of that monopoly was not completed until January 15, 1663). One company, the King's Servants, in 1661 still acting at Gibbons's Tennis Court, was directed by Thomas Killigrew; the other, at the Duke's Theatre, remodelled from Lisle's Tennis Court in Lincoln's Inn Fields (also known colloquially as 'the Opera'), had as manager and patentee Cowley's old friend, Will Davenant. The intimacy of the two is satirized in a stanza from one of the many burlesque elegies composed upon Davenant's death in 1668 and his reception in Elysium:

> Cowley a fair apartment keeps:
> Receiving him with joy he weeps;
> Into his bed Sir William creeps,
> And now in Abraham's bosom sleeps.[1]

But in 1661, Sir William, unchanged as yet by his vicissitudes of fortune, was on the lookout for plays to

[1] Quoted in Bradley and Adams, *Jonson Allusion Book*, p. 338.

fill his playhouse. Cowley had an unproduced comedy. The answer was foregone, and *Cutter of Coleman-Street* was put into rehearsal, after being slightly refurbished and fitted with a few new topical allusions. Whether the share (really the half-share) in the theatre which the playwright disposed of in his will was acquired before or after this event, cannot be ascertained, but the reference in the prologue to ten plays, some revised and some original, which depended on the fate of his own for their production, would suggest that he possessed some private information as to the situation in Davenant's playhouse.

The probability that Cowley, even at this time, was in the intimate confidence of Davenant is increased by a document recently discovered by Leslie Hotson and printed in the appendix of this book.[1] In the records of a Chancery suit filed in 1691 [2] by Alexander Davenant, Sir William's scapegrace son, appears the following passage:

. . . the said Abraham Cowley being an ingenious man and well skilled in poetry, and a familiar acquaintance with the said Sir William Davenant, he the said Sir William Davenant did take his assistance and judgement in writing, correcting, and providing tragedies, comedies, and other poetic entertainments for the stage; and in recompense for the said Mr. Cowley's pains therein did voluntarily permit and suffer him, the said Mr. Cowley, or such as he appointed (but only at the will of him, the said Sir William Davenant), to take such half share of the profits of the said stage during the life of the said Sir William Davenant.

Young Davenant's claim that Cowley's half-share (out of an original total of fifteen shares) was for Davenant's life only, may be dismissed in the light of the later history of that share, which passed into the possession of John Hervey. In fact, Hervey's daughter, in the same

---

[1] Appendix no. 7.
[2] Printed 1687 by error in Hotson's book, p. 221.

lawsuit, stated her belief that Cowley had been Davenant's partner since the beginning of the enterprise and not only held his share under the original paten but also was co-lessee of Dorset Garden with Davenan for a number of years. Whatever the truth of thi opinion of Dame Hervey's, more significant is Alexande Davenant's statement that Cowley had been acting ii the recognized capacity of literary adviser at the Duke' Theatre, and was therefore a person of considerabl power and influence in the theatrical world of the earl Restoration. For these services his half-share, wort between £300 and £400, must have yielded him, accord ing to Hotson's figures,[1] slightly under a pound and half weekly for the usual thirty-three weeks of th season—or between fifteen hundred and two thousan dollars a year in present money. The conservativenes of this estimate is indicated by Dame Hervey's statemen that she believed Cowley to have had a 'fixed interes of three pounds *per day* 'for all the days the playe acted in the said theatre'—an incredible figure. Alex ander Davenant's estimate of the dividends due o this share between 1680 and 1690 is based on a retur of twelve guineas a month, but even this sum is con siderably above Hotson's calculation founded on othe information. At any rate Cowley was deriving a rathe snug income from his association with the drama durin the Restoration.

The cast selected for Cowley's own proposed con tribution to the prosperity of the theatre was of th very best.[2] Colonel Jolly was to be acted by Thom Betterton, already recognized as close to the leadin actor in England; Aurelia was assigned to Mrs. Bette ton, who occupied among the actresses a positic similar to her husband's among the men; and Noke soon to become the most popular of the low comedian took the comic character of Puny. The rest of the cast, as recorded in the *Roscius Anglicanus* of Downes, the prompter of the house, was likewise of the best quality. Davenant spared no pains to give his friend's play a success.

Affairs, however, went wrong from the first.[1] For some reason, real or manufactured, the King could not attend the initial performance, and this fact was of considerable importance, since Cowley could tell from various signs and rumours that his effort was not to be judged without prejudice by the audience. As he wrote later, he was forced to conclude that 'there was something of faction against it'. Finally, a misfortune occurred which prevented him from even attending the premier in person: one of his brothers died, and he therefore felt compelled to remain at home.

Thomas Sprat, however, was of course to be counted on as a competent proxy; and the evening of December 16, 1661, found him at Lincoln's Inn Fields in the company of a young man who had been adding new lustre to Westminster School and Trinity College since Cowley had left them—John Dryden. The acquaintance of Dryden and Sprat had been marked several years before by their joint·publication of elegies on Cromwell; but both were now quite as faithful Royalists as they had ever been Republicans. Up in the gallery, also, sat Sam Pepys, with his 'wife, poor wretch', having just come from dinner but nevertheless fuming a bit since, 'it being the first time, the pay was doubled'.[2] Of the personnel of the remainder of the audience on that eventful night nothing is known, except that, according to Cowley's account, a part of it at least would seem to have been 'packed'. But the gentlemen in general, as mirrored with some humour in the play itself, were attired in periwigs, with broad lace bands about their necks, with dress swords at their belts, and high,

[1] Cf. my article, *R.E.S.*, iv. 18 ff.    [2] Pepys, *Diary*, Dec. 16, 1661.

broad-brimmed, befeathered hats in their hands. And these gentlemen, before the play (and during it too), whiled away the time by ogling the ladies, admiring their curled hair, the black stars, lozenges, and half-moons on their cheeks, their silver-laced shoes, and their ear-rings 'bigger than bouncing pears'—nor were they, indeed, above stealing a glance now and then at a particularly low-cut bodice.

Not even the most carping critic could have found anything to cavil at in the opening scenes between the prim and virtuous hero, Truman, Jr., his heavy domineering father, and the sweet and loyal heroine, Lucia —unless, indeed, the peculiar mixture of prose and blank verse was not racy enough for the new taste. The Puritans were properly reviled, and true love was presented in the most insipidly winning of lights. But when Colonel Jolly appeared, with his boon companions Colonel Cutter and Captain Worm, the storm began to threaten. For Cutter and Worm were braggarts, swaggerers, sharpers—'fellows merry and ingenious enough, and therefore admitted into better companies than they deserve, yet withal too, very scoundrels' [1]— riff-raff and hangers-on of the Cavalier party. But many of the audience, perversely blind to the author's intention, as Cowley wrote when he published the comedy later, took the pair as a deliberate attack on the Royal party in England at the end of the Commonwealth, and began to voice their disapprobation of the play 'before they had seen enough of it to build their dislike upon their judgement'. Ignoring 'the perpetual privilege of satire and comedy to pluck . . . vices and follies, though not . . . persons, out of the sanctuary of any title', these 'enemies of the Muses' pretended to see the play as an attack on the whole party, and not on its 'vermin'.

The situation, moreover, was not improved when it

[1] Cowley, 'Preface' to *Cutter*.

was perceived that Colonel Jolly himself, 'a true gentleman, and one both of considerable quality and sufferings in the Royal party', did not appear as 'a fair and noble character throughout', but submitted 'in his great extremities to wrong his niece for his own relief' by plotting with the two impostors to get her fortune. The criticism was a just one—but only if the play-wright had intended to depict 'the character of a hero', instead of 'an ordinary jovial gentleman' whose sense of honour was not at its highest when his own private welfare was deeply involved.

With such a start it was easy to find new fuel for the flames. Some sharp but astigmatic eyes next spied the fact that the play was loaded with 'profaneness', in both words and thoughts. These persons pretended to be shocked by such passages as the troopers' language in the lively drinking scene at the end of the second act, and were horrified when the Prayer Book called for by Jolly was found to be 'all mouldy' when taken from the cabinet. Aurelia, too, was a very free-spoken and none too scrupulous young lady, with a well-developed penchant for darkened passageways and bedchambers; and Deacon Soaker was discovered too often in the buttery. This criticism seemed to hurt Cowley more than any other—more than the reception of the play as a whole—for was he not the poet who had 'en-deavoured to root out the ordinary weeds of poetry, and to plant it almost wholly with divinity'?

The disturbances on the first night, which probably took the usual form of jeers, hisses, and perhaps a missile or two, obscured the good features of the comedy for most of the audience, although Pepys went home and entered in his diary that it was a 'very good play', without saying one word about its wretched treatment. *Cutter of Coleman-Street* was a lively and rapidly-moving comedy, of the Spanish intrigue type then coming into vogue, and with many elements of farce. These things Cowley himself knew, for he was a good critic. If he made errors from a modern point of view, he made them consciously, with a clear understanding of what he was doing.

It was the lot of the faithful Sprat to break the news of the *débâcle* to his distraught friend, who was waiting in the house of death. The atmosphere was not a favourable one for any sort of news, and for this sort least of all. Sprat, therefore, was probably very glad of the support of his friend Dryden, who at this time was as great an idolizer of Cowley as the most extreme enthusiast in England; to him, the poet was still 'the darling of my youth, the famous Cowley'.[1] The burden of their task must have weighed considerably on the two young men, one thirty and the other twenty-six, and dampened their spirits as they approached the building, though they were also undoubtedly curious as to just how their hero would receive their story.

John Dennis has preserved the tale of their reception, giving it on the authority of Dryden himself, since in 1661 Dennis was but a child, into whose head the idea of theatrical thunder, stolen or otherwise, had not yet entered. But by the time that Dryden regaled the eager ears of Dennis with the anecdote, the vogue of Cowley had passed its height, and his remark was edged with an ironical barb:[2] 'The only play that ever Mr. Cowley writ was barbarously treated the first night, as the late Mr. Dryden has more than once informed me, who has told me that he went to see it with the famous Mr. Sprat, now Bishop of Rochester, and that after the play was done they both made a visit to Mr. Cowley, whom the death of his brother had obliged to keep the house, and that Mr. Cowley received the news of his ill success, not with so much firmness as might have been expected from so great a man'.

[1] Dryden, *Essays*, ii. 108–9.
[2] Dennis, in Durham, *Critical Essays*, pp. 131–2.

VERTUE'S ENGRAVING FROM LELY'S PORTRAIT OF COWLEY

What this lack of firmness consisted of, there is no one to tell. One may doubt whether Cowley actually broke down, but one must also remember that this was but one of a long series of disappointments. Nor is it ordinarily human nature to learn of the failure of an enterprise from which one has expected much, and to put it aside with a brave and careless laugh.

But all was not gloom, black as the first night must have looked. Davenant had confidence in the merits of the play, and would not withdraw it. Cowley perhaps tinkered with some of the speeches, such as that of Lucia at the end of Act I, which has all the earmarks of having been inserted for the special purpose of revealing Cutter and Worm in their proper light. As a result, according to prompter Downes's record, the play, being acted so perfectly well and exact', was 'performed a whole week with a full audience'—a not inconsiderable run in those days. Langbaine and Dennis also unite in saying that the later productions met with universal applause.[1] Nor did the comedy die after these performances. The prologue and epilogue 'Added at Court' show that eventually Charles himself lent his countenance to the entertainment which had first amused him almost two decades before.

From this time on, both *Cutter* and *The Guardian* seem to have been fairly popular, though sometimes the titles were interchanged in referring to the later version alone.[2] The real *Guardian*, however, was revived in Dublin in 1662 or 1663, according to Cowley himself—probably at John Ogilby's second Dublin theatre, which he erected in 1662 and which brought him into some passing trouble because he enticed one of Davenant's actors to desert the Duke's company and join his own. *Cutter* was given again at Lincoln's Inn Fields on August 5, 1668, under the older name; was revived

[1] Langbaine, *Dramatic Poets*, p. 81; Dennis, quoted by Genest, i. 40.
[2] See *R.E.S.*, iv. 20, for basis of following account.

on October 5, 1702, under both titles; was given a ne
prologue to be spoken by Pack and was transferred
Drury Lane on August 1, 1711; and received its fin
recall on November 1, 1723, at the original theatr
Two records, dealing with performances of a *Guardic*
at court on November 17, 1672, and January 8, 167
probably pertain to Cowley's play; and there are son
untrustworthy references to other revivals. At ar
rate, Cowley's one excursion into the profession
theatre held the boards for over sixty years—a recor
not to be despised—and if other causes had not di
couraged him in most of his work he might have gor
on to further comedy-writing with considerable succes
For in this field of literature he had plainly told himse
that he was to conduct his pen, not as a poet, but as
man who had observed ordinary life penetratingly ar
who knew how to make others as well as himself lau;
at its absurdities.

In the meantime certain influences were being p
into action on Cowley's behalf in another quarte
Though the King remained hard of hearing, all of t
available plums did not lie within his control. Cowley
staunchest friend in the government was St. Albar
and the latter's staunchest friend in the royal fami
was Henrietta Maria, who herself had some cause to
grateful to the poet. Now the Queen Mother, althou;
on her return to England she had had to be compensat
in money for the loss of some of her dower lands, st
held the title to many rich estates and manors, whi
could be leased to her favourites for the very trivi
rental fees of ancient reigns, and which could then
re-let or farmed by the lessee with a very satisfacto
profit.

On the first of January, 1661/2, having return
temporarily to France, she sent her warrant to S
Peter Ball, one of the commissioners over her jointu
estates, to make a conveyance of a goodly portion of h

lands in the County of Kent to 'Abraham Cowley, of
the City of London, Esq.'—'for and in consideration of
the good and faithful service done and performed to her
said Majesty by the said Earl of St. Albans and at his
suit and nomination'.[1] The right to these lands, as it
happened, had been forfeited not long before by Robert
Tichborne, one of the regicides, who on the Restoration
of the Stuarts had naturally been attainted of high
treason. As a result of this warrant from Henrietta,
Cowley came into possession of 'all that lordship or manor
of Oldcourt and all lands, meadows, pastures, marshes,
and tithes unto the same belonging or therewith enjoyed
in East Greenwich and West Greenwich in the County of
Kent with their and every of their rights, members, and
appurtenances whatsoever, and also the ballast wharf
there and all other lands, tenements, and hereditaments
whatsoever in East Greenwich, West Greenwich, Deptford, Lewisham, Kidbrooke, Chaleton, Woolwich, and
Beckenham in the said county of Kent, late called
the Queen's lands. . . .' This property, which also included the parsonage of Greenwich, Cowley and his
heirs or assigns were to 'well and sufficiently repair,
support, scour, cleanse, and maintain'—'as well all the
houses, buildings, walls, and coverings as all the hedges,
ditches, fences, enclosures, shores, and banks'. Failure
to make these 'necessary reparations' or to pay the
'ancient rent' within the stipulated period was to result
in the forfeiture of the lease, which was otherwise to
run for eight or nine years—the residue of the grant to
the former occupant. And the rent which made Cowley
master of this estate was six pounds, thirteen shillings,
and fourpence yearly![2]

[1] See appendix no. 4.
[2] The next extant record involving this land is to be found in L. R.
Enrolments (Kent, &c.), 1/117, f. 51. This grant, dated July 15, 1676,
leases the property for ninety-nine years to Sir William Boreman, described as 'the present tenant', for the same rent as Cowley was to

Whether or not he ever occupied his 'lordship' in person is not ascertainable. His exact dwelling-place after the triumphant re-entry of Charles made him for some time a suppliant and hanger-on of the court is doubtful. The 'fruitful part of Kent' where he had pursued his botanical studies during the late Commonwealth may indeed have been near Greenwich or Deptford, and he may have kept his residence there. In Deptford, especially, members of his family were to be found. His brother Thomas was with little doubt the Thomas Cowley who was Clerk of the Cheque there, for the former's will [1] reveals a strong partiality for that town, not only leaving twenty pounds to the poor of the parish and constituting Dr. Breton, minister there, one of his two executors, but also mentioning his cousin, James White, 'late of Deptford'; moreover, the Thomas Cowley who was Clerk of the Cheque administered his duties at Deptford regularly from 1660 to 1667, but in the latter year—in which the poet's brother appeared in Chertsey to inherit Abraham's estate—the name vanishes from the Deptford records.[2] Since John Evelyn also lived in the vicinity, there is little doubt that

pay. Its description of the past history of the land, now part of the possessions of Queen Catherine, does not tally exactly with that in Cowley's indenture, but states that the manor of 'Old Court' was 'demised' by Henrietta Maria to John Hervey of Ickworth on February 25, 1660/1. Cowley's name is not mentioned, except perhaps by implication in the protective clause beginning: 'And notwithstanding the ill reciting of the said several indentures, leases, or grants, or of any other lease, demise, or grant heretofore made of the premises or of any of them to any person or persons whatsoever....' Nor is Hervey's name mentioned in Cowley's indenture. But, in any case, Hervey was one of Cowley's chief patrons, and it is very unlikely that he would put any obstacles in the way of the poet's using his grant, especially since this was of later date than his own.

[1] See appendix no. 3.
[2] Cf. Cal. State Papers, Dom., and Pepys, *Diary*, Nov. 18, 1663. Loiseau, however, thinks that this Thomas Cowley and the stationer were different persons. But could not one man have been stationer and clerk simultaneously?

Cowley was well known in both Greenwich and Deptford, even if he did not actually dwell there during all
this period.

On the other hand, Sprat's statement that in 'his last
seven or eight years' Cowley 'was concealed in his beloved obscurity' is clearly an exaggeration.[1] The poet
was often in London during at least the first part of that
interval, and the indenture between him and the Queen
Mother definitely described him as 'of the City of
London, Esq.' If he had no bachelor domicile of his
own in the metropolis, he probably made the home of
one of his brothers his head-quarters—at least until the
end of 1661, when, according to Dennis's story, one of
these brothers died. This likelihood receives some confirmation from a letter written to Evelyn by Cowley
in 1667, in which the latter asked to have a book
sent to 'my brother's house (that was) in the King's
Yard'.[2]

The name of this particular brother is not known.
He was, however, probably the last survivor of the immediate family, except Thomas and Abraham, for no
others are mentioned in the latter's will in 1665. The
old and dearly loved mother must have died some
years before, and the many elder brothers and sisters all
passed out of sight. Their numerous descendants,
many of whom preserved the names of their relatives in
their own, were most of them named in the wills of both
Abraham and Thomas, whose family spirit remained as
stout as even their father's had been. The house in
the King's Yard had probably been associated with the
Cowleys for a long time—in fact, it was not unlikely the
building in Fleet Street which Aubrey thought to be
Abraham's birthplace. For the 'King's Yard' would
seem to be an abbreviation of the 'King's Head Yard'.[3]

[1] Sprat, 'Account'.                [2] Letter of May 13, 1667.
[3] Cf. G. Cunningham, *London*, p. 244; and contrast P. Cunningham,
Johnson's *Lives*, i. 94, n., and Stebbing, p. 65.

In the seventeenth century, a King's Head Tavern certainly stood on the north side of Fleet Street near Chancery Lane, at the same corner with what is now No. 192. Here Cowley must have spent much of his time, if it were not actually his residence during the first years of the Restoration. Alexander Pope, however, told his friend Spence that Cowley had lived at Battersea before taking up his abode in the first of his homes that can be referred to with assurance, at Barn Elms.[1]

Wherever Cowley lived during the early 'sixties, this hitherto undiscovered Oldcourt indenture, which was officially signed on January 20, 1662/3, and was receipted by Henrietta on February 12, after it had been duly enrolled before the auditor of the County, would indicate that the poet was not so entirely forgotten as he and his friends implied. He was, however, indebted to St. Albans for the grant rather than to the King—or even the Queen Mother. His poem, 'On the Queen' Repairing Somerset House', may nevertheless have sprung partly from his desire to express some of his gratitude for her share in the transaction, although his rival, Waller, also celebrated with similar verses the occasion of her second return to England and the reestablishment of her Roman chapel at her former dwelling-place.[2] There is, however, a suggestion that the words of thanks which the newly restored palace is supposed to address to its royal mistress may be underlaid by the more personal feeling of Cowley himself.

And certainly he was much more interested in the Savoy appointment than in the managing of such property as had come into his possession. For the Savoy was a sinecure, which would necessitate very little labour on his part and would leave him plenty of time

[1] Spence, p. 285.
[2] Loiseau notes that both these poems were registered on Nov. 2 1664; see *Transcript of Registers, 1640-1708*, ii. 349.

or his writing, whereas the manor of Oldcourt would involve him in many anxieties and much personal oversight.

He had little confidence in the achieving of the former longings, however. The general effect of *Cutter of Coleman-Street* had been to confirm the suspicious feeling of the government toward him. Even though he kept himself in alinement with the favourites, such as Colonel Samuel Tuke, by composing a commendatory prologue for the latter's much bepraised tragi-comedy, *The Adventures of Five Hours*, on January 8, 1662/3, he could not overcome the impression he had made. Charles himself had suggested the adaptation to Tuke, and Pepys thought *Othello* 'a mean thing' in comparison with the result.[1] Dryden, too, though making fun of it,[2] was influenced by it. Cowley, therefore, was in the best company. But it was too late. The King had made up his mind, so far as the Savoy was concerned. He had obligations to the Killigrew family to satisfy. Thomas was already a Groom of the Bedchamber. Henry, who had tried to be a dramatist and had then through some obscure channels entered the Church, so far had nothing of any importance. And Lady Shannon, the sister of the two, was a beautiful and approachable woman who had caught Charles's roving eye. Therefore, early in 1663, Dr. Henry Killigrew was appointed Master of the Savoy to succeed Bishop Sheldon, and the new incumbent speedily effected the ruin of the institution, while his sovereign effected the ruin of his sister.[3]

Cowley's state of mind over the whole affair is revealed in one of his best known poems, 'The Complaint'. From this time on, he was 'the melancholy Cowley', as he had thoughtlessly dubbed himself in his lament. He

[1] Pepys, *Diary*, Aug. 20, 1666.
[2] In his preface to *The Wild Gallant*.
[3] Loftie, pp. 144-53.

showed himself transported in a vision back to Cambridge, within 'a bow'r for sorrow made'; and there the Muse, in 'a wondrous hieroglyphic robe', appeared to him and reproached him for his past:

> When I resolved t' exalt thy anointed name
> Among the spiritual lords of peaceful fame,
> Thou, changeling, thou, bewitched with noise and show,
> Wouldst into courts and cities from me go;
> Wouldst see the world abroad, and have a share
> In all the follies and the tumults there;
> Thou wouldst, forsooth, be something in a State,
> And business thou wouldst find, and wouldst create:
>    Business! the frivolous pretence
> Of human lusts to shake off innocence;
>    Business! the grave impertinence;
> Business! the thing which I of all things hate;
> Business! the contradiction of thy fate.

Sparing him nothing in her reminders of the foolishness of his course, she recalled how all but himself had profited from the Restoration, and how he had lost the Savoy, 'The Rachel, for which twice seven years and more' he had served. Yet even when thus baldly confronted with his dilemma, Cowley was unable to resist the perpetual temptation of hope for future favours. He turned on the Muse whose Hannibal he was to have been and mildly remonstrated with her for teaching him 'The Court and better King t' accuse'. Hers, after all, was the guilt for having tinctured his mind with her art while he still lay innocent in the cradle. Regretfully he concluded:

> Whoever this world's happiness would see,
>    Must as entirely cast off thee,
>    As they who only heaven desire
>    Do from the world retire.

His error, his 'gross mistake', was that he had made himself a 'demi-votary'. He had tried to divide himself

between business and art—but he laid the blame on art.
And he ended:

> Kings have long hands, they say, and though I be
> So distant, they may reach at length to me.

'The Complaint' is a depressing document, for it
shows its author in one of his worst lights. Instead of
standing up manfully and accepting his fortune, he is
still willing to palter, conciliate, and flatter. Ready to
abandon court and city life, he is careful to leave the
door on the latch against a possible return. He is weak
when a perfect hero would have been strong. But none
knew better than he how infrequent perfect heroes are,
except in odes and epics.

The spectacle of a leading poet's abasing himself in
this fashion aroused considerable comment. Even the
satirists seem to have been a little saddened by it,
although Cowley was far from alone in his errors. Not
long after this time an anonymous imitation of Suckling's 'A Session of the Poets' was circulated, and later
printed in Dryden's second miscellany. The first
stanza of this satire ran:

> Apollo, concerned to see the transgressions
>   Our paltry poets do daily commit,
> Gave orders once more to summon a sessions,
>   Severely to punish the abuses of wit.

After malicious attacks on Davenant, Buckingham,
Sprat, and others, the unknown critic mournfully
turned his attention to Cowley:

> Savoy-missing Cowley came into the court,
>   Making apologies for his bad play;
> Every one gave him so good a report
>   That Apollo gave heed to all he could say;

> Nor would he have had, 'tis thought, a rebuke,
>   Unless he had done some notable folly:
> Writ verses unjustly in praise of Sam Tuke,
>   Or printed his pitiful Melancholy.

# XV

# THE 'INVISIBLE COLLEGE', HERBS, AND SAINT-ÉVREMOND

WHEN he 'printed his pitiful Melancholy', Cowley had probably already embarked on his scheme for retiring from public life and was living at Barn Elms, just outside of London. The two or three years before he is found here, however, saw the appearance of several works which he had prepared some time earlier. Immediately after the seating of the Stuarts, the gentlemen of the 'Invisible College', now known as the 'Society for the Advancement of Experimental Philosophy', determined to abandon their former obscurity and to make their group the leading element for scientific and intellectual progress under the new regime. Consequently they transferred their head-quarters from Wadham to their previous location at Gresham College, London, and set about canvassing the situation for desirable members, as well as beginning the formulation of the aims of their new society. As early as November 28, 1660, the name of 'Dr.' Cowley was included in a tentative list of persons likely to be interested in such an organization,[1] which already boasted the eminent names of Robert Boyle and Christopher Wren, and was soon to supplement these with Kenelm Digby, whose stay abroad had not at all tamed his exuberant imagination; Charles Scarborough; and Isaac Newton—not to mention the more dilettantish and literary luminaries such as Buckingham, Waller, Evelyn, Denham, Henry More, Tuke, Dryden, and Charles Howard.

Therefore, on February 13, 1660/1, Cowley was proposed for membership, and after a lapse of two weeks, according to the custom, was elected on the fourth of

[1] Birch, *Royal Society*, i. 4.

March.[1] The records, however, peculiarly enough fail to show that he was ever admitted, which was the next regular step in the procedure, or that he attended any of the meetings. This neglect to take advantage of an honour which undoubtedly flattered him greatly and which also bore witness to his standing as a scientific man as well as a wit can be explained only by assuming that he was so much occupied with his suits to the King and other such concerns that he found himself unable to make the required trips to Gresham College. And when a list of Fellows was drawn up and presented to Charles at the time of the granting of the second charter in 1663, Cowley's name was absent.[2]

The poet's keen interest in the Royal Society, as it soon came to be called, appears clearly, however, in *A Proposition for the Advancement of Experimental Philosophy*, which he had written some two or three years before and had apparently left with his friend 'P.P.' for printing during his own stay in France. A copy of this document, in either manuscript or printed form, was perhaps the 'design of founding a college for the promoting of physico-mathematical experimental learning' which, according to the journal of the Society, was discussed after the general meeting of November 28, 1660. At any rate, when 'P.P.' finally issued the *Proposition* he prefaced it with a short address 'To the Honourable Society for the Advancement of Experimental Philosophy', in which he requested that they examine the plan and make 'such additions and alterations' as they should 'think fit', before 'recommending the practice of it to the nation'.[3]

But it also happens that some of the copies of the *Proposition*, bearing the same date as the others, carry a second title-page, with a second title, *A Proposition*

[1] Ibid., i. 16, 17.
[2] Ibid., i. 17, 239; ii. 222. Lumby, p. xx, is in error on this point.
[3] Cf. also Sprat, *Royal Society*, pp. 59–60; Birch, *Royal Society*, i. 17, n.

*for the Advancement of Learning*, and a quotation from
Virgil, 'O fortunati, quorum iam moenia surgunt!'
What reason could Cowley, or his agents, have for these
two differing forms ? Certainly the new page would indicate that the 'walls' of the Society were already rising.
Perhaps, therefore, a few copies of the pamphlet in its
first form were struck off and placed privately before
the members of the group for criticism; then, later, the
new page was added and the work was put at the disposal of the general public.

At any rate, Cowley's plan seems to have been known
to several of London's leading intellectuals before the
pamphlet was officially offered for sale by Henry Herringman in June 1661.[1] For on April 1 Dr. John Worthington
in a letter to his friend Samuel Hartlib inquired, 'What
is meant by that in the news-book, of Dr. Cowley's
proposition for advancing experimental philsophy ?'—
a question to which Hartlib answered, the next day,
'Dr. Cowley's Proposition I have taken special notice of,
but have not as yet seen the book.' On June 24, however, Worthington wrote, 'What doth the society at
Gresham College ? Dr. Cowley's book of Proposals for
the founding of a Philosophical College is dedicated to
them'—whereupon Hartlib replied, 'That which you
mention about Dr. Cowley's Book of Proposals will
oblige me to take more notice of him.' This interchange
may be regarded as a fair specimen of the sort of attention Cowley's work was attracting.[2]

The actual amount of influence exerted on the Royal
Society by the *Proposition* is difficult to estimate. If
Sprat, who was elected to membership in 1663 and was
appointed historiographer soon afterward, may be believed, Cowley's book was of major importance. 'While
they were thus ordering their platform, there came

[1] Kennett, *Register*, i. 489.
[2] See Worthington, *Diary and Correspondence*, i. 284–5, 293, 339,
342.

forth a treatise which very much hastened its contri-
vance: and that was a Proposal by Master Cowley, of
erecting a Philosophical College.'[1] While admitting
that in the two instances of the amount of endowment
required and the addition of educational duties to those
of research the plan was perhaps slightly visionary,
Sprat insisted that otherwise the school was 'every way
practicable', and concluded, 'His purpose in it was like
himself, full of honour and goodness: most of the other
particulars of his draft the Royal Society is now putting
in practice.'

Thus Boswell. On the other hand, Hartlib wrote as
follows to Worthington on August 26, 1661: 'I hear
nothing of Dr. Cowley's Design of a Philosophical
College. I apprehend the Society meeting at Gresham
College is too wise to be thus publicly directed.'[2]
Perhaps both Sprat's friendly puff and Hartlib's ironical
remark may be discounted a bit. Cowley undoubtedly
was regarded as a person of consequence by the members
of the Society itself. His fame and his learning would
make his opinions of value in any such enterprise, and
he had many friends in the group. In simple words, his
project was too ambitious; and the Society had no
funds with which to embark on this or any other advanced educational experiment.

In 1661 likewise, Herringman, at his shop at the sign
of the Blue Anchor in the Lower Walk of the New
Exchange, displayed copies of *A Vision concerning His
Late Pretended Highness, Cromwell the Wicked*—a title
which was later changed to read: *A Discourse by
Way of Vision concerning the Government of Oliver
Cromwell.*[3] The publication of this work, which had
been composed some two or three years earlier, has

---

[1] Sprat, *Royal Society*, pp. 59–60.      [2] Worthington, i. 366.
[3] In the 1668 collected edition. The 1661 edition was registered on
Oct. 29, 1660, as *The Visions and Prophecies concerning England, Scotland,
and Ireland*; see *Transcript of Registers, 1640–1708*, ii. 281.

been regarded as another of Cowley's steps toward mollifying the King, and yet if this was his intention he failed to make it clear to the general public, since the book was issued anonymously.[1] Again, his methods of procedure would seem to have been defective.

But these little brochures were prose. With the exception of his Restoration ode, Cowley—so far as the public was concerned—had kept his five-years-old vow to make himself 'absolutely dead in a poetical capacity'. The itch, however, had remained upon him, and he had continued to salve it privately with both English and Latin verses. Yet the distemper persisted—in fact, it swelled and spread until he saw no other way of allaying it except by seeking an outlet in print. And the work which he selected to open the vein was, interestingly enough, none of his English poems, such as the elegy written 'Upon the Death of the Earl of Balcarres', or his translations, such as the 'Ode. Acme and Septimius out of Catullus', or even the translations from Virgil (the passage from the *Georgics* later included with the essays probably being one of them) which the letter sent from 'Orinda' to 'Poliarchus' on August 20, 1662, shows he had put into familiar circulation.[2] Instead, he chose an original composition in Latin, which he entitled *A. Couleii Plantarum Libri Duo* when he published it in 1662.

It is a significant fact that after his ardent championship of religious poetry in 1656 Cowley wrote no other verse of this nature, with the exception of 'Christ's Passion', an ode based on a Greek original by Masters, of New College, Oxford—and by its position this ode would seem to have been written almost simultaneously with the appearance of the 1656 volume. Of this apostasy Cowley was painfully conscious, as his preface to his new book clearly revealed.

[1] This fact has passed almost unnoticed, perhaps because the *Vision*, like the *Proposition*, is now extremely rare.     [2] Philips, *Letters*, p. 68.

Three charges, he foresaw, might be laid against him.
First, he would be accused of instability, of desultoriness,
since, after only 'a day or two's journey', he had left
'mighty matters'—that is, the *Davideis*—but a third
finished. This charge he answered by tacit admission of
having tired of his subject. 'I thus employed myself'
(in the words of Nahum Tate's translation of the Latin) [1]
'not so much out of counsel as the fury of my mind; for
I am not able to do nothing, and had no other diversion
of my troubles; therefore through a wearisomeness of
human affairs to these more pleasing solaces of literature
(made agreeable to me by custom and nature) my sick
mind betakes itself; and not long after from an irksome-
ness of the selfsame things, it changes its course and
turns off to some other theme.'

Second, he would be reproached as a renegade and
traitor to the very cause he had crusaded for. 'When
thou thyself, say they, hast thus declared with the
approbation of all good men, and given an example in
thy *Davideis* for others to imitate, dost thou, like an
apostate Jew loathing manna, return to the leeks and
garlic of Egypt ? After the appearance of Christ himself
in thy verse, and imposing silence on the oracles of
demons, shall we again hear the voice of Apollo from
thy profane tripod ?' This charge demanded a more ingenious defence, for no matter what Cowley's mind was
groping toward, his heart never abandoned its conventional piety. And the answer which he evolved for
having taken plants for his subject and treated them
partly in the mode of classical authors, was this: 'I
esteem that which celebrates the wonderful works of
Providence not to be far distant from a sacred poem.
Nothing can be found more admirable in nature than
the virtues of several plants; therefore amongst other
things of a more noble strain, the Divine Poet upon
that account praises the Deity, "Who brings forth

[1] Published in 1689.

grass upon the mountains, and herbs for the use of man".'

Last, many would ask why he had broken his oath and written at all. To this poser he could do no more than append an imitation of Horace's familiar epistles, which he had composed for his old Westminster and Trinity friend, Robert Creswell, now not only a preacher 'Whose thundering sermons make the pulpit shake' but also a versifier in his own right. In short, Cowley admitted that he had no excuse. In spite of thrice taking hellebore and exercising all other precautions when the moon shone upon him, he was unable to escape the madness borne upon her rays. Understanding and forgiveness were all that he could request.

These two books on plants, which were actually two books on herbs, were the chief result of Cowley's scientific studies in Kent. According to a marginal note in the preface, they were written 'paulo ante foelicissimum Regis reditum'—that is, probably in 1659. He had been led to their composition by a wonder as to why, with such a copious and attractive body of material, none of the great poets had chosen to display, in verse, their veneration for plants. They had loved the gardens, the fields, and the woods, but they had failed to celebrate in any detail the herb life with which these were populated.

As a matter of fact, however, Cowley's own work, or poetical herbal, is written from the medical rather than the botanical point of view. The problem immediately arose as to how such seemingly barren material could be made interesting, and not remain a mere collection of versified facts; and he reached his solution, not in any highly original manner, but by a simple personification. The first book became a rather miscellaneous budget, in which such plants as maidenhair, sage, wormwood, scurvy-grass, duck's meat, and rosemary each spoke in monologue and revealed its uses and virtues, as well as many of the classical and vulgar old wives' tales associated with it. The second displayed more invention, inasmuch as it was unified by dealing wholly with, as Tate phrased it, 'such chiefly as come under the female province and are serviceable in generation or birth', and also had a thread of narrative running through it. According to the imaginary situation, an assembly of all the herbs of this nature in the 'physic garden' at Oxford was called by their president, mugwort, who thereupon led the discussion of their various problems, powers, and difficulties. After pennyroyal, plantain, birthwort, laurel, myrrh, and others had spoken, the meeting was suddenly surprised and broken up early in the dawn by the unlocking of the gate by the distraught gardener, Robert, who had come to gather sowbread for his wife, who had prematurely fallen into childbirth.

All these little treatises, some serious, some humorous, some instructive, some entertaining, Cowley embellished with diverse bits of quaint herb lore or with erotic tales drawn from Ovid and Catullus. Pliny and Fernelius, too, furnished him with annotations and authority for statements which he felt might otherwise be regarded as too imaginative and incredible; and references to other more scientific works were introduced in marginal notes. As for Cowley's Latin style, Sprat wrote: 'The two first books treat of herbs, in a style resembling the elegies of Ovid and Tibullus in the sweetness of the verse, but excelling them in the strength of the fancy and vigour of the sense.'[1] Few have questioned Cowley's Latinity. It was an ability on which he had always prided himself, and which he had not been able to exercise since the days of his college compositions, his *Naufragium Joculare*, and his *Davideidos*. In fact, while working on his *Plantarum Duo Libri* he must have fancied himself back in his youth, living the bucolic life for which one side of him had always yearned. 'You are not',

[1] Sprat, 'Account'.

he warned his readers, 'therefore to expect in a work of this nature the majesty of an heroic style (which I never found any plant to speak in), for I propose not here to fly, but only to make some walks in my garden, partly for health's sake, and partly for recreation.' [1]

Cowley was very fond of his new little volume, and presented copies of it to several of his friends. The letter which accompanied his gift to the Rev. Dr. Richard Busby, the famous and revered 'whipping master' who had succeeded Osbaldeston at Westminster, shows that Cowley had kept up his connexion with his old school: [2]

Sir,

I should have made you this mean present before, but that I have been out of town; and as some things are too great, so this is too little to be sent far. If I were not well acquainted with your candour, and your particular favour to me, it would be madness to venture this criminal in the presence of so great and so long-practised a judge of these matters. It may be a fitter entertainment for some of your scholars than for yourself, and is a more proportionable companion for the hyssop than the cedars of Lebanon. I ask, therefore, your pardon for this liberty; and am, with great respect, Sir, your most humble and most faithful servant,

A. Cowley.

A second copy went to the Bodleian, and a third—the most interesting of all now extant—to Sir Alexander Fraizer, the personal physician of King Charles. The ornate Latin verses which Cowley inscribed in this book, now in the possession of Mr. John Sparrow, [3] indicate that Fraizer attended the poet during an illness which may have been rather serious and perhaps occurred

[1] Tate's translation.

[2] First printed in *Gentleman's Magazine*, lvii (1787), 847; reprinted in Nichols, *Illustrations*, iv (second series), 395; and sold for £30 at Sotheby's auction on Nov. 18, 1929.

[3] Sparrow, *London Mercury*, xx (1929), 398–9.

while he was composing his botanical works and studying herbs and flowers. The acquaintance of the two
men probably went back to a much earlier period,
since Sir Alexander was very likely the 'Dr. Fraser'
described in Cowley's letter of November 18, 1650, as
having been one of several men banished from Scotland
at that time for an uprising in favour of the young
King.

With the *beau monde* of London Cowley's place was
secure, no matter how he was regarded and treated
politically. His opinion was sought on literary matters,
and his criticisms were considered as more or less
Delphic. Anecdotes were built about them and often
circulated, probably to the accompaniment of knowing
nods and smiles, through the *salons* and fashionable parks.
Seldom, however, was his judgement expressed in any
but the most friendly and kindly of manners. As Sprat
said, 'He never oppressed any man's parts, nor ever put
any man out of countenance'; or, more specifically,
'Quorum mores aut scripta minus probabat, eos non
vituperando aut illudendo sed monendo, favendo, et
etiam laudando corrigebat.' [1] This method is perhaps
best illustrated in the anecdote about Ned Howard,
preserved by both Alexander Pope and the *Tatler*.[2]

Edward Howard was the least endowed of the
brothers of Sir Robert Howard, Dryden's brother-in-
law and the Crites of the 'Essay of Dramatic Poesy',
but his will to be a poet, like Sir Robert's to be a heroic
dramatist, was untamable. The *Tatler* takes up the
story from this point: 'A certain author brought a poem
to Mr. Cowley for his perusal and judgement of the
performance, which he demanded at the next visit with
a poetaster's assurance; and Mr. Cowley, with his usual
modesty, desired that he would be pleased to look a
little to the grammar of it. "To the grammar of it!

[1] Sprat, 'Account' and 'De Vita'.
[2] Pope, 'Letter to a Noble Lord'; *Tatler*, no. 234.

What do you mean, sir, would you send me to school again?" "Why, Mr. H——, would it do you any harm?" '

The mildness of this rebuke may be contrasted with the scathing irony of Sprat's poem, 'To a Person of Honour upon His Incomparable, Incomprehensible Poem, Entitled "The British Princes" '. There is no telling whether or not 'The British Princes' was the poem submitted for Cowley's criticism, but any poem by Ned Howard would have displayed the same qualities.

On all subjects, Cowley was a sensitive man. In one of his essays, for instance,[1] he tells how he had been 'drawn twice or thrice by company to go to Bedlam' and had been expected to enjoy the 'fantastical extravagancies' of the madmen there. But he had always returned home, not only melancholy, but positively sick with the sight. He could never explain the callousness of most human beings to such afflictions.

Cowley's modesty, also, made a strong impression on all of his associates, accustomed as they were to the self-confidence and self-assertion of most of the gallants and poets of their day. Even when, with strange blind spots in his critical vision, he sometimes disagreed with his friends on certain literary matters, he did so gently and quietly. Dryden, for example, tells the story of how Cowley, on the request of the Earl of Leicester (who had come out of his retirement at Penshurst to be sworn a member of the Privy Council), read over the works of Chaucer and declared him 'a dry, old-fashioned wit, not worth reviving'. Dryden, as it happened, was already planning his version of the *Fables*, but this fact did not prevent him from remarking charitably, 'Mr Cowley was too modest to set up for a dictator; and being shocked perhaps with his old style, never examined into the depth of his good sense'.[2]

[1] 'Dangers of an Honest Man in Much Company'.
[2] Dryden, *Essays*, ii. 265.

No, Cowley was not a dictator, not a Dr. Johnson, though he had one of the first Boswells in literary biography. He could dazzle his friends with his pen, but not with his lips. The contrast between his writing and his speaking soon passed into a tradition. Aubrey wrote that Cowley 'discoursed very ill and with hesitation'.[1] Denham's epigram became famous:

> Had Cowley ne'er spoke, Killigrew ne'er writ,
> Combined in one, they'd made a matchless wit.[2]

The twenty-fourth *Guardian* gave the tradition its final form: 'There is not, methinks, an handsomer thing said of Mr. Cowley in his whole life than that none but his intimate friends ever discovered he was a great poet by his discourse.' Perhaps herein lies the explanation of Pope's tale about Cowley's morose behaviour in company toward the end of his life, especially when women appeared. 'In the latter part of his life,' said Pope to Spence, 'he showed a sort of aversion for women, and would leave the room when they came in.'[3] This grumpy conduct Pope attributed to Cowley's 'disappointment in love'; but the whole story lacks confirmation from any first-hand source. Cowley made his best appearance in his private sitting-room, not in audience chambers and reception halls. Faithorne's well-known engraving of him at this period of his life shows him to have been a handsome and dignified gentleman, with a frank and friendly countenance; but the face is not a vivacious one.

Yet the most brilliant men of the day prized his acquaintance, perhaps partly because their own showiness was effectively set off by his reticence. And not the least flashing of these illustrious lights was the French exile, M. de Saint-Évremond, whose eccentric career, jarred from its normal orbit not long before by his

[1] Aubrey, *Brief Lives*, i. 190.
[2] Wood, *Ath. Oxon.*, iv, i. 694.          [3] Spence, pp. 285-6.

embroilment with Mazarin over the terms of the
Spanish treaty, had brought him to London in the train
of the Comte de Soissons for the purpose of felicitating
Charles on his restoration. Saint-Évremond, whose
*libertin* writings and dashing military career as well as
his affair with the celebrated Ninon de l'Enclos had
made him one of the most spectacular figures in Europe,
had naturally been embraced at once by the wittiest
and gayest group in the English court. Many of them
he had already known while they, not long before, had
been exiled in France. It was turn and turn about.
Buckingham, St. Albans, Ormonde, Arlington, Digby,
and the rest of the royal favourites made him one of
themselves. His ignorance of English on his arrival
formed no hindrance to their intimacy, for they were as
much at home in French as in their native tongue. His
wit, his epicurean notions of pleasure, his sceptical
philosophy, appealed to them. None of them but admired his manners, his nimbleness and penetration of
mind, and his delicate way of flattering the ladies
without submitting himself to their power. Just past
fifty years of age, he was still capable of being the *beau
idéal* of many a young courtier who already saw his own
future in Saint-Évremond's past.

The closest of the Frenchman's friends in London
were d'Aubigny and Buckingham. These three, according to the life of Saint-Évremond written by his
friend Pierre Bayle, saw each other almost every day.
It was inevitable, therefore, that Saint-Évremond and
Cowley should become acquainted, since the latter was
also one of the frequenters of Buckingham's house.
Among the 'gens de lettres les plus distingués en Angleterre', wrote Bayle, Saint-Évremond fraternized with
Digby and Hobbes, but more particularly with Cowley
and Waller. For the two poets had 'infiniment de
l'esprit', as plainly appeared in their poetry.[1]

[1] Bayle, *Saint-Évremond*, i. 59; cf. Silvestre, ibid., i. 268.

Though Cowley never referred directly to Saint-Évremond in his writings, the presence of the Frenchman, with his *libertin* doctrines and epicurean leanings, must have affected the impressionable Englishman at this particular juncture in his career. There would be reminders of the philosophical theories of Gassendi and the scepticism of Montaigne—reminders of the natural hedonism which his French sojourn had begun to develop in him years before. The atmosphere of Buckingham's circle, outwardly in orthodox submission to the Established Church, would also foster the same attitude of mind, if not of action. For despite Cowley's constant association with many of the most dissipated of the Restoration wits and gallants, rumour never whispered a syllable against the integrity of his character or the purity of his life. It is in his writings alone that the signs of his moderate epicurean philosophy appear.

One of Buckingham's chief diversions—which he treated in much the same manner as he did his political duties—was the drama. Saint-Évremond also favoured himself as a playwright, in a dilettantish way, and so it was not long before the two, with the help of d'Aubigny, found themselves engaged on a satirical comedy, *Sir Politic Wouldbe, or Le Pretendu Politique*, for which each furnished part of the characters, while Saint-Évremond gave 'la forme' to the whole.[1] Though there is nothing to connect Cowley's name with this enterprise, he must certainly have known about it and taken a diplomatic interest in it, for his liking for the drama was keen.

But whether or not Cowley collaborated in this Anglo-French comedy by offering criticisms or suggesting lines, he very likely had the tip of a finger, if no more, in another of his Duke's dramatic projects of the time. Buckingham loved ridicule; and his sharp tongue and high-handed manner brought him the requisite material

[1] Bayle, i. 59.

in the way of enemies on which to expend it. He also
liked to work in collaboration—for a sneer or a jibe in
one's private study with no one to hear it loses half its
savour. Consequently, in 1662 or 1663 he had commenced the satirical burlesque which still stands out as
among the most amusing of its type in English literature.
*The Rehearsal* was originally directed against poor noseless Will Davenant, with whom the Duke had recently
grown irritated. Before it was produced, almost a
decade later, however, it had shifted its attack to Sir
Robert Howard and then to John Dryden himself; and
six or eight assistants to Buckingham during that period
have been named by different critics at different times.
The Duke, indeed, seems to have conducted a sort of
dramatic carpenter shop, in which characters, scenes,
and lines were shaped, spoiled, finished, or rejected as
in any such establishment. Cowley's part in the work,
indeed, could never have been very great, though his
best friends were deep in it:

> Intelligence was brought, the Court being set,
>     That a Play Tripartite was very near made;
> Where malicious Mart Clifford and spiritual Sprat
>     Were joined with their Duke, a peer of the trade.

So the author of 'Savoy-missing Cowley' wrote in the
fourth stanza of his poem, after having referred to
Davenant in the second.[1] Cowley's name did not
appear in this context. It would, however, be rather
surprising to find him quite absent from a project involving Sprat and Clifford as well as Buckingham, and
the 1712 preface to Waller's poems gives the necessary
clue.[2] For, according to the editor, Waller and Cowley
had also been drawn into Buckingham's undertaking,
as well as 'some other wits', among whom Dr. Johnson
mentions 'Hudibras' Butler.[3] If, however, Cowley did

---

[1] In Dryden, *Second Part of Miscellany Poems*, pp. 89–90.
[2] 'Preface' to Waller's *Poems* (1712), p. 37.
[3] Johnson, *Lives*, i. 282, 368.

To    John Evelyn

Happy art Thou, whom God dos Bless
W^th y^e full choice of theire own Happines!
And Happier yet becaus thou'rt Blest
With prudence how to choos the Best!
In Books and Gardens thou hast plac'd aright
(Things w^ch thou well dost understand;
And both dost make w^th thy laborious hand)
Thy noble, innocent delight;
And in thy virtuous Wife, wher thou again dost meet
Both pleasurs, mor refin'd and sweet,
The fairst Garden in her looks,
And in her Mind the wisest Books,
Oh who would change thes soft yet solid joys
For empty Shows, and senceless Noise;
And all w^ch rank Ambition breds,
w^ch seem such beauteous Flowrs, and are such poisonous Weeds?

A Cowley

A HOLOGRAPH COPY OF COWLEY'S POEM TO EVELYN, WITH
A VIEW OF COWLEY'S HOUSE

lend his comic gifts to his patron, it is to be concluded that his contribution was nominal only. For this sort of personal satire was not at all consistent with his character, and till the day of his death he had only friendship for Davenant, to whom he left twenty pounds in his will.

# XVI

## THE GENTLEMAN GARDENER

BY the beginning of 1663 Fortune had called the turn for Abraham Cowley. It had taken her long to teach him his lesson, but, to his credit, when he finally became convinced of his error, he set firmly to work to remodel his life, undeterred by any contrary, though friendly, advice. To be sure, his plans, in nebulous form, had been gestating for many years. In his boyhood he had pretended to envy Horace and his Sabine cottage. But he had yielded to his academic and patriotic ambitions. During his French exile he had meditated an escape to the American colonies, where he had thought that life could be nourished by reading poetry and philosophy. But when Will Davenant had started off on his expedition to the New World, Cowley was not found as a passenger, a member of the crew, or a stowaway. Now, however, bitter experience had shown him that court advancement was definitely blocked for him; and in addition he had learned that the ways of monarchs and their henchmen are not always those of which even *l'homme moyen sensuel* can approve. His decision was, then, partly the result of necessity, partly the result of desire.

Among Cowley's essays is found one entitled 'The Danger of Procrastination', with the secondary title, *'A Letter to Mr. S. L.'* This essay—which is actually a personal letter, and was probably never intended for publication—was clearly written before Cowley had abandoned the metropolis for ever. 'I am glad', he began, 'that you approve and applaud my design of withdrawing myself from all tumult and business of the world, and consecrating the little rest of my time to those studies to which Nature had so motherly inclined

COWLEY'S HOUSE AT CHERTSEY IN 1797, FROM A SEPIA DRAWING
BY HENRY DE CORT

me, and from which Fortune, like a step-mother, has so long detained me.' After this preliminary he at once went on to defend the virtues of immediate action against the arguments of his mysterious correspondent, whose letter, in spite of its general tone of approval, had advised a 'Festina lente' policy which (with an implication of Royal relenting) might even yet lead to a state described as 'Otium cum dignitate'. But these and 'three or four other more of your new Latin sentences' Cowley overwhelmed with a battery of his own, from Horace, Varro, Caesar, Persius, Martial, and the events of the late Civil War.

> To-morrow you will live, you always cry;
> In what far country does this morrow lie
> That 'tis so mighty long ere it arrive?
> Beyond the Indies does this morrow live?
> 'Tis so far fetched, this morrow, that I fear
> 'Twill be both very old and very dear.
> To-morrow I will live, the fool does say;
> To-day itself's too late, the wise lived yesterday.

This letter is worth attention for several reasons. In the first place, it shows that Cowley is again not looking to the future for happiness, as all good Christians do, but to the present, which, to be sure, soon becomes the past. But the wise man, he preaches (and he tells an anecdote from Epicurus in his essay also), is the one who enjoys his life while he is living it. In the second place, the letter is a definite link between Cowley's epistolary and essay styles, in which the most attractive side of his character is revealed. And in the third place, it would seem to be one of the 'lost' collection of familiar letters which 'spiritual Sprat' later wrote to 'malicious Mart Clifford' that he had suppressed, because he believed that in writings of this private nature 'the souls of men should appear undressed: and in that negligent habit they may be fit to be seen by one or two in a chamber, but not to go abroad into the

streets.'[1] Coleridge was not the first, or the last, to sniff at
the prudery in this literary theory,[2] which Sprat had consciously developed in reaction against the indelicacy—
as he would regard it—of the French practice, which
would be the more likely to publish the correspondence
the more personal it was.

For who was '*Mr. S. L.*'? Certainly he was a definite
person with a definite personality, which is clearly
evolved in the letter. He and Cowley 'love' Cicero
'very much'; they have had friendly arguments about
Persius, 'who, you use to say, you do not know
whether he be a good poet or no, because you cannot
understand him, and whom therefore, I say, I know to
be not a good poet'; and Martial is the correspondent's
'special good friend'. The two initials fit none of
Cowley's known acquaintances, the 'L' being of course
the puzzling letter. 'Mr. S.' would positively shout
'Mr. Sprat', in spite of the latter's avowed scruples concerning the printing of such missives. The literary
tastes are such as a young cleric with an Oxford education and a reputation as a classical scholar would be
likely to have. Moreover, in his Latin life of Cowley
Sprat later used the phrase 'vivendi aliquando *in otio
cum dignitate*' in a description of Cowley's retirement;
and in his English life he admitted that he had for a
while attempted to dissuade Cowley from his hermitical
schemes. Only the 'L' prevents Sprat from becoming
a liar and a hypocrite, although an easily forgivable one.
But in the first folio of Cowley's *Works*, prepared
directly under Sprat's supervision, the 'S.' is in roman
type and the 'L.' in italic. The enigma thereupon grows
more enigmatic, but it might be stated, for what the
fact is worth, that in 1662 Sprat had become prebendary of Lincoln cathedral. Could the letter have been

[1] Sprat, 'Account'.
[2] See my article, 'The Letters of Abraham Cowley', *M.L.N.*, xliii.
369 ff.

addressed to 'Mr. Sprat of Lincoln'? And if it were not written to Mr. Sprat, how did it come into his possession?

The spot to which Cowley betook himself in his flight from 'business' in 1663, was Barn Elms, a quiet old estate across the Thames in Surrey—not far south-west of 'the monster, London', in miles, but quite removed from it in atmosphere in the days when green meadows and pastures commenced to show themselves almost as soon as Westminster and the city walls were passed. The country here was flat and low-lying, but rich and fertile for that very reason; and its flatness was redeemed by the wooded character of the land, which was responsible for the name of Barn Elms. When William Howitt, in 1847, made the sentimental pilgrimage to the place which he describes in *Homes and Haunts of the Most Eminent British Poets*, he found that many of the elms had even then become only large and mossy stumps, but that enough of them, together with old mulberry trees, evergreens, and hedges, remained intact to give an impression of aristocratic antiquity 'almost too goodly for our ideas of the fortunes of a poet' and according 'more truly with the prestige of a successful lawyer'.[1]

Cowley, however, probably never lived in the manor house itself, which at this time was leased to Master John Cartwright. On May 5, 1659, the *Mercurius Politicus* had advertised 'Barn-elms House' as to let, and had suggested that it might be divided into 'two convenient dwellings'. This hint the Cartwrights very probably complied with when they regained their ease after the Restoration. The manor had once been known as 'Queen Elizabeth's Dairy', and had been the scene of various 'rural' entertainments of Elizabeth's court. The names of Sir Francis Walsingham and of the young Earl of Essex were associated with it as those of residents. But Cowley slept among the shadows

[1] Howitt, pp. 71-3.

of none of these great deceased. Although the records of the canons of St. Paul's, to whom the land has belonged since the time of King Athelstan, show no lease of any kind or portion to Abraham Cowley, Howitt found by inquiry that the poet's temporary residence had 'long been pulled down', although the main villa still stood. From the meagre information he could gather, moreover, Cowley's house 'seems to have stood near the present stable-yard', though the 'walls of the old gardens still remain'.[1]

Living in these quiet old grounds, however, Cowley had not entirely cut himself off from the life of which he had wearied. The Elms were still a fashionable resort for courtiers when they wished to seem rustic without too much exertion. Pepys, after rowing up the river one day, 'walked the length of the Elms, and with great pleasure saw some gallant ladies and people come with their bottles, and basket, and chairs, and form, to sup under the trees by the waterside, which was mighty pleasant'.[2] Music, either vocal or on the lute, very likely followed. Orinda's poem, 'Upon the Graving of Her Name upon a Tree in Barn Elms Walks', may have been a result of a stroll along the promenade after a visit to her admired Cowley in the company of Poliarchus, whom she had called her 'Valentine' in a letter not long before. Barn Elms had other uses, too. Five years after Cowley's arrival and one after his death, the Duke of Buckingham met the Earl of Shrewsbury in a duel in the park and killed him, while the Countess of Shrewsbury, in a page's garb, stood by and held the horse of her paramour. It is possible, also, that the house in which Cowley lived was the one which Jacob Tonson, to whom the rights over Cowley's works passed early in the eighteenth century, resided in and used for the meetings of that club of choice wits, the famous Kit Cat.

[1] Contrast G. Cunningham, *London*, p. 26.
[2] Pepys, May 26, 1667.

John Evelyn continued to be one of the poet's most intimate friends, and visited him at least twice at Barnes, as his diary records—once on May 14, 1663, and again on January 2, 1664. And when the two men could not see one another, they were accustomed to exchange notes, and even gifts, having to do with their favourite hobby—gardening. One of these letters was discovered in the well-known chirographer, T. Astle's, collection and printed by Isaac Disraeli in 1812;[1] it is now in the British Museum. Dating his letter March 29, 1663, Cowley wrote in his quaintly formal style:

Sir,

There is nothing more pleasant than to see kindness in a person for whom we have great esteem and respect (no, not the sight of your garden in May, or even the having such a one), which makes me more obliged to return you my most humble thanks for the testimonies I have lately received of yours, both by your letter and your presents. I have already sowed such of your seeds as I thought most proper upon a hot-bed, but cannot find in all my books a catalogue of these plants which require that culture, nor of such as must be set in pots, which defects and all others, I hope shortly to see supplied; that is, I hope to see shortly your work of Horticulture finished and published,[2] and long to be in all things your disciple, as I am in all things now,

Sir, your most humble and most obedient servant,

A. Cowley.

Deference being always one of the most delicate sorts of flattery, it is no wonder that Evelyn called the other his 'excellent and ingenious friend' when mentioning him in his diary.

Cowley was at last, then, realizing his heart's desire. Following his scientific training as a botanist, he was becoming an enthusiastic amateur gardener. In confessing his discipleship under Evelyn, moreover, he took

[1] Disraeli, i. 57–8, n.
[2] Note that Evelyn dedicated the second edition of his *Kalendarium Hortense* to Cowley.

one of the best tutors available in his day, as his reference to the garden at Sayes Court acknowledges. Being, indeed, so eager to acquire the knowledge that he lacked and Evelyn possessed, he went so far as to borrow the manuscript of his friend's *Kalendarium Hortense*, not yet in print, and to transcribe it for his guidance on such precarious problems as had to do with the use of hot-beds versus flower-pots.[1] His heart was set on becoming as much of a horticultural savant as his limited resources would allow.

And after all, taste and leisure are the chief requirements for success in this pursuit, and Cowley now had both. He could experiment with topiary, if he wished, and clip or pleach his hedges into pyramids, peacocks, or gryphons. He could plant sun-dials of flowers opening at the different hours of the day, ending with primroses at dusk. He could cultivate bees, and grow his own honey. In the autumn, according to the directions in Evelyn's 'Acetaria' (a discourse on herb gardens and the making of salads),[2] he could go snailing along the walls under his fruit trees. Or, either for his own epicurean palate or for the connoisseurs among his few visitors, he could concoct a 'sallet' in conformity with Evelyn's own specifications, watching especially 'the discreet choice and mixture of the oxoleon, . . . so as neither the prodigal, niggard, nor insipid' should preside; drying and cleaning the greenage lightly in a cloth so that it should not be bruised; selecting the best Tewksbury mustard for the sauce; mixing the oil and the egg in careful proportions; using naught but a knife 'of silver, and by no means of steel'; and finally placing the whole on the table in a dish 'of porcelain or of the Holland Delft ware'. All should 'fall into their places like the notes in music, in which there should be nothing harsh or grating', wrote Sir John; 'and though admitting some discords (to dis-

[1] See dedication mentioned above.
[2] Evelyn, *Misc. Writings*, p. 765 ff.

tinguish and illustrate the rest), striking in the more
sprightly and sometimes gentler notes reconciles all
dissonances and melts them into an agreeable composition.' Cowley could well have thought of his own
life while manufacturing a salad according to Sir John
Evelyn's prescription.

The withdrawal of England's most famous poet into
such comparative obscurity as that of Barn Elms
naturally elicited considerable comment, which has
never died down. The faithful Orinda, from her rocky
retreat in Wales, straightway penned a profuse Pindaric
'Ode upon Mr. Abraham Cowley's Retirement', in
which she thanked him for having shown her the
hollowness of the world and made her free. But later
opinion—with the natural exception of Thomas Sprat
—was slyly inclined to the belief that Cowley, Aesop-
like, had called the grapes sour because they were in-
accessible. This opinion culminated a century later in
Dr. Johnson, who wrote in the *Rambler* that Cowley's
initial scheme was one 'to which the imagination of a
girl upon the loss of her first lover could scarcely have
given way',[1] and who ended by saying, in his *Lives of
the Poets*: 'Yet let neither our reverence for a genius,
nor our pity for a sufferer, dispose us to forget that, if
his activity was virtue, his retreat was cowardice.'[2]

But Cowley now sincerely regarded himself as beyond
the whisperings of the world, malicious or otherwise.
He could putter in his garden or prune his fruit trees,
read the philosophy of others or write his own into his
copybook, as he saw fit. In the meantime, however, he
had arranged for the publication of some of his older
works which had remained unprinted under his supervision, although they had all been made public in some
form or other. The natural impulse to defend *Cutter of
Coleman-Street* against its maligners had led him to

[1] *Rambler*, nos. 6 and 202. See also *Spectator*, no. 613.
[2] Johnson, *Lives*, i. 10.

prepare a lengthy and eloquent preface, dealing with
the function of comedy in general and the purpose of this
comedy in particular. This preface he had published,
together with the play itself, before October 13, 1663,
since Orinda refers to it in a letter of that date.[1] About
the same time, too, Herringman had brought out *Verses,
Lately Written upon Several Occasions*, with a brief fore-
word explaining that the necessity had been forced upon
the poet by the recent appearance of an unauthorized
edition of these poems in Dublin. And certain it is
that these occasional verses are far from including all
that Cowley had written since 1656, for many new additions to the section were made by Sprat in 1668. On
the other hand, six translations from Horace, Virgil,
Claudian, and Martial were later removed from this
group and assimilated into the essays.

This verse collection was also in the bookstalls by
November, since on the eighteenth of that month
Samuel Pepys entered in his journal, 'I walked home
again, reading of a little book of new poems of Cowley's
given me by his brother.' Since Pepys had spent the
day at Deptford, where in fulfilment of his duties as
clerk of the acts in the Navy Office he had paid off
several ships, the brother was undoubtedly Thomas
Cowley, clerk of the cheque there.

The new sense of freedom springing from his retreat
at Barn Elms produced a sort of reaction, almost of
laziness, in Cowley. He was by no means an old man—
only in his middle forties, in fact—but a natural tendency toward indolence, combined with an opportunity
for indulging it, was too much for him, and he courted
the Muse very infrequently during his two years at
Barnes. He had at last sacrificed the one half of his life
in accordance with her requirements—he was no longer
a 'demi-votary'—but little of his new-found time was
spent before her altar. And what he did dedicate to her

[1] Philips, *Letters*, pp. 194-5.

was mostly but an oblique sort of worship of his new goddess, Flora.

The chief literary result of the Barn Elms period was seemingly the continuation of the work on plants, the third and fourth books of which were concerned with flowers, as the first and second had been with herbs. Moreover, for variety, Cowley selected Catullus and Horace for the models of his verse, as Sprat has perhaps unnecessarily pointed out.[1] There is, indeed, much more diversity of numbers in these two books than in the first two, and the author has selected his effects to harmonize with the freshness and daintiness of his blossoms. And for the essential unifying factor of plot, he has again made use of the conventional debate or disputation motive, and conceived a sort of Court of Flowers, at which Flora, for diversion's sake, would attempt to choose a Vice-Goddess who should rank next to herself. In their seasonal order, then, the flowers (not mortal and perishable, as we know them, but the 'ideas' of flowers, as Plato saw them) presented their claims. In the third book the blossoms of the winter and spring, from 'Helleborus Niger' to the rose, offered their cases, followed in the fourth book by the blooms of the summer and autumn, from the pansy to the amaranth. But, as in the case of the gynecological herbs, the court terminated without a decision: Flora, a Roman goddess, with so many illustrious competitors before her, begged the question by decreeing a 'Respublica Florum', on the Roman model, with two consuls and four praetors to be selected every year. Every flower—as in a true democracy—therefore thinking that she would eventually hold one of these offices, all were satisfied; and the book, given a slightly scientific cast by its annotations from such horticulturists as Parkinson, Lauremberg, and Gerard, was closed.

On June 11, 1664, Cowley was admitted by Cam-

[1] Sprat, 'Account'.

R

bridge 'ad eundem gradum apud nos quo fuit apud Oxonienses'.[1] The degree was probably that of M.D., since Cowley already held his M.A. from his first university. His standing as a scientific man therefore continued to be recognized.

Shortly after this time, he wrote what is perhaps his only extant occasional poem of this period. In March 1664 Mrs. Philips had come up to London with an almost completed translation of Corneille's *Horace*. Her friends were also attempting to persuade her to allow an authorized edition of her poems to be made, but she was so hypersensitive and still so much upset over an unlicensed collection that had been printed just before that she continued to refuse. And then, in June, she was attacked by a virulent form of small-pox. She died on June 22. Cowley showed his grief by his ode 'On the Death of Mrs. Katherine Philips', in which he reiterated his former praises of her beauty, her superiority to Sappho, and her virtue and wit. But more than aught else he associated the theme of friendship with her name. This virtue she had practised so well on earth that she would feel no stranger in heaven, her new 'glad world of poetry and love'.

Artificial and conceited as the elegy is in many ways, it displays some genuine sorrow on Cowley's part, although Orinda had never been as intimate with him as she had with Waller.[2] He must also have looked upon her death with some personal emotion inasmuch as he had himself only recently recovered from the first serious illness he had ever had. On the whole, he possessed an excellent constitution. But the neighbourhood around Barn Elms, though pleasantly attractive in the summer, was not so healthful in the winter. It was rather damp and marshy, and was exposed to the river breezes; and the cold weather aggravated its bad

---

[1] Bliss, quoting Baker, in Wood's *Fasti, Ath. Oxon.*, iv, ii. 210 n.

[2] Note her references in her *Letters*, &c.

qualities.[1] Consequently Cowley soon caught what Sprat called 'a dangerous and lingering fever', from which he never entirely recovered, 'though his mind was restored to its perfect vigour'.[2] On November 18, 1663, after his conversation with Thomas Cowley at Deptford, Pepys wrote: 'Abraham do lie, it seems, very sick still, but like to recover.' But the worst of this first attack was over by January 2, 1664, since on that day Evelyn travelled 'To Barn Elms, to see Abraham Cowley after his sickness; and returned that evening to London'.

Nevertheless, the poet was rightly worried by his experience, and resolved to change his residence as soon as possible. The location of a suitable spot, however, consumed some time; and especially since his two noble patrons were again interesting themselves on his behalf, he did not wish to move too quickly. It was not until the spring of 1665, therefore, that he abandoned Barn Elms and the gardens he had cultivated so lovingly, and established himself at Chertsey, twenty miles farther up the river.

[1] Baker, *Biographia Dramatica*, i. 101.        [2] Sprat, 'Account'.

# XVII

## THE SABINE FARM

FROM an amateur gardener at Barn Elms, Abraham Cowley became, in a modest way, a country gentleman at Chertsey.[1] The story of his 'elevation' is fairly well known, but is tantalizingly vague, if not actually erroneous, in many of its details.

Sprat, as usual, is blandly indefinite: 'But upon the settlement of the peace of our nation, . . . he then obtained a plentiful estate, by the favour of my Lord St. Albans and the bounty of my Lord Duke of Buckingham; to whom he was always most dear, and whom he ever respected as his principal patrons.'[2] There is no recrimination here—not even a hint that the aid was a bit slow in arriving. Both Sprat and Cowley were quick to forget the pinchings of the past in the comforts of the present—and besides, a mere chaplain was much wiser to flatter his immediate patron than to disparage his sovereign.

Wood being almost equally vague, contenting himself with remarking that the 'plentiful estate' was 'a lease of a farm held of the Queen Dowager at Chertsey in Surrey',[3] it is necessary to go to Aubrey's memorandum for the most vivid account of the affair. Aubrey can always be depended upon to dramatize his story, even when he is forced to rely on his imagination for his material. The *Brief Lives* contains two versions of the proceedings, which may be pieced together as follows: 'When his Majesty returned, the Duke of Buckingham, hearing that at Chertsey was a good farm of about . . . *li.*

[1] His name, however, can be associated with the town as early as January 21, 1660/1, since on that date he, with St. Albans and Wintour, witnessed a lease of part of Chertsey Manor to Robert Hembrick and John Brookehaven. See L.R. Enrolments (Kent, &c.), 1/114, f. 44b.

[2] Sprat, 'Account'.     [3] Wood, *Fasti*, in *Ath. Oxon.*, iv, ii. 209-10.

per annum, belonging to the Queen Mother, goes to the
Earl of St. Albans and the commissioners to take a lease
of it.' 'Said the Earl to him, "That is beneath your Grace
to take a lease." "That is all one," quoth he, "I desire
to have the favour to buy it for my money." He bought
it, and then freely bestowed it on his beloved Cowley.'[1]

Just when this transaction was made, or how much
it cost the kind-hearted Duke, it is impossible to say. In
reality, it was probably never made as Aubrey and Wood
described it. Stebbing, too, unless he was lucky enough
to have found the indenture which has escaped every
other searcher's eye, must have been exercising his
fecund imagination when he asserted that Cowley got
'a lease for life' on this manor in 1661, at a rental of
£50 a year.[2] But if Stebbing knew nothing about the
Oldcourt grant, he probably knew nothing about this.
As a matter of fact, the only extant document directly
linking any Cowley with property in Chertsey is one
dated April 2, 1668, and recording that after the
expiration of a term of sixteen and a half years Cowley's
brother Thomas was to be granted a lease of fourteen
and a half years upon the manor known as Chertsey
Beamond, with all its carefully specified pastures,
marshes, dovecotes, and dungcarts. Thomas, however,
never lived to pay the Crown his yearly rental of nineteen
pounds, sixteen shillings, and eight pence, plus thirty
loads of hay and thirty quarters of great oats to be
delivered at the royal barn at Hampton Court or
Oatlands.[3] He survived his brother by only two years.

The probability that the manor of Chertsey Beamond
and Abraham Cowley's domicile at Chertsey were the
same should, moreover, be given strong consideration.
This manor, which was known as both 'Chertsey' and
'Chertsey Beamond' or 'Beaumont',[4] had been granted

[1] Aubrey, *Brief Lives*, i. 189–90.   [2] Stebbing, p. 71.
[3] See L.R. Enrolments (Kent, &c.), 1/115 (vol. 23), ff. 195–8.
[4] For its history, see *Victoria History of County of Surrey*, iii. 406–7.

to Henrietta Maria by Charles I. But on January 29,
1660/1, it had been re-leased for twenty-one years to
Cowley's old friend and patron, John Hervey,[1] who as
it happened might also have been one of the 'commissioners' of Aubrey's tale. Thomas Cowley's indenture,
it will be noted, was to take effect after the expiration of Hervey's term, and its wording would imply
that Thomas was then already dwelling on the farm.
The negative evidence, then, would suggest that
Abraham, unlike his brother, never held a formal lease
to any of the Crown lands at Chertsey, but that he had
simply gone there to live on Hervey's manor, perhaps
paying rent for it himself, or perhaps letting Buckingham do so for him. The reference of Alexander Davenant to a debt owed by Abraham to Hervey is also
worth noting in this connexion,[2] as are the facts that
Sprat said nothing about Chertsey in his allusion to the
'plentiful estate', and that Cowley himself used the
phrase 'a hired house and garden' in his essay, 'The
Garden'.

The missing link is supplied by an indenture dated
almost simultaneously with the arrival of Cowley and
all his belongings in Surrey, but having nothing at all
to do with that county—an indenture which should
considerably modify all future pictures of the last part
of the poet's life, as it would have modified all past ones if
it had been known. For Cowley must have been in quite
comfortable circumstances while he lived at Chertsey.
He had the income from the sale of his various works; he
had a half-share in Davenant's theatre; he had his
fellowship at Trinity; he had Henrietta Maria's grant
of the Manor of Oldcourt to lease for his profit; he
had his farm at Chertsey, which may or may not have

---

[1] See L.R. Enrolments (Kent, &c.), 1/114, ff. 72 b–74 b. Note, also,
that the manor of Oldcourt had likewise been associated with Hervey's
name.

[2] See Davenant's suit against Dame Hervey, in appendix no. 7.

Photograph by F. Frith & Co., Ltd.

CHERTSEY. COWLEY'S HOUSE IN THE 20TH CENTURY

been paid for by one of his patrons;—and he had joint rights in a valuable piece of property in London itself, owned this time not by the Queen Mother but by Charles himself, and deeded to Cowley and his heirs in a perpetual lease, the rent of which was to be met by St. Albans and his descendants.

Among the Land Revenue Enrolments, dated April 1, 1665, is to be found a document labelled: 'A graunte made to Baptist May and Abraham Cowley to them and their heires fforever of the Baylywicke of St. James, &c. ...'[1] The land involved was known, more specifically, as the Pall Mall Field, lying in the Manor of St. James in the Fields, Middlesex—in other words, adjoining St. James Park and the King's own Mansion House of St. James. Bab May, in recognition of his services, was also made Keeper of the Privy Purse in 1665, and his share in this grant has long been known,[2] though for some reason Cowley's has been overlooked. What the staid poet thought of being partner to Pepys's 'court pimp' will never be known, but it may be assumed that the two men did not see much of each other.

This plot of ground, several acres in extent, had had an interesting history. In March 1661 Henrietta's commissioners, headed by St. Albans and Kenelm Digby, had made two indentures, leasing the whole Manor of St. James in the Fields to John Hervey and John Coell for a combined period of thirty-one years. In the next year, Charles had confirmed the Pall Mall Field to be part of the Manor, and had extended their lease on this particular section up to the year 1720. Seemingly the profit from the business was to come from the erecting and renting of 'thirteen or fourteen great and good houses' there, subject to the approval of the King and his agents; but Charles soon discovered that

[1] The enrolment of the above-described patent; found in L.R., Essex, Hertford, Middlesex, &c., 12 (62), ff. 12b–15.
[2] See *Dict. Nat. Biog.* under 'May'.

'men are unwilling to build such great houses for any term or estate but that of inheritance'.

It was here that Cowley and May entered the affair, for 'in consideration of the many good and acceptable services to us done and performed by the said Henry, Earl of St. Albans, and for other good considerations us thereunto moving', Charles granted 'unto our trusty and well-beloved Baptist May and Abraham Cowley', their heirs and assigns, a perpetual lease to fifteen or twenty specified pieces of land within the Pall Mall Field, contingent only upon the regular yearly payment of four score pounds by the Earl of St. Albans or his successors. The implication that Cowley and May would immediately proceed to erect the expected buildings would indicate that the two had money of their own to invest. Certainly it is unlikely that St. Albans would construct the houses as well as pay the rent, merely to please his favourites.

In addition, for the sum of forty shillings a year, Charles granted the same two men, for fifty-five years, the right to lease out to tenants, many of whom had already made such a request, that part of the common highway running between Charing Cross and the Mansion House of St. James which had not already been granted to Sir Philip Warwick and Cowley's old friend, Sir John Denham. The only royal stipulation was that no buildings be erected on any of these pieces of land which might prove 'occasion of annoyance' to the King's own domiciles or prómenades in the neighbourhood.

Finally, the indenture consciously and explicitly refrained from mentioning any set value for the lands leased, but one would conclude, from the tone of the description, that good managers would be able to derive an income of two hundred pounds from them as a minimum, and probably much more.[1]  Alexander

[1] The fact that this indenture was still in force in 1674 is demon-

Pope hazarded the guess that Cowley's total revenue never exceeded three hundred pounds a year.[1] There seems, however, to have been a personal application in Cowley's own remark, in 'Of Greatness', that 'When you have pared away all the vanity, what solid and natural contentment does there remain which may not be had with five hundred pounds a year?' Five hundred pounds a year in the seventeenth century was equal to four or five thousand to-day. Thomas Cowley, Abraham's heir, disposed of an estate of almost three thousand pounds in specific bequests alone. Abraham, indeed, could not have lived in the magnificent style of dukes and earls and king's favourites, but he had no cause to complain. Nor did he ever express himself as acutely dissatisfied, after he had unburdened himself of 'The Complaint'.

As a gentleman farmer, with several tenants under him, Cowley at first found his life a piquant mixture of major joys and minor vexations. But he never lost his sly, mildly ironical sense of humour at his own expense, as all his references to his life at Chertsey testify. His inimitable picture of his disastrous arrival at his new home has been preserved by Francis Peck, in the form of a letter written by Cowley to Sprat on May 21, 1665,[2] and extant only because of a commendable carelessness on the latter's part in failing to destroy all his correspondence, as he had guaranteed to do:

'The first night that I came hither I caught so great a cold, with a defluxion of rheum, as made me keep my chamber ten days. And, two days after, had such a bruise on my ribs with a fall that I am yet unable to

strated by a new lease dated Sept. 10 of that year. In it St. Albans agrees to return the Manor of St. James to Hervey and Coell after several terms then in being should expire. The lease of Cowley and May is referred to several times. See L.R. Enrolments (Essex, &c.), 1/62 (vol. 4), ff. 59–65.

[1] Spence, p. 13.　　　　　[2] Peck, *Collection*, pp. 81–2.

move or turn myself in my bed. This is my personal
fortune here to begin with. And besides, I can get no
money from my tenants and have my meadows eaten
up every night by cattle put in by my neighbours.
What this signifies, or may come to in time, God
knows; if it be ominous, it can end in nothing less than
hanging. Another misfortune has been, and stranger
than all the rest, that you have broke your word with
me and failed to come, even though you told Mr. Bois
that you would. This is what they call *Monstri simile*.
I do hope to recover my late hurt so far within five
or six days (though it be uncertain yet whether I shall
ever recover it) as to walk about again. And then,
methinks, you and I and *the Dean* might be very merry
upon St. Anne's Hill. You might very conveniently
come hither the way of Hampton Town, lying there
one night. I write this in pain, and can say no more:
*Verbum sapienti.*'

These forebodings, however, were not fully realized
Cowley, although weakened by his former fever at
Barnes, did recover from his 'defluxion of rheum' and
even from his bruised ribs. In spite of his bachelorhood
he was seemingly well taken care of, and had a real
affection for his two servants. Though his maid, Mary
never entered into literature as did Herrick's Prue
Cowley left her twenty pounds and all his 'wearing
linen' in his will—the equivalent of three or four years
wages; and his serving man, Thomas Waldron, received
ten pounds 'and most of my wearing clothes at my
brother's choice'. Cowley was a good and kind master
as Sprat's Latin life carefully pointed out.

As for 'Mr. Bois' and '*the Dean*', they must remain
*personae ignotae*. The name Bois appears in Pepys,[1] and
also in the records of St. John's College, Cambridge;
but Cowley does not tell enough about his friend to
allow the drawing of any conclusions. And '*the Dean*'

[1] *Diary*, Aug. 20, 1664.                    [2] See Peck, p. 93 ff.

T, must abide

too, must abide in obscurity, although it is more than probable that he, Sprat, and Cowley later had their picnics on the pleasant, heathy sides of St. Anne's Hill, which commanded the river and the whole level countryside. If the decanal title was not intended simply as a jocose allusion to some mutual friend with ambitions for preferment, it is, however, possible that Cowley was referring to some member of the great Benedictine Abbey at Chertsey, which had even then begun to fall into ruin. Or he may have been the 'Mr. George Ent' who, according to Aubrey, 'lived in his [Cowley's] house at Chertsey in the great plague, 1665', and later showed the antiquarian a copy of Cowley's 'Virgilian Lots' verses in the poet's own handwriting.[1]

The disillusionments of landlordism, on the other hand, continued. Cowley, almost enjoying his own discomfiture, could not keep them out of his writings. 'The Dangers of an Honest Man in Much Company' confesses his stupefaction:

One would think that all mankind had bound themselves by an oath to do all the wickedness they can; that they had all (as the Scripture speaks) sold themselves to sin: the difference only is, that some are a little more crafty (and but a little, God knows) in making of the bargain. I thought when I went first to dwell in the country that without doubt I should have met there with the simplicity of the old Poetical Golden Age: I thought to have found no inhabitants there but such as the shepherds of Sir Phil. Sidney in Arcadia, or of Monsieur d'Urfé upon the banks of Lignon; and began to consider with myself which way I might recommend no less to posterity the happiness and innocence of the men of Chertsey; but to confess the truth, I perceived quickly, by infallible demonstrations, that I was still in old England, and not in Arcadia or La Forrest; that if I could not content myself with anything less than exact fidelity in human conversation, I had almost as soon go back and seek for it in the Court, or the Exchange, or Westminster Hall.

[1] Aubrey, *Anecdotes*, pp. 109–10.

This recurring mood was the result, as much as anything else, of the feeling that, after all, any improvements or reforms which he might make in his lands would be applied to the property of another and not to anything which was actually his own. So he confessed to Evelyn, when writing 'The Garden': ' . . . I stick still in the inn of a hired house and garden, among weeds and rubbish; and without that pleasantest work of human industry, the improvement of something which we call (not very properly, but yet we call) our own.' This moping humour, nevertheless, was transient, and his genuine feelings are to be inferred with at least as much reliability from such passages as the one in 'Of Greatness' wherein he paints the pleasures of five hundred pounds a year: a few good horses and servants; a sufficiency and a choice of food; warm and comely garments, though not so many as the tailor or *valet de chambre* would like; a 'convenient brick house, with decent wainscot, and pretty forest-work hangings'; herb, flower, and fruit gardens; and 'water every whit as clear and wholesome as if it darted from the breasts of a marble nymph or the urn of a river-god'.

Yes, Cowley, while his health remained good, came as close to realizing his Sabine farm ideals as Providence usually allows men to do with such hopes. Horace himself probably had more annoyances than he found it convenient to confess. Chertsey was as rural and 'solitary' as Cowley's temperament could well have borne, despite his literary yearnings for an out-and-out anchorite's life. His home, situated in Guildford Street at the west end of the village and called the Porch House,[1] was a comfortable building of seven or eight rooms, so solidly constructed of timber and brick, that, though considerably altered, it stood until 1926, when it was torn down to make room for a row of 'flats' and shops. One of the bedchambers was wainscoted with

---

[1] Cf. Manning and Bray, *Surrey*, xix, 207.

panels of oak, and the banisters of the staircase were of
solid oak, rather rudely carved. Cowley's study was a
small closet.

The local fame which must have attached to the
house at once because of its famous though idiosyn-
cratic occupant with his addiction to versifying has also
endured. The place is frequently mentioned in the
literature of pilgrim admirers. In 1752 William Stukely,
investigating the old monastery of the town, 'viewed
the house in Chertsey where Mr. Cowley the poet lived
and died, as they say. It is a good old timber house of a
tolerable model. There is a large garden; a brook,
arising at St. Anne's Hill, runs by the side. They talk
of a pretty summer-house which he built, which was
demolished not long since; and of a seat under a sycamore tree by the brook; which are mentioned in his
poems. There are very good fish-ponds too of his
making.'[1]  In 1792 an account in the *Gentleman's
Magazine* noted that the house had passed into the
possession of Richard Clarke, alderman of London[2]
(perhaps a descendant of the Clarkes who were Cowley's
kinsmen, since he also presented Trinity College with a
portrait of the poet).[3]  Clarke in 1786 had pulled down
the porch because it projected over the street, had filled
up the rather marshy fish-ponds, and, by not occupying
the building for a while, had allowed it to fall somewhat
into decay. By the time that Manning and Bray had
made their survey of Surrey early in the next century,
however, Clarke had completely repaired and remodelled
the building, and took great pride in it, as his contribution of many views of the house and engraved portraits
of the poet to their great folio history shows.[4]  He also
let a stone tablet into the outer wall of the room in
which Cowley had died, with the partial inscription,

[1] Cf. *Gent. Mag.*, lxvii. 199.          [2] Ibid., lxii. 28.
[3] See Appendix, p. 331.
[4] Manning and Bray, xix. 209 *passim*.

paraphrased from Pope's *Windsor Forest*, 'Here the last accents flowed from Cowley's tongue.' From this date on, engravings and woodcuts are frequent.[1]

Not until two hundred and fifty-nine years after the poet's death did the citizens of Chertsey so lose their fundamental British reverence for shrines as to allow the old Porch House to be pulled down and its site to be devoted to the new Goddess of Commerce.

[1] See Howitt's *Homes and Haunts*, Hall's *Chertsey and Its Neighbourhood* in 1853, Hazlitt's completion of Johnson's *Lives* in 1854 (with a careless reversal of the Barn Elms and Chertsey houses), and Cox's *Rambles in Surrey* in 1910.

# XVIII

# MONTAIGNE, EPICURUS, AND PRIMITIVE CHRISTIANITY

THE thoroughly bucolic surroundings at Chertsey, unlike the modified suburbanity of Barn Elms, at once began to stimulate Cowley to a new intellectual, or at least emotional, activity. Old projects which were dangling before him incomplete commenced to prick his conscience, and his head began to swarm with more new ideas than he could have enfleshed in many years. As Sprat rightly said, his mind was restored to its perfect vigour, though his body remained frail.

The last two books on plants were among the first things which he completed, and Sprat is sporadically right in maintaining that they show no diminution of their author's powers. Again, Cowley changed his Latin style, for now he was dealing with the more 'lofty' subject of trees, and Virgil's *Georgics* seemed the most appropriate model.[1] In book five, then, he recounted a contest between the fruit trees of the Old and New Worlds, held before the goddess Pomona at a banquet which she gave the gods on one of the Fortunate Isles. With mingled learning and humour he related how the tournament bade fair to break up in a fist fight between Omelochilus and Bacchus over the merits of the cocoa-tree, until Apollo stilled the tumult by striking such chords on his lyre as were heard when chaos first danced itself into the created universe. This book Cowley ended with a panegyric on Columbus and the New World, which had obviously always fascinated him, and with a far-sighted (and perhaps debatable) prophecy that the passage of the years would transfer the supremacy of national virtue and power from Europe to the Americas.

[1] Sprat, 'Account'.

The final book, though entitled *Sylva*, was a tacit confession either that Cowley had tired of his botanical excursions or that he felt the necessity of uttering some new paean in praise of Charles, Henrietta, Buckingham, and England. For this concluding section has very little to do with trees. As Sprat said, rather unctuously, 'For making the British oak to preside in the assembly of the forest trees, upon that occasion he enlarges on the history of our late troubles, the King's affliction and return, and the beginning of the Dutch War: and manages all in a style that (to say all in a word) is equal to the greatness and valour of the English nation.'[1] In this buttered flattery, with its mixture of legendary and authentic history, the passage of most interest is probably that in which Cowley, on his oath, but with the licence of a poet, describes a recollection of his own tenth year, in which the prodigious vision of two armies in full battle among the clouds gave warning to all England of the horrors of the Civil War to come.

Concerning Cowley's inner thoughts and uncon- summated plans during his last years, only Sprat's record remains. The young cleric was closer to his idol than was any other man, and therefore perhaps mirrored him as well as Cowley could have done him- self. The distortions which are present in parts of the re- flection are probably due to certain contradictions in the character of the original which Cowley himself could not have reconciled, since he had not perceived them.

One of the most ambitious of his projects, under- taken at the earnest solicitation of his friends, was the composition of what was seemingly to be called a *Discourse concerning Style*. 'In this', according to Sprat, 'he had designed to give an account of the proper sorts of writing, that were fit for all manner of arguments; to compare the perfections and imperfections of the authors of antiquity with those of this present age; and

[1] Sprat, 'Account'.

ABRAHAMUS COULEIUS
Anglorum Pindarus, Flaccus Maro,
Deliciæ Decus Desiderium Ævi sui,
Hic justa situs est.
Aurea dum volitant late tua scripta per orbem
Et Famâ æternùm vivis, Divine Poeta,
Hic placidâ jaceas requie Custodiat urnam
Cana Fides vigilentq; perenni Lampade Musæ,
Sit sacer ille locus, Nec quis temerarius ausit
Sacrilegâ turbare manu Venerabile Bustum,
Intacti maneant, maneant per secula Dulces
COULEII cineres, serventq; immobile Saxum
Sic voves.
Votumq; suum apud Posteros sacratum esse vo-
luit,Qui viro incomparabili posuit sepulcrale marmor
GEORGIUS DUX BUCKINGAMLÆ.

Excessit è vita Anno Æt.49 et honorifica pompa
elatus exÆdibus Buckinghamianis viris illustri-
bus omnium Ordinum exequias celebranti
bus sepultus est Die 3ᵗ M.Augusti Ao.Dⁱ 1667.

AN ADAPTATION OF COWLEY'S MONUMENT IN
WESTMINSTER ABBEY

to deduce all down to the particular use of the English genius and language.'[1] In other words, the work was to be a sort of theoretical and practical handbook of writing, with perhaps a foretaste of the Ancients *v.* Moderns controversy; and in it Cowley was to emerge as the critic, whereas before he had been known only as the creative writer.[2] As Sprat averred, 'This subject he was very fit to perform, it being most proper for him to be the judge who had been the best practiser.' This statement—or at least the first part of it—does not seem to be too much of an exaggeration. Scattered throughout Cowley's works, as well as concentrated in his prefaces, are a surprising number of critical remarks of considerable intelligence, in view of the adolescent state of criticism in his day. In general, in his liberality and his scorn of 'authority' as the ultimate guide, he belongs to the school of the youthful Corneille and of Dryden. He was both scientific and imaginative, objective and subjective. Nature, he believed, was more important than Art; and imitation was to be directly of the thing presented, with no intermediaries. He held that poetry should delight before it instructed. And he believed that, to be successful, the poet should steadfastly study philosophy, both natural and theoretical.

His fate, however, again ruled against him, so far as his project was concerned. 'But he scarce lived to draw the first lines of it', mourned Sprat. 'All the footsteps that I can find remaining of it are only some indigested characters of ancient and modern authors.' And of course he never thought of preserving these, since, like the personal correspondence, they were not dressed 'to go abroad into the streets'.

An integral part of this interest in English literature was Cowley's interest in the English language. Perhaps in echo of the recently formed French Academy, several members of the Royal Society had discussed the pos-

[1] Ibid.                    [2] Cf. my article in *R.E.S.*, ii. 385–404.

sibility of an English organization contrived to perfect
and standardize the language of the British. Sprat
referred to these proposals in his *History of the Royal
Society*,[1] but a letter of Evelyn to Pepys, August 12,
1689,[2] gives the most complete account of the affair and
of Cowley's part in it: 'And indeed such was once
designed since the restoration of Charles the Second
(1665) and in order to it three or four meetings
were begun at Gray's Inn, by Mr. Cowley, Dr. Sprat,
Mr. Waller, the D. of Buckingham, Mart. Clifford,
Mr. Dryden, and some other promoters of it. But by
the death of the incomparable Mr. Cowley, distance and
inconvenience of the place, the contagion, and other
circumstances intervening, it crumbled away and came
to nothing.'

In all the new movements Cowley was somehow to
be found. He had a naturally inquisitive mind, and he
set out to satisfy it, wherever possible. His whole retirement, indeed, he told Sprat he planned to devote to
a 'search into the secrets of divine and human knowledge, and to communicate what he should observe.'[3]
It was because of this intention that he dedicated himself so whole-heartedly to the study of natural science.
The seeds of a vague deism were perhaps in his conviction that an understanding of Nature would aid him
in understanding God. 'The whole compass of the
Creation, and all the wonderful effects of the Divine
Wisdom, were the constant prospect of his senses and
his thoughts.' His attitude was at least a generally
teleological one.

It is not unlikely that the last of Cowley's projects—
which seems to have worried the loyal Churchman,
Sprat, a bit—was a direct outgrowth of this sort of intellectual activity. This plan demanded an examination
and a review of the 'original principles of the primitive

[1] Sprat, *Royal Society*, pp. 40–5.
[2] Evelyn, *Diary*, iv. 310.          [3] Sprat, 'Account'.

church'—not, Sprat hastened to add, because Cowley was inclined 'to any uncertainty or doubt' or because he was not 'in his practice exactly obedient to the use and precepts of our church'. His only reason, springing from his observations of the many controversies and divisions of Christendom, was the laudable desire of 'every wise man' to establish 'his mind in the faith he professed'. To this end, Cowley planned an intensive study of the lives of Christ and the apostles 'and their immediate successors, for four or five centuries'. This limit he chose because thereafter, he believed, 'interest and policy prevailed over devotion'. Finding in this remark an excellent opportunity for drawing a modern parallel, Sprat quickly added, 'And besides, such a work, coming from one that was no divine, might have been very useful for this age, wherein it is one of the principal cavils against religion that it is only a matter of interest, and only supported for the gain of a particular profession'.

Sprat, nevertheless, permitted no doubt to enter his mind as to the eventual haven in which his friend would arrive. His most extreme admission concerning Cowley's plan was to the effect that 'He hoped to have absolutely compassed it in three or four years, and when that was done, there to have fixed for ever, without any shaking or alteration in his judgement'. But the human mind is sometimes a dark place, and even its owner does not always know the thoughts that are lurking there. And perhaps Cowley would, as Sprat predicted, have ended upon the bedrock of the Church of England, with his doubts at rest and his faith confirmed. Or perhaps he would have provided himself with one set of ideas for Sundays and other feasts and fasts, and with another for the privacy of his study. He would not, indeed, have been the first of his contemporaries to fashion a sort of protective colouring of theological conformity, while his whole inner life and many of his outer actions were motivated by quite different doctrines. Even the great Hobbes, with his terrifying moustaches—which, as Aubrey said, bristled upward naturally, because of their owner's pugnacious disposition—even the great Hobbes had found it possible to profess adherence to the state religion because of the practical value of such an institution in government. And Francis Bacon, too, had built up a weighty system of philosophy quite apart from his theology. Abraham Cowley, then, many ranks below these two idols of his as a thinker, may never have recognized that all was not well with his professed and his actual guides to life and conduct. He may never have recognized that he was faced with another dilemma; and yet the dilemma was there.

Most of Cowley's critics have united with Pope in calling his essays the true 'language of his heart'; [1] and it is in these essays that his philosophical tendencies while at Chertsey appear. [2] In Sprat's words, Cowley intended them 'as a real character of his own thoughts, upon the point of his retirement', and to them he expected to add 'many others', the whole collection eventually to be dedicated to the Earl of St. Albans as 'a kind of apology for having left human affairs in the strength of his age, when he might still have been serviceable to his country'. [3]

Though there may be slight grounds for argument as to the exact date when Cowley began composing his essays, there is no satisfactory evidence for believing that any of them, with the exception of the 'Letter to Mr. S. L.', were written before 1665. Beginning with 'Of Liberty', many of them were stuffed with such terms and phrases as 'tenants-at-will', 'quit-rent', 'stiles', 'bridges', and 'lanes'—a vocabulary which would

[1] Pope, 'First Epistle of Second Book of Horace.'
[2] Cf. my article, 'The Essays of Abraham Cowley', *J.E.G.P.*, xxix. 114–30.     [3] Sprat, 'Account'.

very likely spring naturally to the lips of a tyro farmer like Cowley. The rather 'advanced' discussion, in 'Of Agriculture', of the desirability of establishing an agricultural course in the colleges, parallel to the existent curricula in medicine and law, was very likely actuated by the ignorance of that subject which he discovered in both himself and his new tenants—though the idea was not novel to him, inasmuch as he had touched briefly on it in his *Proposition.* 'The Dangers of an Honest Man in Much Company' referred to Chertsey outright. The paraphrase of Horace in 'Of Greatness' alluded indirectly to the two comets which had plunged superstitious London into a not unjust fear in December 1664 and April 1665. 'Of Obscurity' quoted from *The Poems of Horace,* edited and partly translated by Alexander Brome in 1666. 'The Garden' was originally written as a letter to Evelyn, dated from Chertsey on August 16, 1666;[1] it was a complimentary acknowledgement of Evelyn's intention to dedicate the second edition of the *Kalendarium Hortense* to Cowley, and was printed, verse and prose, with later editions of Evelyn's work. 'Of Myself' was obviously one of the last to be written, because of its valedictory-like tone and its *résumé* of the author's whole life. Of the remainder of the essays, some made use of classical translations and paraphrases which Cowley had already printed in 1663, and 'Of Agriculture' also gave an English version of the opening of his own as yet unpublished fourth book on plants. The whole series, indeed, is so closely bound together by similarity of material and by cross-references that (with the exception of the two letters, which may have been inserted later by Sprat to fill out the prose group) it seems to be but one continued discourse, embellished by an almost equal amount of verse.

The eleven essays, published posthumously in Cowley's collected works as 'Several Discourses by Way of

[1] Printed in Evelyn's *Misc. Writings,* pp. xvi, 435, 442.

Essays, in Verse and Prose', have as their central theme the topic which always becomes a favourite one with the poets as soon as a nation begins to focus itself in its urban centres and to grow away from its earlier agricultural and pastoral life. 'Of Liberty' announces the subject, which is then turned and shifted about in a variety of positions and lights so that the reader may examine it in all its facets; that is, to consider the 'liberty of a private man in being master of his own time and actions, as far as may consist with the laws of God and of his country . . ., and to inquire what estate of life does best seat us in the possession of it'. It is the city versus the country, and naturally Cowley can see only evil growing from the conditions of city life. True liberty is to be found exclusively in a life of 'moderate plenty' in some retreat far from the 'hives' of men.

This lesson of the Aristotelian 'Golden Mean' is re-inforced in many essays, but most notably in Cowley's description of the ideally happy person in 'Of Obscurity': he is 'a person who has a moderate mind and fortune, and lives in the conversation of two or three agreeable friends, with little commerce in the world besides, who is esteemed well enough by his few neighbours that know him; and is truly irreproachable by anybody, and so, after a healthful quiet life, before the great inconveniencies of old age, goes more silently out of it than he came in (for I would not have him so much as cry in the *Exit*).' And this is the same person speaking who had shouted out in the key poem of his chief volume:

> What shall I do to be for ever known,
> And make the age to come my own?

and had then proceeded to advertise his decision to become the Muse's Hannibal! Did he intend a public recantation when he wrote, in 'Of Solitude', 'And happy had it been for Hannibal if adversity could have taught him as much wisdom as was learnt by Scipio from the highest prosperities?' The poetical Hannibal had clearly

earned his lesson, though the military Hannibal had
failed.

What was it which had sent Cowley off into this sort
of writing—in prose—since he could have used (and
did use) the same sort of material for versifying? Was
it the discovery that the essay would allow him—
virtually the first in English—to introduce the same
intimate note and colloquial style as he had been accustomed to use in his familiar letters; to substitute
humour, personal experiences, pithy sayings, literary
and historical anecdotes and examples, for the over-
ornamentation and elaborate figures of speech which
had defaced so much of his poetry? Or was he simply
putting into practice once more his favourite theory
of imitation or emulation, and, as many have suggested,
was only attempting to acclimate the Sieur de Mon-
aigne to an English environment?

Cowley's acquaintance with Montaigne's essays is
undeniable. Twice he alludes to them in his own—once
in 'Of Solitude' and once in 'Of Greatness'; and a dozen
or more passages in the English essays are strangely
reminiscential of the French. Cowley knew Mon-
aigne's 'Of Solitude' so thoroughly that he seems to
have re-worked ideas from it, perhaps unconsciously in
some cases, into his own 'Of Solitude', 'The Dangers of
an Honest Man in Much Company', 'The Shortness of
Life and Uncertainty of Riches', 'Of Liberty', and
'The Danger of Procrastination'. Similarly, Montaigne's
'Of the Inconvenience of Greatness' and 'Of Glory'
have projected their shadows upon 'Of Greatness' and
'Of Obscurity', respectively. And finally, Cowley's
egotism, his I-speaking, especially in 'Of Myself', had
been anticipated by Montaigne in a score of places,
though the completeness and number of the latter's
personal revelations far exceeded anything that Cowley
ever attempted—or would have considered decent.

And yet the atmospheres of the two series of essays

are quite different, no matter how many ideas or stylistic hints may have been borrowed by Cowley. The situation is an illustration of the powers of transformation by temperament. Montaigne is nervous, quick, unstable—buzzing discontentedly from place to place. Cowley, on the other hand, even in the midst of his reflections on the world's ill-treatment, moves in an air of freshness and real pastoral tranquillity. Though, on the facts of their lives alone, Cowley is the one who should seem peevish, there is actually more of this feeling pervading the three books of Montaigne's essays.

But Montaigne is not, after all, the only influence discernible in Cowley's 'discourses'. Bacon is there, too, as might be expected in a disciple, in a small way, of the great Lord Chancellor. Cowley's first essay, 'Of Liberty', shows clear traces of the Baconian technique in its sententious announcement of its topic; in its division of material into three parts and its discussion and illustration of each; in its use of examples, 'sentences', and apothegms; and in its lack of any strongly personal element. 'Of Avarice', probably written later than the other, is in some respects a reversion to Baconian methods, although the author had escaped from them in the intervening essays. In 'Of Solitude', too, Cowley used the same comparison between the solitude of a god and that of a wild beast as Bacon had used in 'Of Friendship', although of course both men may have derived directly from Aristotle.

Cowley's thoughts, however, had not been confined to Montaigne or Bacon while he was setting down his essays in the privacy of his new house or under the sycamore in his garden, although perhaps the normal tone of scepticism and materialism in these two men may have had a general permeating effect. An analysis of the authors whom he referred to by name is very illuminating. Out of a possible forty-five, thirty-one are Roman or Greek, seven are Biblical, and seven are modern—two of the last being French, one Italian, and four English. Of the classical authors, Horace is mentioned by far the most often, with Martial next, and Virgil close behind. On their heels comes Epicurus, with his friends and followers, Metrodorus, Democritus, and Lucretius, also frequently alluded to by anecdote and quotation. The Epicurean bias of the group is indisputable, for the hedonistic philosophers and poets have been filling Cowley's mind, and their doctrine—pleasure as the ultimate goal of life—is his. In his youth his philosophical tendencies had been in the same direction, but now, in his middle age, they have matured and come out into the open.

Although Cowley never says, 'Carpe diem!' outright with Horace, he quotes other just as characteristic adjurations to enjoy the present. 'From a short life cut off all hopes that grow too long', he paraphrases in 'The Shortness of Life and Uncertainty of Riches'. Or,

> To-morrow let my sun his beams display
> Or in clouds hide them: I have lived to-day,

he quotes his own boyish rendering of Horace in 'Of Myself'; and then clinches it with a new admonition from Martial:

> Be satisfied and pleased with what thou art;
> Act cheerfully and well th' allotted part;
> Enjoy the present hour, be thankful for the past,
> And neither fear, nor wish, th' approaches of the last.

As even these brief passages would show, Cowley's Epicureanism was not the vulgar one of 'Eat, drink, and be merry, for to-morrow we die'. It was not even of the Cyrenaic type of Aristippus, which advocated a living and searching for what Pater centuries after was to call the 'vivid moments' of life. Rather it was the Golden Mean as Horace saw it—moderation in the indulgence of the mind as well as all the senses—no slighting or over-development of any part of one's being

at the expense of any other. Although Cowley sometimes used the terms 'Epicure' and 'Epicurean' in the
loose, popular sense, he never actually distorted them,
and twice he discussed the real doctrines of Epicurus so
definitely that his study of them is clear. In 'Of Liberty',
in a passage on voluptuousness, he wrote: 'Metrodorus
said that he had learnt ἀληθῶς γαστρὶ χαρίζεσθαι, to give
his belly just thanks for all his pleasures. This by the
calumniators of Epicurus his philosophy was objected
as one of the most scandalous of all their sayings; which,
according to my charitable understanding, may admit
a very virtuous sense, which is, that he thanked his own
belly for that moderation in the customary appetites of
it which can only give a man liberty and happiness in
this world'. And when, in 'The Garden', he wrote his
ode for Evelyn, the translator of Lucretius and of La
Mothe le Vayer, he spoke even more plainly:

> When Epicurus to the world had taught
>   That pleasure was the chiefest good
> (And was perhaps i' th' right, if rightly understood),
>   His life he to his doctrine brought,
> And in a garden's shade that sovereign pleasure sought:
> Whoever a true Epicure would be,
> May there find cheap and virtuous luxury.

These are the lines upon which Richard Hurd, a
century later, based his assertion that Cowley knew the
writings of Pierre Gassendi on Epicurus.[1] And yet,
peculiarly enough, Cowley never referred, in any
specific way, to any of the chief modern writers on
Epicurus, such as Diogenes Laertius, Walter Charleton,
or Gassendi. Charleton, however, was a prominent
Royalist, a physician-in-ordinary to both the Charles's,
and a member of the Royal Society. Sprat, moreover,
at the very time that Cowley was writing, was admiring
the brilliance of Gassendi in his own *Observations on
Monsieur de Sorbier's Voyage into England*; and it seems

[1] Hurd, *Cowley*, ii. 137.

very probable that the two friends discussed the Frenchman's tenets together. If so, neither appears to have found anything incompatible with his Anglican creed in these strongly non-ascetic doctrines which placed happiness in the present world far above possible happiness in an uncertain future life in heaven. But then, Gassendi and Charleton themselves were Christian Epicureans, who had somehow trained their philosophy and their theology to lie down quietly together.

On the other hand, since the ideas of Epicurus must be learned mostly at second hand, because almost none of the original works are extant, Cowley must have got his knowledge somewhere. And he does name several other possible sources. These are, chiefly, Lucretius and Cicero—the *De Natura Deorum* of the latter being one of the prescribed texts of his ideal college, as explained in his *Proposition*. Finally, he was naturally familiar with Plutarch, who has also preserved fragments of Epicurean thought, only—like Cicero—to refute them. It seems scarcely necessary to add that Montaigne's works are also thoroughly impregnated with Epicurean belief.

And so for two years Abraham Cowley lived in Chertsey, a model of steadiness and orthodoxy to all who knew him, respected for his piety and purity even by those of his friends who could never again obtain these qualities for themselves. Would his study of the origins of the Christian church, if completed, have betrayed any signs of the ethical code which really governed his life? Or would he have remained like most of the rest of his generation—a conventional outward Christian, untroubled by any pains of conscience?

# XIX

## NEXT TO CHAUCER AND SPENSER

MOST of Cowley's poetic output in English during the period of his 'retirement' was eventually diverted to the essays—and some of his Latin verses, too, are also to be found there in an English dress. Among these are the Sapphics, 'Solitudo' and 'Ode', printed in *Poemata Latina* and also appearing in an English version at the end of 'Of Solitude' and 'The Shortness of Life and Uncertainty of Riches' respectively. This sort of juggling Cowley seems to have been rather addicted to, perhaps partly for amusement and partly for practice in the spare hours of his own solitude. Certainly he regarded Latin as a sort of second mother tongue, and was always turning the one into the other, as his epistle, '*A.C.* Cliffordo, *S.D.*', and his contributions to Brome's collection of translations from Horace would indicate.

One poem which might well have forced a passage into the essays, however, never found its way there—though it is extant in a Latin form also. Cowley's 'Hymn. To Light' could have been written only after he had watched the 'winged arrows' shoot from the 'golden quiver of the sky' for a long succession of fresh, bright dawns in the country; had felt them frighten away 'sleep, the lazy owl of night'; and had even seen how they could turn the face of 'cloudy care' itself into a 'gentle, beamy smile'.

> When, Goddess, thou lift'st up thy wakened head
> > Out of the Morning's purple bed,
> > Thy quire of birds about thee play
> And all the joyful world salutes the rising day . . . .

> All the world's bravery that delights our eyes
> > Is but thy sev'ral liveries;
> > Thou the rich dye on them bestow'st;
> Thy nimble pencil paints this landscape as thou go'st.

A crimson garment in the rose thou wear'st;
A crown of studded gold thou bear'st;
The virgin lilies in their white
Are clad but with the lawn of almost naked light.

The violet, Spring's little infant, stands
Girt in thy purple swaddling-bands;
On the fair tulip thou dost dote;
Thou cloth'st it in a gay and parti-coloured coat.

Nature to Cowley was a pretty thing—not a profoundly inspiring or even a stirring thing, but a source of constant pleasure and beauty, of which he could finally drink his fill. Light, the 'first-born of Chaos', enhanced these charms, though thoughtlessly she shone on gold as well and made it more tempting to the inconsiderate. But despite the moralizing, the poem is one of the best Cowley ever wrote. In its epithetical felicity it vies with 'Beauty' and the double poem on Hope; its paradoxes are apt and as little protuberant as those in the essays; and the conceits, if they are conceits at all, are no more recondite than the one at the end, wherein light is conceived as a 'clear river' pouring from the vast ocean of the sky and gathering in pools and lakes only where its course is opposed by some firm body such as the earth.

The last known poem from Cowley's pen—the last of any importance, at least—is his great Pindaric, 'To the Royal Society'—an ode which seems to promise that Sprat's prediction concerning the new phase of his friend's writing would have been fulfilled. The genesis of the poem can easily be traced. By 1665 the Royal Society, in spite of the jibes and mockery of many sceptics, had grown so lusty as to be convinced that it had a history and that that history was important enough to be written. As a consequence, Thomas Sprat was elected historiographer, was given access to the records, and promptly embarked on his task.

Because of the Plague and the Fire, however, the printing of the book was delayed, although much of the type
had already been set up.  But by the spring of 1666/7
conditions had become sufficiently settled for the work
to be resumed.

This situation is made clear by an interchange of
letters between Cowley and Evelyn, secretary of the
Society, the letters being preserved among the latter's
correspondence.[1]  On March 12, Evelyn wrote to his
friend at Chertsey, for two reasons: first, to explain that
his 'trifling essay' on *Public Employment . . . Preferred
to Solitude*, recently published, was not to be taken
seriously, as would only too clearly appear from a comparison of it with Sir George Mackenzie's *Moral Essay
upon Solitude, Preferring it to Public Employment*, to
which it was designed as a sort of *tour de force* of reply;
and second, to call Cowley's attention to the 'eulogies'
which 'our good friend' Sprat was publishing on the
Royal Society, and to request, in the name of the
Society, 'an ode from the best of poets upon the noblest
argument'.  So much absorbed was Evelyn in his purpose
of vindicating the group from the 'satire and the songs
of drunkards' which had been giving it considerable un-
desirable publicity that he ventured to sketch out a
plan for Cowley to follow in his poem.

It was two months almost to the day before Cowley
answered, with a profuse apology for his 'rudeness' in
delaying his reply so long.  His only excuse was his
'laziness in finishing the copy of verses upon the Royal
Society, for which I was engaged before by Mr. Sprat's
desire and encouraged since by you'.  In other words,
contrary to Grosart's statement, Evelyn was not
primarily responsible for the ode which appeared that
same year in the *History of the Royal Society*, but Sprat
was.  This fact may have slightly increased Cowley's
diffidence in having to inform the former that the com-

---

[1] Evelyn, iii. 194 ff.; also Grosart, *Cowley*, i. lxxvii–viii.

prehensive suggestions he had made for the poem were not quite practicable 'for one copy of verses', but that Sprat, who had seen Evelyn's letter, assured him that all these points, together with 'the praises of particular persons', had been taken care of in the history itself— which, as a matter of fact, turned out to be a panegyrical enough affair to satisfy even Evelyn's desires.

The poem which Cowley produced was, in a sense, his version of the history of philosophy, a 'male-virtue',

> the great and only heir
> Of all that human knowledge which has been
> Unforfeited by Man's rebellious sin.

The poet can distinguish only two periods in this history—the one before Bacon and the other beginning with him. Reverting for a moment to the ideas in his earlier poems, 'The Tree of Knowledge', 'Reason', and 'Life and Fame', on the constricting effect of the philosophies which for three or four thousand years had merely wandered among the 'labyrinths of ever-fresh discourse', he embarked on an impassioned attack upon authority. Only the coming of Francis Bacon put to rout this ghost-like body of authority and no longer suffered men to be misled by the shadows of dead people. For Bacon drew the mind from 'words, which are but pictures of the thought', to 'things, the mind's right object'. It was as the direct successors and perfecters of Bacon's researches that Cowley praised the Royal Society and its already great accomplishments. And it is by this alinement that he shows irrevocably what direction his own future researches and writings would have followed.

But the poet's health had never been good since the fever had attacked him at Barn Elms. Its departure, moreover, had left him weak and susceptible to colds and other ailments. Disease in its most frightful form, the Plague, was also stalking abroad, and Cowley, though having left the environs of London before the scourge reached its height, was naturally put in mind of his own mortality.

On the eighteenth of September 1665, he therefore summoned his servant, Thomas Waldron, and John Symonds, a wheelwright of the village, to witness his will.[1] After the conventional preamble concerning his own health and understanding, as well as his sins and his weakness of belief, he left all his 'worldly goods, moneys, and chattels' to his bachelor brother Thomas, with the exception of certain legacies first to be paid out of the estate 'which it hath pleased God to bestow upon me much above my deserts'. These bequests are interesting because they show that Cowley never forgot—or lost— a friend. In addition to making provisions for several kinsfolk and for his own and his brother's servants, he disposed of the following gifts: Thomas Fotherby, one hundred pounds, 'which [I] beseech him to accept of as a small remembrance of his ancient kindness to me'; Davenant, twenty pounds; Scarborough, twenty pounds; Dr. Thomas Croyden, an old Trinity friend, twenty pounds; Clifford, twenty pounds; Robert Crane, D.D., another old Westminster and Trinity friend and still a Fellow at Trinity, 'a ring of five pounds'; John Hervey, 'my share and interest in his Highness the Duke of York's Theatre' (in payment of a debt, as Alexander Davenant vindictively charged in his chancery suit);[2] and 'the right Honourable the Earl of St. Albans, my Lord and once kind master, a ring of ten pounds, only in memory of my duty and affection to him'.

To Trinity College itself, in case any payments from his Fellowship were due, he left the resultant sum to be expended on books for the library. This desire was faithfully carried out, for two years after his death the following record appeared among the Trinity 'Extra-

[1] Appendix no. 2.                    [2] See appendix no. 7.

ordinaries': 'To Mr. Alestry for books given by Dr. Cowley to the Library, £51'.[1] This statement seems to have bothered Lumby somewhat, though without cause, for James Allstrey was a leading London publisher, from whom the books had obviously been bought.

Another bequest of some interest was that of twenty pounds to the poor of Chertsey. Although this proof of Cowley's kindness and charity is representative, John Aubrey has nevertheless erred in giving him more credit for such benevolence than he deserved.[2] Aubrey's story, which he said he had from 'Mr. Dunning of London, a scrivener, who is an acquaintance of Dr. Cowley's brother', was to the effect that every year the will set aside 'so much . . . to be paid for the enlarging of poor prisoners cast into gaol by cruel creditors for some debt'. As a matter of fact, in a slightly altered form this was one of the provisions of Thomas Cowley's will, which also left thirty pounds to the Chertsey poor and two hundred to be divided equally among 'twenty such widows that are really poor'.[3]

Finally, Abraham requested his 'dear friend Mr. Thomas Sprat to trouble himself with the collection and revision of all such writings of mine (whether printed before or not) as he shall think fit to be published, beseeching him not to let any pass which he shall judge unworthy of the name of his friend, and most especially nothing (if anything of that kind have escaped my pen) which may give the least offence in point of religion or good manners'. And 'in consideration of this unpleasant task' Cowley bequeathed Sprat all his library, and a sum of twenty pounds. Sprat, nevertheless, seems to have been pleased by the commission and, when the time came, to have undertaken it with enthusiasm. The permission, however, to revise both manuscripts and printed works he availed himself of only slightly,

[1] Lumby, p. xx.    [2] Aubrey, *Brief Lives*, i. 190–1.
[3] Appendix no. 3.

T

if his 'improvements' in the latter may be taken as a criterion of the former.[1]

For a time, Cowley appeared to have drawn his will prematurely. After his recovery from his fall and his 'defluxion of rheum', he enjoyed a period of almost two years of comparatively good health, during which he did some of his best writing. He took occasional trips into London and to the court, as Pepys's anecdote about Killigrew and King Charles, entered in his journal for December 7, 1666, shows. He entertained the select few of his friends who were willing to undergo the inconveniences of the country. Sprat was of course the most frequent of these visitors, and at these times the two often discussed plans for future editions of Cowley's works. At the last of these meetings, a third friend, Thomas Cook (to whom Cowley left twenty pounds in his will), was also present, and the conversation apparently turned on the subject which the poet could never quite forget, in spite of his resolutions— the reason for the miscarriage of his public career.[2] The passage which he felt had been most misinterpreted and had done his reputation the most harm was the 'disloyal' recantation in the 1656 preface. So deep an impression had this incident made upon him that he informed his two visitors of his intention of removing the offending passage from the next edition of his works, which he seems even then to have been planning. At the same interview, too, he appears to have told his prospective literary executor of his design to dedicate his essays to St. Albans.

Then, at the beginning of the year 1667, Cowley fell into another sickness, which the doctors diagnosed as diabetes.[3] For about three months he suffered under this, but at the end of that time it showed signs of yielding to their treatment. If so, it of course could not

[1] See Sparrow, *R.E.S.*, iii. 22–7
[2] Sprat, 'Account'.
[3] Sprat, 'De Vita'.

have been real diabetes; but if Cowley was actually a
victim of this disease, the fact would go far toward ac-
counting for his periodical attacks of melancholy and
his frequent fancies of persecution. Eventually, however, he left his bed, and again took up his daily round
of writing and farm-management. Perhaps, however,
he suspected his fate. Certainly his essay, 'Of Myself',
which contains a sort of *résumé* of his whole career and
character up to the very end of his life, strikes such a
farewell note as to seem to have been written in the
very midst of these afflictions.

In the middle of the summer he went out one day to
supervise the reaping in one of his meadows. The field
was larger than his labourers had anticipated, but they
stayed at their work until evening came—and Cowley
stayed with them, forgetting the effect which the
dampness arising from the river and the night air might
have on him, as it had before at Barn Elms. Consequently, he was again attacked by illness, which at
first he neglected and treated only with such home-
made remedies as he would use for a bad cold. These
failing—and he himself thus failing when his own medical
skill was brought to the test—he called in the neighbouring physicians who had attended him before. It
was too late. For a fortnight he lay sick. His disease,
which, because of Sprat's description of its symptoms
and its eventual 'stoppage of his breast and throat',[1]
would appear to have been pneumonia, held him fast,
and on July 28 he died.[2]

The only dissenting voice to this account of the circumstances of Cowley's death is that of Alexander Pope,
who told the following scandalous tale to Spence:[3]
'He died at Chertsey; and his death was occasioned by
a mean accident, whilst his great friend, Dean Sprat,
was with him on a visit there. They had been together

[1] Sprat, 'Account'.
[2] See *London Gazette*, Aug. 4, 1667.          [3] Spence, p. 13.

to see a neighbour of Cowley's, who (according to the fashion of those times) made them too welcome. They did not set out for their walk home till it was too late, and had drank so deep that they lay out in the fields all night. This gave Cowley the fever that carried him off. The parish still talk of the drunken Dean.' But this malicious story bears within itself its own confutation. For even if Sprat was capable of deliberately lying about his last meeting with Cowley, he did not acquire the title of Dean until 1683. What Pope's motives were, or how the tale was fabricated, need not be gone into here.

London, however, received the news as befitted the death of the man whom all of its leading wits, divines, and gallants united in praising as the greatest poet of the English nation—some, indeed, not baulking at including all races and all ages in the comparison. Cowley's body was floated down the river from Chertsey to Wallingford House, Buckingham's home in Whitehall, and on August 3 the funeral was held with all pomp and magnificence. The next day the *London Gazette* contained the following account of the ceremony: 'Yesterday, in the evening, the body of Mr. Abraham Cowley, who died the 28th past, was conveyed from Wallingford House to Westminster Abbey, accompanied by divers persons of eminent quality who came to perform this last office to one who had been the great ornament of our nation, as well by the candour of his life as the excellency of his writings.' Evelyn, with his taste for describing public spectacles, made a brief but graphic entry in his diary: 'Went to Mr. Cowley's funeral, whose corpse lay at Wallingford House and was thence conveyed to Westminster Abbey in a hearse with six horses and all funeral decency, near one hundred coaches of noblemen and persons of quality following, among them all the wits of the town, divers bishops and clergymen'.[1] As a final touch, Aubrey stated that

[1] Evelyn, *Diary*, Aug. 3, 1667. See also Aug. 1.

Buckingham himself held a tassel of the pall.[1] It was Buckingham, too, who immediately announced that he would erect a marble monument to his friend, who now lay buried next to Chaucer and Spenser.[2] This promise, however, was not redeemed until May 1675 [3]—and even then, according to a veiled hint in Tom Brown's 'London,' the Duke neglected to pay for his memorial.[4] On the tombstone was placed what is perhaps the most florid of all Latin exequial eulogies, composed, according to various guesses, by Sprat, Clifford, Scarborough, or even Dr. Thomas Gale.[5] Here Cowley is for ever immortalized as 'Anglorum Pindus, Flaccus, Maro, Deliciae Decus, Desiderium Aevi Sui', and the world is told that the tombstone will live for ever, because his dust is beneath it.

When the rites were completed, King Charles was heard to remark heartily that Mr. Cowley had not left a better man behind him in England;[6] but he omitted all reference to the Savoy or any similar appointment. Yet in spite of the splendour of the funeral, the inveterate man-about-town, Samuel Pepys, had to wait until he made a visit to the bookseller's at the New Exchange on August 10 and met Denham there before he heard of Cowley's demise. However, two days later he recorded that he had overheard Bishop Ward of Exeter, Bishop Morley of Winchester, and Dr. Bates lamenting the dead man as 'the best poet of our nation, and as good a man'.

But no one who pretended to admire literature could remain in ignorance long. Elegies were hastily made and circulated by the poet's friends, and by others who had

[1] Aubrey, *Brief Lives*, i. 190.
[2] The Register of Westminster Abbey, however, does not record the actual burial until Aug. 17.                         [3] Wood, iv, ii. 213.
[4] Brown, *Works*, iii. 22, interpreted by P. Cunningham in Johnson's *Lives*, i. 50, n.
[5] Aubrey, *Brief Lives*, i. 190; P. Cunningham, i. 50, n.; Grosart, *Cowley*, i. cxl; Wood, iv, ii. 213.                         [6] Johnson, *Lives*, i. 17–18.

only read his works.  Denham was one of the first of the former,[1] and Scarborough was another.[2]  Sprat also apparently wrote a long elegy, 'On the Death and to the Memory of Mr. Abraham Cowley', which curiously enough he did not insert in the edition he was supervising; nor does it seem ever to have been printed.[3]  By the time the eighth edition of Cowley's works, with various additions of his juvenilia, translations of his Latin poems on plants, &c., had appeared in 1693, the list of printed eulogies included the names of Orrery, Denham, Thomas Higgons, Thomas Flatman, and Samuel Wesley; and Nahum Tate, Aphra Behn, and others had paid their tribute to him while translating his Latin so that it would be accessible to every English reader.

What Cowley would have thought of the extravagance of these elegies can only be surmised.  The authors probably in this case meant what they said, although most seventeenth-century verse tributes are not to be trusted much farther than most funeral sermons.  However, when one recalls the reiterated wishes that Cowley had made in his essays to pass out of the world even more quietly than he had entered it, one wonders whether his own 'Epitaphium Vivi Auctoris', composed at Chertsey and thus Englished by William Cullen Bryant,[4] might not have made a more fitting inscription for a monument to be placed in a spot somewhere less overrun than Westminster Abbey:

*The Living Author's Epitaph*

Here, Stranger, in this lowly spot,
    The buried Cowley finds at last
Rest from the labours of his lot,
    And leaves life's follies with the past.

[1] Printed in later editions of Cowley.

[2] Wood, iv, ii. 98.  Poem not extant.

[3] See MS. Eng. Poet. e. 4, ff. 49–57, in Bodleian.  A blank space for the first two stanzas has been left in this copy.

[4] Bryant, *N. Am. Rev.*, cxxiv, 380–1.  A version by Addison appears in Chalmers, ix. 536.

In not unseemly low estate,
  Nor meanly slothful, though retired,
Well hath the poet learned to hate
  The wealth by staring crowds admired.

Yea, speak of him as dead; for see
  How little earth is now his share;
And, Stranger, pray that light may be
  Its burden, and may bring no care.

Strow flowers; they please the living dead;
  Here roses ere they wither strow;
And o'er his yet warm ashes shed
  The sweetest-smelling herbs that grow.

# XX

# THE LAST OF THE METAPHYSICAL RACE

ABRAHAM COWLEY, according to the classifiers of literature, was a Metaphysical Poet. In the opinion of Dr. Samuel Johnson, the none too flattering godfather who fastened the name upon him, he was 'almost the last of that race, and undoubtedly the best'.[1] Yet in the preceding pages he has been designated by that term only once or twice—and then in quotation. The abstention was deliberate.

If Cowley had been addressed as a 'Metaphysical Poet' in his lifetime, he would have looked mystified and then, in his polite manner, have asked for elucidation. In one of his essays, in fact, he had remarked that as for metaphysic he did not 'know whether it be anything or no'.[2] To have the word fastened on him for eternity— or as much of eternity as would be his—would therefore prove just a bit disturbing. But if the phrase had been then explained as meaning belonging to the 'School of Donne', he might have nodded hesitantly—but very doubtfully. For in his autobiography, 'Of Myself', he had classed himself, initially at least, as a Spenserian. Moreover, if Clarendon is to be believed, he had later accredited his success to the example of Ben Jonson.[3] It would have been much less surprising to Cowley to be put with the disciples of Spenser or with the Sons of Ben than with the School of Donne. For, in a very real sense, groups of conscious and avowed followers of Spenser and Jonson had existed. But there never was a School of Donne until later critics and historians manufactured it for ease of classification. Almost none of the poets who have been associated as 'Metaphysical' claimed Donne as their master.

[1] Johnson, *Lives*, i. 35.    [2] 'Of Agriculture'.    [3] Clarendon, *Life*, i. 34.

Dryden was, more or less involuntarily, responsible for the whole situation.[1] In his 'Original and Progress of Satire' he had spoken of Donne as one who 'affects the metaphysics, not only in his satires, but in his amorous verses, where nature only should reign, and perplexes the minds of the fair sex with nice speculations of philosophy when he should engage their hearts and entertain them with the softnesses of love'; and then had added, 'In this (if I may be pardoned for so bold a truth) Mr. Cowley has copied him to a fault; to great a one, in my opinion, that it throws his *Mistress* infinitely below his Pindarics and his latter compositions, which are undoubtedly the best of his poems, and the most correct.' Dryden, therefore, associated Donne and Cowley on only one ground: their use of 'metaphysics' in their love poetry.    His remark, however, was promptly taken up and repeated by writers like Sir Thomas Pope Blount, John Oldmixon, Elijah Fenton, Alexander Pope, and others throughout the eighteenth century, most of them being satisfied not to elaborate on it to any extent—all except Pope, who increased the 'school' by enrolling Davenant and Sprat as 'scholars'. But in all these cases the word 'metaphysical' had a close relationship to metaphysics as a branch of philosophy, tenuous and scholastic though that philosophy might be.

At the same time, however, parallel with this correct use of the word to apply to subject matter and content, another use came more and more into currency.    This may be represented by one quotation from Lord Chesterfield and one from Joseph Warton.    On February 8, 1750, Chesterfield wrote to his son: 'The *Pastor Fido* of Guarini is so celebrated that you should read it; but in reading it, you will judge of the great propriety of the characters. A parcel of shepherds and shepherdesses, with True Pastoral Simplicity, talk metaphysics, epigrams, *concetti*, and quibbles by the hour to

[1] Cf. my article, *M.L.N.*, xxxvii. 11–17.

each other.' This new and contemptuous association for the word 'metaphysics' occurs even more clearly in a passage from Joseph Warton's *An Essay on the Writings and Genius of Pope*: 'And indeed to speak the truth, there appears to be little valuable in Petrarch, except the purity of his diction. His sentiments, even of love, are metaphysical and far-fetched.' In other words, 'metaphysical' has become connected with certain qualities of manner or style—with conceits, far-fetched figures of speech, plays on words, abstruse and extravagant allusions, and mere elaborateness and over-decoration in the expression of an idea.

Dr. Johnson, unfortunately for succeeding critics and readers, was familiar with both uses, but confused the two. He knew that Donne and Cowley were full of fantastic conceits, and also that they were fond of raising philosophical speculations; he therefore looked through his list for the poets of the seventeenth century who indulged their ingenuity and wit in the first of these two fashions; found Marino, Donne, Cowley, Cleveland, Suckling, Waller, Denham, and Milton; rejected the last four so far as the majority of their works were concerned; and called the resulting motley group the 'Metaphysical Poets'. Moreover, he applied the term to all of their works, and not simply to the relatively few in which Dryden had discerned the metaphysical 'taint'—chiefly because in these, Dryden thought, philosophy was out of place. Consequently, from Johnson's time down, to the 'great vulgar' (as Cowley called the mob) 'metaphysical poetry' has meant poetry compounded of ridiculous conceits and ostentatious learning; and the utmost efforts of a few clearer-sighted critics have been unable to free the general reader from the conviction that all the poets whom Johnson, and others misled by him, have branded with this term are for ever cast into outer darkness, where they have ceased even to gnash their teeth.

But the ease with which Johnson and others discovered examples of what they insisted on calling the
metaphysical style would indicate that Cowley was
merely the inheritor or last important representative
of some wide-spread and deeply-rooted tendency of his
times. The search for the origins of this style has led
scholars into all sorts of labyrinths and obscure corners.
In England the desire for novel and *recherché* expression had evolved Euphuism and its counter-movement,
Arcadianism. In France it had evolved the affectations
of Ronsard and his Pléiade, of du Bartas, and of the
*précieuses*. In Italy it had evolved Marino and *secentismo*.
In Spain it had evolved Góngora and Gongorism. The
interrelationships of these groups are uncertain, and
in some cases the movements were actually opposed
to each other. No chronological order can be established. It is probable that each nation would have
developed the same symptoms if shut off hermetically
from all intercourse with its compeers.

Moreover, the only appreciable difference between
these various styles was a shifting of emphasis, a placing
of greater stress upon certain elements than upon others,
which were usually also present. Elisha Kane, in
*Gongorism and the Golden Age*,[1] has summed these
elements up as thoroughly as one could desire, and his
summary may well apply to all varieties of this sort of
writing: 'To recapitulate the constituents of gongorism,
it may be said that this flamboyant style is made up of a
number of elements which may roughly be grouped
under two heads: affectation in language, or cultism;
and affectation in thought, or conceptism—with the

[1] The studies of Morris W. Croll on the prose aspect of the same
general phenomenon also contain much valuable information for the
student of poetry. They are as follows: ' "Attic Prose" in the Seventeenth
Century', *Studies in Philology*, xviii (1921), 79–128; 'Muret and the
History of "Attic Prose" ', *P.M.L.A.*, xxxix (1924), 254–309; and articles
in *Schelling Anniversary Papers* and *Studies in English Philology: A
Miscellany in Honour of Frederick Klaeber*.

understanding, of course, that the two classes are not
distinct, but blended. As to separate elements, those
which seem most definitely cultist are neologisms,
hyperbates, bombast, and involved sentences. Other
components which may be either cultist, conceptist
or both, are the architectonic devices of rhetoric and
the use of bizarre figures of speech, epecially metaphors,
puns, paradoxes, personification, and allegory. Finally
there are traits which incline usually, though not
invariably, to conceptism, and these are the pedantic
ornamentations of thought secured by obscure references and mythological allusions.'[1] The combination
of 'cultism' and 'conceptism' into a single form is, then,
approximately what Addison was to call 'Mixt Wit',
'which consists partly in the resemblance of ideas and
partly in the resemblance of words', and of which he
selected Cowley as the chief English example—though
at the same time he was careful to state that the same
poet possessed as much 'True Wit' as any genius who
ever wrote.[2]

Now these stylistic qualities, in differing proportions,
are to be found almost universally distributed so far as
geography or period is concerned. Putting to shame his
predecessors, who had traced such rococo characteristics
only to the decay of medieval Latin, to Guevara, to
Marcus Aurelius, and to Ovid and Martial, Kane has
found the same sort of 'meretricious verse' in the
Skalds of Iceland, Arabic lyrists of the Dark Ages, Pro-
vençal poets of the *Trobar clus*, and the decadent Greeks
of Alexandria. With such an inheritance unconsciously
upon his shoulders, it would have been absurd to treat
Abraham Cowley merely or even primarily as a representative baroque writer, or even as a representative
'Metaphysical Poet'. Addison and Dr. Johnson have
already culled the best—or worst—specimens of his
'Mixt Wit' and his most startling conceits. Enough has

---

[1] Kane, pp. 40–1.    [2] *Spectator*, no. 62.

already been written about him from this point of view.
But Addison and even Johnson—the latter very grudg-
ngly—were forced to admit the presence of many other
admirable traits in their poet. Cowley is more interest-
ng as an individual, as a personality, than as a representative 'Metaphysical' writer.

The true critic judges a man primarily by his successes, not by his mistakes. Sometimes, indeed, mistakes may be taken for successes, and praise may be
awarded for what is later recognized as an error. In
such cases, time is essential for a fair and complete
appraisal, but eventually the sifting process will be
accomplished. A study of the development of Cowley's
reputation therefore not only discloses what have been
generally selected as his best works, but also gives an
interesting commentary on the progress of taste from
his time to the present.[1]

The poem on which Cowley had originally based his
greatest hopes, the work which had been announced in
type twice as large as any other on the title-page of his
1656 volume, is now the most inert of all. The epic
*Davideis* was hailed in Cowley's own day and for some
years after as one of the chief lights of English poetry.
By the beginning of the eighteenth century, however,
it was being read chiefly by the clergy like Dr. Samuel
Woodford and Dr. Henry Felton, and the more pious
among their flocks. By the end of the eighteenth
century it was dead, and was forgotten except by such
schoolmasters and professors of rhetoric and aesthetics
as George Campbell and James Beattie, who rifled its
corpse of various examples of hyperbolic description
and incongruous thinking. The body has never been
revived. Cowley himself confessed that he had been
bored by his epic.

*The Mistress* and certain lyrics possessing similar

[1] The basis for the following summary may be found in my article
in *P.M.L.A.*, xxxviii. 588–641.

stylistic distinctions were the earliest of Cowley's works to be attacked with vigour. This attack, inaugurated by Dryden, came to its focus at the hands of Addison, Pope, Oldmixon, Johnson, and the Scotch schoolmasters, Kames and Blair, and then fell off toward the end of the century as the Romantic revival gathered way. Hurd, Headley, and others did their work so well that the nineteenth century was prepared for admirers like Lamb and Grosart. And in the twentieth century, instead of shuddering at such grotesqueries, an editor like John Sparrow has the boldness to make the bulk of his anthology of Cowley's poems these same lyrics which the early eighteenth century had scorned and ridiculed, because of their lack of simplicity and their faulty 'numbers'.

The Pindaric or irregular ode, loose in versification and 'soaring' in spirit, was mildly questioned by Dryden and severely assailed by Congreve—but both critics almost entirely exempted Cowley from their strictures on the *genre* in general. Not until the end of the eighteenth century, after Gilbert West, Gray, and others had shown what the odes of Pindar really were, did Cowley's own experiments come in for their share of the censure which had long been given their mimickers. But even after the critics had turned against them —if imitation is truly the sincerest form of flattery— Cowley's Pindarics continued to please the poets, who have not yet ceased to publish irregular odes.

In his classical paraphrases and translations, however, Cowley had the most consistent success and continuous praise. His Anacreontics and his versions of Horace, Martial, and the rest have almost never been found fault with from his day to this. The easy, familiar spirit of these ancient poets seemed to strike sympathetic harmonies in his own soul, and he rose to his most permanent heights when he did not try to soar at all.

As a consequence, the most unforeseen development in Cowley's reputation appeared in his prose work. In his own time and during the Restoration his essays, his prefaces, his prose pamphlets, and his two prose plays were scarcely known or mentioned. But as soon as the periodical essayists began to write, Cowley's prose emerged from its obscurity. At first it was merely quoted or alluded to without comment, but soon this sort of tacit approval proved insufficient, until in 1759 Oliver Goldsmith wrote: 'The time seems to be at hand when justice will be done to Mr. Cowley's prose as well as poetical writings.' To this opinion there was no dissenting voice. Hurd, Joseph Warton, Johnson himself, joined in the chorus of praise which has not yet ceased. For, said Hurd in 1764, in reference to Pope's phrase, 'so long as these *Essays* remain, they will oblige all honest men to "love the language of his heart".'

The attitude of the Neo-Classicists toward such a writer as Cowley is easy to understand. At first admiring him for his moral and intellectual qualities, they soon began to grow disturbed by the lack of simplicity in the expression of his ideas and in the seeming lack of polish in some of his verse. 'This age of taste' demanded that its literature be clear, elegant, and urbane; that it shun the extravagant and the *outré*; that it fix on the natural and the normal instead of the individual and the striking. Reason made a stronger appeal than emotion. The fact that Cowley had written several pieces with these Neo-Classical requirements served to keep him read by a limited group while greater poets such as Donne were stuffed away on the highest and dustiest shelf. Cowley's simple and frivolous little ballad, 'The Chronicle', was, like the Anacreontics, always admired. As for his didactic quality and his ability to condense ideas, Dr. Johnson had once withered Boswell—as Boswell himself records—by crying, 'There is more sense in a line of Cowley than in a page (or a sentence, or

ten lines—I am not quite certain of the very phrase) of
Pope.'

With the advent of the reactionists, however, new
qualities were discovered in Cowley's poetry. Hurd
was charmed by the 'sensible reflecting melancholy'
which infused so many of the verses in the essays or such
a poem as 'The Complaint', as well as by the graceful
'unforced gaiety' of many lighter poems. The *Monthly
Review* in 1773 went even farther by showing how
Hurd, like Pope, had gone astray in ascribing Cowley's
power merely 'to that moral air and tender sensibility
of mind which are discoverable in his writings'. For,
said the reviewer, 'the real cause why they still please is
what Mr. Pope could not judge of, because he was a
stranger to it. It is enthusiasm—the genuine spirit of
enthusiasm that breathes through all those pages where
the poet is not professedly in chase of wit'. Thus,
though the new 'liberals' could appreciate the quaint-
ness, the imagination, and the originality in Cowley
which had been deplored by their predecessors, they too
recognized that much of his work was permanently dis-
figured by conceits and 'learned puerilities'. But their
discriminative powers had been sharpened also by contact with the solid and useful works of their contemporaries. Their critical eyes could see more because
they were further opened.

The nineteenth century, on the whole, did not continue the development of this appreciation to quite the
completion which might have been expected. Lamb, of
course, loved Cowley for his flavour of oddity, eccentri-
city, and companionableness.[1] Wordsworth called him
an 'able writer and amiable man'.[2] Hazlitt, lecturing
on Dryden and Pope, described him as 'melancholy and
fantastical'—'a great man, not a great poet'.[3] But the
Romantics did not read him as they did even the minor

[1] Lamb, 'Detached Thoughts on Books and Reading', &c.
[2] Wordsworth, *Prose Works*, ii. 114–15.    [3] Hazlitt, *Works*, v. 84

works of Milton, whose fame he had eclipsed while
both were alive. The latter half of the century, indeed,
was enlivened by the friendly squabble between
Edmund Gosse and the Rev. Alexander Grosart as
to which of them was the last or the greatest of
Cowley's admirers.[1] Nevertheless, Grosart's assertion
that Cowley has always had, and always will have, 'an
inner circle of readers and students' seems to be tenable
even to-day. The historians and critics, with the help
of posterity, have begun to understand what Cowley
stood for and what he accomplished. 'Metaphysical
poetry', even in the Johnsonian sense, seems almost to
be coming into fashion. It is highly dangerous not to
agree that John Donne was one of the major English
poets. H. J. C. Grierson is not afraid to publish an
anthology and label it defiantly, *Metaphysical Poetry*.
And John Sparrow has dared to print *The Mistress, with
Other Select Poems of Abraham Cowley*.

What, briefly, are Cowley's claims on the attention
of every one who pretends to an appreciation of and a
regard for English literature? In his youth, with boyish
enthusiasm and confidence, he set out to scale the Alps
of poetry—to be the 'Muse's Hannibal'. The uncertainty and the lack of firmness in his own character,
however, combined with the political conditions of his
time, prevented him from achieving this ambition. In
fact, by the end of his life, which had consisted of
a series of dilemmas muddled through rather than
solved, he had renounced ambition. He had reached
his Italy not by conquering the Alps but by going around
them. His haven, nevertheless, was just as bright, just
as sunny, as if he had come to it as victor rather than
vanquished. He had some regrets, to be sure, but these
were growing dimmer and dimmer in his memory—
when he died, before he had reached the age of fifty.

But during his career of almost forty years of writing,

[1] Grosart, *Cowley*, pp. xxxiii–iv.

he had made more marks in English literature than most
men would dare to hope for. He was perhaps the most
precocious of English poets, anticipating even Pope in
the early maturing of his genius. He composed—or at
least commenced—the first religious epic in English
anticipating Milton by several years. He was the
popularizer—almost the inventor—of the Pindaric or
irregular ode; and he was therefore a liberal influence
on versification. Although he also wrote and helped to
develop the couplet, he would probably have been in
the van of the *vers librists* if he had lived in the second
decade of the twentieth century. As part of his innovations with Pindar, too, he developed his theory of
translation, which, in its emphasis on 'naturalization
into the new language and culture by 'compensating
the work for what it had inevitably lost in transit, was a
fresh and original idea. Similarly, he was an incipien
critic, next to Davenant perhaps the most importan
one between Jonson and Dryden, and his scientifi
views on the influence of climate, social and politica
environment, &c., on the writer lead directly to the
deterministic creed of Taine. He held various advance
ideas on education and science; he had planned a prac
tical school to be based primarily on the sciences with
out neglecting the humanities; and he was an influentia
factor in the formation of the Royal Society. He was th
first in English to write essays in which self-revelatio
and the establishment of an intimate bond betwee
reader and author was a prime aim; and he wrote
familiar, colloquial prose which was among the bes
styles in his century.

Finally, if he had lived, he might have become
'Metaphysical Poet' in the true sense of the term. Fo
Abraham Cowley was continually growing. Things c
importance were happening in his mind up to the da
of his death. His interest in natural science and philo
sophy, his reverence for Bacon and Hobbes, his implic

Epicureanism, combined with his fluency of expression, all gave promise that he might some day have written something which would really have deserved the term metaphysical poetry. For one thing is certain: he had long ago outgrown the phase in which his eager desire was to surprise his readers with the ingenuities of burning glasses of ice, of trees withered from the carving of a lover's heart upon them, of strange deifications of the 'monster, woman'. In his maturity he seemed to be reaching out toward a kind of writing which should be emotional as well as learned, imaginative as well as intellectual—something which should interpret the universe and man, rather than the artificialities of life, as he had before seen them.

# APPENDIX

## DOCUMENTS RELATING TO ABRAHAM COWLEY
## OR HIS FAMILY

(In the following pages no attempt has been made to re-
produce errors made by the original writers or scribes and
then corrected by them. Because of the exigencies of typography, the various curls and other signs of abbreviation
and contraction have been omitted and the superscribed
letters have been brought level with the line. But when-
ever the resulting abbreviation has seemed to promise
difficulty of interpretation, the missing letters have been
supplied in brackets on the first appearance of the word
in each document.)

# THE WILL OF THOMAS COWLEY, FATHER OF ABRAHAM COWLEY

*(The original will, preserved at Somerset House, is followed here. Grosart has followed the copy from the register, 82 Meade, in the Prerogative Court of Canterbury.)*

I Thome Cowley

In the name of god Amen the ffoure & twentith daye of Julye Anno d[o]m[in]i 1618. And in the Sixtenth yere of the raigne of o[u]r souraigne Lorde Kinge James of England ffraunce & Ireland and of Scotland thone & ffyfteth I Thomas Cooley Citizen & Stacyonr of London & of the p[ar]ishe of St. Michell at querne london beinge sicke in bodye but in good & p[er]fecte memory thankes be god doe make this my last will & testamt. in mannr & forme followinge that is to saye ffirst I comit my soule to the Almighty god wth full assurance of remission of all my sinnes throughe the merritts & passion of Jesus Christ my savior & redeemer And my body to be buried at the discresion of my executor hereafter named And As for the disposinge of that worldly estate As god hath bestowed vppon me (my debtes beinge sattysfyed) I give devise & bequeth the same in mannr & forme followinge that is to saye ffirste my will & mynde is that wheras god hath blessed me wth Sixe Children besides the Childe or Children wch Thomasyn my wife now goeth wthall, vizt. Peeter Cooley Audrey Cooley John Cooley William Cooley Katheryn Cooley and Thomas Cooley and to the Childe or Children wch my wife goeth wthall I giue & bequeth to eurye of them seurally the some of One hundred & ffourtye poundes apeece of lawfull money of England and if either or any of them shall happen to dye or decease this mortall lyve that then his her or their porcon soe deceasinge to be equally devided amongest the rest of them survivinge to be payd at their seurll ages of one & twenty yeres or daye of marriage Item I giue & bequeath vnto my sisters Children Richard Milwood & Margery Milwood to either of them ffyve poundes of lawfull money of England Item I giue & bequeath to Elizath [*sic*] Peirce my sister ffyve poundes of lawfull money of England. Item I giue & bequeath vnto my brothers in lawe Humphrey Clarke & Humphrey Clare; and Henry Morton & Rowland Squyer to eurye of them ffyve poundes of lawfull money of England And Doe make them ou[e]rseers of this my laste will & testamt desiring them to be Aydinge & assistinge to my beloved wife my executor hereafter named. The reste & reasidue of my estate my debtes fully sattysfyed my legacyes p[er]formed & my funerall discharged I giue & bequeath vnto Thamesyn Cooley my deere & welbeloved wife who I make my full & sole executrix of this my laste will and testamt In witnes whereof I haue herevnto set my hand & seale the daye & yere above written.

Thomas
Cowley

Sealed published and Declared by the aboue named Thomas Cowley the Testator the fower and twentieth daie of July 1618 for his last will & Testamt in the p[re]s[e]nce of vs

John Sharpe
Georg Brittridge

*The copy has the following record of probate, the formula on the original being a condensation and abbreviation of this, with the additional signature 'Audree' at the end:)*

Probatum fuit Testamentum suprascriptum apud London coram Mag[ist]ro Edmundo Pope legum doctore Surrogato venerabilis viri D[omi]ni Johannes Bennet militis legum etiam Doctoris Curie Prerogative Cantuariensis Magri custodj sive comissarij legitime constituto vndecimo die Mensis Augusti Anno Dni millesimo sexcentesimo Decimo octavo Juram[en]to. Thomasine Cowley Relicte dicti Defuncti et Executrice in eodem Testamento nominat[u]r Cui Commissr fuit administraco bonorum Jurium et Creditorum dicti Defuncti de bene et fideliter administrand[um], &c. Ad Sancta Dei Evangelia Jurat.

## II

## THE WILL OF ABRAHAM COWLEY

*(The original will, preserved at Somerset House, is followed, rathe:*
*than the form which Grosart has copied from Cunningham.)*

In the name of God Almighty, to whom bee forever all glory
Amen. I Abraham Cowley of Chertsea in the County of Surry
beeing at present by Gods mercy in perfect health and vnder
standing, and well considering the vncertainty of human Life
most especially in theise times of sicknes and mortality, do i»
attendance of Gods blessed pleasure concerning my life or death
make and declare this my Last Will and Testament, as followith

I humbly recommend my Soul to yt great God from whom
had it, beseaching him to receive it into his bosome for the merit
of his Sonne, the Saviour of Sinners, amoungst whom I am one c
ye greatest, and my Body to ye Earth from whence it came, i
hopes of a happy Resurrection, O Lord I beleive, help my un
beleif, O Lord I repent, pardon the weaknes of my Repentanc(

All my worldly goods, moneys, and Chattels, I bequeath t
my Brother Thomas Cowley, whom I do hereby constitute m
sole Heyr and Executr. hee paying out of yt estate wch it ha
pleased God to bestow vpon mee much above my deserts, thei
ensuing Legacies.

I leave to my Neveu    [*sic*] Cowley (if hee bee yet alive) te
pounds. To my Cosen Beniamin Hind towards his education i
Learning fivety pounds, To my Cosen    [*sic*] Gauton of Nutfei)
in Surrey for ye same vse of his eldest sonne, fivety pounds. T
my Cosen Mary Gauton twenty pounds; To Mr. Thom;
Fotherby of Canterbury Esqr. one hundred pounds, wch [:
beseech him to accept of as a small remembrance of his ancie\
kindnes to mee. To Sr. Will Davenant twenty pounds, to M
Mart. Clifford twenty pounds, to Mr. Thomas Sprat twen»
pounds, to Mr. Thomas Cook twenty pounds, To Dr. Charl‹
Scarburgh twenty pounds, to Dr. Thomas Croyden twen»
pounds, To my Mayd Mary (besides what I ow her, and all n
wearing Linen) twenty pounds. To my servant Thomas Waldr‹
ten pounds and most of my wearing clothes at my Brothe
choise. To Mary my Brothers Mayd five pounds. To the poor ‹

the Town of Chertsea twenty pounds. I do farther leave to the
Honble. Iohn Hervey of Ickworth, Esqr. my share and interest
in his Highns. the Duke of Yorks Theater, and to ye right
Honble. the Earl of St Albans, my Lord, and once kind Master,
a Ring of ten pounds, onely in memory of my duty and affection
to him, not beeing able to give any thing worthy his acceptance, nor hee (God bee praised) in need of any gifts from such
persons as I.

If any thing bee due to mee from Trinity College I leave it to
bee bestowed in books vpon yt Library, and I leave besides to
Dr Robert Crane Fellow of ye sd College a Ring of five pounds
valew as a small token of o[u]r freindship.

I desire my dear Freind Mr Thomas Sprat to trouble himself
wth ye Collection and Revision of all such writings of mine
(whither printed before or not) as hee shall think fit to bee
published, Beseeching him not to let any passe wch hee shall
iudge vnworthy of ye name of his Freind, and most especially
nothing (if any thing of yt kind have escaped my pen) wch may
give the least offence in point of Religion or good Manners.
And in consideration of this vnpleasant task I desire him to
accept of my Study of Books.

This I declare to bee my Last Will and Testament. Lord
have mercy vpon my Soul. Made, Written by my own hand
signd and Sealed, At Chertsea, this 18 day of September, 1665.

Abraham Cowley

Signed and Sealed in
   ye presence of
      Thomas Waldron

The mark of Iohn Symonds [*mark*]
   Wheelwright, of Chertsey

*(The copy—104 Carr—has the following record of probate, the
formula on the original being a condensation and abbreviation of
this:)*

Probatum fuit Testamentum suprascriptum apud ades Exo-
nienses scituat[is] in le strand in Comitatu Midd[se]x coram
Petro Lane artium magistro surrogato venerabilis et egregij viri
Domini Willimj Merick milit[i]s legum doctoris Curiæ Prero-
gativa Cantuariensis magistri Custodis sive commissarij l[egi]-

t[i]me constituti Vltimo die mensis Augusti Anno Dnj Mill[es]imo
Sexcentisimo sexagesimo septimo Juramento Thomæ Cowley
fratris dicti defuncti et executoris in huiusmodi Testamento
nominat Cui Commissa fuit administraco omnium et singulorum
bonorum Jurium et creditorum dicti defuncti de bene et
fidel[ite]r administrand[um] eadem Ad sancta dei Evangelia
Jurat.

(*On the original also appears the following.*)

Ulto: die mensis Augusti 1667.
Thomas Cowley Executor intronominatus
Jurat coram me
    Pet: Lane Surr

# III

## THE WILL OF THOMAS COWLEY, BROTHER
## OF ABRAHAM COWLEY

(*The original will, preserved at Somerset House, has been followed
here, rather than the copy from the register, 102 Coke, in the
Prerogative Court of Canterbury.*)

In the Name of God to whom bee Glory for euer Amen: I
Thomas Cowley of Chertsey in ye County of Surrey being by
Gods mercy in p[er]fitt Health both of Body & mind do make
and declare this to bee my Last will and Testemt. I humbly
recom[m]end my Soule to Almighty God, my Body to ye Earth
from whence it came hoping through ye merrits of o[u]r
L[or]d & Sauiour Jesus Christ to have a ioyfull resurrection at
ye last day: First I desier yt the Legacies giuen by my late
deare Brother Abraham Cowley in his last will not yett payd
bee iustly performed. I giue and bequeath vnto my Kinsman
Roger Cowley now beyond ye Seas (if hee bee aliue) and his
Children lawfully begotten the sum[m]e of one thowsand pounds
if hee and his Children be dead at ye time of my decease then
ye said Thousand pounds to bee disposed of to such charritable
vses as my Executors & ouerseers shall thinke good. To the
Children of my Cosen Humphrey Clark equally deuided two
hundred pounds To the two Sonns of my Cosen Henry Gawton
one hundred pounds. To the Children of my Cosen Will[ia]m

Gawton deceased to each of them fourty pounds. To my sister
in Law Eleanor Cowley twenty fiue pounds. To Joseph Hynd
her Sonne twenty fiue pounds and to Beniamen Hynd her Sonne
fiuety pounds. To the dumbe Daughter of my Cosen James
White late of Deptford fiuety pounds. To my Cosen Barrow at
Oxford ten pounds. To Mr Thomas Cowley Draper twenty
pounds and to him more for silke to pay at my death twenty
pounds. To Mr. Willyam Cowley of Dodleston by Chester ten
pounds. To my Mayd Mary Hazzard fiuety pounds. To the
two twins of my freind Mr. Thomas Turner Moses & Aron each
twenty pounds. To my servant Thomas Waldron if liuing with
mee at ye time of my death fourty pounds or if with consent
gonn from mee ten pounds. To the poore of the parrish of
Deptford twenty pounds. To the poore of ye parrish of Chertsey
thirty pounds. To the poore of ye parrish of Lambeth
thirty pownds. To the Company of Stationers towards the new
building of there Hall one hundred pounds or if built in plate:
to Christ Church Hospitall one hundred pounds. To St.
Thomas Hospitall in Southwark one hundred pounds. To ye
poore prisoners of Ludgate Kings bench & Marshallsees for ye
discharge of such as are kept for any debt vnder tenn pounds one
hundred and fiuetie pounds To twenty such widdows yt are
really poore and soe proued to bee to my Executrs. & ouerseers
the sume of two hundred pounds equally deuided. To my
ffreind Mr. Henry Wagstaffe for a ring fiue pounds To my
freind Mr. Humphrey Robinson at Oxford for a Ring fiue pounds.
To the Minister of that parrish where it shall please God my
Body shalbee interred fiue pounds. To Mr. Thomas Spratt
and Capt. Giles Trauers whome I desier to bee Ouerseers that
this my will bee performed to each of them fiuety pounds. To
Dr Breton Minister of Deptford and to Mr Jeremiah fforman
of London merchant whom I doe heereby ordayne and appoint
my Executors of this my last will & Testement to each one
hundred pounds. That after funerall Charges which I desier to
bee moderate & leaue it to ye discretion of my said Executrs and
all charges which the said Executrs shalbee at in ye sale of all
goods and chattells or otherwise concerning this trust that what
shalbee receiued over and aboue the premises bee disposed of to
such Charitable vses as my said Executrs & Ouerseers shall agree
& thinke fitt. In Witnesse whereof I haue heere sett to my hand

and seale dated this twentieth day of May one thousand six hundred sixty and nine being Ascention day:

Thomas Cowley.

*(The following depositions appear in the original only:)*

1°: Sept. 1669°

Quodie Compl. personalit[e]r Maria Hassard et fecit fidem That the Testator Thomas Cowley lieing very weake of body but of perfect mind & sound memory did on Wensday Night ye Eleaventh of August 1669 call this Deponent to him & told her yt he had made his will and settled his estate thereby and for his Executors had nominated and Made Doctor Breeton & Jeremiah fforman Merchant and Mr Thomas Spratt & Capt. Giles Trauers Overseers thereof.

Signum
Maria [*mark*] Hassard

Eod[em] die   Compl. personalit[e]r Egidius Travers et fecit
fidem That on Wensday ye 11° Aug[us]ti 1669 in
1 Sept. 1669/Maria ye afternoone hee discourseing wth the Testator
Hassard et Egidius Thomas Cowley he the sd Testator did say and
Travers Jurat sup-
[er] veritate yr al- Declare to this Deponent that he had made
legtor coram me his will And this deponent further sayeth yt
Rich: Lloyd Sur: after the death of ye sd deceased hee this depo-
nent togather wth seurall other persons searching for writeings of ye deceaseds in a Cabbinett where most things of concernment vsed to lie did find this paper writeing in a black box perporting a will being all written wth ye proper hand writeing of ye sd testator Sealed wth ye seale & subscribed wth. his Name as now it is

Giles Trauers.

Probat[u]m apud ades Exon[iense]s &c primo die mensis sep[temb]ris Anno Dni 1669 Coram ven[era]b[i]li viro Richardo Lloyd leg[u]m d[o]c[t]ore surr[ogat]o &c Juramentis

Roberti Breton Sacrae Theologiæ Professoris et Jeremiah
fforman Ex[ecuto]rum &c quibus &c de bene &c Jura[n]t.

1° Sept. 1669

Executores infrano[m]i[n]at[i] Jura[n]t coram me
Rich: Lloyd: Sur.

## IV

## GRANT OF THE MANOR OF OLDCOURT TO ABRAHAM COWLEY

(*From the Land Revenue Enrolments—Kent, Surrey, Sussex, &c.*
*L.R. 1/114, vol. 22.*)

Henritte Marie R.

*This Indenture* made the twentieth day of January in the ffower-
teenth yeare of the Reigne of our souereigne Lord Charles the
second by the grace of god of England Scotland ffrance and
Ireland king defender of the faith &c Annoque Dom[in]i one
Thousand six hundred sixtie and Two *Betweene* the most high
and Exellent Princes Henritt Marie by the grace of god Queene
of England scotland ffrance and Ireland Mother of the said
Kings Ma[jes]tie that now is, of the one part and Abraham Cowley of the Citty of London Esqr of the other parte: *Whereas*:
the Right hono[r]able Henry Earle of st Albans Sr Kenelme
Digby Sr John Wintor Sr Charles Harbord Sr Robert Long
Sr Peter Ball and Sr Henry Wood doe stand and are possessed
(amongst other things) of and in the Lordship or Manor of Oldcourt and the Lands Tenem[en]ts and Hereditaments hereafter
menconed for the terme of diverse yeares yett vnexpired Vpon
Trust and Confidence To and ffor the onely Vse and beniffitt
of the said Most Excellent Princesse Queen Henritte Marie ffor
her life as part of her Jointure; *And Whereas* the said Mannor
of Oldcourt the parsonage and Tithes of Greenwich the Ballast
wharfe there. Marshes Woods and other lands Tenemts and
Hereditamts lyeing and being in East Greenwich; West Greenwich Deptford Lewisham Kidbrooke Chaleton Eltham Woolwich
Chislehurst; and Beckenham in the said County of Kent were
heretofore graunted by Kinge James by his Letters pattents
beareing date the eight and Twentieth day of ffebruary in the
ninth yeare of his said Maties Reigne: over England. To John
Eldred and William Whitmore ffor the Terme of sixty yeares from

thence next ffollowing which said Lease by meaene assignemts or Conveyances in the Law afterwards Came vnto Robert Tichburne or some other person or persons Jn Trust for him and being by him since fforfeited ffor high Treason whereof hee is Attainted whereby and by graunt (amongst other things) of the goods and Chattells of all persons attainted of high Treason within her said ma[jes]t[y]s Jointure or any parte of it; by her dearest Lord King Charles the first by his Letters pattents beareing date the ninth day of March in the sixth yeare of his Reigne to her made dureing her life. The Residue of the said Terme belongeth to her said Matie *Now this Jndenture Wittnesseth* That the said Most Execellent princess Queen Henriette Marie of her especiall grace Certeine Knowledge and meere mocon aswell for and in Consideracon of the good and ffaithfull seruice done and performed to her said Matie by the said Earle of st Albans and at his suite and nominacon As alsoe of the yearly rent and Covenants hereinafter referred and agreed to bee paid and performed *hath* graunted Leased Sett and to farme letten and by theise pr[e]sents doth graunt sett and to ffarme lett vnto the said Abraham Cowley his executors Administrators and assignes *All* that Lordship or mannor of Oldcourte and all lands Meadowes Pastures Marshes and Tithes vnto the same belonging or therewith enioyed in Eastgreenwich and West Greenwich in the County of Kent with their and every of their rights members and appurtenances whatsoever and alsoe the Balast wharfe there and all other Lands Tenemts woods and hereditamts whatsoever in East Greenwich West Greenwich Kidbrooke Eltham woolwich Beckenham and Chislehurst and all lands Tenemts Meadowes ffeedings pastures and woods in East Greenwich West Greenwich Deptford Lewisham Kidbrooke Chaleton woolwich and Beckenham in the said County of Kent late called the Queenes lands heretofore demised to Robert Viscount Cranborne menconed to be to geather by the perticuler thereof of the yearely rent or value of six pounds thirteen shillings and foure pence and of the cleare yearely vallue (Reprizes thereof deducted) of six pounds Eleauen shillings & ffowre pence And after graunted by the said late Kinge James to the said John Eldred and William Whitmore ffor the Terme of three-score yeares as aforesaid vnder the yearly rent of six pounds Thirtene shillings and ffoure pence as by the same grant thereof made (amongst other things therein Conteined) it doth and may more att large appeare and were parcell of the possessions graunted to our late sovereigne Lord King Charles the first and his heires Kings of England for ever before his comeing to the Crowne, by his said late Maties most deare ffather Kinge James of Blessed memory and after granted by the late King Charles or other his Trustees, to her said Matie or Trustees for her Matie as parte of her Jointure and all her right title tearme interest Claime and demand therein by vertue of the said Attainder and grant to her made by the said recited Letters Pattents dated the ninth of march aforesaid: *To haue and to hould* the said Manors Lordships Lands Tenements and hereditamts and all and Singular other the pr[e]misses before in and by theise prsents demissed or meant menconed or intend to bee demised with their and every of their rights liberties members and appurtenances vnto the said Abraham Cowley his executors Administrators and assignes from the second day of January in the yeare of our lord one Thousand six hundred sixty and one, for and dureing all the rest and residue of the said Terme and vnto the full end of the said Tearme vnto the said John Eldred and William Whitmore granted or menconed to bee granted; to them by his said late Matie Kinge James as aforesaid yett to come and vnexpired vnder the Rents Couenants and agreements therein conteined *yeilding* and payeing therefore yearely and every yeare dureing the said terme hereby demised the yearly rent or sume of six Pounds Thirteene shillings and ffoure pence of lawfull money of England and all other rents suites and Services reserved in or by the said letters Pattents made to the said John Eldred and William Whitmore. Att the ffeasts of the anunciacon of the blessed Virgin st mary and st Michall the Archangell in euery yeare dureing the said terme to be paid vnto the hands of her said Maties Bayleiffes or Receivor generall of the prmisses for the tyme being, by even and equal porcons dureing the said terme hereby granted to and for the vse of the said most Execellent Princesse Queene Henriette marie dureing her life and after her decease vnto the Bayleiffe or Receivor generall of the Kings Most Excellent Matie his heires and successors of the premisses ffor the time being by euen and equal porcons dureing the said terme hereby granted *And* the said Abraham Cowley ffor himselfe his executors administrators and assignes

and for every of them doth Couenant promise and agree to and
with the said Most Excellent Princesse Queene Henriette Marie
her executors administrators and assignes and to and with every
of them by theise prsents That hee the said Abraham Cowley his
executors administrators and assignes and every of them shall
and will at his their or some of their proper Costes and charges
from time to time and at all times dureing the said Terme
hereby demised well and sufficiently repair suport scoure clense
and maintaine as well all the howses buildings walls and Coveer-
ings as all the hedges ditches ffences inclosures shoares and
Bankes of and belonging to the Premisses and all òther necessary
Reparacons whatsoever of the Premisses and the Premisses soe
well and sufficiently repaired and amended in the end or other
determinacon of this prsent demisse shall leaue avoyd and yeild
vp: *Provided* allwayes That if it shall happen dureing the said
Terme hereby demissed the said yearely rent of six Pounds
thirteen shillings ffourepence in and by theise prsents reserved
to bee behind or vnpaied in part or in all by the space of
fforty dayes next after either of the said ffeastes in which the
same ought to be paid being lawfully demanded by her or her
Matis Receivors Baliffes or others therevnto Authorized That
then and from thenceforth it shall bee lawfull for them to re-
enter into all and singuler the Premises and that from thenceforth the said demisse and lease thereof hereby made and every
Article Couenant Clause and agreemt therein Conteined shalbe
vtterly voide ffrustrate and of none effect Anything in theise
prsents Conteined to the Contrary thereof in anywise notwithstanding: *Provided* asoe [*sic*] That if it happen this prsent demise
not to bee inrolled within one yeare now next and emediatly
ffollowing before the Auditor of the said County where the
prmisses are ffor the time being then alsoe the Lease and denise
[*sic*] hereby made shalbee voide and of none Effect in the law;
*Jn Wittness* whereof to the one parte of theise prsent Jndentures
the said Most Excellent Princesse Queen Henritte Marie hath
caused her greate seale to bee affixed and to the other parte
thereof the said Abraham Cowley his hand and Seale hath sett
the day and yeare first aboue Written

May it please yo[u]r Matie
    This containeth a grant from yor Matie to Abraham Cowley

Esqr (att the direcon and notacon of the Earle of st Albans) of
all that Lordship and manor of oldcourt in the County of Kent
and of the Ballast wharfe and all lands tenemts hereditamts to
the said Lord shipe or Manor belonging for the residue of a
terme of 60 yeares graunted by his Matie King James vnto John
Eldred and William whitmore wch said terme by meane Conveyances came vnto Robert Tichborne and by him since forfeited for Treason and belonging to your [sic] and vnder the
auncient Rent of 6li 13s. 4d. And is done by vertue of yr maties
warrant vnder yor Maties Signe Manuell to mee directed date
1° January 1661;

4to. Aprilis 1663 exr:

>)3 ffebruary 1662) By her Maties Com[man]d
>)Peter Ball) John Wintour
>Recepi ffeb. 12 1662 HR

## V

## GRANT OF THE PALL MALL FIELD TO ABRAHAM COWLEY AND BAPTIST MAY

*(The following excerpt is taken from Patent Roll 3077, 17 Charles II,
Part 6. This differs only slightly, chiefly in spelling, from the
Land Revenue Enrolments—Essex, Hertford, Middlesex, &c.
Liber 12 (62), ff. 12–15.*

*The first one third of the document is devoted to a description of two
previous indentures, one of March 27, 1661, in which Henrietta
Maria's commissioners granted the Manor of St. James in the
Fields (Middlesex) to John Harvey and John Coell for a period
of twenty-one years at a yearly rent of £37 6d.; and the other of
March 28, 1661, between the same parties extending the lease
for ten years more at the same rent. Since there seemed to be some
question as to the inclusion of the Pall Mall Field or Close in this
property, on September 28, 1662, Charles II confirmed the Field
to be part of the manor, on the request of St. Albans, Harvey, and
Coell. Moreover, to begin in 1691, he gave the latter two a lease
of the field for twenty-nine years at a yearly rent of £5. Permission was also accorded them to build on this property such*

x

*edifices as the King or his agents should direct and they should see*
*fit. The new indenture then continued as follows:)*

. . . And whereas wee have designed a place in the said Pall Mall
ffeild Whereon thirteene or ffoureteene great and good houses
which will compasse the said place are to stand. And wee being
informed that men are unwilling to build such greate houses for
any terme or estate but that of Inheritance *Now Know* yee that
Wee for and in consideracon of the many good and acceptable
services to us done and performed by the said Henry Earle of
Saint Albans and for other good consideracons us thereunto
moveing of our especiall grace certaine Knowledge and meere
mocon have given and graunted and by these presents att and by
the nominacon of the said Earle doe for us our heires and Successors give and graunt unto our trusty and welbeloved Baptist
May and Abraham Cowley Esquires their heires and Assignes,
the severall peices or parcells of ground herein after menconed
(that is to say) All that peice or pcell of ground conteyning by
estimacon 200 feete in front being or reputed to bee one
moyety or halfe part of the West side of a great Square place in
the said ffeild called the Pall Mall Feild staked out with the
depth to the high Way leading Northward from St. James gate
And alsoe all those two slipps or parcells of ground lyeing and
being on the Southside of the said great square place and of the
Northside of the Streete called or knowne by the name of the
Pall Mall streete also Saint Katherines streete each of the said
slipps or parcells of ground conteyning by estimacon in length
210 feete and in depth 60 feete or thereabouts. And alsoe all that
peice or parcell of ground lyeing and being on the West end of
the said two slipps or parcells of Ground and on the North side
of the said streete called the Pall Mall streete also Saint Katherine streete, equall to the breadth of the said two slipps or parcells of ground With the depth to the high Way leading Northward from Saint James house. And alsoe all that peice or
parcell of ground conteyning by Estimacon 200 feete or thereabout being the other moyety or halfe part of the West side of
the said great square place With 200 feete in depth And alsoe all
that peice or parcell of ground lyeing betweene the West and
North side of the said great square place or ground being a
square of 200 feete or thereabouts Whereupon stables are designed and intended to bee built to and for the houses to bee

built upon the severall parcells of ground aforesaid and alsoe all
that peice or parcell of ground conteyning by estimacon 210
feete in front or thereabouts, being or reputed to bee one
moyety or halfe parte of the North side of the said square place
With the depth to the first streete Northward And all that
peice or parcell of ground conteyning by estimacon 210 feete in
front or thereabouts being the other moyety or halfe parte of
the Northside of the said great Square place With the depth alsoe
to the first streete Northward, and alsoe all that peice or parcell
of ground lyeing betweene the North and East sides of the said
great Square place being a square of 200 feete or thereabouts
Whereupon stables are designed to bee built to and for the houses
intended to bee built on the severall parcells of ground last menconed And alsoe all that peice or parcell of ground conteyning
by estimacon 200 feete in front and 200 feete in depth being or
reputed to bee one moyety or halfe parte of the East side
of the said great square place And alsoe all that peice or
parcell of ground conteyning by estimacon 200 feete in front
and 200 feete in depth being or reputed to bee the other
moyety or halfe parte of the said East side of the said great
square place All which said severall peices or parcells of
ground and premisses herein before menconed and intended
to bee hereby graunted as aforesaid are parcell or reputed
parcell of the said close or ffeild called Pall Mall ffeild
and premisses in and by the said severall recited Indentures
demised as aforesaid And together With the square place or
parcell of ground hereafter menconed and intended to bee
accepted doe conteine in the whole by estimacon twelve acres
three roodes and two and Twenty pearches or thereabouts.
And all our Estate right title interest clayme and demand
Whatsoever of in and unto the premisses herein before menconed and intended to bee hereby graunted and every parte and
parcell thereof And the Revercon and Revercons Remainder and
Remainders together With the yearely and other rents Revenues
and proffitts of the premisses and of every parte and parcell
thereof (except and out of these presents and the graunt hereby
made alwaies reserved and foreprized[)] All that peice or parcell
of ground being a square place and designed for a Markett place
and wherein a Markett house is intended to bee erected conteyning in length from East to West 262 feete and in breadth

from North to South 195 feete and 4 inches or thereabouts And alsoe all streetes high Wayes and publique pathes and passages to bee made and laid out in by or through the premisses or any parte or parcell partes or parcells thereof To have and to hold the said severall peeces or parcells of ground and all and singuler other the premisses herein before menconed and intended to bee hereby graunted With their Appurtenances unto the said Baptist May and Abraham Cowley and their heires to the use of the said Baptist May and Abraham Cowley and of their heires and Assignes for ever. Yeilding and paying And the said Henry Earle of Saint Albans for himselfe his heires Executors and Administrators doth hereby Covenant and graunt to and with us our heires and Successors to yeild and pay unto us our heires and Successors att the receipt of the Exchequer att Westminster the yearely rent or sum[m]e of ffourescore pounds of lawfull money of England together with the said severall yearely Rents or Sum[m]es of money in or by the said severall recited Indentures or leases respectively reserved or payable as aforesaid Which are hereby agreed intended and declared to remaine and continue to bee paid and payable during the continuance of the said leases respectively according to the purport and intent of the reservacons and agreements in the same severall leases conteyned the said yearely rent of ffourescore pounds to bee paid att the ffeast of Saint Michaell the Archangell and the Annunciacon of the blessed Virgin Mary by even and equall porcons the first payment thereof to begin and bee made att the ffeast of Saint Michaell the Archangell which shalbee in the yeare of our lord Christ one thousand six hundred sixty and six Provided alwayes that if the said yearely rent of ffourescore pounds hereby reserved as aforesaid shall att any tyme or times hereafter. bee behind or unpaid by the space of fforty dayes next over. or after. either. of the said ffeast dayes Whereon the same is herein before appointed to be paid That then and from thenceforth the Graunt hereby made of the premisses unto the [sic] Baptist May and Abraham Cowley their heires and Assignes of the premisses as aforesaid shall cease determine and bee voyd. Any thing to the contrary notwithstanding And whereas sundry of the Tennants of that Rowe of houses which are scituate and being on the South syde of the said streete called Pall Mall Streete also Saint Katherines Streete have humbly besought us that leases may bee graunted to them of the ground sometymes vsed as the Com[m]on high Way from Charing Crosse to our Mansion house of Saint James and lyeing betweene their said houses and the Wall of our said Parke of Saint James Whereunto wee are graciously pleased to condiscend *Now* know yee therefore that Wee for the consideracons aforesayd and of our more ample grace certaine knowledge and meere mocon have graunted leased sett and to ffarme letten and by these presents (att and by the like nominacon of the said Earle) doe graunt lease sett and to ffarme lett unto the said Baptist May and Abraham Cowley their Executors and Assignes All that part of the said Ground heretofore used as a Com[m]on High Way which doth extend from that parte or parcell thereof Which Wee have already graunted to our Trusty and Welbeloved Sir Phillipp Warwicke, Knight on the East to that other parte or parcell thereof Which wee have likewise already graunted to our Trusty and Welbeloved Sir John Denham Knight of the Bath on the West. To have and to hould the same unto the said Baptist May and Abraham Cowley their Executors Administrators and Assignes from the ffeast of Saint Michaell the Archangell which was in the twelfth yeare of our Raigne for and during and unto the full end and tearme of threescore yeares from thence next ensueing and fully to bee compleate and ended To the intent that leases may bee made and graunted to the severall Tennants thereof as is desired yeilding and paying therefore yearely and every yeare during the said Tearme unto us our heires and Successors in the receipt of the Exchequer att Westminster the yearely rent or Sume of fforty shillings of lawfull money of England Att the ffeast of the Annunciacon of the blessed virgin Mary and Saint Michaell the Archangell by even and equal porcons. The first payment thereof to beginn and bee made att the ffeast of the Annunciacon of the blessed virgin Mary now next comeing. Provided alwayes And our Royall Will and pleasure is That the said Baptist May and Abraham Cowley their Executors Administrators or Assignes or any of them shall not att any tyme or tymes hereafter erect sett or build or cause permitt or suffer. to bee erected sett upp or built any houses Edifices or Buildings Whatsoever, upon any parte or partes of the premisses last menconed and hereby intended to bee demised as aforesaid Which shall or may annoy or prejudice or bee occasion of annoyance or prejudice to our

said house called Saint James House or our said parke called
Saint James Parke or any our houses Edifices or buildings in
about or belonging to them or either of them And that they the
said Baptist May and Ab.aham Cowley their heires or Assignes
or either or any of them shall not or may not att any tyme or tymes
hereafter erect frame build or sett upp or cause to bee erected
framed built or sett upp any houses Edifices or buildings in or
upon any parte or partes of the said severall peices or parcells
of ground and premisses herein before menconed and intended
to bee hereby graunted unto the said Baptist May and Abraham
Cowley their heires and Assignes as aforesaid, But such only as
shall bee according to such designes and plotts and in such manner
and forme as Wee our heires and successors shall by Warrant
under our or their Signe manuell or privy Signett direct and
appoint and not otherwise any thing to the contrary in any wise
notwithstanding Provided alsoe that if the said yearely Rent of
fforty shillings hereby reserved and payable as aforesaid shalbee
behinde or unpaid in part or in all by the space of fforty dayes
next after either of the said ffeast dayes Whereon the same is
herein before appointed to bee paid That then and from thenceforth the demise and lease hereby made of the said part of the
said high way and premisses last menconed shall cease determine
and bee utterly voyd Any thing herein before conteyned to the
contrary notwithstanding Provided further that if these our
letters Patent bee not inrolled before the Auditor of the said
County of Middlesex for the tyme being within one yeare next
after the date hereof Then these presents and the severall
Graunts hereby made shall cease determine and bee utterly
voyd any thing herein before conteyned to the contrary notwithstanding And our further Will and pleasure is And Wee doe
by these presents for us our heires and Successors Declare and
graunt that these our letters Patents or the Inrollment thereof
shalbee in and by all things firme good valid and effectuall in the
lawe to all intents and purposes Notwithstanding the not reciting or menconing or ill or not true reciting or menconing of
the said severall recited Indentures or letters patents or of any
of them or of any the graunts Clauses matters or things in them
or any of them specifyed or conteyned or of any other letters
Patents or graunts heretofore made or graunted of the premisses
or any of them or any parte or parcell thereof by us or any of our

Royall Progenitors or Predecessors unto any person or persons Whatsoever. And notwithstanding noe Inquisicon or Office hath beene had or taken of or concerning the premisses before the makeing of these presents or that the true and certaine yearely vallue thereof is not herein sett forth and expressed, And notwithstanding the not namning [*sic*] or menconing or not true or certaine naming describing or menconing of the premisses or any of them or any parte or parcell partes or parcells thereof or of the severall quantityes extents meetes or bounds thereof or of any parte or partes thereof or of any parish place or County wherein the same are scittuate lyeing or being And notwithstanding the Statute made in the Parliament held in the ffirst Yeare of the Reigne of our late Royall Predecessor King Henry the fourth and notw[i]th[standin]g. the Statute made in the Parliament held in the 18th yeare of our late Royall Predecessor King Henry VIII, Or any other Act Statute Provision incertainty Imperfeccon or other matter or thing to the contrary in any wise notwthsg although expresse mencon &c.

In Witnesse &c. Witnes the King att Westmr. the first day of Aprill.

p[er] b[re]ve de privato sigillo

*(The following ending in the enrolment differs somewhat from the ending of the patent:)*

*Although* expresse mencon of ye true yearely value or certainty of ye premises or of any of them or of any other guifts or graunts by us or any of our progenitors or predecessors heretofore made to ye sd Baptist May and Abraham Cowley in theise presents is not made or any statute Act Ordinance provicon proclamacon or Restriccon heretofore had made enacted ordained or provided or any other matter cause or thinge whatsoever to ye contrary notwithstanding *In Wittnes* whereof wee haue caused theis our L[ett]res to be made pattents Wittnes our selfe at Westminister the ffirst day of Aprill in the Seaventeenth yeare of our Raigne.

By writt of privy Seale

Vyner

## VI

## 'CANT' LETTERS SUPPOSED TO HAVE PASSED BETWEEN COWLEY AND HIS CORRESPONDENTS IN PARIS

*(MS. Clarendon 51.f.211, 51.f.248, and 51.f.277, in the Bodleian. All dated 1656 in the Calendar of Clarendon MSS., and attributed to Cowley.)*

A.

London ye 21 of Apr.

Sr

I have I had [*sic*] Conference wth severall of yr Friends about yr business and I hope I shall bee able to give yu good account of ye particulars about ye latter end of ye Term, I feare I shall scarce see Mr Martin, nor can I yett heare of Mr. Helmington [*or* Felmington], Mr Ascud [Ascot ?] is verry ready to doe his vtmost in yt business wee talkt of by ye way, but yu know it was onely my proposition, and as yett I have noe order from Mr Conyers to offer any rewards or encouragements either in particular or Generall, pray lett mee know something in ys particular wth all possible speed for I find there may bee good done in yt, pray present my humblest seruice to Mr Ellis and lett him know I have delivered his Lre. I meet wth some verry discreet and knowing, yt are peremptory in ye story of Mr Osborn making love passionately to Mrs Conyers, yu had best lett Mr Ellis her Friend know it, yt hee may in time advise her, yet hee is not so courtly to others; for hee takes all violent courses to disoblige both his own and Mrs Conyers Friends, I shall not fayle yu a post now, though I have not yett a [*sic*] heard a word from you

I am

Yrs most Faithfully

J T

[*Endorsed*] 21st April

B.

London, ye 27th

Deare Nic,

This is ye 3d and noe return yett, I cannot imagine ye mis cariage of any, and therefore I doe not repeat my business,

have now to tell you yt I sent Mr Smith to Mr Green about Mr
Conyers business, and I had ys return to ye main particular; yf
hee will not fayle to send him satisfaction monye wth all convenient speed, by Mr Redshaw I beleeve hee will not doe it, for
I left him free to doe it his own way, as I always doe, thoughe I
would faine strike my friend into trading, some of yr friends I
beleeve will, make choyce of him, ye premisses I pray signifie to
Mr Ellis wth my humble service. I beleeve Mr Redshaw will
bee vpon his Journey towards yu wthin a fortnight at farthest
vnlesse hee have further instructions, wch hee doth not desire,
for hee longs to bee in yr parts, I expect a return from Mr Leke
on Saterday next, pray lett me know by ye next if yu will meet
Redshaw at Roan or Diep, and whether yu can direct mee or
noe to whom I must supers[c]ribe ye Gloves, I heare a report of
Mr Parsons leaving yu, if it bee soe, I would gladly comply wth
his time, for yu know his company might be advantageous to
mee  My Deare Friend instruct mee how I may appeare

Yrs<br>J H

[*Addressed*] A Monsieur Monsieur [*sic*] Le Fleure, Tailleur
Francois dans le Fauxbourg St Germains A Paris

[*Endorsed*] This is Mr Cow: letter to mee.
        Mr. Cow. to Mr Armourer 27th. Apr.

[*Seal*: A sheaf of corn.]

C.

Sr

I much wonder I heard not from yu ys post I have writt 4 and
reced none, Mr Thompson is returned from Leke and goe [*sic*]
to morrow towards Mr Allen, Mr. Leke is willing to accommodate
Mr Conyers but ye proportion I know not, nor ye way, for tis
by his sonn, whoe is in yr parts, I doe not know why I stay, after
next week, for I shall have dispatcht, what is possible for mee, if
I gett yu any gloves Ile bring them along wth mee, I expect ye
next weeke yrs in answer to all mine, my service to Tom  A Di

Yrs most Faithfully<br>W: R

May day
[*Addressed*] For Mr Binns
[*Endorsed*] 1st May

## VII

## CHANCERY SUIT BETWEEN ALEXANDER DAVENANT AND DAME ELIZABETH HARVEY OVER COWLEY'S HALF-SHARE IN THE DUKE'S THEATRE

(*Nos. 62 and 63 of the Hotson Chancery Photostats in the Harvard College Library, C8 348/95 and C8 560/39. Originals in Public Record Office.*)

A.                              7mo Novem: 1691

*The Right honourable the Lords Com[missione]rs for the Custody of the Great Seale of England*
Powell

*Humbly* Complaineing sheweth unto your Lordshipps your Orator Alexander Davenant of London Gent that our late Soveraigne Lord King Charles the second by his Letters patents under the Great Seale of England beareing Date the fifteenth day of January in the fourteenth Yeare of his Reigne for the Consideracons therein menconed did give and grant unto Sr William Davenant Knight since dec[eas]ed your Orators father licence and authority to Erect and build A Playhouse or Theatre in any place within the Cittyes of London and Westminster wherein Tragidies Comedies Plays Operaes Musick Seanes and all other intertainments of the Stage whatsoever might be shown and presented And further our said late Soveraigne Lord in and by his said letters patents for himselfe his heires and successors did grant unto the said Sr William Davenant his heires and Assignes full power licence and authority from tyme to tyme to gather together Entertaine Governe and keep playe[r]s and persons to Exercise and Act Tradedies [*sic*] Comedies Playes Operaes And other performances of the Stage for the honest recreation of such as should desier to see the same And that itt might be Lawfull for the said Sr William Davenant his heires and Assigns to take and receive Great Expences of Scenes musicke And such new Decorations as had not formerly been used as by the said latters Patents now of Record in this Honourable Court may more att large Appeare And your Orator further sheweth that the said Sr William Davenant att his great Charges and

Expences by virtue of the said Letters Patents did Erect and build A Playhouse or Theatre in Dorsett Garden neer ffleet street London and did gather together and Entertaine Players and persons who Acted in the Carrying on the Designe of the said Letters Patents all his life tyme afterwards whereby A Considerable proffitt did Accrue to him towards his paines and Charges thereabouts And your Orator further sheweth that the said Sr William Davenant Departed this life in or about the Month of      [sic] which was in the yeare of our Lord one thousand six hundred sixty and nine after whose Death the said licence and authority in and by the said Letters Patents granted for continueing of Stage Playes and other like representacons as Aforesaid Vested in Charles Davenant Esqr Eldest son and heir of the said Sr William Davenant by virtue of the said Letters Patents And the said Charles Davenant being then in his minority And under the Age of one and twenty yeares Dame Mary Davenant his Mother and Guardian and Relict of the said Sr William Davenant in right of the said Charles Davenant did take upon her the Management of the said Theatre dureing the minority of the said Charles Davenant And your Orator further sheweth that the said Charles Davenant haveing Attained to his full Age And our said Soveraigne Lord King Charles the second haveing granted the like Letters Patents to one Thomas Killigrew for Erecting A Playhouse in Covent Garden called the Kings Playhouse And haveing A Company of Players thereto belongeing on or about the ffourth day of May in the Yeare of our Lord one thousand six hundred Eighty and two Jtt was Agreed between the said Charles Davenant and his Trustees and one Charles Killigrew who then was authorized to Execute the Power granted in and by the said last menconed Letters Patents and who was fully authorized and had Good and sufficient power and authority to make sure Agreement that the said two Companies of Players should be united and become as one Company belongeing to one Theatre And the said Mr Charles Killigrew was to have some shares of the Proffitts thereby Ariseing in such manner as between the said Charles Davenant And the said Mr Killigrew was Agreed And yor Orator ffurther sheweth that afterwards (to witt) about the thirtieth day of August in the Yeare of our Lord God one thousand six hundred Eighty and seaven your Orators said brother and his Trustees ffor valuable Consideracons

and in due and sufficient manner did Assigne and Convey to
your Orator and his Trustees and their heires and Assignes ffor
Ever the said Playhouse or Theatre in Dorsett Court all the
power licence and Authority in and by the said first menconed
Letters Patents granted and all their Shares of and in the
benefitt of the said Agreement for union of the said two Com-
panies of Players to and for the Sole benefitt of your Orator and
his heires Exe[cuto]rs Adm[inistrato]rs and Assignes for Ever
And your Orator hath Ever since Enjoyed the same accordingly
And your Orator further sheweth that about the begining of
March last the Honourable Dame Elizabeth Harvey of London
Widdow for and on the behalfe of Elizabeth Harvey Widdow
Relict and Executrix of the last Will and testament of John
Harvey late of        [sic] Esqr Deceased did clayme A Moiety or
halfe of one Share in twenty Shares to be Devided of the Clear
Proffitts of that Company of Players which Acrued by virtue of
the ffirst Letters Patents granted to the said Sr William Dave-
nant Alleadgeing and pretendeing that the said Sr William
Davenant in his life tyme had absolutely and for Ever Granted
such Share of the said proffitts of the said Theatre unto Abraham
Cowley Esqr Deceased who Assigned the same Absolutely as he
Alleadged to the said John Harvey since Deceased which matter
yo[u]r Orator was then A stranger to and knew not the truth
thereof but att that tyme was induced to give some Creditt
thereunto in regard yo[u]r Orator had been informed that the
said John Harvey for some tyme did receive such halfe share of
the Proffitts of the said Theatre Whereupon and upon the said
Dame Elizabeth Harvey her Affirmeing that the said Elizabeth
Harvey Widdow as Executrix of the said John Harvey was
really intituled to such halfe Share and that she the said Dame
Elizabeth Harvey was Authorized sufficiently to treat with your
Orator touching the said Claime And to sell or dispose of the
said halfe Share for the said Eliz. Harvey the Executrix And
seemeing very desirous to sell the same And soe farr Concerneing
herselfe therein as that she did declare she would take itt as a
great kiendnesse if your Orator would Comply with her proposalls
and Purchase the same Whereupon yo[u]r Orator was prevailed
with And trusting to the Affirmacons and Assureances of the
said Dame Elizabeth Harvey overhastily and unadvisedly before
he had made strict Enquiry into the said Elizabeth Harvey the

Executrixs right or tittle to any Share of the proffitts of the said
Theatre (to witt) On or about the third day of March last did
Agree to give A thousand pounds for the Absolute Purchase of
the said half Share for ever and Arreareages thereof payable as
followeth That is to say your Orator was to pay four hundred
pounds thereof upon the fourth day of May then next Ensueing
And then was to Enter into two bonds Each of the penalty of
six hundred pounds and with Condicon to pay three hundred
pounds upon the twenty first day of June then next and the
other with Condicon to pay three hundred pounds more upon
the twenty first day of August then next And yo[u]r Orator
was to have a good tittle to the said halfe share And the full
benefitt thereof for Ever Conveyed to him by the said Elizabeth
Harvey the Executrix And in [*illegible*] thereunto the said Elizabeth Harvey the Executrix was to Release all Demands to your
Orator to the said ffourth day of May And she the said Dame
Elizabeth Harvey was to procure the Right Honourable Ralph
Earle of Montague together with herselfe to Enter into bond to
your Orator of the penalty of two thousand pounds that such
good tittle should be made to your Orator of the said halfe
Share And the benefitt thereof for Ever as Aforesaid att the
tyme of payment of the said four hundred pounds And Articles
should have been made accordingly And your Orator further
sheweth unto your Lordshipps that Articles were drawne which
your Orator then apprehended had been made accordingly to
the said Agreement And thereupon your Orator did signe &
Seale the same And Expected the sd Eliz: Harvey Widdow
should & would have produced her Deeds or Evidences to mani-
fest her tittle soe as yo[u]r Ora[to]rs Councell might have advised
thereupon And that yo[u]r Ora[to]r should not have parted wth
his money without such good Assureance as afforesd *But now soe
itt is* may itt please yo[u]r Lordshipps that the said Articles
as itt seemes are soe penned as in Strictness in Lawe your Orator
thereby is onely to have & Enjoye the said Eliz: Harvey the
Executrix her pretended halfe Share onely for her life Against
any Claime to be made by her onely whereas yo[u]r Orator
[*saith* ?] the true intent of the said Agreement was to have had
such halfe Share Conveyed to him & to his heires Exers Admrs &
Assignes for Ever And now itt seems that one Sr Thomas Harvey
Knight is Coexecutor with the said Eliz: Harvey Widdow And

threatens to sue yo[u]r Ora[to]r about the sd Share And will not Agree that yo[u]r Ora[to]r should pay the sd moneyes according to the said Articles nor will he joyne in makeing yo[u]r Ora[to]r any Assureance of the said halfe Shares nor will they or Either of them nor as yo[u]r Ora[to]r beleives can they shew any tittle they have to any such Share And yo[u]r Ora[to]r since the sd Agreement haveing made strict Jnquiry into the Transaccons which have been between the sd Sr William Davenant & the sd Abraham Cowley and the sd John Harvey deceased touching the said halfe Share of the Cleere proffitts of the said Sr William Davenants late Theatre & Company of Players hath lately since the sd Agreement And not before discovered And the truth is that the sd Elizabeth Harvey Widdow And Sr Thomas Harvey or Either of them as Exers of the said John Harvey or otherwise have noe right or tittle att all to any such Share of the proffitts of the said Theatre as they pretend to or any other share whatsoever but the sd Abraham Cowley being an Jngenious Man And well skilled in Poetry And A familiar Accquaintance wth the sd Sr William Davenant he the sd Sr William Davenant Did take his Assistance & Judgment in Writeing Correcting & provideing Tragedies Comedies And other Poeticke Entertainements for the stage And in recompence for the sd Mr Cowleyes paines therein did voluntarily permit and suffer him the said Mr. Cowley or such as he appointed but onely att the Will of him the sd Sr William Davenant to take such halfe Share of the proffitts of the said Stage dureing the life of the said Sr William Davenant which neverthelesse was Continued to him the sd Abraham Cowley aforesd [*after ?*] Sr William Davenants death untill the tyme of his the said Mr Cowleyes death [*Cowley actually died first*] but such halfe share was not Conveyed or Assigned to the said Abraham Cowley for Ever or for any other Certaine tyme or Terme or for any money paid for the Purchase thereof or other Consideracon then as Aforesaid And was to have noe longer Continuance than he the said Mr. Cowley lived And was serviceable to the Theatre and players as Aforesaid much lesse the said Abraham Cowley any power to dispose thereof after his Death Neverthelesse as itt seems the said Abraham Cowley being indebted to the said John Harvey in his life tyme about three hundred pounds or some other sume of money the said John Harvey did procure himselfe

to be deputed by the said Abraham Cowley to receive some
moneys out of the said Playhouse as belonging to the said halfe
Share towards payment of the said debt And under Colour of
Such Deputacon the sd John Harvey pretendeing some greater
right then such Deputacon did prevaile with the Receiver of the
said Playhouse money to lett him receive the said halfe Share
And Accordingly the said John Harvey sometyme dureing the
Jnfancy of the said Charles Davenant when the Right of the
said Charles Davenant was not duely understood or inspected
into in that particular did receive the said halfe share And he the
said John Harvey by such receipt imbursed himselfe A far
greater sume of money then was due to him from the said
Abraham Cowley for all which moneyes soe by him received
after the death of the said Abraham Cowley the Exers of the said
John Harvey as your Orator is Advised ought to come to Accompt
with yo[u]r Ora[to]r as Assignee of the the [*sic*] sd Charles
Davenant your Orator now standeing in the place of the
said Charles Davenant And being Expressly intituled by his
Agreement and Assignement from the said Charles Davenant
to recover and receive all such sumes of money as had been
unjustly or unduely received by any person And there fore
the Proffitts of the said Theatre dureing the Minority of the
said Charles Davenant the said Executors ought to refund the
same or to make yo[u]r Ora[to]r Satisfaccon therefore he the
said John Harvey haveing left them A plentifull personall
Estate more then sufficient to pay his Debts which they the
said Exers doe Enjoye And yo[u]r Ora[to]r further sheweth that
Dame Eliz: Harvey hath not nor Ever had any sufficient
authority to Release [*illegible*] yo[u]r Ora[to]r of the sd Jo.
Harvey Exers Demands touching the Arreares of the sd halfe
Share if any right the Exers had to such halfe Share wch yo[u]r
Ora[to]r does not Admitt nor is such halfe Share of the proffitts
of ye sd Theatre since the said vnion & great improvemts have
been made therof wch the sd Mr Cowley or the sd John Harvey
never were Concerned in worth more to be Purchased to have
for Ever then the sume of And yett ye sd Articles are soe penned
as if yo[u]r Ora[to]r should have ye sume but for the life of ye
said Eliz: Harvey Vid: Wherein yo[u]r Ora[to]r was Surprized
And yett the sd Dame Eliz: Harvey hath lately putt ye sd
Articles in Suite ag[ains]t yo[u]r Ora[to]r And threatens to

prosecute & levy the sd sume of 1000 li. of yo[u]r Ora[to]r
Although she neverthelesse hath or cann[ot ?] make any tittle to
yo[u]r Ora[to]r of or in ye said halfe Share wch doeings of the sd
Dame Eliz: Harvey are Contrary to Equity & good Conscience
& doe tend to yo[u]r Ora[to]rs great Oppression & Jnjury In
tender Consideracon thereof & for as much as yo[u]r Ora[to]r
hath noe remedy in ye pr[e]misses att or by ye strict Rules of
Lawe And ye rather for that yo[u]r Ora[to]rs Wittnesses wch
Could prove ye truth of ye premissess are some of them dead &
others in Remote parts beyond the Seas unknown to yo[u]r
Ora[to]r so as yo[u]r Orator cannot have ye benefitt of their
Testimony att any tryall att Lawe to be had Concerneing ye
premisses but is properly releivable before yo[u]r Lordshipps in
this most Honourable Court *To the End* therefore that the said
Dame Eliz: Harvey Eliz. Harvey Widdow & Sr Thomas Harvey
may upon their severall Corporall Oathes sett forth & discover
what state Jnterest or tittle the sd Abraham Cowley or Iohn
Harvey deceased had or ye sd Eliz: Harvey did or the sd Sr
Thomas Harvey have or any of them hath in any Share or halfe
Share of ye proffitts of the sd Theatre & Company of Player
late ye sd Sr William Davenants. And from whome & howe &
by wh[a]t Conveyances & for wh[a]t Consideracon they had or
have or doe Claime ye same & may sett forth the Dates & Contents of such Conveyances if any they have And to ye End ye sd
Dame Eliz: Harvey shall discover & sett forth whether yo[u]r
Orator did not treat & Agree wth her on ye behalfe of ye sd
Eliz: Harvey Vid. to have ye sd half Share for Ever & on wh[a]t
Consideracon And for whose benefitt ye sd Articles were made
& ye sd 1000 li. to be paid & whether she did not Affirm th[a]t
ye sd Eliz: Harvey Vid had A good right & tittle to the same &
may sett forth ye Authority she had to treat & Agree wth yo[u]r
Ora[to]r thereabout & to ye End ye sd Dame Eliz: Harvey
Eliz: Harvey Vid & Sr Tho: Harvey may true & direct Answe
make to all & Every ye matters Aforesd as if hereagaine Jnterro
gated And more particularly th[a]t ye sd Sr Tho: Harvey may
sett forth & declare whether he gave ye sd Dame Eliz: Harvey
any Authority to treat wth yo[u]r Ora[to]r touching ye pre
misses or knew thereof att ye tyme of ye sd Agreem[en]t o
Articles And th[a]t the sd Articles may be delivered up to b
Cancelled And th[a]t ye sd Eliz: Harvey Vid & Sr Thoma

Harvey may Either owne th[a]t they have sufficient Assetts to Answ[e]r yo[u]r Ora[to]rs Demands or may discover all the particulars natures Kiends qualities & true values of ye personall Estate of ye sd John Harvey wch he was intituled to att ye tyme of his Death & wh[a]t is become of ye same & may sett forth & discover from wh[a]t tyme & to what tyme ye sd Jo: Harvey their Testator did receive or take the sd halfe Share of ye proffitts of ye sd Theatre or any part thereof & what ye same amounted to weekly or otherwise dureing th[a]t tyme And may Accompt wth yo[u]r Orator for the same & refund to pay wh[a]t hath been soe received or had by him ye sd John Harvey or them or any other person or persons on their or any of their behalfes or to their use or benefitt & that yo[u]r Ora[to]r may be relieved in all & Every ye pr[e]misses according to Equity *May itt please* yo[u]r Lordshipps ye pr[e]misses Considered to grant to yo[u]r Orator ye Kings Majesties most Gratious Writt or Writts of Subpena to them ye sd Dame Elizabeth Harvey Elizabeth Harvey Widdow And Sr Thomas Harvey to be directed Commandeing them thereby att A Certaine day & under A Certaine paine therein to be limitted personally to be and appeare before yo[u]r Lordshipps in this Court then and there to Answere the premisses And further to stand to & abide such further Order & Decree therein as to yo[u]r Lordspps shall seem meete And your Orator shall Ever pray &c

Tho: Powys<br>Jo: Warkhouse

B.

Jurat decimo sexto

Garth

Novemr 1691 coram me

Miles Cooke

*The Sevrall Answere of the Honor[a]ble Dame Elizabeth Harvey Vid one of the def[endan]ts to the Bill of Compl[ain]t of Alexander Davenant gent Compl[ainan]t.*

*This* Deft now & at all times hereafter saveing and reserveing to her selfe all Advantages of Excepcon to the manifold [*illegible*] Insufficiencies & other faults and Imperfeccons of the Complts Bill of Complt & of the matters & things therein Contained for a full true plaine perfect and direct Answere to soe much thereof

Y

as this deft is Advised doth any way mat.ially concerne her this defendt to make Answere unto she Answereth and saith that she believes it may be true that King Charles the second did grant Lycence to Sr Willm Davenant the Complts late father to Erect the Playhouse in the Complts said bill menconed called the Dukes Theatre but beleives the Lycence was granted as well to Abraham Cowley in the bill named as to the said Sr Willm Davenant or els in trust for the said Abraham Cowley And this deft beleives the said Sr Willm Davenant & the said Abraham Cowley together did take a Lease of Dorsett Court or Garden for a great number of yeares and did Erect a Theatre or Playhouse thereon as in the said Bill is menconed or els a Lease thereof was taken in trust for them And this deft beleives the said Abraham Cowley had such a certaine ffixed Interest in the said Theatre or playhouse that he might dispose thereof as he pleased & as would Survive to his Executors or Admors in case he had not disposed thereof And this deft saith she doth not know what share or Interest the said Abraham Cowley had in the said Theatre or playhouse but beleives he was to have & allwayes had three pounds per day for all the dayes the Players Acted in the said Theatre And this deft further saith that the said Abraham Cowley by his last will & testamt in Writeing beareing date the eighteenth day of September in the yeare of our Lord One thousand Six hundred Sixty five did devise to the Honorble Iohn Harvey of Ickworth Esqr his share & Int.est in his highness the Duke of Yorkes Theatre as by the said last will of the said Abraham Cowley relacon being thereunto had & to which for more certainety herein this deft referreth her selfe doth and may more fully appeare And this deft Verily beleives that the said Iohn Harvey from the death of the said Abraham Cowley till his owne death being about fifteene yeares did receive and Injoy the said Abraham Cowleys share of the proffitts of the said Playhouse And this deft further saith that she beleives the said Iohn Harvey by his last will & testamt in writeing beareing date the eighteenth day of August in the yeare of our Lord One thousand Six hundred Seaventy six did devise (int.alia) all his terme and the proffitts of the said Playhouse or Theatre to the said other deft the Honorble Elizabeth Harvey widow dureing the terme of her n[atu]rall life And after her decease to the other deft Sr Thomas Harvey & thereof made the said

Elizabeth Harvey his Relict and the said Sr Thomas Harvey
Executors as by the said will relacon being thereunto had & to
which for more certaintety therein this deft referreth her selfe
doth and may more at large appeare And this deft further saith
the said Iohn Harvey soon after the make [*sic*] the said will that
is to say about the month of Ianuary in the yeare of our Lord
one thousand six hundred Seaventy nine dyed by Virtue of
which wills as this deft is Advised the other deft Elizabeth Harvey
became Intituled to the said Abraham Cowleys share of the
rents and proffitts of the said Playhouse or Theatre And the deft
beleives she did demand an Account thereof & that no Account
was given to her while she staid in England only in or about
the month of Iuly in the yeare of our Lord One thousand Six
hundred and eighty there was paid to her or to her vse one
hundred pounds in part for the rent or p[ro]ffitts of the Playhouse but whether the sume was soe paid by Dame Mary his
Relict or by Charles Davenant in the Bill named this deft doth
not know And this deft further saith that soon after the death of
the said Iohn Harvey there grew differences betweene the other
deft Sr Thomas Harvey and Elizabeth Harvey & sutes were
betweene them vpon which the said Elizabeth Harvey left
England And the said Elizabeth Harvey engaged and Imployed
this deft to manage her whole estate & all her affaires here in
England and to receive the rents Jssues and proffitts thereof
And to lett and dispose thereof as this deft should think fitt &
to receive all arreares & all other debts due to her & to discharge
and Release the same and to be be [*sic*] Attorney in all & ev[e]ry
other matters & things to her any wise belonging to act receive
& manage and to accquitt or discharge any person or persons
whatsoev[e]r as fully and effectually as if the said Elizabeth
Harvey were personally p[re]sent & gen[e]rally to doe all other
things requisite & neccessary for the managemt of her estate
And made this deft Sufficient Authorityes in writeing to that
purpose beareing date on or about the nineteenth day of Iune
in the yeare of our Lord One thousand Six hundred eighty six
whereby she did ratifie allow & confirme all that this deft should
lawfully doe or cause to be done in Execucon of the prmisses to
which letter of Attorney this deft doth referr her selfe And
accordingly this deft did take vpon her the sole managemt of the
said other deft Elizabeth Harveys estate & affaires in England

And did very much Sollicite the Complt to come to An account
with her for the said Elizabeths Jnt.est in the said Playhouse or
Theatre & her share in the proffitts thereof And after much
tyme spent & many Sollicitacons for that purpose The Complt
in or about Ianuary last did send this deft an Account thereof
a true Coppy whereof this deft hath caused to be Annexed to
this her Answere & makes the same part thereof & prayes the
same may be soe taken by which account it appeares there was
due to the other deft Elizabeth for the rents and proffitts of the
said Playhouse or Theatre the sum[m]e of Six hundred forty
four pounds fourteene shillings as by the said Account all of the
Complts owne writeing as this deft verily beleives now in this
defts Custody or power ready to be p[ro]duced and to which for
more certainety herein this deft referreth herselfe doth and may
appeare And this deft further saith that she did not treat with
the Complt her selfe but Imployed one mr Willm Poetts her
Agent to treat with him And the said mr Poetts accquainted
this deft that the Complt was not willing to pay the Arreares
due on the said Account but would Ad to it a biger sum[m]e soe
as he might be secured agt the other deft Elizabeth Harvey
claimeing any further Int.est therein or share of the proffitts
dureing her life And therevpon after many treaties an Agreemt
was made touching the same & reduced to Writeing and is in
these words following Vzt March the third One thousand Six
hundred and ninety then Agreed betweene Alexander Davenant
Esqr of the one part And the Honorble Dame Elizabeth
Harvey of the other part as followeth Jmpr[im]is the said Alexander Davenant doth hereby Covent. and Agree to pay to the
said Dame Elizabeth Harvey four hundred pounds of lawfull
money of England vpon the fourth day of May next & then to
euter into two bonds to the said Dame Elizabeth Harvey in the
penalty of six hundred pounds and with Condicon to pay three
hundred pounds vpon the one & twentieth of Iune next & the
other with Condicon to pay three hundred pounds more to the
said Dame Elizabeth Harvey vpon the one & twentieth day of
August next both which bonds are to be without Int.est. Item
the said Dame Elizabeth Harvey in consideracon thereof doth
Covent. and Agree with the said Alexander Davenant that vpon
his paymt of the said four hundred pounds she as Attorney of the
honorble Elizabeth Harvey widow Relict of Iohn Harvey Esqr

decd shall & will execute a Release to the said Alexander
Davenant of all claimes and demands whatsoevr from the
beginning of the world [?] to the said fourth of May next And
allso that she will procure the Right Honorble Ralph Earle of
Mountague & shall allso her selfe enter into one bond of two
thousand pounds penalty to the said Alexander Davenant
with Condicon to save him harmeless from any claime that
shall or may be made by the said Elizabeth Harvey widow her
Executors or Admors agt him the said Alexander Davenant his
heires Executors or Admors for or by reason of any share or
Jnt.est in the Theatre or playhouse in Salisbury Court or any
arreares of proffitts thereof now due or Incurred or that shall
Jncurr or grow due to her from the time of the death of the said
John Harvey to the time of the death of the said Elizabeth
Harvey his Relict Jn Witness whereof the said partyes have
Jnterchangeably sett to theire hands & Seales the day and yeare
above said *Alex: Davenant* as by the said Agreemt ready to be
pduced vnder the Complts hand & Seale relacon being thereunto had & to which for more certainety therein this deft
referreth her selfe doth & may appeare And this deft further
saith she did duly execute one part of the said Agreemt & the
said Complt did as she is Informed & doubts not but to prove
duly execute the other part thereof And this deft was ready to
receive the said four hundred pounds Agreed to be paid by the
said Agreemt & to Execute such release as is therein menconed
And shee & the said Right Honorble Ralph Earle of Mountague
were and still are ready to enter into such bond as in the said
Agreemt is Agreed to be given but the Complt faileing in the
paymt of the said four hundred pounds & in giveing such bonds
as by the Agreemt he ought to have done she this deft after
sevrall requests made to the Complt to perform the said Agreemt
and his refusall soe to doe hath Comenced two sevrall Accons
vpon the said Agreemt one an Accon of debt for four hundred
pounds And the other an Accon of Covent. for not entring into
the said bonds according to the said Agreemt as she beleives &
is Advised is lawfull for her to doe And hopes she shall be at
libty to psente the same And this deft saith it may be true albeit
she doth not know the same that Sr Willm Davenants share &
Int.est in the said Playhouse or Theatre by Virtue of the said
Letters Patents or otherwise after his Death might vest in Charles

Davenant the Complts Brother in the bill named but whether
he was a minor at the death of the said Sr William or that the
said Dame Mary did manage the same for the said Charles or in
his right dureing his minority or for any other time this deft
knoweth not nor doth this deft know that the said late King
Charles the Second granted the like letters Patents unto Thomas
Killigrew in the bill named to erect a Playhouse in Covent
garden nor that any such Agreemt was or were made Betweene
the said Charles Davenant in this bill named & Charles Killigrew in the said bill likewise named that the said two Companyes
of Players should be vnited and become as one Company belonging to one Theatre or otherwise nor what shares of the proffitts thereby arriseing the said Charles Killigrew was to have
thereby And this deft saith it may be true that the said Charles
Davenant and his trustees have Assigned to the Complt & his
trustees but referrs her selfe to such Assignmt as to the Contents
thereof if any such there be And this deft confesseth that in
right of the said other deft Elizabeth Harvey widow untill the
said Agreemt was Sealed she did claime such share & int.est in
the rents & proffitts of the said Playhouse or Theatre as the said
Abraham Cowley & Iohn Harvey had therein & an account for
the same from the death of the said Iohn Harvey but which
Allegacons were made vpon the said treaty this deft knoweth
not in regard she did not treat with the Complt her selfe but
she beleives such treaty & Agreemt was made for the said Elizabeth Harveys share of the rents and proffitts of the said Theatre
or Playhouse which was then in arreare or which should or might
incurr or grow due at any time afterwards dureing the said
Elizabeth Harveys life & not otherwise And this deft insists she
had a good power & Authority to discharge the Arreares then
Due & for the residue of the said Elizabeth Harveys life the
Complt did not rely vpon any power this deft had to sell the
same but vpon the security of this deft And the said Earle of
Mountagu agreed to be given by the said Agreemt to Indemp-
nifie the Complt agt her the said Elizabeth Harveys claime And
this deft saith the said Agreemt was no other nor was intended
to be any other then what is Conteined in the said writeing
herein before sett forth as she is informed by her said Agent that
made the same on her behalfe and as she verily beleives for that
her said Agent had no power to make any other Agreemt nor

the said Elizabeth Harvey any other Estate or Int.est in the said
Theatre And this deft denyes that she was forward to sell the
said Elizabeth Harveys Int.est for her life in the said Playhouse
nor would she have made the said Agreemt above sett forth
if she could have been paid the said Arreares without sute but
to Avoid a sute for the said Arreares & Considering the other
deft Elizabeth Harvey was of great Age she this deft did consent to the said Agreemt & vpon no other Account or motive
whatsoevr And denyes that the said Agreemt was otherwise or
for any other estate or Int.est then as is herein before sett forth
& this deft saith she beleives the Complt was not surprized in
makeing the said Agreemt nor that he made the same over
hastily for she saith she hath vsed all faire means for sevrall
yeares to bring him to an account for the said Arreares and she
doubts not but the Complt well knew the said Elizabeths title
before he delivred or sent to this depont. the said Account of
the Arrears hereunto Annexed And this depont. saith that the
other deft Sr Thomas Harvey as she beleives is well satisfied in
the said Elizabeths right dureing her life for that he never made
any Claime or prtence thereunto since the death of the said Iohn
Harvey that evr this deft heard off And this deft denyes that the
said Elizabeth Harvey was to Convey her share or Int.est in the
said Playhouse to the Complt for evr or that she was to Execute
any release thereof or of all demands or otherwise to the Complt
then in the said Agreemt is Conteined And this deft denyes that
she or the said Earle of Mountagu were to enter into any other
bond or bonds to the Complt then in the said Agreemt is menconed And this deft beleives the said Articles were drawn according to the said Agreemt & not otherwise And this deft saith
what deeds & evidences are of the said Elizabeth Harveys said
share (otherwise [?] the said wills of the said Abraham Cowley
& Iohn Harvey) are in the hands of the said other deft Sr
Thomas Harvey as this deft beleives And this deft denyes the
said Elizabeth Harvey or any for her was to pduce the same to
make any assurance thereof vpon paymt of the said four hundred
pounds or otherwise And this deft saith that she beleives the
other deft Sr Thomas Harvey hath not done nor can doe anything to hinder the Complt from Executeing the said Agreemt
made with this deft, nor is it mat.iall he should Ioyne in any
Conveyance thereof nor is the Complt now at lib[er]ty to Ques-

tion the title of the said Elizabeth Harvey to the said Arreares
& share of the said Playhouse dureing her life he or those vnder
whome he Claimes haveing paid her part thereof as aforesaid &
he haveing delivred this deft an Account of the said Arreares
and submitted by the said Agreemt to make this deft in her
right a Satisfaccon for the same And this deft saith she cannot
sett forth any other right title or Int.est of the said Abraham
Cowley or the said Iohn Harvey or the other deft Elizabeth
Harvey to the said share of the said Playhouse or Theatre then
by the said wills and possession as aforesaid she haveing no deeds
concerning the same And this deft saith that the other deft Sr
Thomas Harvey never did give this deft any Authority to treat
with the Complt for the said Elizabeth Harveys right nor needed
this deft any such Authority but this deft saith she has a good
Authority as she is ad [*illegible*] to receive the said Arreares and
discharge the same as aforesaid And she is Advised that is all
that was neccessary for her to have to make the said Agreemt
with the Complt And this deft saith she doth not know Exactly
from what time to what time the said Iohn Harvey recd the
share of the said Theatre or Playhouse nor what the same
Amounted unto but beleives it was from the time of the said
Abraham Cowleys death to his owne death which hapned
about the tenth day of January in the yeare or our Lord one
thousand Six hundred Seaventy nine & which as this deft
beleives was about fifteene yeares as aforesaid And this deft
denyes all vnlawfull Confederacy and Combinacon with the
other defts or any or either of them or any of the purposes in the
bill Charged without that that [*sic*] any other matter or thing in
the Complts bill of Complt conteined mat.iall or effectuall in the
law for her this deft to make Answere unto & not herein and
hereby well & suffitiently Answered unto confessed or Avoided
travrsed or denyed is true to the knowledge of her this deft All
which matters & things this deft is ready to aver maintaine &
prove as this Honorble Court shall A [*illegible*] And humbly
Prayes to be hence dismissed with her reasonable Costs in this
sute most wrongfully sustained

                                                    Tho: Daile

C.

Garth

*The Schedule* to which this Answere reffers

|  | li | s | d |
|---|---|---|---|
| From March the 15th 1680 to Ianuary the 20th 1690. Wee have played 72 Months att 12li:12s:00 d Ls Month amounts to | 907: | 04: | 00 |
| Tenn Years ground Rent to be deducted at 12li:5s: the Year . | 122: | 10: | 00 |
| Tenn Years Repaires att 40li . | 040: | 00: | 00 |
| Paid in Moneys to Mr Chaynter as by Note . | 100: | 00: | 00 |
|  | 262: | 10: | 00 |
| If the Accot: were to be delivrd on Oath this is the Ballance | 644: | 14: | 00 |

Miles Cooke

# A NOTE ON THE EXTANT PAINTINGS AND ENGRAVINGS OF ABRAHAM COWLEY

THE earliest extant likeness of Abraham Cowley is an engraving made by Robert Vaughan for the 1633 edition of *Poetical Blossoms*. It has been reproduced in the present volume because it is a distinctly better artistic performance than the anonymous engraving in the 1636 edition, which was reused in the 1637, as well as in *Love's Riddle* in 1638. Another view of Cowley as a boy appears in the fourth and later editions of the juvenilia, beginning in 1681.

William Faithorne's excellent engraving for the 1668 *Works* is probably the best known of any, and is reproduced here as a frontispiece. It was re-engraved by him in 1687. The original is now in the Bodleian Gallery. Faithorne also classicized the same view for the edition of *Poemata Latina* in 1668. Faithorne's work was adapted by I. de Leeuw for Tonson's editions in 1707 and 1710. Alais also adapted it for Grosart in 1881.

Zinck's enamel miniature, originally in Horace Walpole's collection at Strawberry Hill, has had a long history. An engraving was done by 'H.P.' for Hurd's selected edition of Cowley in 1772, but a new plate was made by John Hall for the 1777 edition. The latter view was followed in Johnson's edition in 1779, and in Sparrow's *Mistress* in 1926. Another engraving was made by J. Romney for a selection in 1809; this has been used in the augmented edition of Manning and Bray's *Surrey*.

Sir Peter Lely's portrait is in the National Gallery in London. George Vertue's engraving in Tonson's 1721 edition follows Lely. Two versions by Vertue also appear in Manning and Bray, and one of these is reproduced in the present volume.

Bell's edition of Cowley in his *Poets of Great Britain* (1777) contains an inferior engraving by Cook, labelled 'From an original in Lord Chesterfield's collection'.

Houbraken's well-known series of poets contains an engraving of Cowley.

At Trinity College, Cambridge, there are three portraits, for detailed information about which I am indebted to J. P. Thomson, Esq., of the College. One is a painting by Stephen Slaughter, made in 1741 and given to Trinity by T. Townshend in 1752. An adaptation of this was engraved by W. H. Worthington in 1821. The painter and source of the second portrait are unknown. It is in oils, and seems to be based on Faithorne. The third portrait is the most interesting. It is a crayon drawing by an unknown artist, and was given to the college on August 1, 1824, by Richard Clarke, of London and Chertsey. According to a note in the Trinity College Library, from Wordsworth to Sedgwick, Clarke said that the picture had belonged to Sir Thomas Browne and that he, Clarke, had brought it from Norwich. But Aldis Wright's letter to Grosart (in Grosart's edition, i. cxli–ii) is worth noting, for it calls attention to Cowley's juvenile elegy to his cousin of the same name as the donor, Richard Clarke. The suggestion of course is that the picture remained in the Clarkes' possession from the early seventeenth century. Certainly if the two Richard Clarkes belonged to the same family, the interest of the later Richard in Cowley would be explained. An engraving of this drawing was made by James Basire in 1813, and printed in Manning and Bray. This has been reprinted in the present volume, because it seems to be authentic, by internal evidence if no more. Grosart appears to have been unusually blind when he stated that he could distinguish no similarity between this view of Cowley at twenty and the other well-authenticated portraits. Feature by feature, however, Clarke's crayon can be checked off against the faces drawn by Faithorne and Lely; the resemblance, in fact, is much stronger here than it is in Zinck's miniature.

Grosart also mentions a portrait at Bothwell Castle, which formerly belonged to Clarendon, but of this likeness I have no information.

# BIBLIOGRAPHY

*The following printed works have been used in the preparation of this biography:*

ALDINGTON, RICHARD.
'Cowley and the French Epicureans', *New Statesman*, xviii (1921), 133–4.

AUBREY, JOHN.
'*Brief Lives*', *Chiefly of Contemporaries, Set Down by John Aubrey, between the Years 1669 and 1696*. Ed. Andrew Clark. Oxford, 1898. 2 vols. (Contains interesting gossip and some valuable biographical data.)
Extracts from his contemplated *Remains of Gentilism and Judaism* (Lansdowne MS., No. 231). In Camden Society's *Anecdotes and Traditions, Illustrative of Early English History and Literature, Derived from Manuscript Sources*. London, 1839.

BAKER, DAVID ERSKINE.
*Biographia Dramatica, or, A Companion to the Playhouse*. London, 1782. 2 vols.

BALDWIN, THOMAS WHITFIELD.
*The Organization and Personnel of the Shakespearean Company*. Princeton, 1927.

BALL, W. W. ROUSE, and VENN, J. A.
*Admissions to Trinity College, Cambridge*. London, 1911–16. Vol. II.

BARGRAVE, JOHN.
*Pope Alexander the Seventh and the College of Cardinals*. Ed. J. C. Robertson for the Camden Society, 1867.

BARNES, JOSHUA (ed.)
*Anacreontius, Poeta Lyricus, Summa Cura et Diligentia ad Fidem Etiam Vet. MS. Vatican. Emendatus. . . . Item Anacreontis Vita, &c.* Cantabrigiae, 1705.

BEATTIE, JAMES.
*Essays: On Poetry and Music, as They Affect the Mind; On Laughter, and Ludicrous Composition; On the Usefulness of Classical Learning.* Edinburgh, 1776.

BELLAMY, D[ANIEL], Sr. and Jr.
*Miscellanies in Prose and Verse*. London, 1740–1. 2 vols.

BIRCH, THOMAS (ed.).
*A Collection of the State Papers of John Thurloe, Esq., Secretary, First, to the Council of State, and Afterwards to the Two Protectors, Oliver and Richard Cromwell*. 7 vols. London, 1742. Vol. V.
*The History of the Royal Society of London for Improving of Natural Knowledge. . . .* London, 1756. Vol. I.

BLAIR, HUGH.
*Lectures on Rhetoric and Belles Lettres.* London, 1783. 3 vols.

BLOUNT, THOMAS POPE.
*De Re Poetica, or Remarks upon Poetry, with Characters and Censures of the Most Considerable Poets. . . .* London, 1694.

BOSWELL, JAMES.
*Boswell's Life of Johnson. Including Boswell's Journal of a Tour to the Hebrides and Johnson's Diary of a Journey into North Wales.* Ed. G. B. Hill, Oxford, 1887. 6 vols.

BRADLEY, JESSE FRANKLIN, and ADAMS, JOSEPH QUINCY.
*The Jonson Allusion-Book. A Collection of Allusions to Ben Jonson from 1597–1700.* In *Cornell Studies in English,* vol. VI. New Haven, 1922.

BRETT, G. S.
*The Philosophy of Gassendi.* London, 1908.

BROME, ALEXANDER (ed.).
*The Poems of Horace, . . . by Several Persons.* London, 1666.

BROWN, THOMAS.
*Works, Serious and Comical, in Prose and Verse.* London, 1707–8. Vol. III.

BRUCE, JOHN.
Note on Cowley's 'To Sir William Davenant', *Notes and Queries,* First series, xii (1855), 66.

BRYANT, WILLIAM CULLEN.
'Abraham Cowley', *North American Review,* cxxiv (1877), 368–82.

*Calendar of State Papers, Domestic Series, of the Reign of Charles II, 1661–2, Preserved in the State Paper Department of Her Majesty's Public Record Office.* Ed. Mary A. E. Green. London, 1861.
*Of the Reign of James I, 1603–10.*

CAMPBELL, GEORGE.
*The Philosophy of Rhetoric.* Edinburgh, 1776. 2 vols.

CAMPBELL, KILLIS.
'Notes on Davenant's Life', *Modern Language Notes,* xviii (1903), 238–9

CARPENTER, WILLIAM HOOKHAM.
*Pictorial Notices: Consisting of a Memoir of Sir Anthony Van Dyck, with a Descriptive Catalogue of the Etchings Executed by Him: and a Variety of Interesting Particulars Relating to Other Artists Patronized by Charles I, Collected from Original Documents in Her Majesty's State Paper Office, the Office of Public Records, and Other Sources.* London, 1844. (Contains Van Dyck's will.)

*Certain Passages of Every Dayes Intelligence, from the Army, and His Highness the Lord Protector and His Council,* April 13–20, 1655.

CHALMERS, ALEXANDER.
*The Works of the English Poets.* London, 1810. 21 vols.

CHESTER, JOSEPH LEMUEL (ed.).
*The Marriage, Baptismal, and Burial Registers of the Collegiate Church of Abbey of St. Peter, Westminster.* London, 1876. Vol. X of Publications of the Harleian Society.

CHESTERFIELD, EARL OF [PHILIP STANHOPE].
*Letters to His Son.* New York, 1917. 2 vols.

CLARENDON, EDWARD, EARL OF.
*The History of the Rebellion and Civil Wars in England, to Which Is Now Added an Historical View of the Affairs of Ireland.* Oxford, 1816. 3 vols.
*The Life of, in Which Is Included a Continuation of His History of the Grand Rebellion.* Oxford, 1827. 3 vols.

CONGREVE, WILLIAM.
*Works.* Birmingham, 1761. Vol. III.

COOPER, CHARLES HENRY.
*Annals of Cambridge.* Cambridge, 1842–53. Vol. III.

COWLEY, ABRAHAM.
The following list contains only the most important editions or selections of his work:
*The Mistresse or Seuerall Copies of Love-Verses.* London, 1647.
*Poems: Viz. I. Miscellanies, II. The Mistress, or, Love Verses, III. Pindarique Odes, and IV. Davideis, or, a Sacred Poem of the Troubles of David.* London, 1656.
*The Works of Mr Abraham Cowley. Consisting of Those Which Were Formerly Printed: And Those Which He Design'd for the Press, Now Published out of the Authors Original Copies.* London, 1668.
*Abrahami Couleij Angli, Poemata Latina. In Quibus Continentur, Sex Libri Plantarum, Viz. Duo Herbarum. Florum. Sylvarum. Et Unus Miscellaneorum.* Londini, 1668.
*A Poem on the Late Civil War.* London, 1679.
*The Works of Mr. Abraham Cowley. Being What Was Written and Published by Himself in His Younger Years. And Now Reprinted Together.* London, 1681. Fourth edition. (This was published by Harper and Tonson, and is not the same as the fourth edition in the regular series by Herringman.)
*The Works of Mr. Abraham Cowley. Consisting of Those Which Were Formerly Printed: And Those Which He Design'd for the Press. Now Published out of the Author's Original Copies. To This Edition Are Added, Cutter of Coleman-Street: And Several Commendatory Copies of Verses on the Author, by Persons of Honour. As Also a Table to the Whole Works, Never Before Printed.* London, 1693. Eighth Edition. Also contains *His Six Books of Plants, Never Before Printed in English.* London, 1689.

*The Works of Mr. Abraham Cowley: Consisting of Those Which Were Formerly Printed, And Those Which He Design'd for the Press. Now Published out of the Author's Original Copies. With the Cutter of Coleman-Street. To which Are Added, Some Verses by the Author, Never Before Printed.* London, 1700. Ninth edition.

'Letters by the Famous Mr. Abraham Cowley (Then Secretary to My Lord Jermyn) during King Charles the Second's Exile; Written from Paris to Mr. Henry Bennet, Afterwards Earl of Arlington'. *Miscellanea Aulica: or, a Collection of State-Treatises, Never Before Publish'd.* London, 1702.

*The Works of Mr. Abraham Cowley . . . Adorn'd with Cuts.* London, 1707–8. Tenth Edition. 3 vols. in octavo.

*The Works of Mr. Abraham Cowley . . .* London, 1710–11. Eleventh edition. 3 vols.

*Select Works in Verse and Prose, of Mr. A. Cowley.* Ed. Richard Hurd. London, 1772. 2 vols. Also 3rd ed., 1777.

*The Works of the English Poets. With Prefaces, Biographical and Critical.* Ed. Samuel Johnson. London, 1779. Vol. I.

*A Complete Edition of the Poets of Great Britain.* Ed. Robert Anderson. London and Edinburgh, 1792. Vol. V.

*Prose Works of Abraham Cowley, Esq. Including His Essays in Verse and Prose.* London, 1826.

*The Complete Works in Verse and Prose of Abraham Cowley. Now for the First Time Collected and Edited: with Memorial-Introduction and Notes and Illustrations, Portraits, &c.* Ed. A. B. Grosart for the Chertsey Worthies' Library. Edinburgh, 1881. 2 vols.

*Essays and Selected Verse of Abraham Cowley.* Ed. J. M. Attenborough. London and New York, n.d.

*Cowley's Prose Works.* Ed. J. Rawson Lumby. Cambridge, 1887. (Contains some biographical material.)

*The English Writings of Abraham Cowley.* Ed. A. R. Waller for the Cambridge English Classics. Cambridge, 1905–6. 2 vols.

*The Essays and Other Prose Writings.* Ed. Alfred B. Gough. Oxford, 1915. (Contains some biographical material.)

*Cowley's Essays.* A revision of Lumby's *Cowley's Prose Works*, by Arthur Tilley. Cambridge, 1923.

*The Mistress, with Other Select Poems of Abraham Cowley, 1618–1667.* Ed. John Sparrow. London, 1926. (Contains some new biographical material.)

Cox, J. Charles.
*Rambles in Surrey.* London, 1910.

Crashaw, Richard.
*The Poems, English, Latin and Greek, of Richard Crashaw.* Ed. L. C. Martin. Oxford, 1927.

CROLL, MORRIS W.
    ' " Attic Prose" in the Seventeenth Century', *Studies in Philology*, xviii (1921), 79–128.
    'Muret and the History of " Attic" Prose', *P.M.L.A.*, xxxix (1924), 254–309.
    'Lipsius, Montaigne, Bacon', in *Schelling Anniversary Papers*. 1923.
    Article in *Studies in English Philology: A Miscellany in Honor of Frederick Klaeber*. Minneapolis, 1929.

CUNNINGHAM, GEORGE H.
    *London. Being a Comprehensive Survey of the History, Tradition and Historical Associations of Buildings and Monuments under Streets in Alphabetical Order*. London and Toronto, 1927.

CUNNINGHAM, PETER.
    *Shakespeare Society Papers*. London, 1845. Vol. II. (pp. 146–50 contain the first printing of Abraham Cowley's will.)

DAVENANT, WILLIAM.
    *A Discourse upon Gondibert: An Heroick Poem. With an Answer to It by Mr. Hobbs*. Paris, 1650.
    *Gondibert: An Heroick Poem*. London, 1651.

DENHAM, JOHN.
    *The Poetical Works of Edmund Waller and Sir John Denham*. Ed. C. C. Clarke. Edinburgh, 1869.

DENNIS, JOHN.
    'The Grounds of Criticism in Poetry' and 'A Large Account of the Taste in Poetry'. In *Critical Essays of the XVIIIth Century (1700–25)*. Ed. Willard Higley Durham. New Haven, 1915.

DIGBY, KENELM.
    *Private Memoirs of Kenelm Digby, Gentleman of the Bedchamber to King Charles the First. With a Life, Complete*. London, 1827.

DISRAELI, ISAAC.
    *The Calamities and Quarrels of Authors: With Some Inquiries Respecting Their Moral and Literary Characters, and Memoirs of Our Literary History*. London, 1812. 2 vols. (Contains some biographical speculations and a letter.)

DOWNES, JOHN.
    *Roscius Anglicanus, or, An Historical Review of the Stage . . . from 1660, to 1706*. London, 1708.

DRYDEN, JOHN.
    *Essays of*. Ed. W. P. Ker. Oxford, 1900. 2 vols.
    *The Second Part of Miscellany Poems*. Ed. Dryden. London, 1727 (fifth ed.).
    *The Works of John Dryden*. Ed. Walter Scott and George Saintsbury. Edinburgh, 1882–93. 18 vols.

EVELYN, JOHN.
*Diary and Correspondence of John Evelyn.* Ed. Wm. Bray and John Forster. London, 1881. 4 vols.
*The Miscellaneous Writings of John Evelyn, Esq., F.R.S., Now First Collected, with Occasional Notes by William Upcott of the London Institution.* London, 1825. (Contains the original of Cowley's 'The Garden'.)

FELTON, HENRY.
*A Dissertation on Reading the Classics, and Forming a Just Style.* London, 1713.

FENTON, ELIJAH.
'Observations on Some of Mr. Waller's Poems.' In *Works of Edmund Waller, Esq., in Verse and Prose, Published by Mr. Fenton.* London, 1729.

FIRTH, C. H.
'Cowley at the Restoration', *The Academy,* no. 1118, xliv (1893), 296.

FOSTER, J. (ed.).
*London Marriage Licences, 1521–1869.* From Excerpts by Col. Chester. London, 1887.

[GENEST, J.]
*Some Account of the English Stage from the Restoration in 1660 to 1830.* Bath, 1832. 10 vols.
*Gentleman's Magazine : and Historical Chronicle, The.* London, 1731–1800.

GILDON, CHARLES.
*Miscellany Poems upon Several Occasions, Consisting of Original Poems by the Late Duke of Buckingham, Mr. Cowley, Mr. Milton, Mr. Prior, Mrs. Behn, Mr. Tho. Brown, &c.* London, 1692.

'GODFREY, ELIZABETH' [JESSIE BEDFORD].
*Home Life under the Stuarts, 1603–79.* London, 1925.

GOLDSMITH, OLIVER.
*The Works of Oliver Goldsmith.* Ed. J. W. M. Gibbs. London, 1885–6. 5 vols.

GOSSE, EDMUND.
*Seventeenth Century Studies.* New York, 1897. (The essay on Cowley is enthusiastically written, but full of inaccuracies.)

GRAY, THOMAS.
*The Poetical Works of Thomas Gray, with a Life by the Rev. John Mitford.* London, 1885.

GRIERSON, HERBERT J. C. (ed.).
*Metaphysical Lyrics & Poems of the Seventeenth Century. Donne to Butler.* Oxford, 1921.

HALL, MRS. S. C.
*Chertsey and Its Neighbourhood.* 1853.

z

HARBAGE, ALFRED.
*Thomas Killigrew, Cavalier Dramatist, 1612–83.* Philadelphia, 1930.
HASTED, EDWARD.
*The History and Topographical Survey of the County of Kent.* Canterbury, 1778–9. Vol. I.
HAYNES, HENRIETTA.
*Henrietta Maria.* New York and London, 1912.
HAZLITT, WILLIAM.
*The Collected Works of William Hazlitt.* Ed. A. R. Waller and Arnold Glover. London, 1902–6. 12 vols.
HEADLEY, HENRY.
*Select Beauties of Ancient English Poetry.* London, 1787. 2 vols.
HEARNE, THOMAS.
*Remarks and Collections of Thomas Hearne.* Prepared for the Oxford Historical Society. Oxford, 1885–1914. Vol. I.
HENRIETTA MARIA, QUEEN.
*Letters of Queen Henrietta Maria, Including Her Private Correspondence with Charles the First.* Ed. Mary Anne Everett Green. London, 1857.
*Lettres Inédites de Henriette-Marie, Reine d'Angleterre.* Publiée par Le Comte de Baillon. Paris, 1884.
HISTORICAL MSS. COMMISSION.
*Reports of the —.* London, 1874 ff.
HOBBES, THOMAS.
*Leviathan.* Ed. A. R. Waller. Cambridge, 1904.
HOTSON, LESLIE.
*The Commonwealth and Restoration Stage.* Cambridge, Harvard University Press, 1928.
HOWITT, WILLIAM.
*Homes and Haunts of the Most Eminent British Poets. The Illustrations Engraved by H. W. Hewet.* New York, 1847.
HURD, RICHARD.
*Moral and Political Dialogues; with Letters on Chivalry and Romance.* London, 1771. 3 vols.
JACOB, GILES.
*The Poetical Register, or, The Lives and Characters of the English Dramatick Poets with an Account of Their Writings.* London, 1719.
*An Historical Account of the Lives and Writings of Our Most Considerable English Poets. . . .* London, 1721.
[JOHNSON, CHARLES.]
*Fortune in Her Wits.* London, 1705.
JOHNSON, SAMUEL.
*Lives of the Most Eminent English Poets. With Notes Corrective and Explanatory by Peter Cunningham, F.S.A.* London, 1854. Vol. I.

*Johnson's Lives of the British Poets. Completed by William* [C.] *Hazlitt.* London, 1854. Vol. II.

*The Lives of the English Poets.* Ed. G. B. Hill. Oxford, 1905. 3 vols. (Contains valuable biographical annotations.)

*The Works of Samuel Johnson, Ll.D.* Ed. Arthur Murphy, with notes by others. London, 1806. Vol. X.

KAMES, LORD (HENRY HOME).
*Elements of Criticism.* London, 1762.

KANE, ELISHA K.
*Gongorism and the Golden Age. A Study of Exuberance and Unrestraint in the Arts.* Chapel Hill, 1928.

KENNETT, WHITE.]
*A Register and Chronicle Ecclesiastical and Civil: Containing Matters of Fact, Delivered in the Words of the Most Authentick Books, Papers, and Records; Digested in Exact Order of Time. With Proper Notes and References towards Discovering and Connecting the True History of England from the Restauration of King Charles II.* London, 1728.

LAKE, EDWARD.
*The Diary of Dr. Edward Lake,* quoted by Peter Cunningham, 'Cowley', *Johnson's Lives,* I, and by A. B. Grosart in his ed. of Cowley, ii. 353.

LAMB, CHARLES.
*The Works of Charles and Mary Lamb.* Ed. E. V. Lucas. London, 1903. 6 vols.

LLOYD, DAVID.
*Memoirs of . . . Those . . . That Suffered by Death . . . for the Protestant Religion . . . from the Year 1637 to the year 1660.* London, 1668.

LOFTIE, WILLIAM JOHN.
*Memorials of the Savoy. The Palace: The Hospital: The Chapel.* London, 1878.

*London Gazette, The.* August 1–5, 1667.

MACKENZIE, GEORGE.
*Works.* Edinburgh, 1716. 2 vols.

MANNING, OWEN, and BRAY, WILLIAM.
*The History and Antiquities of the County of Surrey; Compiled from the Best and Most Authentic Historians, Valuable Records, and Manuscripts, in the Public Offices and Libraries, and in Private Hands, with a Facsimile of Domesday . . .* 1804–14. 3 vols. folio, later extended to 7 vols. (Contains a large number of views of Cowley's home at Chertsey, and several interesting portraits.)

*The History and Topography of the County of Surrey, Compiled and Described from the Most Authentic Manuscript Records and Historians; Commenced by the Rev. Owen Manning, S.T.B., Rector of Pepperharrow, and Vicar of Godalming. Continued and Enlarged by William Bray, of Shire, F.S.A. Illustrated by Upwards of Six Thousand Drawings, Prints, Maps, and Plans; Portraits of Eminent Personages, Born or Resident in the County; Architectural and Other Delineations of the Churches, Monastic Edifices, and Old Manor Houses; Pedigrees, and Heraldic Insignia of Families, &c.* Islington, 1847. Vol. xix. (There are many original drawings, &c., in this edition which are not in the earlier editions, the collection having been formed by Richard Percival.)

MARKHAM, CLEMENTS R.
*The Life of the Great Lord Fairfax, Commander-in-Chief of the Army of the Parliament of England.* London, 1870.

McBRYDE, JOHN McLAREN, JR.
*A Study of Cowley's Davideis.* Johns Hopkins, 1899 (reprinted from *Journal of Germanic Philology*, ii, No. 4).

McKERROW, R. B.
*A Dictionary of Printers and Booksellers in England, Scotland, and Ireland, and of Foreign Printers of English Books, 1557-1640.* London, 1910.

*Mercurius Politicus. Comprising the Sum of All Intelligence, with the Affairs and Designs Now on Foot in the Three Nations of England, Scotland, and Ireland.* August 12-19, 1655; May 5, 1659.

MONTAIGNE, MICHEL DE.
*Les Essais de Michel de Montaigne.* Bordeaux, 1906-20.

*Monthly Review, The.* London, 1749-1800.

MULLINGER, JAMES BASS.
*Cambridge Characteristics in the Seventeenth Century; or The Studies of the University and Their Influence on the Character and Writings of the Most Distinguished Graduates during That Period.* London, 1867.

NICHOLAS, SIR EDWARD.
*The Nicholas Papers. Correspondence of Sir Edward Nicholas.* . . . Ed. George F. Warner. London, Camden Society, 1886-1920. 4 vols.

NICHOLS, JOHN.
*Literary Anecdotes of the Eighteenth Century; Comprizing Biographical Memoirs of William Bowyer, Printer, F.S.A., and Many of His Learned Friends* .... London, 1812-15. 9 vols.
*Illustrations of the Literary History of the Eighteenth Century. Consisting of Authentic Memoirs and Original Letters of Eminent Persons; and Intended as a Sequel to the Literary Anecdotes.* London, 1817. 8 vols.

*Notes and Queries.*

[OLDMIXON, JOHN (translator and adapter).]
*The Arts of Logick and Rhetorick, Illustrated by Examples Taken out of the Best Authors, Antient and Modern, in All the Polite Languages. Interpreted and Explain'd by That Learned and Judicious Critick, Father Bouhours. To Which Are Added, Parallel Quotations out of the Most Eminent English Authors in Verse and Prose: Wherein the Like Observations Are Made on Their Beauties and Blemishes, in All the Various Kinds of Thoughts and Expression.* London, 1728.

OSBORNE, DOROTHY.
*Letters from Dorothy Osborne to Sir William Temple (1652–4).* Ed. Edward Abbott Parry. London, n.d.

PECK, FRANCIS.
*A Collection of Curious Historical Pieces.* London, 1740. (This is the second part of his *Memoirs of the Life and Actions of Oliver Cromwell* ... and contains Cowley's letter to Sprat in 1665.)

PEPYS, SAMUEL.
*The Diary of Samuel Pepys, M.A., F.R.S.; Clerk of the Acts and Secretary to the Admiralty.* Ed. Henry B. Wheatley. London, 1904–5. 8 vols.

*Perfect Diurnall of Some Passages and Proceedings of, and in Relation to, the Armies in England, Scotland, and Ireland, The.* April 16–23, 1655.

*Perfect Proceedings of State-Affaires. In England, Scotland, and Ireland, with the Transactions of Other Nations.* April 12–26, 1655.

PERRENS, F. T.
*Les Libertins en France au XVIIe Siècle.* Paris, 1896.

[PHILIPS, KATHERINE.]
*Letters from Orinda to Poliarchus.* London, 1705.
*Poems.* In George Saintsbury, *Minor Poets of the Caroline Period.* Oxford, 1905–21. Vol. I.

PLOMER, H. R.
*Dictionary of Booksellers and Printers Who Were at Work in England, Scotland and Ireland from 1641 to 1667.* London, 1907.

POPE, ALEXANDER.
*The Works of Alexander Pope. Including Several Hundred Unpublished Letters, and Other New Materials.* Ed. J. W. Croker, W. Elwin, and W. J. Courthope. London, 1871–86. 10 vols.

POWICKE, FREDERICK J.
*The Cambridge Platonists—A Study.* London and Toronto, 1926.

PRIDEAUX, HUMPHREY.
*The Judgement of Dr. Prideaux, in Condemning the Murder of Julius Caesar, by the Conspirators, as a Most Villanous Act, Maintain'd: And the Sophistry in the London Journals of December, the 2nd, and 9th, Expos'd. With Some Political Remarks on the Roman Government.* London, 1721.

PRYNNE, WILLIAM.
*Legenda Lignea*. London, 1653.
REYNOLDS, MYRA.
*The Learned Lady in England, 1650–1760*. Boston and New York, 1920.
SAINT-ÉVREMOND, CHARLES DE MARGUETEL DE SAINT-DENIS, SIEUR DE.
*Œuvres de Monsieur de Saint-Évremond, avec la Vie de l'Auteur, par Monsieur des Maiseaux, Membre de la Société Royale*. Also contains material by P. Silvestre and Pierre Bayle. 1753. Vol. I.
S[ANDYS], G[EORGE].
*Ovid's Metamorphosis Englished, Mythologized, and Represented in Figures. An Essay to the Translation of Virgil's Aeneis*. Oxford, 1632.
SARGEAUNT, JOHN.
*Annals of Westminster School*. London, 1898. (Among other information, this also contains a juvenile poem by Cowley given in none of the editions. The MS. is now in the British Museum.)
SHAFER, ROBERT.
*The English Ode to 1660*. Princeton, 1918.
SMITH, G. C. MOORE.
*College Plays Performed in the University of Cambridge*. Cambridge, 1923.
*Some Account of the Life and Writings of the Right Reverend Father in God, Thomas Sprat, D.D., Late Lord Bishop of Rochester, and Dean of Westminster. With a True Copy of His Last Will and Testament*. London, 1715.
SPARROW, JOHN.
'The Text of Cowley's *Mistress*', *Review of English Studies*, iii (1927). 22–7.
'Cowley's *Plantarum Libri Duo*: A Presentation Copy', *The London Mercury*, xx (1929), 398–9.
*Spectator, The*. Ed. G. Gregory Smith. New York, 1912. 4 vols.
SPENCE, JOSEPH.
*Anecdotes, Observations, and Characters, of Books and Men, Collected from the Conversation of Mr. Pope, and Other Eminent Persons of His Time*. Ed. Samuel Weller Singer. London, 1820.
SPINGARN, J. E. (ed.),
*Critical Essays of the Seventeenth Century*. Oxford, 1908. 3 vols.
SPRAT, THOMAS.
'An Account of the Life and Writings of Mr. Abraham Cowley. Written to Mr. M. Clifford.' In *The Works of Mr. Abraham Cowley*. London, 1668.
'De Vita & Scriptis A. Couleii, Martino Cliffordo, So. T. Sprat, S.' In *Abrahami Couleij Angli, Poemata Latina*. London, 1668.

*The History of the Royal Society of London, for the Improving of Natural Knowledge*. London, 1667.

*Observations on Monsieur de Sorbier's Voyage into England*. London, 1665. (The book is in the form of a letter to Christopher Wren, dated August 1, 1664.)

'Upon the Poems of the English Ovid, Anacreon, Pindar, and Virgil, Abraham Cowley.' *Poems.* In Alexander Chalmers, *The Works of the English Poets* (London, 1810), Vol. IX.

STATIONERS' COMPANY.

*A Transcript of the Registers of the Company of the Stationers of London, 1554–1640 A.D.* Ed. Edward Arber. London and Birmingham, 1875–94. 5 vols.

*A Transcript of the Registers of the Worshipful Company of Stationers; from 1640–1708 A.D.* London, 1913. 3 vols.

STEBBING, WILLIAM.

*Some Verdicts of History Reviewed.* London, 1887. (The essay on Cowley contains some interesting speculations.)

STEPHEN, LESLIE.

'Abraham Cowley'. *Dictionary of National Biography.* New York and London, 1887. xii. 379–82.

TATE, N[AHUM], ed.

*Poems by Several Hands, and on Several Occasions. Collected by N. Tate.* [The title on p. 1 reads: *A New Collection of Poems. Written by Several Authors.*] (Contains a poem by Cowley which has never been reprinted in its original form.)

TAYLOR, I[DA] A.

*The Life of Queen Henrietta Maria.* London, 1905. 2 vols.

*Victoria History of the County of Surrey, The.* Ed. H. E. Malden, &c. London, 1902.

WALKER, JOHN.

*An Attempt towards Recovering an Account of the Numbers and Sufferings of the Clergy of the Church of England, Heads of Colleges, Fellows, Scholars, &c. Who Were Sequester'd, Harass'd, &c. in the Late Times of the Grand Rebellion* .... Part II contains a list of those who were put or kept out of their preferments in churches, colleges, &c. 1714.

WALLER, EDMUND.

*Poems, &c. Written upon Several Occasions, and to Several Persons.* London, 1712. Also ed. G. Thorn-Drury. London and N.Y., 1901. 2 vols.

WALTON, IZAAK.

*The Lives of Donne, Wotton, Hooker, Herbert, and Sanderson.* Ed. Alexander Young, following Zouch. Boston and Cambridge, 1832. 2 vols.

WARTON, JOSEPH.
*An Essay on the Genius and Writings of Pope.* London, 1756–82. 2 vols.

*Weekly Intelligencer. Of the Commonwealth. Faithfully Communicating All Affairs Both Martial and Civil, The.* April 17–May 1, 1655.

*Weekly Post, The.* April 17–24, 1655.

WELCH, JOSEPH.
*The List of the Queen's Scholars of St. Peter's College, Westminster, Admitted on That Foundation since 1663; and of Such As Have Been Thence Elected to Christ Church, Oxford, and Trinity College, Cambridge, from the Foundation by Queen Elizabeth, 1561, to the Present Time.* A new edition 'By an Old King's Scholar' [Charles Bagot Phillimore]. London, 1852.

WELLWOOD, JAMES.
*Memoirs of the Most Material Transactions in England for the Last Hundred Years, Preceding the Revolution in 1688.* London, 1700.

WEST, GILBERT.
*Odes of Pindar, with Several Other Pieces in Prose and Verse, Translated from the Greek . . . .* London, 1766.

WOOD, ANTHONY À.
*Athenae Oxonienses. An Exact History of All the Writers and Bishops Who Have Had Their Education in the University of Oxford from 1500 to 1690. To Which Are Added the Fasti or Annals of the Said University.* Ed. Philip Bliss. London, 1813–20. 4 vols.

WOODFORD, SAMUEL.
*A Paraphrase upon the Canticles.* London, 1679.

WORDSWORTH, WILLIAM.
*The Prose Works of William Wordsworth.* Ed. A. B. Grosart. London, 1876. 3 vols.

WORTHINGTON, JOHN.
*The Diary and Correspondence of Dr. John Worthington, Master of Jesus College, Cambridge, Vice-Chancellor of the University of Cambridge, &c., &c.* Edited by James Crossley and R. C. Christie for the Chetham Society, 1847–86. Vols. XIII, XXXVI, CXIV of *Remains, Historical and Literary, Connected with the Palatine Counties of Lancashire and Chester.*

YARNALL, EMMA A.
*Abraham Cowley.* Berne, 1897.

*The following Manuscript sources have also been used:*
Bodleian:
Clarendon MSS. for 1646, 1650, and 1656.
Rawlinson MS. Poet. 246.
Tanner MS. 69, f. 137.

Bodleian:
  MS. Carte. 30; 213.
  MS. Eng. Poet. e. 4.
  MS. Rawlinson. A. 328, f. 35; A. 328, f. 122; A. 44, f. 33b; A. 16,
    f. 351; D. 912, f. 562.
British Museum:
  Addit. MSS. 33596, ff. 21–32.
  Royal MSS. 12 A. xiii; 12 A. lviii.
  Addit. MSS. 19399, 23113.
Public Record Office:
  Chancery Proceedings. C8. 348/95; C8.560/39.
  Land Revenue Enrolments. Kent, Surrey, Sussex, &c.: L. R.
    1/114.22; 1/115.23. Essex, Hertford, Middlesex, &c.: Liber 12
    (62), ff. 12b–15. L.R. (Essex, &c.) 1/62 (vol. iv), ff. 59–65.
  Patent Rolls. 17 Chas. II, Part 6, Roll 3077.
  Prerogative Court of Canterbury. Register 102 Coke; 104 Carr;
    82 Meade; 109 Plymouth; 145 Shaller.
  Somerset House. Wills of Thomas Cowley, Sr. and Jr.; and Abraham
    Cowley.
  State Paper Office. Jas. I, vol. 32, no. 30; Chas. II, vol. 47, no. 94.

*The following articles by the present author contain more detailed infor-
mation bearing on certain phases of the foregoing study:*

'Abraham Cowley as Dramatist', *The Review of English Studies*, iv.
  (1928), 1–24.
'Abraham Cowley's *Discourse concerning Style*', *The Review of English
  Studies*, ii (1926), 385–404.
'The Essays of Abraham Cowley', *The Journal of English and Germanic
  Philology*, xxix (1930), 114–30.
'The Letters of Abraham Cowley', *Modern Language Notes*, xliii (1928),
  369–75. (Should be supplemented by the present work.)
'The Relation of Cowley's "Pindarics" to Pindar's Odes', *Modern Philo-
  logy*, xix (1921), 107–9.
'The Reputation of Abraham Cowley (1660–1800)', *Publications of the
  Modern Language Association of America*, xxxviii (1923), 588–641.
'The Reputation of the "Metaphysical Poets" during the Age of Johnson
  and the Romantic Revival', *Studies in Philology*, xxii (1925), 81–132.
'The Reputation of the "Metaphysical Poets" during the Age of Pope',
  *Philological Quarterly*, iv (1925), 161–79.
'The Reputation of the "Metaphysical Poets" during the Seventeenth
  Century', *The Journal of English and Germanic Philology*, xxiii
  (1924), 173–98.
'The Term "Metaphysical Poets" before Johnson', *Modern Language
  Notes*, xxxvii (1922), 11–17.

# INDEX

This index lists all of the proper names in this volume (including those of authors mentioned in the footnotes), as well as a few of the most important topics treated. The titles of reference books are generally not given; see the bibliography for their authors.

Horace, 14, 19, 31, 64, 96, 108, 138,
139, 169, 222, 232, 233, 240, 241,
252, 260, 261, 265, 268, 277, 286,
333.
*Horace*, 242.
Horton, 22.
Hotson, Leslie, vi, 201, 202, 314, 338.
Houbraken, Jacob, 330.
Howard, Charles, 216.
Howard, Edward, 225, 226.
Howard, Sir Robert, 225.
Howitt, William, 235, 236, 254, 338.
*Hudibras*, 230.
'Humours', 33, 73.
Huns, 84.
Hurd, Bishop Richard, 19, 77, 92, 93,
185, 266, 286, 287, 288, 330, 334,
338.
Hyacinth, 24.
Hyde, Edward (*see also* Clarendon),
59, 70, 80, 94, 118, 119, 120, 129,
160, 161, 162, 190, 199.
Hyde Park, 80.
'Hymn. To Light', 268.

IAMBLICHUS, 58.
Iceland, 284.
Ickworth, 45, 210, 297, 322.
*Ignoramus*, 32.
Imitation, 137, 138, 257, 263.
'In Commendation of the Time We
Live In', 25.
Income, v, 246–7, 249.
'Inconstant, The', 104.
Indies, 233.
'Innocent Ill, The', 165.
Innocent X, Pope, 99, 133.
Inns of Court, 28.
'Invisible College, The', 183, 185, 216.
Ireland, 90, 121, 123, 140, 147, 182,
219, 294, 301, 334, 340, 341.
Ironsides, The, 170.
Isaiah, 155.
Isburd, Alice, 2.
Isocrates, 14.
Israel, 154, 155.
Italy and Italian, 19, 33, 49, 97, 122,
125, 126, 133, 137, 139, 186, 265,
283, 289.

JACOB, Giles, 175, 176, 177.
James I, King, 16, 32, 294, 301, 302,
305, 333, 345.
James II, King (*see also* Duke of
York), 119, 120, 131.
Japan, 126.
Jermyn, Baron Henry (*see also* St.
Albans), 45, 76, 88, 90, 91, 92, 93,
94, 95, 96, 110, 113, 114, 115, 118,
119, 120, 126, 128, 129, 131, 142,
144, 146, 162, 187, 188, 190, 191,
194, 334.
Jermyn, Susan, 45.
Jersey, 91, 115, 118, 123, 128, 129,
130, 135.
Jesus (*see also* Christ), 41, 294, 296,
298.
Jesus College, Cambridge, 79, 344.
Jews, 221.
Johnson, Charles, 338.
Johnson, Dr. Samuel, 7, 8, 19, 23, 37,
40, 42, 46, 49, 51, 62, 66, 69, 79,
101, 105, 106, 108, 116, 121, 163,
193, 196, 211, 227, 230, 239, 254,
279, 280, 282, 283, 284, 285, 286,
287, 289, 330, 333, 334, 338, 339,
345.
Johnson, W., 65.
Jolly, Colonel, 202, 204, 205.
Jonathan, 50, 140.
Jonson, Ben, 12, 17, 29, 30, 33, 59, 71,
73, 77, 135, 153, 199, 200, 280, 290,
333.
Jordan, John, 16.
Joyner, William, 131.
Judges, 154.
Julius Caesar. *See* Caesar.

KALENDARIUM *Hortense*, 237,
238, 261.
Kames, Lord (Henry Home), 286, 339.
Kane, Elisha K., 283, 284, 339.
Kennett, Bishop White, 218, 339.
Kent, 20, 169, 170, 183, 209, 210,
212, 222, 244, 245, 246, 301, 302,
305, 338, 345.
Kepler, Johann, 96.
Ker, W. P., 7, 336.
Kercherus, 69.